From Plantation to Ghetto

FROM
PLANTATION

by AUGUST MEIER
and ELLIOTT RUDWICK

TO
GHETTO

THIRD EDITION

American Century Series

Hill and Wang   *New York*

A division of Farrar, Straus and Giroux

Consulting editor: Aïda DiPace Donald

Copyright © 1966, 1970, 1976 by August Meier and Elliott Rudwick
All rights reserved
Published simultaneously in Canada by McGraw-Hill Ryerson Ltd., Toronto

ISBN (clothbound edition): 0–8090–4792–6
ISBN (paperback edition): 0–8090–0122–5

First edition, October 1966
Revised edition, July 1970
Third edition, 1976

Printed in the United States of America

Library of Congress Cataloging in Publication Data

Meier, August.
    From plantation to ghetto.

    (American century series)
    Bibliography: p.
    Includes index.
    1. Negroes—History.   I. Rudwick, Elliott M.,
joint author.   II. Title.
E185.M4   1976   973'.04'96073   75–43729

For ROBERT CURVIN
AND LOUIS R. HARLAN

Preface

In this book we have attempted an analytical, interpretive, and interdisciplinary history rather than a narrative account. We have assumed that the reader will have a knowledge of the facts of American history and we have focused less on what whites were doing about blacks than on what Negroes themselves were doing. Moreover, certain topics have been omitted altogether, and special emphasis has been placed on ideologies, institutional developments, patterns of interracial violence, and protest movements.

Gloria Marshall of the anthropology department of the University of Michigan very carefully read and criticized the first chapter, which greatly benefited from her suggestions. William H. Pease and Jane H. Pease of the history department at the University of Maine kindly let us have a copy of their paper, "Antislavery Ambivalence: Immediatism, Expediency, and Race," prior to its publication. James M. McPherson of the history department at Princeton University very generously went through his notes and supplied us with data on black participation in the abolitionist movement from 1861 to 1870. In the preparation of the final chapter of this new edition we were greatly indebted to Alex Poinsett, senior editor at *Ebony* magazine, for an illuminating interview and for permitting us to see his unpublished manuscript on black politics. The discussion of interracial violence during Reconstruction owes much to the research of two graduate students of ours, Melinda Martin Hennessey and the late Gerald T. Martin.

We wish to thank Professor Robert Curvin of the political

science department of Brooklyn College for his perceptive criticism of an earlier version of Chapter VIII. We are indebted to Mrs. Barbara Hostetler for doing much of the typing. Finally we wish to express our deep appreciation to the Kent State University Center for Urban Regionalism and its director, Eugene P. Wenninger, for facilitating the preparation of this edition.

AUGUST MEIER
ELLIOTT RUDWICK

Contents

From Plantation to Ghetto

I

The West African Heritage and Afro-American History

THE BLACK EXPERIENCE in the United States has been largely shaped by two contrasting environments. The first was the Southern staple-producing farm and plantation, on which the vast majority of pre-twentieth-century Negroes worked, in the beginning as slaves and later as sharecroppers. The second was the urban ghetto, predominantly a twentieth-century creation, which grew primarily as a consequence of the migration of rural Negroes to the cities of the South and North.

Thus black life and culture in America have developed within the context of a subordinate status whose leading institutional manifestations have been the plantation and the ghetto. Within these two environments, created by a dominant majority, blacks have both assimilated the culture of the whites and developed what is widely regarded as a distinct, though loosely

3

defined, subculture. On the one hand, Negroes adopted the egalitarian values of the American democratic creed and the middle-class values regarding wealth and upward mobility; on the other hand, their ideologies and institutions differed from those of the whites because blacks had to cope with the reality that democracy, economic opportunity, and social acceptance were not extended to them.

Wishing to be fully accepted as American citizens, yet alienated from the larger society, Negroes have been looked upon, and have looked upon themselves, as a separate ethnic group within that society. One facet of this ethnocentrism has been an awareness that exclusion from the mainstream of American life was related to their African origin.

1

What the African background has meant for blacks in the United States can be discussed under two major categories. One is an analysis of the ways in which American blacks have perceived and felt about Africa. The other is an investigation of the degree to which the distinctive aspects of the American Negro subculture may in part be derived from African ways of life.

Over the years black Americans have displayed a broad range of views and attitudes about Africa, many of them laden with considerable ambivalence. Race prejudice and discrimination compelled Negroes to identify themselves as being of African descent, yet because the white conceptions of black inferiority and African savagery were absorbed by many Negroes, they displayed embarrassment over the allegedly primitive culture of the ancestral continent. At one extreme was the tiny handful of individuals who said that as Americans they had no more interest in Africa than they had in any other foreign land. At the other extreme was the minority—at times a substantial one—who rejected completely the possibility of achieving a satisfactory existence in the United States and advocated colonization, or the return of black Americans to the African homeland. Between these there was a broad spectrum of opinions. Practically universal among articulate nineteenth-century blacks was a pride in the accomplishments of ancient Africa, particularly Egypt. Equally universal was the view of contemporary Africa as heathen and savage. But it was generally believed that Afro-Americans, supposedly the most civilized portion of the black race, had a special duty and responsibility to assist in the uplift and moral and spiritual redemption of the homeland. Some thought of commercial ventures as playing a part in this mission, but for the most part the stress was on the role that Negro churches should play in sending missionaries to civilize and Christianize the allegedly immoral, primitive, and idolatrous inhabitants of Africa. Exclusively nationalist sentiments, looking toward the establishment of a new national homeland in Africa for oppressed black Americans, were less commonly held but, nevertheless, existed throughout the history of Negroes in America and, at certain times, flowered into highly significant and dramatic movements. From time to time eminent black intellectuals have espoused colonization or emigration; yet its chief appeal has been to the poorest class of blacks—the group which has been the most alienated from society and, therefore, the group most likely to identify with Africa.

Such was the range of views among nineteenth-century Afro-Americans. They had wide currency until the present generation. But as early as the turn of the century, W. E. B. Du Bois, the sociologist, historian, and noted protest leader, enunciated a new approach. Possessed of a deep emotional commitment to Africa and people of color throughout the world, Du Bois was probably the first American Negro to express the idea of Pan-Africanism: the belief that all people of African descent had common interests and should work together in the struggle for their freedom. He also appears to have been the first American author to describe the great medieval kingdoms of West Africa, and he was among the first to regard the nonliterate societies of sub-Saharan Africa as possessing complex and sophisticated cultures. Finally, he was apparently the first person to suggest that the culture of black Americans had been substantially influenced by the cultures of Africa.

Du Bois was well versed in the literature produced by European explorers and historians. His early writings on Africa were thoroughly imbued with the new knowledge that was a by-product of European penetration and conquest of the African interior in the late nineteenth century. Since then, historians and anthropologists have added greatly to and refined our knowledge of African history and culture. It took time, however, for Du Bois's picture to spread, even among Negroes. Although Carter G. Woodson, the influential scholar and propagandist for the study of the Negro's past and the founder of the *Journal of Negro History*, expressed similar ideas, few indeed accepted Du Bois's suggestion that American Negro culture owed much to the African way of life. Du Bois's views on this subject were based more on mystical yearnings than on hard factual data; it was not until Melville J. Herskovits in 1941 published his *Myth of the Negro Past*, based on extensive empirical research, that the thesis became widely debated.

The title of Herskovits's book suggests very well the viewpoint, not only of whites, but also—until very recent decades—of most blacks regarding the African past. Ordinarily when blacks expressed pride in Africa they pointed to the antique past. The myth that Du Bois, Woodson, and Herskovits were bent on destroying was a dual one: (1) that the ancestral cultures of the black Americans were primitive, with Africans making no contributions to the culture of the world; and (2) that under the slave regime practically all evidence of African culture—except perhaps for some survivals in music and dance—had been destroyed.

Having set forth the myth, let us now turn to a brief presentation of some of the salient facts.

2

Africa south of the Sahara was known to medieval Muslims as the *Beled es-Sudan*, or "Land of the Blacks." Today the term "Sudan" is restricted to the broad belt of grassland lying south of the Sahara and north of the tropical rain forest that occupies the Guinea Coast and the Congo River Basin. The peoples who became the chief source of the Negro population in the New World resided in the forested area and in the southern portions of the western Sudan. The chief theater of operation for the transatlantic slave trade was along the West African coast between Senegal and Angola. Some slaves came from deep in the interior, but ordinarily the range of the slave trade lay within three hundred miles of the coast. Thus the great majority of Negroes who were brought to the New World came primarily from the area drained by the Senegal, Gambia, Volta, Niger, and Congo Rivers.

The theater of much of the Sudanese cultural history that we are about to relate was actually located to the north of the area from which New World Negroes came. Yet we cannot separate the history of the southern Sudan from that of the northern Sudan. Moreover, the institutions of the Sudanese societies had important influences on the societies of the Guinea Coast, and some of the most important slave-trading kingdoms encompassed territory in both the rain forest and the Sudan. It therefore seems appropriate to begin the story of the American Negro's African heritage with a brief sketch of the cultural history of the western Sudan.

Modern scholarship places the western Sudan among the important creative centers in the development of human culture—along with the ancient Near East, the Indus and Yellow River valleys, and Mesoamerica. In each of these places an unusually high agricultural productivity achieved during the Neolithic period sustained a relatively dense population and thus ultimately led to a profound transformation in social institutions. In each case the social complexities arising out of the increasing number of inhabitants resulted in the development of social classes, urban centers, and despotic theocratic monarchies.

The importance of the domestication of plants and animals as a catalyst for these institutional changes cannot be overestimated. It is possible that, as the anthropologist George Peter Murdock has suggested, the western Sudan was among those centers in which agriculture was an indigenous invention, thus duplicating the achievement of the inhabitants of Southwest

Asia, Mesoamerica, and possibly other places. The staple grains of the Sudanese complex of crops, comparable to the wheat and barley of the Near East and the maize of the New World, were pearl millet and sorghum. Among the other important cultivated crops probably first domesticated in the western Sudan were okra, the kola tree (the original source of the stimulant in cola drinks), the watermelon, sesame, and cotton. Murdock's thesis, based chiefly upon plant distributions and data from historical linguistics, has not yet found support in the slim archaeological investigation thus far done in West Africa. Others insist that the knowledge and techniques of plant cultivation were not developed independently in the western Sudan but diffused into this area from Southwest Asia, via Egypt. Whatever archaeologists eventually find in regard to the origins of agriculture in West Africa, subsequent cultural development in the Sudan paralleled that which occurred in Mesopotamia and Egypt, in China and India, and in Mexico and Peru. By the second millennium B.C., according to Murdock, or by the opening of the Christian era, according to more conservative authorities, the Sudan had developed large-scale, complex kingdoms.

An important factor in the proliferation of urban societies and empires in the western Sudan was the trans-Saharan trade. Though little of certainty can be established about this commerce during the early millennia, it is known that the introduction of the camel during Roman times greatly facilitated it. Three major routes emerged in the western half of the Sahara Desert. Of these the most important, until the end of the sixteenth century, ran from Sijilmasa in present-day Morocco to the Upper Niger River area. The prominence of this route was based on the proximity of its southern terminal entrepôts to Wangara, the gold-producing territory around the headwaters of the Senegal and Niger Rivers. The principal southbound commodity was salt, an item in scarce supply in the Sudan but plentiful at the Taghaza salt mines in the Sahara Desert. Lesser, but important, items in the traffic were Negro slaves from the Sudan and luxury textiles from the Mediterranean. Control of the Wangara goldfields was a leading consideration in the

West Africa

minds of the empire builders of the western Sudan. The significance of this, the westernmost route, is evident in the fact that
the prosperity of the three most important and largest states in
early West African history—Ghana, Mali, and Songhai—was
largely based upon this traffic in gold and slaves, salt and cloth.
Each in turn controlled the southern entrepôts of the Moroccan trade, most notably the city of Timbuktu. Timbuktu, on
the edge of the desert, close to the Niger at the most northern
point on its course, by the end of the twelfth century had
become the major international market where the products of
the Niger Valley were exchanged for those of northern Africa.
It also became the leading commercial and intellectual center of
West Africa.

The earliest West African state of which we have any written
account (and archaeological work has barely begun) was the
empire of Ghana. The state was founded, probably in the
fourth century A.D., by the Soninke people on the southern
fringe of the Sahara, where they were in a position to benefit
from the caravan trade between Morocco and Wangara.
Though the exact boundaries of the kingdom are in dispute, it
is generally agreed that Ghana was located north and west of
the great bend in the Niger River, the empire at its height (in
the tenth century) extending as far west as the upper portion of
the Senegal River. The rulers were pagan, though the capital,
Kumbi-Kumbi, consisted of two towns—one pagan, which contained the fortified residence of the king and his court, and the
other Muslim. Arabic was the written language of the empire,
and both Muslims and pagans held high office.

For some time before its downfall the kingdom of Ghana had
been threatened by the Islamized Berber peoples to the north
and west, and in 1076 it was conquered by the Berber Almoravides, originally a Muslim sect in the lower Senegal Valley.
The Almoravides empire lasted a century, and for a brief period
stretched from the Sudan almost to the Pyrenees. Though
within a dozen years the Soninke peoples had regained their
independence, the place of the former kingdom of Ghana was
now occupied by a number of warring states. Finally, in 1240,

the ancient capital Kumbi-Kumbi was completely destroyed by the rising kingdom of Mali.

Mali, which thus gave the *coup de grâce* to the history of Ghana, shared the center of the Sudanese stage with the kingdom of Songhai from the thirteenth to the fifteenth century. Both had obscure origins, dating back perhaps to the seventh century A.D. The original territory of Mali was located on the Upper Niger, west of the Great Bend. Songhai's capital was situated on the middle section of the river, east of the Great Bend. Both states were converted to Islam in the eleventh century, and the economic prosperity of both was based chiefly upon their importance as trade entrepôts. Little is known about the history of Songhai, which gradually expanded north and south along the Niger River, until the fourteenth century, but Mali had achieved prominence before the middle of the thirteenth century. Ultimately the Mali empire stretched from almost the Atlantic eastward beyond the Niger, and from the Sahara to the rain forest. It reached its apogee under the illustrious Mansa Musa (1307–32), who annexed Songhai. Even prior to this addition to his kingdom, Mansa Musa had dazzled the Mediterranean world with an elaborate pilgrimage to Mecca. His retinue of sixty thousand and his lavish gifts of gold made his name a legend among both Muslim and Christian nations.

After the middle of the fourteenth century, Mali entered into a long decline, while Songhai, which had regained its independence shortly after the death of Mansa Musa, gradually established itself as the leading power in the western Sudan. Under Askia Muhammad I (1493–1528), who acquired the remnants of the Mali empire and invaded the Hausa states to the east, Songhai, whose territories reached nearly to the Atlantic and almost to Lake Chad, became the largest empire in West African history. With Askia's encouragement of trade and learning, Songhai enjoyed an enormous prosperity, and the University of Sankore at Timbuktu became one of the great centers of learning in the Muslim world. Despite its imposing magnificence, however, the Songhai empire was shattered by the Moroccan invasion of 1591 and the western Sudan was divided among several smaller kingdoms.

To the south, the inhabitants of the rain forest along the Guinea Coast followed a similar pattern in their cultural history, except that many important developments came considerably later. Since Sudanese crops were not suitable for cultivation in the tropical forest, other foods had to be domesticated, and different agricultural techniques were needed. Agriculture seems to have come to the Guinea Coast by the time of the Christian era. The staple crops were not grains but root crops—chiefly yams. Once the Bantu-speaking peoples of the Lower Niger Valley became farmers, they were equipped to cultivate the Congo River Basin. The early centuries of the Christian era witnessed the Bantu migration into central and then eastern and southern Africa and the displacement of the food-gathering Pygmies and Bushmen as the Bantu took over almost all of the southern half of the continent. The subsequent increase in population among the rain-forest peoples by the second millennium A.D. made possible the establishment of despotic states modeled upon the political institutions of the Sudanese kingdoms to the north. They shared with them certain institutional and ritual forms, including the important role played by the queen-mother or queen-sister, which were unknown outside of Africa. Thus the European slave-trading nations dealt not only with coastal tribes but also with proud kingdoms like those of the Mani-Congo in present-day Zaïre and Angola, and of the Ashanti, the Yoruba, and the Dahomeans, whose boundaries stretched from the Guinea Coast into the southern Sudan.

3

West African societies in the slave-trade area ranged from small tribes to large kingdoms of a million or more; from small groups where kinship ties were the source of all authority to large states with complex political institutions. These societies were characterized by economic specialization and a monetary system based on the cowrie shell to facilitate trade. The larger ones had a system of social classes and a hierarchical territorial political organization. Interlacing and underpinning these political, economic, and social class arrangements were a deeply rooted and intricate kinship system extending from family to clan, and an elaborate web of religious belief involving the individual, the kinship groupings, and the entire society. Although these societies differed widely among themselves, their many basic cultural similarities make it possible to form some valid generalizations about the cultural background of New World Negroes. While in the discussion that follows our examples will be drawn from the larger and more complex of these societies, such as the Dahomeans, the Ashanti, the Mossi, and the Yoruba, most of what we say, except for the class structure and political institutions, applies generally to the ancestral peoples of the New World blacks.

Throughout the entire area the economy was basically agricultural, although along the coast there was some fishing and, inland, poultry was raised as the main source of meat. Farming was done with the hoe, men ordinarily doing the heavy work of breaking the soil. Among the Ashanti both sexes cultivated the crops; the Dahomeans allocated this work to women, while among the Yoruba most of it was done by men. Larger, heavier tasks were performed cooperatively by the men. Among the Dahomeans, for example, fields were cleared and houses built by a voluntary cooperative male group known as the *dokpwe*. The *dokpwe* also played an important role in funeral services; thus it was an institution with both religious and economic functions.

Economic specialization involved the elaboration of a number of crafts, most notably ironworking, weaving, wood carving, basketry, pottery making, and bronze casting. The craftsmen's products often had an aesthetic function, and have been much admired by Western artists and art critics since the turn of the century. Especially notable were the bronze and brass castings made by the *cire-perdue* process. Craftsmen in most of the societies were organized into craft guilds, ordinarily along kinship lines, which set prices and often acted as mutual-aid societies. Among the Yoruba the guilds of craftsmen and women traders exercised considerable political influence on the town councils.

Much of the internal commerce of each West African society was in the hands of women, some of whom were producer-traders, while other women were nonproducing middlemen. In most West African societies local and interregional trade was facilitated by the existence of complex systems of markets, held daily and periodically in villages as well as in towns. External trade was controlled by the royal heads of state. Among the Ashanti and in Dahomey the right to trade in certain items—notably slaves, gold, and European imports—required personal authorization from the king, who levied fees for granting such privileges. The West African societies thus had an unusually elaborate economic organization for nonliterate peoples, an economic organization comparable, for example, to those of the Inca and Aztec empires in the New World.

The larger societies were characterized by specialization not only in economic pursuits but in other spheres of life as well, and there developed a degree of social stratification sufficient to lead some scholars to characterize them as possessing a class structure analogous to that in Western societies. Thus in Dahomey there was an elaborate hierarchy. At the bottom were the slaves, chiefly war captives. The children of slaves—except for those on the king's estates, where a kind of hereditary serfdom existed—were absorbed into the families of their owners. The backbone of the society was a class of free farmers and artisans. At approximately the same social level were the ordinary temple priests and diviners. The upper class consisted of the higher elements in the priesthood and the king's officials. Because members of the royal clan were not permitted to hold office, these functionaries were drawn from the ranks of the freemen. At the top stood the large but parasitical royal clan, whose members did no work, and at the apex was the monarch himself.

In general, land in West African societies was owned in perpetuity by corporate kin groups who would alienate it only on the rarest occasions. Individual members inherited or were apportioned land for their own use, and they owned and could freely dispose of the goods they produced. In all kingdoms of West Africa the land was considered to "belong" ultimately to the paramount ruler, a consideration that signified recognition of the king's sacred authority over and responsibility for the kinship groupings and territorial units making up his domain.

The system of land ownership is only one indication of the importance of the family and larger kinship groupings in African societies.* Highly complex groups formed on the basis of descent and of marriage and residence were important in matters of politics and religion as well as in matters of livelihood and inheritance. And as is the case in most societies, certain of these kinship groups were the primary agents through which individuals learned the norms and values of their cultures.

Descent was usually traced either matrilineally or patrilineally. In a matrilineal society, all those males and females whose descent was traced through a line of mothers to a single female ancestor formed a descent group or lineage. In a patrilineal society, all those persons descended from a common ancestor through a line of fathers formed a lineage. Groups of lineages tracing their descent from a common ancestor formed a clan. In many cases the members of each clan believed themselves descended from a divine animal ancestor; thus in Dahomey the royal clan claimed descent from a leopard. Exceedingly important as members of all these kinship groupings were the dead ancestors. They were revered and given sacrifices. They had power to work evil or good for their relatives and descendants. The people believed that their ancestors participated intimately in the conduct and guidance of family, lineage, and clan affairs. The clan head, as a rule its oldest living male member, served as the link between the ancestors and the living and therefore exercised considerable power over the clan's members. Among

* Because African kinship systems are complex and very different from those in Western societies, the following discussion is somewhat technical. We thought a correct treatment preferable to an oversimplified and therefore distorted one.

the Dahomeans he controlled the use of the communal lands of
the clan, could force the clan members to work the lands, was
consulted in all marriages, and was treated with ritualistic
respect.

Ordinarily the West African *family* group was what anthropologists term an "extended family." It comprised two or more
generations of adults descended from a common ancestor, their
spouses, and their children, all sharing a single residential unit,
often termed a compound. A compound frequently consisted of
a group of dwellings enclosing a courtyard, often with a fence
surrounding the entire group of buildings. Polygyny was everywhere recognized as a suitable or preferred form of marriage. In
a number of societies, such as Yoruba and Dahomey, each wife
had a separate room or dwelling within the compound, living
with her husband in rotation with his other wives. In patrilineal
societies the *extended family* occupying a compound typically
comprised a man, his wives and children (i.e., sons and unmar-
ried daughters), his brothers and their wives and children, and
his adult sons and their wives and children. Although the adult
sisters and daughters of men in such a household would ordinarily marry into other extended families, they would still retain
membership in their father's lineage, while their husband and
children belonged to other lineages. A comparable situation
occurred in matrilineal societies, such as the Ashanti, except
that a man and his wives often lived with, and were considered
as belonging to, the extended family headed by his maternal
uncle.

In both patrilineal and matrilineal societies the head of an
extended family was usually one of the oldest males. Typically
he exercised considerable power over the members of the
household. When the head of a compound died, the next
younger brother, or the eldest son, or the oldest male in the
household succeeded him. When the size of a family became
too large to be supported by the land resources in the compound, a younger brother or son would establish a new household in the same or a different community. This household
continued to acknowledge its relationship to the parent com-

pound, however, and the various members of the newly formed
residence remained members of their original descent groups or
lineages.

Political units varied in character from autonomous villages
to despotic centralized monarchies. More than any of the other
societies in the West African slaving area, Dahomey resembled
the European absolute monarchy. At the base of its political
pyramid was the local village chief, appointed by the king but
to some extent responsive to the family heads who formed the
village council. The villages and towns were grouped into twelve
districts, each governed by a royally appointed official with fiscal
and administrative functions. The king was nearly an absolute
ruler, a sacred figure, mediating between the people and the
powerful royal ancestors. The king himself chose his heir from
among his eligible sons. He was the highest judicial officer and
had the final decision on appeals brought from cases heard by
lesser officials. He appointed all of his administrators. Chief
among them were the royal executioner, who exercised the
power of a prime minister; the official in charge of the princely
class; the governor of the coastal region, who also dealt with the
European traders; the chief gatekeeper, who supervised the
officers and residents of the royal palace and headed an espio-
nage system; the commander in chief of the army; the minister
of the interior, who supervised markets, agricultural operations,
and the ingenious system of tax collections; and the royal
treasurer.

Women played an important role in the administration of
political affairs in Dahomey. Each major official had a female
counterpart known as his "mother," who took precedence over
him at court and supervised his work. When officials reported
to the king, groups of women were present whose duty it was to
remember what had been transacted. Women also had an important role in the army, and, since they were technically regarded as wives of the king, these female soldiers were kept
secluded from all men.

Dahomey was a more centralized and absolute monarchy
than its contemporaries. Elsewhere the sacred rulers of the

larger societies had not achieved this concentration of power. Chieftains of villages and town subdivisions were often selected by the council of local family heads from among the members of a particular lineage in which the right to this office inhered. Provincial governors and the king himself were chosen in a similar way by a council consisting of the heads of the powerful lineages in the provincial or national capitals. Often the queen-sister or the queen-mother was a powerful figure in her own right, with lands and slaves of her own and considerable influence over the king. Among the Ashanti she actually nominated the king. In most cases a king's council had at its disposal a recognized procedure by which it might depose a ruler. Among the Yoruba, when his council sent him an ostrich egg, the *Alafin*, ruler of Oyo and paramount ruler of all Yorubaland, knew he was expected to commit suicide. This limitation on the king's power, the elective nature of the office, the interregnum between the death of one ruler and the appointment of his successor, and the decentralized nature of the political hierarchy were responsible for centrifugal forces in most West African monarchies that gave them a quasi-feudal appearance. Although we lack the information to verify the hypothesis, it is likely that this characteristic was also true of the earlier Sudanese empires, which Mediterranean travelers described as constantly threatened by rebellious vassal states.

Religion permeated West African cultures. Typically there were complex notions regarding a person's souls or spiritual attributes. Elaborate funeral services were the rule because the spirits of the dead ancestors were regarded as sacred beings, powerful in determining the destiny of kinship groups and states. Great gods, sometimes arranged in groups or pantheons, as well as numerous lesser, local deities, also had their roles in determining the course of human affairs. Elaboration of religious beliefs was carried to especially great lengths among the Dahomeans, but a brief examination of their ideas and practices illuminates the religious life of West Africa generally.

The Dahomeans held that each individual had five different souls or spiritual attributes, one of which survived as an independent soul after a person died. Impressive ceremonies were held periodically to deify the dead ancestors. There were also annual rituals honoring and worshipping them, the rites including frenzied dancing and animal sacrifices. The yearly "custom" for the royal ancestors was an especially important occasion, since they were the guardians of the state. At these events and after the death of a king, criminals and captured prisoners of war were among the sacrifices. Like peoples in many parts of the world, the Dahomeans believed that a human being was the most valuable sacrifice they could offer to a revered and powerful deity.

The Dahomean great gods were organized into three pantheons—Sky, Earth, and Thunder. The most important deity of all was Mawu, the Moon Goddess, who presided over the Sky pantheon with her husband, Lisa, the Sun God. They were the parents of the other chief deities—including Sagbata, head of the Earth pantheon, who was responsible for bringing crop abundance, and Xevioso, head of the Thunder pantheon, with control over rain and fire, rivers and oceans. Connected with the worship of the great gods was a belief in fate. One could effect a change in his destiny by offering sacrifices to Legba, the trickster god, who relayed to the other deities Mawu's directions concerning the execution of men's destinies. Each pantheon had its own cult, its own priests, its own group of adherents. Initiation into a cult came only after a long period of training, and in the final ceremonies the initiate performed a frenzied dance, during which he was regarded as being literally possessed by the deity, who "rode" on his head and inspired his motions. Finally there was *Da*, the serpent, symbolizing the sentient, elusive, moving aspect of life, the dynamic element in the world, and evident in fortune, smoke, roots, and the umbilical cord.

4

As we have already noted, although Du Bois and Woodson believed that Africanisms were present in American black culture, it was the work of the anthropologist and Africanist Melville J. Herskovits that made this thesis a focus of controversy among students of American Negro life and culture. Not only did Herskovits insist that Africanisms existed in the Afro-American subculture, but he held also that some of these cultural traits had been transmitted to the whites. Herskovits's method was basically that of making a comparative analysis of West African cultures, the cultures of blacks in the Caribbean area and Brazil, and the patterns of life among what the sociologist Charles S. Johnson has called the "folk Negro" in the United States. Supported by impressive ethnographic fieldwork both in West Africa and in black peasant communities in the West Indies and Dutch Guiana, Herskovits's findings commanded attention. Scholars agree that in Brazil and the Caribbean area much of African culture has survived and that in those countries there has been a synthesis of African and European cultural traditions. African religious and familial institutions, linguistic elements and folktales, mutual-aid societies, and musical and dance forms have had a marked effect on the life of New World Negroes south of the United States. Haitian *vodun*, for example, is a syncretism of Catholic and African religious beliefs and practices, with various African gods being equated with Catholic saints. (*Vodun*, rendered in English as *voodoo*, is itself a Dahomean word meaning "deity.") Thus was repeated the age-old process of religious syncretism, of which Christianity, combining as it does elements of Judaism, Hellenistic philosophy, and Oriental mystery religions, is itself a superb example.

Controversy arises as to the degree to which African survivals are to be found in the United States, where Herskovits himself held that they were less common than in the Caribbean and Brazil. The higher proportion of whites to blacks in the sections where slavery held sway, the absence of mountains or jungle fastnesses where escaped slaves could develop a stable community without white interference, and the generally more repressive slave codes in the United States, which made it difficult or impossible for slaves to maintain social and religious organizations of their own, all militated against the survival of Africanisms. Yet Herskovits believed he had identified numerous evidences of such survivals.

For certain items, Herskovits's claims are incontrovertible. Since Lorenzo Turner's epoch-making book *Africanisms in the Gullah Dialect* (1949), it is accepted that the peculiarities of vocabulary and syntax among the inhabitants of the coastal Sea Islands of South Carolina and Georgia—where Africanisms are undoubtedly strongest because of the relative isolation of Negro communities—were derived from Africa and not, as was once widely held, from archaic dialects of sixteenth-century England. African influence upon American Negro music and dance, both of which have diffused into the culture of the white population, is also generally recognized and accepted. Much of lower-class black folklore, magic, and medicine—especially of a generation and more ago—can be traced to African origins. Much of the content in Joel Chandler Harris's Uncle Remus tales, doctored though it was for white audiences, is genuine folk material with African roots. Notable in this connection are the stories revolving around the rabbit, who, as an animal trickster, is a central figure in African folklore. Herskovits also asserts that similarities between mutual-benefit societies and funerary practices in the United States and those in West Africa demonstrate African survivals, though proof for this is more difficult to establish. Where the chief controversy arises, however, is over Herskovits's assertions regarding religion and family life.

E. Franklin Frazier, in his *Negro Family in the United States* (1939), one of the classics of American sociological literature, described what he called a matriarchal pattern that is frequently found among lower-income black families. These are extended families in which the central figure is the mother or the grandmother. She functions as an authority figure and as a breadwinner and is the one who holds the family together. Such families are often characterized by marital instability and desertion on the part of the husband. Herskovits held that this pattern developed out of the adjustment of African family institutions to the brutalizing conditions of Negro life in America. He

referred to the importance of women in African societies, especially their economic role, not only as farmers, but even more
significantly as the chief traders in the village and urban markets (a situation that exists in Haiti today). He referred also to
the prevalence in African societies of polygynous family systems
and to the custom of each of a man's wives having her own
dwelling. In such situations, Herskovits held, the bonds of identification and affection—even in patrilineal societies—were between the children and their mother rather than between the
children and their father.

There are of course alternative explanations for the prevalence of the matriarchal or, to follow modern anthropological
usage, matrifocal family patterns among lower-income black
people. Some scholars have held that they are the heritage of
slavery, for if any family bonds were respected by the slaveowners, they were usually those between mothers and their
young children. Other researchers have used a psychoanalytic
approach and have stressed white society's emotional emascula-
tion of the black male. Whatever the origins of the matrifocal
patterns and their acceptance among lower-class Negroes, the
twentieth-century urban environment has served to perpetuate
them. Historically the lower-class black woman found it easier
than a man to obtain and hold a job. The husband, unable to
fulfill the economic functions expected of a man in our society
and unable to accept the social inadequacy that his wife's superior earning power suggested, would often desert his family.
Thus both authority in the family and responsibility for its
economic support are often shouldered by the woman. The
matrifocal family, one in which a woman is head of the household, has been, therefore, a functional adjustment to social realities rather than a survival of Africanisms. Support for this view
comes from West Indies studies. While recent scholarship on
black Americans has not been concerned with testing Herskovits's thesis, investigations in the West Indies have either im-
plicitly or explicitly criticized his views on the black family.
There, family patterns appear to be well correlated with economic factors. Investigators of Negro life in the West Indies

accord slavery a role in originating and/or perpetuating matrifocal patterns but view their persistence in some places today as
mainly rooted in modern economic and social conditions.

As for religious survivals, Herskovits maintains that the religious hysteria characteristic of lower-class evangelical churches
and pentecostal sects, among both whites and blacks, reflects
the influence of the intensely emotional and frenzied African
ceremonies. The phenomenon of religious "possession," in
which the enthusiast feels united with a deity, is well known to
anthropologists. Its manifestations range from epileptic fits
among the Arabians and the Siberian shamans, through the
visions of the ancient Near Eastern Christian hermits, to
trances of Hindu mystics, to the fantasies induced among
American Indians by starvation, self-mutilation, or drugs, to
"getting religion" by the sanctified among the Holy Rollers,
spiritual Baptists, and similar groups. Among American Negroes
this phenomenon is especially common in lower-class Baptist
and Methodist Churches, the pentecostal sects, and such cults
as Daddy Grace's House of Prayer for All People. Similar forms
of religious possession are found among the white sects and
cults and Baptist churches that are the counterparts of the black
lower-class religious institutions. Herskovits, calling attention to
the emotional type of religious service that came with the Great
Revival of the early nineteenth century, attributed the particular patterns of religious hysteria that developed at camp meetings and revival services to contact with slaves who attended
such gatherings. His thesis is that here, as in Haiti, we find a
form of religious syncretism. Herskovits also saw syncretism in
the high proportion of blacks, perhaps as many as two thirds,
belonging to the Baptist Church. Pointing to the importance of
the river cults in West African religion, he held that slaves
flocked to the Baptist Church because of the similarity between
West African practices and the total immersion required for
initiation into the Baptist Church, a rite found also among the
pentecostal sects and such cults as those of Elder Micheaux and
Daddy Grace.

Frazier, who was Herskovits's most articulate critic, regarded such interpretations as nonsense. Most Negroes, he insisted, became Methodists and Baptists because these churches were the only ones that really proselytized among blacks, as they had a general interest in society's downtrodden people. Baptists especially appealed to Negroes, he wrote, because their highly decentralized form of church organization and congregational autonomy made it possible for blacks to govern their own institutions and assume leadership positions without difficulty. Moreover, there is a functional explanation for the emotional character of worship in most lower-class black churches. The evangelical churches have always appealed primarily to lower-class people because of the escape that "getting religion" offers from the burdens of everyday reality. Frazier argued that every significant aspect of lower-class Negro religious life can be explained as arising out of the social milieu in which American blacks found themselves, without recourse to explanations in terms of African survivals.

It can be argued of course that the aspects of African culture which have survived in the United States are those which have had a functional value; that the African family institutions were modified and adapted to meet the exigencies of life for the slave and the freedman in America; and that the African forms of religious possession fulfilled important needs for the oppressed black people and indeed for lower-class whites as well. Actually there is no necessary contradiction between Herskovits's emphasis upon the persistence of African cultural traditions and the functional explanations offered by sociologists like Charles S. Johnson and E. Franklin Frazier.

Whether the distinctive cultural characteristics of the black community are viewed as survivals of an African heritage or as functional adjustments to the specific situation in which American blacks found themselves, the Afro-American way of life is a subculture, a variety of the larger American culture. Unlike the cultures of black peasants and urban masses in countries to the south, what survives of African culture in the United States is relatively limited. Such Africanisms as persist are not evenly distributed among all groups in the black population. They proved strongest among the rural Sea Islanders of Georgia and South Carolina, where contact with whites was extremely limited, and in the permissive atmosphere of Latin-oriented Louisiana, where vestiges of African "voodoo" existed until recent years. Such Africanisms as do remain are characteristic of the life of the lower classes rather than the middle and upper classes. As with other ethnic minorities in our society, those Negroes who have moved up the economic and social ladder have, as part of the process of upward mobility, assimilated white middle-class ways in speech, family life, religious services, and values far more than did lower-class blacks.

Herskovits's thesis certainly remains a provocative and suggestive one. Some of his contentions are undoubtedly correct and there is no argument about them. But in its more controversial aspects, no definite conclusions can be drawn concerning its validity in explaining the existence of a black subculture in America.

Herskovits's ideas originally evoked a stormy response from most articulate Negroes and from most whites interested in race relations. These people were busy fighting the charges that blacks were inferior to whites and therefore unable to assimilate white American culture and adjust to white American middle-class society. Black intellectuals like the sociologists Charles S. Johnson and E. Franklin Frazier described distinctive patterns of life among the black lower classes as being responses to the social oppression and economic degradation that they suffered. Beginning with the late 1950's, however, Herskovits's thesis has been more hospitably received. The rise to independence and power on the part of the new African nations gave American blacks new feelings of identification with and pride in the ancestral continent. Prominent scholars belonging to the American Society for African Culture (AMSAC) embraced the theory of *négritude* propounded by the international parent body, the Society for African Culture, with headquarters in France. This theory holds that the descendants of Africans everywhere in the world exhibit in their culture and in their thought certain ineradicable evidences of their African origin. The stirrings and achievements of the black revolution in the United States have also stimulated among American Negroes a new feeling of racial identity—of accepting themselves as blacks rather than trying to imitate whites—and, concomitantly, a new interest in the race's past.

What then is the significance of the African—especially the West African—cultural heritage for American Negro history? Undoubtedly it contributed something to the quality of black life and institutions in the United States; and to some extent it provided materials that American blacks refashioned to cope with the problems they faced in the New World. Throughout American history, Africa provided for American Negroes an ancestral homeland with which they identified in various ways and to various degrees. Not until the middle of the twentieth century, however, did the rise of African nations to independence and international influence make large numbers of blacks genuinely proud of their West African heritage. Both the changing role of Africa and the civil-rights revolution gave Afro-Americans a new sense of identity. As a result articulate blacks became more receptive to the idea that Africanisms survived in their way of life.

Thus, changes on the world scene and in the blacks' status in the United States have made acceptance of Herskovits's thesis far more widespread among black Americans and, for that matter, among American whites as well. We shall do well to keep his views in mind, and we shall have occasion to refer to them again. Nevertheless, the major forces shaping Negro life in the United States, from the first use of black men on the tobacco farms of Virginia to the civil-rights revolution spawned in the modern cities, lay in the American environment. It is mainly to the plantation and the ghetto that we shall have to turn if we are to understand Afro-American life and history.

II

Black Men in Agrarian America:
Slavery and the Plantation

1

THE INSTITUTION OF SLAVERY had long been known in both southern Europe and Africa, but the rise of the European traffic in African slaves was the product of two major developments in the fifteenth and sixteenth centuries: the emergence of the national monarchies facing the Atlantic and the Commercial Revolution.

Quite naturally, the new nations sought wealth and empire in Africa and the New World. Once Spain and Portugal had broken the commercial preeminence of the Italian city-states, Holland, France, and England successfully entered the contest for a share of the African trade and for empires in the Americas. Soon Africa became the major source of labor for the exploitation of the tropical and semitropical regions of the New World.

27

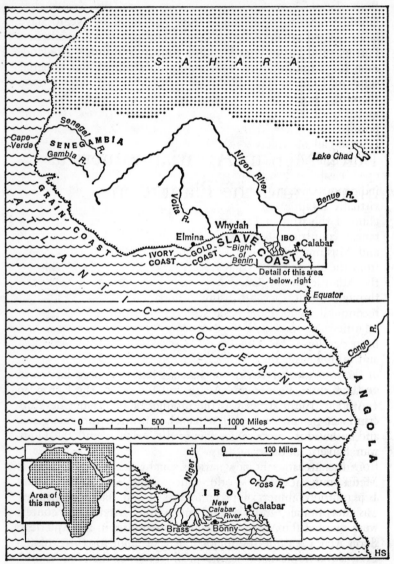

The Slave Coast

Both the slave trade itself and, even more, the wealth that flowed from American staple crops cultivated by Negro slave labor created much of the prosperity and power that made first Portugal and Spain, later Holland, France, and finally England, each for a span of time a dominant commercial and imperial state in Europe. The African slave trade and slavery were, therefore, major factors in the quickening of European commerce, industry, and banking and in the shift of economic power from the Mediterranean countries to northwestern Europe—all of which constituted the Commercial Revolution.

The European traffic in slaves with sub-Saharan Africa developed easily and without opposition because slavery was an indigenous institution on both continents. While slavery had virtually disappeared from northwestern Europe after the decline of the Roman Empire, it continued to exist in Mediterranean countries. During the later Middle Ages both Christians and Muslims engaged in a thriving slave trade that extended from the shores of the Black Sea to the countries bordering on the Atlantic Ocean. On the Iberian Peninsula slavery persisted through the medieval Muslim occupation and the Christian reconquest. Indeed the basic structure of both the later transatlantic slave trade and the New World plantation system had been developed by Italian merchants trading in the Black Sea and raising sugar on Sicily, Cyprus, and Crete. At the opening of the fourteenth century, in fact, Negro slaves could be found on the Cyprus sugar plantations.

Among West African peoples, sources of slaves included criminals, people pawned by their lineages as security for loans and enslaved if the debts were not repaid, and captives taken in war. Slavery in these noncapitalist societies differed markedly from the highly exploitive system developed by Europeans on Mediterranean and New World plantations. The use of slaves as plantation laborers on the vast estates of the Dahomean king was exceptional. Some, in societies like Dahomey and Ashanti, were sacrificed to the powerful royal ancestors. But as a rule slaves were employed as domestic or household servants. Moreover, slaves in African societies had certain rights. Among the

Ashanti they could marry free people, even royalty; they could own property (even other slaves); and they could not be killed without the king's permission. In the kingdom of Benin in coastal Nigeria, slaves or their children were permitted to earn enough to purchase their freedom. Slaves of the Dahomeans, the Ashanti, and the Ibo of the Niger Delta commonly achieved free status through adoption into the families of their masters. Rulers among the Yoruba and the Muslim Hausa states of northern Nigeria frequently chose slaves for high official positions. Among the Dahomeans, kings sometimes selected the son of a favorite slave wife to succeed to the throne.

The Portuguese were the first Europeans to engage in the slave traffic with sub-Saharan Africa. During the Middle Ages, gold from the Wangara area had reached Europe through Arab intermediaries trading at Timbuktu, and the origin of European trade in West African slaves was actually subsidiary to Prince Henry of Portugal's attempt to tap the Sudanese gold marts. Thus, at first the European trade with Africa resembled the older trans-Saharan traffic; not until the end of the seventeenth century did slaves become the primary object of interest. In 1441 the first cargo of gold and slaves arrived in Lisbon. By 1482 the Portuguese had explored the coast as far as Angola and erected a fort at Elmina on what later became known as the Gold Coast (modern Ghana). By the end of the century Spain had recognized Portugal's claim to exclusive trading rights in Guinea.

The Guinea Coast that presented itself to the Portuguese slavers and their successors was an inaccessible stretch of land offering few harbors. The mouths of its navigable rivers were obstructed by sandbars that proved a perennial problem to the traders. Between the area around the Senegal and Gambia Rivers (Senegambia), which was the major source of slaves during the fifteenth and sixteenth centuries, and Angola, which became a leading source by the nineteenth century, lay the heart of the slave-trading belt during the seventeenth and eighteenth centuries. Europeans divided this belt into four main sections, each named after what was at first its leading export: the Grain Coast, from Sierra Leone to Cape Palmas, source of the grains of melegueta pepper; the Ivory Coast, from Cape Palmas to modern Ghana; the Gold Coast, a stretch of about 160 miles; and finally the Slave Coast, extending from the Volta River to the Niger Delta and beyond and including the coastal areas of modern Dahomey, Togo, and Nigeria.

The Portuguese, like other nations later, conducted a lively trade with Africa in gold, slaves, pepper, and ivory. In the fifteenth century, substantial numbers of Negroes were brought into both Spain and Portugal. In these two countries Africans were accorded the protection that the law and the church had historically provided for slaves. There were no bars to emancipation or intermarriage, and eventually the Africans' descendants were absorbed into the general population. A few achieved distinction—the most notable was Juan Latino, who became a Latin professor and humanist at the University of Granada in the sixteenth century. Negroes, usually as servants, accompanied many of the Spanish explorers. Estevanico, the most famous of the Negro explorers, played a major role on the expedition searching for the Seven Cities of Cíbola. Subsequently black people were with the French Jesuit missionaries in the exploration of Canada.

After the discovery of the New World, the slave trade soon became a major enterprise. Without the labor supply derived from Africa the economic development of the Americas would have been greatly retarded. The sparse Indian population on the Caribbean islands was enslaved first and died out under the brutal conditions. The earliest Negro slaves brought to the New World arrived at the beginning of the sixteenth century. Because of the rapid spread of sugar cultivation introduced first in Brazil, the slave trade grew rapidly. Roughly a century later, between 1620 and 1650, the English, Dutch, and French all secured firm footholds in the Caribbean. After the introduction of sugar cultivation in their colonies during the 1640's, the slave trade expanded. All three of these northern European powers turned to it with zest, seeking to supply their own colonies with slaves and to encroach upon the Spanish colonial market as well.

It was the Dutch who first really challenged the Portuguese monopoly. In 1611 they built a fort on the Gold Coast and before the middle of the century drove out the Portuguese, who thereafter confined their operations to Angola. During the second half of the seventeenth century the Gold Coast became an arena of intense competition among the European powers. The peak of the slave trade was reached in the eighteenth century. By then the major share of the traffic had shifted from the Gold Coast to the Slave Coast, with England becoming the leading slaving power.

For two centuries the European powers conducted the traffic through chartered monopolies. The first English company to engage seriously in the slave trade was the Royal Adventurers into Africa, chartered by the crown in 1660 and reorganized in 1672 as the Royal African Company. The company imported gold, ivory, and dyewood directly from Africa into England and purchased slaves for the New World. In 1698, following the trend among all the slave-trading powers, England ended the monopoly of the Royal African Company and inaugurated an era of free competition, which produced a dramatic increase in the slave trade and brought real wealth to the country. In addition to servicing the needs of the English colonies, British shippers became major suppliers for the colonies of other European powers, so that during the late eighteenth century, British merchants, chiefly from Liverpool, were handling roughly half the European slave traffic.

The dissolution of the Royal African Company's monopoly was also commercially advantageous to merchants in the English mainland colonies. Some of them had engaged in the slave traffic since early in the seventeenth century. Because the British companies chartered for the Guinea trade were interested mainly in supplying the lucrative sugar-producing West Indies, rather than in satisfying the lesser demands of the continental colonies, throughout the seventeenth century most of the slaves brought to the mainland came from the Caribbean. With the end of the Royal African Company's dominance, the number of slaves imported into the continental colonies increased sharply. During the last thirty years of the seventeenth century, the slave population of Virginia grew slowly from around 2,000 to 6,000. In the first decade after the end of the monopoly in 1698, 6,369 slaves were brought into the colony. As the demand for slave labor in the southern continental colonies grew, it became profitable to bring entire shiploads of blacks directly from Africa. During the eighteenth century the sources of slaves for British North America were principally African.

Merchants in all sections of the mainland provinces participated in the slave trade, but preeminent were those from the Massachusetts and Rhode Island seaports. Rhode Island entered the slave trade much later than Massachusetts, probably around the beginning of the eighteenth century. By mid-century Newport and Providence surpassed their rivals in Boston and Salem. From then until the official closing of the slave trade in 1808, the traffic flourished in Rhode Island and formed the basis of some of the greatest fortunes in the state.

In Africa itself the commerce in slaves developed into a relatively complex operation. Because the African rulers valued their inland monopoly, Europeans were generally confined to the coast; only in Senegambia did they penetrate far inland to trade. It was rare for Europeans themselves to engage in raids to obtain captives. Not that they had any scruples—some of the earliest traders did in fact participate in raids—but Europeans found it easier to depend for their supply upon African rulers and merchants.

European settlements, in the form of forts and sporadically occupied trading posts known as factories, were commonest in Senegambia and on the Gold Coast. At both types of establishments agents bought slaves and held them until the arrival of one or more slave ships. Along the Grain and Ivory Coasts, where no forts or factories were established, the Africans used smoke signals to indicate their readiness to trade. They came out to the European ships in canoes or, sometimes, waited on shore for a party from the ship. Along the Slave Coast the Africans successfully discouraged European fortifications. Near its western end was Whydah, where all the principal slaving nations of Europe maintained representatives. Here the ruler permitted only mud forts and forbade establishing them within three miles of the sea. In the Bight of Benin and in Calabar, where European forts and factories were absent, the river estuaries and the numerous mouths of the Niger provided safe places in which to conduct the traffic directly from the slave ships.

A slaving ship usually spent several months picking up captives on the shores of Africa, stopping first at one place and then another. The supply was uneven and a vessel might wait many weeks until the slaves were brought from the interior. Europeans found that a wide variety of goods was essential for trading, and since the demand for them differed from place to place, the prudent trader selected his stock with care. Among the most important goods used in exchange for slaves were cowrie shells and cotton cloth obtained from the East India Company; iron bars; firearms; gunpowder; brass rings, which were cut into pieces to make bracelets and collars; and liquor. On the Gold Coast alone 150 items were required; the almost exclusive dependence of the eighteenth-century Rhode Island traders on rum was highly unusual.

Warfare was the major source of slaves for the African rulers and merchants who traded for European goods. The traffic was originally a by-product of war, but given the insatiable demands of the European powers and the steady rise in the number of slaves sent to the New World, a number of scholars have assumed that by the eighteenth century the trade itself had become the major cause of military conflict among the West African states. The most recent scholarship, however, noting the marked variations over time in the availability of slaves from any particular area, suggests that enslavement continued to occur principally as a by-product of wars fought for other reasons rather than as a result of systematic slave-catching expeditions. Kidnapping was another significant source; lesser sources included enslavement for debts and crimes. In the Ibo area, east of the Niger River, slaves were obtained through oracles, of which the Aro Chukwu was easily the most powerful. Because political organization did not extend beyond the village level among the Ibos, the trading settlements of the Aro people, who had established colonies at river crossings and intersections along the interior trade routes, became the sites of courts where individuals and clans sought adjustment of their disputes. The Chukwu deity, serving as the highest court of appeal, levied fines on guilty parties, which were paid in slaves. The Ibos believed that these captives were eaten by the god, though actually they were sold to the coastal merchants. Where the coastal rulers did not conduct wars for slaves, merchants who dealt with Europeans bought slaves for resale at the interior markets. By whatever means they were obtained, the slaves intended for overseas trade were tied or fettered together and often marched hundreds of miles to sea. Along the Lower Niger River they were bound to the floors of canoes for the voyage downstream.

When a slave ship arrived it was first necessary to present a gift (or "dash") to the local ruler or his officials. Before commencing to trade with the African merchants, the Europeans were required to buy the king's slaves at an inflated price. The king also levied a tax (or "comey") on all slaves and goods obtained from African traders. Once the ruler's slaves had been sold, the whites could then bargain with the private traders. If there were not enough slaves immediately available, the Europeans often advanced the goods necessary to enable coastal middlemen to travel to interior slave markets. The European merchant's physician carefully examined the slaves in order to avoid purchasing ill, maimed, or elderly people. In the Niger Delta and Cross River—at Brass, Bonny, and Calabar—the slaves were immediately put on board the ship at anchor in the river estuary. In Whydah, on the other hand, where the trade was very well organized first by the king of Whydah and later by the king of Dahomey, who placed the province under a powerful viceroy, the traders were compelled to keep the slaves in the king's barracoons (temporary prisons) until the condition of the surf permitted transfer to the waiting ships. The king of course profited handsomely from payments charged for this service. In these barracoons the traders took the precaution of branding their slaves on the breast with a hot iron to prevent the king from substituting captives of poor quality.

Slaves thus obtained by the Europeans frequently displayed overt resistance. Although carefully guarded, they sometimes jumped overboard in attempts to escape. When not eaten by sharks, which nearly always surrounded slave ships, they might deliberately drown themselves if in danger of recapture by the slaveowners. Some slaves mutinied aboard ship, especially while the vessel was still anchored off the African shore. For example, on the *Nancy*, lying at anchor at New Calabar in 1769 with 132 slaves, the Negroes revolted, attacking several of the crew, whose members fired upon the slaves, killing six and wounding others. When Africans onshore heard the gunfire, large numbers of them surrounded the vessel in their canoes. Finding her poorly manned, they rescued all the slaves and plundered the ship of everything on board, leaving it a complete wreck. Slave mutinies were rarer in mid-ocean, yet a number of them occurred. For example, on the *Narborough* in 1753, some blacks who had been given considerable freedom so that they could help run the ship obtained firearms and massacred all of the white crew except a few members who were forced to steer the craft back to Bonny.

By far the worst part of the slave's journey was the "Middle Passage" from the African coast to the West Indies or the American mainland. This voyage generally lasted between forty and sixty days, and the overcrowded conditions were indescribable. Most eighteenth-century slave ships had two decks with the 'tween-deck space reserved for slaves. In a Newport slaver the average height between decks was three feet ten inches. Men, women, and children were each placed in separate compartments on the slave deck, the men bound together with iron ankle fetters. The slaves were made to lie with their backs on the deck, the men secured to chains or iron rods attached to the deck, squeezed so tightly together that the space allowed to each person was about sixteen inches wide and five and a half feet long. In the Liverpool ships toward the end of the century, the average height between the decks was five feet two inches. This permitted even worse crowding, for a shelf extending six to nine feet from the sides of the ship was placed midway between the two decks, and both the lower deck and the shelf were packed tightly with slaves. On the small sloops and schooners that lacked 'tween decks, the slaves were placed on a temporary platform of rough boards laid over the barrels in the hold. There are recorded instances where the space between such a "deck" and the one above was less than two feet. Most of the ships used after the trade had been outlawed were of this type, and during this later period of great risks and greater profits, slaves were stowed closer than ever, forced to lie on their sides, back to back, spoon-fashion. Where the space between decks was two feet or more, the slaves were placed sitting up in rows or crowded into each other's laps.

Conditions like these were described by eyewitnesses. Alexander Falconbridge, an eighteenth-century ship's surgeon, wrote:

> . . . In favourable weather they are fed upon deck, but in bad weather the food is given them below. Numberless quarrels take place among them during the meals, more especially when they are put upon short allowance, which frequently happens, if the passage from the coast of Guinea to the West India islands, proves of unusual length. . . . Exercise being deemed necessary for the preservation of their health, they are sometimes obliged to dance, when the weather will permit their coming on deck. If they go about it reluctantly, or do not move with agility, they are flogged. . . . The poor wretches are frequently compelled to sing also. . . .
> The hardships and inconveniences suffered by the negroes during the passage, are scarcely to be enumerated or conceived . . . the exclusion of the fresh air is among the most intolerable. For the purpose of admitting this needful refreshment, most of the ships in the slave trade are provided, between the decks, with five or six air-ports on each side of the ship. . . . But whenever the

sea is rough, and the rain heavy, it becomes necessary to shut these, and every other conveyance by which the air is admitted. The fresh air being excluded, the negroes['] rooms very soon grow intolerably hot. The confined air, rendered noxious by the effluvia exhaled from the bodies, and by being repeatedly breathed, soon produces fevers and fluxes, which generally carries off great numbers of them. . . . the floor of the rooms, was so covered with blood and mucus which had proceeded from them in consequence of the flux [i.e., dysentery], that it resembled a slaughter-house. It is not in the power of human imagination to picture to itself a situation more dreadful or disgusting. Numbers of the slaves having fainted, they were carried upon deck, where several of them died. . . . The surgeon, upon going between decks in the morning, to examine the situation of the slaves, frequently finds several dead, and among the men, sometimes a dead and living negro fastened by their irons together. When this is the case, they are brought upon the deck, and being laid on the grating, the living negro is disengaged, and the dead one thrown overboard.

The mortality from the bloody flux (dysentery), smallpox, and other diseases was often considerable. There are cases on record where whole shiploads, including the entire crew, went blind from ophthalmia, first contracted by the slaves in their filthy and crowded conditions. Very sick Negroes were sometimes thrown overboard, as the underwriters would not pay for slaves who died on the ship. Although one authority estimates that, on the average, slave losses en route were about 16 percent, there were many cases where one half to two thirds of the slaves on a ship were dead by the time it arrived at the West Indies.

Given the incomplete and scattered nature of the data, it is difficult to estimate the total number of slaves brought from Africa to the New World. Philip Curtin, the first person systematically to analyze and synthesize the available evidence, estimates that between nine and ten million Africans reached the New World in the three and a half centuries of the transatlantic slave trade—perhaps 1.5 million before 1700, about six million in the eighteenth century, and approximately two million in the nineteenth century. Of the total, less than 5 percent were imported into British North America. Thus the United States received only a minor share of the Africans obtained for the transatlantic slave trade, the bulk of whom went to Brazil and the Caribbean. Therefore, the fortunes of the Newport slave traders rested on the traffic with the West Indies.

Contrary to popular impression and despite the social disruption it caused, the transatlantic trade did not generally lead to a breakdown in West African social and political organization. In Angola, it is true, the Portuguese slave trade led to the disintegration of the extensive Mani-Congo kingdom. Because its ruler opposed the traffic, the Portuguese turned to his provincial officials, who supplied slaves in exchange for firearms that enabled them to challenge their king's authority. In West Africa, from the Gold Coast to the Niger Delta and Old Calabar, the overseas slave traffic encouraged the development of a substantial mercantile group whose fortunes were based on the slave trade. Where Europeans found strong despotic kingdoms, and rulers willing to supply their wants, the trade thrived from the start. Where these did not exist in West Africa, the slave traffic called them into being, or, as in the Niger Delta, stimulated the establishment of oligarchic and monarchical city-states. With the profits derived from the trade, and more particularly with the firearms obtained from Europeans in exchange for slaves, old rulers strengthened their power, and new autocratic kingdoms, such as Dahomey and Ashanti, arose. The role of firearms was crucial. Just as the Moroccans had quickly destroyed the Songhai empire in the sixteenth century because the latter lacked guns, so the strategically placed societies of the rain forest and the southern Sudan were able to overpower their poorly armed neighbors.

It is difficult to ascertain with any degree of precision how profitable the slave trade was. Complete records are lacking; profits and losses fluctuated from one voyage to another, depending on the prices both in Africa and in America and on the numbers surviving the transatlantic crossing. Recent research suggests that profits may not have been as great as they were once believed, but voyages with monetary returns ranging from one third to one half or more on the original investment were frequent. In the late eighteenth century Liverpool profits of 100 percent and more were not uncommon. Not only was the slave trade profitable in itself, but it was the base upon which the colonial industry and commerce of European powers rested. In the plantations of the New World, it supplied labor for cultivating the staple crops of sugar, cotton, tobacco, and indigo. The slave traffic was an important incentive to English industry and to agriculture, fishing, and rum manufacture in the northern colonies on the mainland.

The Middle Passage received its name because it was regarded as the middle leg of the system of triangular trading that by the eighteenth century became such a prominent feature of the slave traffic. From England various manufactured products—chiefly textiles, metal goods, and liquor—were exported to Africa, where they were exchanged for slaves. From the proceeds of slaves sold in the West Indies, sugar was bought and shipped to England. Each leg of the voyage was a profitable venture, and the whole business stimulated the shipbuilding, textile, and metallurgical industries. Colonial merchants also found the triangular trade exceedingly profitable. New England rum was exchanged for slaves in Africa, molasses was obtained with the proceeds in the West Indies, and in turn was manufactured into rum for use in the fur trade with the Indians, for sailors on the fishing fleets, and for further trade with Africa.

Officially the African slave traffic was outlawed by European countries during the early nineteenth century, but it actually persisted illicitly. In 1807 both England and the United States enacted legislation that the African slave trade would be illegal effective January 1, 1808. By 1850 other European nations involved in the traffic had followed suit, and Brazil, the largest market for African slavers, had joined the list. England, the world's leading naval power, was a prime force in obtaining the cooperation of countries like Spain and Portugal, which permitted the British Navy the right to search suspicious ships carrying their flags. The African coastal waters could have been patrolled with a fair degree of effectiveness if the United States had seriously tried to suppress the trade. The United States, however, would neither give England the right to search vessels flying the American flag nor herself dispatch enough ships to handle the matter. Searches by the United States Navy were spasmodic, and cases brought to court in the United States were often lost through legal technicalities because of sympathetic judges in both the North and South. Consequently, the flag of the United States became the most desirable one for slave traders; during the 1850's nearly all slave ships carried it.

Because slavery in the French West Indies ended during the Revolutionary and Napoleonic eras, and because England had outlawed slavery in her colonies in 1833, the principal markets for this illicit trade were Brazil and Cuba. It is impossible to know how many slaves were smuggled into the United States. According to a recent estimate, perhaps fifty thousand reached this country between 1808 and 1860. There is evidence that slaves from Africa were being landed on the Georgia coast in American vessels as late as 1858 and 1859. Unquestionably it was United States policy—or lack of it—that largely was responsible for the continuation of this commerce. Not until 1862, when the Lincoln Administration signed a treaty giving the British the right of search and seizure was the trade destroyed.

2

The first Negroes who landed at Jamestown in 1619, probably in a Dutch warship that had seized them from a Spanish slaver, did not become slaves but were assimilated into the system of indentured servitude that existed in the colony. The data are too meager for a clear picture of the development of black-white relations in seventeenth-century Virginia, but it appears that gradually, over the next half century, two interrelated developments occurred: the degradation of black men to an inferior position in society and the emergence of a system of slavery. Fragmentary evidence indicates that by 1640 black servants in Virginia occupied a status distinctly subordinate to white bondsmen. Not until the 1660's, however, was a rudimentary slave code enacted. This pattern of events stood in marked contrast with the situation in the British West Indies, where, around 1640, under the influence of the Spanish and Portuguese models, a full-blown system of plantation slavery swiftly matured.

In Virginia as early as 1630 a white man was sentenced to a sound whipping for having sexual relations with a black woman. A decade later a court case involving three runaway servants suggests that some black people might already have been slaves. All three received thirty lashes. The two who were white were sentenced to an additional year of service for their masters and three years for the colony, but the black was assigned to servitude for life. In the same year the Virginia House of Burgesses specifically denied Negroes the right to bear arms. In 1643 it passed a law declaring that black female servants over sixteen—but not white servants—were to be included among the tithables. The House also placed limitations on the terms of indentured servants, specifically omitting Negroes. The next year, asked to determine the legal status of a particular black servant who had been sold as "a slave for-ever," this assembly decided that he should only "serve as other Christian servants do." But clearly he had already served an unusually long period—twenty-one years. In the 1640's inventories of estates showed that Negroes were consistently listed as more valuable than white servants. The number of years remaining to be served ordinarily appeared in the case of whites, but no such notations were made for blacks. Virginia court cases of the early 1650's indicate that in selling black servants life servitude was specified, as well as the fact that their offspring inherited their status.

By the mid-seventeenth century, then, court decisions were reflecting the existence of slavery. Negroes entering the colony thereafter lacked indentures, and slavery was limited to people of African ancestry. Nevertheless there were anomalies. Some of the earlier black indentured servants not only gained their freedom but bought Negro servants of their own and acquired considerable property. For example, Anthony Johnson, who came to the colony perhaps in 1621, appears to have been free a year or so later and by 1651 imported five servants on whose headrights he received 250 acres in Northampton County. Richard Johnson, a carpenter, imported two white servants in 1654, for which he obtained 100 acres. A third black was granted 550 acres after importing eleven people. Ironically, one of the earliest decisions holding a Negro bound to life servitude involved a plaintiff who sued Anthony Johnson in 1654.

Such cases were exceptional. Blacks by this time were customarily slaves. But the first law referring to slavery was an act of 1661, decreeing that if a white servant fled with a black, the former was required to make up the time missed by the latter. The very casualness of this rather incidental reference makes it apparent that Negro slavery had been the custom for some time. The following year, reversing the English common law providing that children followed the status of their fathers, the Virginia House of Burgesses enacted a statute declaring that children born in the colony would be bond or free according to the status of their mothers. Even yet, however, some doubt existed about holding Christians in perpetual bondage, and legislation settling the matter was passed in 1667. This law decreed that "baptism doth not alter the condition of the person as to his bondage or freedom."

At that time white servants still formed the backbone of the farm labor force. In 1671 there were two thousand black slaves in Virginia and six thousand white servants out of a total population of forty thousand. With the development of large-scale plantation agriculture toward the latter part of the century and the ending of the Royal African Company's monopoly of the slave trade in 1698, Negro slavery rapidly took precedence over white servitude.

The evolution of Negro servitude in Maryland closely paralleled that of Virginia, but in Carolina, founded later, there was no such period of uncertainty. Negro slavery was expressly provided for in the Fundamental Constitutions of 1669 and from the beginning was actively encouraged by the proprietors. In Georgia, founded in 1733, the proprietors first excluded slavery on what they judged to be sound mercantilist grounds. Impressed by the example of South Carolina, however, the settlers clamored for slaves and permission was granted in 1750.

The characteristics of the different staple crops cultivated in the colonial South influenced the size of farming units and the concentration of the black population. Tobacco was the staple crop in the Chesapeake Bay colonies of Virginia and Maryland and in North Carolina. In South Carolina plantation agriculture did not really develop until the introduction of rice cultivation at the end of the seventeenth century. The evidence suggests that whites failed in their first attempts at rice cultivation. Ironically, it is likely that slaves familiar with its technology in Africa made possible its successful cultivation in tidewater South Carolina, thus accelerating the rapid expansion of slavery there in the first part of the eighteenth century. Later, after the middle of the century, indigo also became a major crop. After Georgia was opened to slavery, the cultivation of these two crops quickly spread to that colony. Of necessity, rice and indigo were concentrated in the low-lying, moist, and hot Sea Islands and coastal lands. Tobacco could be grown in the hilly back country and to a considerable extent was cultivated on small units by white farmers with few or no slaves. On the other hand, the technology of rice cultivation, with its extensive irrigation system, promoted large plantations and the use of slave labor. During the 1780's, the average size of slaveholdings in the counties surrounding Charleston, South Carolina, was about three times the average holding in the principal plantation counties of Maryland and Virginia. In 1790 the largest slaveholder in the tobacco colonies, the noted signer of the Declaration of Independence, Charles Carroll of Carrollton, held 316 chattels, while in the Charleston district one planter held 695 and five owned over 300 slaves apiece. The black population was chiefly concentrated in the tidewater areas of the Chesapeake colonies, South Carolina, and Georgia, where the largest plantations were located. In such counties Negroes in fact outnumbered whites, although South Carolina was the only colony where slaves were consistently in the majority throughout the eighteenth century.

With the increase in the numbers of blacks, the fear of lawlessness and insurrection rose, leading to the passage of stringent slave codes regulating their activity. There were also sporadic attempts in Virginia and South Carolina to limit the importation of slaves (efforts often disallowed by the king's Privy Council). While the codes varied from colony to colony, generally they provided that slaves could not carry arms, own property, or leave their plantation without a written pass. Murder, rape, arson, and in some cases robbery, were capital crimes; common punishments for lesser offenses were maiming, whipping, or branding. After insurrectionary plots were discovered in the Charleston area in 1739 and 1740, South Carolina strengthened its slave code, sharply limiting the assembling of slaves and prohibiting the sale of liquor to them. The policy of increasing the severity of the legal restrictions upon slaves—and sometimes on free Negroes as well—was almost universally employed throughout the period of slavery as a response to servile rebellions.

North of Chesapeake Bay, slave labor was not so economically profitable, and slavery never secured as firm a foothold. New Jersey and New York were both familiar with slavery on a small scale during the period of Dutch settlement. Indeed the Dutch West India Company, itself a major slave-trading organization, and the Dutch government hoped to stimulate agriculture by encouraging the importation of slaves into New Netherlands. Importations increased noticeably under the English, but in both these colonies slavery never involved large-scale plantation agriculture. In New York there was a widespread distribution of small slaveholders, Negroes forming about 12 percent of the population during the eighteenth century. In both colonies Negroes worked in a wide variety of occupations—as farm laborers, domestic servants, miners, and artisans (ironworkers, carpenters, coopers, tanners, shoemakers, millers). Although bondage in New Jersey and New York was far less harsh than in the South, their slave codes were not very different from those of the tobacco and rice colonies. A slave revolt of serious proportions in New York City in 1712, and hysteria over a possible, but unproved, conspiracy in the same city in 1741, guaranteed that the codes would be kept as severe as those in the South.

Although at the end of the eighteenth century the Pennsylvania Quakers were in the vanguard of the antislavery movement, certain Quaker merchants had played a significant role in the slave trade. The institution of African servitude was firmly rooted in Pennsylvania during most of the colonial period. In the southern part of the colony, slavery on a small scale developed in the early 1700's and retained its viability there into the second half of the century, though not for economic reasons. Rather, the possession of slaves, used chiefly in domestic capacities, was valued as an aristocratic status symbol. In the colony's urban center, Philadelphia, on the other hand, slaves were far more important economically. Slave importations there reached a peak during the Seven Years War (1756–63), when the supply of indentured servants was cut off and black bondsmen provided important services as mechanics and artisans. Though the slave code does not seem to have been too different from that of other colonies, contemporary reports indicate that slavery in Pennsylvania was relatively mild and the slaves were permitted considerable latitude in their activities.

The New England colonies, important though their role was in the slave trade, valued black labor even less than the middle colonies. There is evidence of the presence of Negro servitude in each of the four New England colonies (Massachusetts, Connecticut, Rhode Island, and New Hampshire) by the middle of the seventeenth century, but by 1700, blacks numbered only about one thousand in a population estimated at ninety thousand. At no time did Negroes constitute as much as 5 percent of the people in any of these colonies, with the exception of Rhode Island, where blacks were recorded in 1749 as being 11 percent of the population. This was the one New England colony where something resembling the plantation system of the South developed.

Since New Englanders were in close commercial contact with the West Indies, Negro servitude there did not go through the lengthy evolutionary process that had been the case in Virginia and Maryland. The first shipment of West Indian slaves probably arrived at Massachusetts Bay in 1638; three years later, the colony recognized slavery in the Body of Liberties of 1641. This law was later adopted by Plymouth and Connecticut. Perhaps because of the libertarian spirit of its founder, Roger Williams, Rhode Island proved to be something of an exception; its law of 1652 prohibited enslavement and limited involuntary servitude to a period of ten years. But this statute was openly violated and in 1708 slavery received legal recognition.

New England's economy was diversified and so was the Negro's work. Many black people were employed on small farms, but in the fertile Narragansett area of Rhode Island, they were used on the large dairy and cattle-raising estates by the local landed aristocracy known as the Narragansett planters. The number of slaves on these farms ranged from five to forty, and although most of them were in dairying, others raised sheep and cultivated vegetables or tobacco. New England Negroes also worked as house servants and coachmen; as laborers in shipbuilding, lumbering, ironworking, cooperage, distilling, and other industries; as skilled artisans in blacksmith and carpenter shops, tanneries, and printing shops; as apprentices to doctors, and even as physicians themselves.

Slavery in New England was the mildest in the colonies. Because the Puritan slave code was modeled on the Old Testament slave law, it afforded greater recognition to the slaves as persons and permitted them more legal rights than did slave codes elsewhere. There were the usual limitations on the slave's behavior of course—rules designed as elsewhere to prevent conspiracies and robberies. Slaves were forbidden on the streets at night after nine; they could not strike a white person. The sale of liquor to them was prohibited. Unlike the colonies to the south and except for capital punishment for a limited number of crimes, punishment was confined to whipping; there was no maiming, dismemberment, or branding. As property, slaves were subject to taxation like other goods and chattels; they could be bought, sold, and inherited. On the other hand, masters were specifically forbidden to kill their slaves (though no master ever appears to have been executed for doing so); slaves could acquire, hold, and transfer property; they could offer testimony against whites even in cases in which black people were not involved (in contrast to the South and New York, where this was explicitly forbidden); they were entitled to a jury trial (though they could not serve on juries). Slaves were expected to obey the sexual standards legally set for whites. Marriages were duly solemnized and legally recorded in the same manner as for whites, yet slave families were frequently broken up through sales and the settlement of wills. Masters could be as cruel in New England as elsewhere, but relationships tended to be paternalistic, as in Pennsylvania, where most slaves were either household retainers or worked closely with masters in shop and field. Slaves could not vote, of course, but they held mock elections in each of the New England colonies at which a black "governor" was chosen amid much festivity. Apparently these "governors" exercised some control over the slaves and appointed "judges" and "sheriffs" to handle minor violations.

In New England more attention was paid to the slaves' religious conversion and education than in any of the other colonies. How many became Christian is not known, but these converts faced the usual contradictions. For example, those who were considered members of the Congregationalist Church did not vote in church affairs and sat in a rear section or in the gallery. Some Negroes were so well trained by their masters that they managed farms and stores and had charge of ships and warehouses. Newport Gardner, a slave of Caleb Gardner of Newport, Rhode Island, received music lessons and soon became so proficient that he opened a music school and taught both blacks and whites. A few slaves turned to literary compositions. The most famous of these was poetess Phillis Wheatley, purchased as a young girl when she was brought from Africa in 1761 by a mistress who taught her to read and write.

Clearly slavery in New England was not of the same order as in the South or even in New York and Pennsylvania. The fact that slaves could even sue their masters not only signified a status superior to that of the slaves farther south but helped pave the way for emancipation. In the 1760's and 1770's a number of individual black people successfully sued for their freedom in the Massachusetts courts. Though they uniformly won these suits, the procedure was slow and expensive. Such legal decisions applied only to the individuals who brought the action and therefore left the mass of slaves untouched. Yet these cases established a pattern, and in 1783, in the noted *Quok Walker* case, the state supreme court declared slavery in Massachusetts unconstitutional.

3

Quok Walker was liberated on the grounds that since the preamble to the state constitution of 1780 declared that all men were born free and equal, slavery was illegal. To the Massachusetts Supreme Court, the ideology of the American Revolution was fundamental law and not an abstraction. Indeed, the Revolutionary era proved to be, relatively speaking, a pinnacle of antislavery sentiment and racial egalitarianism.

Negroes themselves, especially in New England, cited the principles of the Declaration of Independence in requesting an end to their servitude. In January 1777, a group of Massachusetts slaves petitioned the state legislature, claiming a natural God-given right to freedom and asserting "that Every Principle from which Amarica has Acted in the Cours of their unhappy Difficulties with Great Briton Pleads Stronger than A thousand arguments in favours of your pet[it]ioners. . . ." During the Revolutionary War a number of white Americans, especially in the North, such as John Jay and Abigail Adams, were seriously concerned with the moral issue involved in slavery. Farther south, slaveowners like George Washington and Thomas Jefferson looked forward to its gradual abolition. Only in South Carolina and Georgia was support for the slavery system undiminished.

The antislavery and racially egalitarian tendencies of the Revolutionary era resulted from four converging streams of influence. One, of course, was political: the struggle for independence against English tyranny. Another was economic: slavery in the North had never been especially remunerative anyway, and in the tobacco counties of Virginia, Maryland, and North Carolina fluctuating prices and declining fertility of the land tended to make the plantation regime only marginally profitable.

Antislavery enthusiasm was also fed by two major intellectual traditions. One was the eighteenth-century European Enlightenment. Rooted in John Locke's environmentalist psychology and defense of individualism and revolution, the ideals of the Enlightenment, with its belief in human liberty, natural rights, egalitarianism, cosmopolitanism, and human progress, provided as much justification for antislavery and the cause of the free Negro as for the Revolution itself. The two leading American representatives of the Enlightenment, Thomas Jefferson and Benjamin Franklin, were both much concerned about the problems of slavery and the future of blacks in American society.

The ideals of the Enlightenment coalesced with an older stream of religious antislavery thinking in America. The earliest opponents of the slave trade and slavery were a handful of religious thinkers, chiefly Quakers. It was primarily the eighteenth-century Quaker pamphleteers John Woolman and Anthony Benezet who brought the issues before the public. In 1754–5 the Pennsylvania Yearly Meeting of Friends decreed that persons engaged in buying or selling slaves would be expelled. In 1775 they helped to found the first antislavery society in America, and the following year ruled that all members must emancipate their slaves. Friends meetings in the tobacco belt were drawn to the same decision, and even some substantial slaveholders among them emancipated their slaves rather than leave the church. The Quakers also exercised considerable influence in New England, where, joined by a Puritan stream, the movement against slavery gained great momentum during the years prior to the Revolution.

It should be noted that white antislavery men were not necessarily believers in the psychological equality of the races.

Many actually accepted the notion of black inferiority and advocated colonization, or the expatriation of blacks, as the only satisfactory solution to the race problem. Thomas Jefferson well illustrated the ambivalences and contradictions of many of even the most advanced thinkers on the subject. Jefferson, through inheritance and matrimony, became a large slaveholder, owning well over two hundred blacks. To Jefferson, slavery was a moral evil, unjust to Negroes and deleterious to the character of whites. From his first term in the House of Burgesses he had displayed a strong interest in facilitating the manumission of slaves. Although he greatly favored a program of gradual emancipation, Jefferson personally freed only a few of his own slaves, and these were mostly closely related to him by ties of kinship. Moreover, Jefferson did not conceive of the two races living in the same nation on an equal and harmonious plane. White prejudice, black remembrance of oppression, and "the real distinction which nature has made" would "divide us into parties, and produce convulsions, which will probably never end but in the extermination of one or the other race." While not dogmatic on the subject of racial differences in ability, he suspected that blacks might be "inferior to the whites in the endowments both of mind and body." Although strong circumstantial evidence supports the claim made by the children of Jefferson's slave Sally Hemings that he was their father, Jefferson himself expressed fear of the race mixture that he believed would follow emancipation. Not surprisingly, therefore, he proposed that freed Negroes be settled in their own society in the interior of the continent, far removed from the whites. On the other hand, he was interested in evidence of Negro ability. In 1791, as Secretary of State, he appointed the black mathematician and almanac maker Benjamin Banneker of Maryland to the staff of the commission that surveyed the site for the national capital. To Banneker he wrote, "Nobody wishes more than I do to see such proofs as you exhibit that nature has given to our black brethren talents equal to those of the other colours of men, and that the appearance of a want of them is owing merely to the degraded condition of their existence both in Africa and

America." But to some others Jefferson took a different line, voicing a suspicion that much of Banneker's work had been produced by a white friend. Until the very end of his life, Jefferson retained his ambivalent attitudes about Negroes.

The inconsistencies that marked the thinking of Jefferson, who to this day symbolizes more than any other man the idealism of the Revolutionary era, were mirrored in the conduct of the Revolutionary War itself. Despite the more favorable climate, prejudice and discrimination still abounded, as the policies about the use of black soldiers demonstrate. All the colonies had laws excluding Negroes from militia service, but, as in crises during the French and Indian Wars, in the first battles of the Revolution in the spring of 1775 these laws were overlooked. In fact a number of Massachusetts slaves were freed to fight in the army. By summer, however, Washington and his staff ordered the termination of black recruitment, and during the winter of 1775–6 both the states and the Continental Congress acted to prohibit their enlistment. The protests of free Negroes were mostly in vain. The British had no such qualms, and Lord Dunmore, governor of Virginia, promised freedom to slaves who fought alongside the British. Though the Southern slaveholders were frightened, and though large numbers of Negroes from Georgia, South Carolina, and Virginia did join the English, recent scholarship has discounted the effect that Dunmore's proclamation of 1775 was formerly supposed to have had in prompting a reversal of American policy regarding the use of black troops. Beginning in 1777, nevertheless, the manpower problems compelled state after state—and in 1779 the Continental Congress—to reconsider the earlier stand. By the end of the war, both Congress and most of the states promised that slaves who enlisted would receive freedom when their military service was over. Only Georgia and South Carolina, despite urgent pleading from Congress and the military, prohibited black enlistments entirely.

Freedom through service in the armed forces was only one of the fruits Negroes gained from the Revolution. The movement to emancipate slaves made considerable headway in the North-

ern states and the upper South. The antislavery society founded
in Pennsylvania in 1775 was reorganized in 1787 with Benjamin
Franklin named as president. In 1785 antislavery men founded
the New York Society for Promoting the Manumission of
Slaves, with John Jay as president. By 1792 antislavery societies
existed in each of the states from Massachusetts to Virginia. All
of them attacked the slave trade and most pleaded for the
eventual abolition of slavery. Some, however, agreeing with
Jefferson on the future of the two races in America, advocated
the deportation of free blacks from the United States.

Moreover, Northern states took steps to free their slaves.
State legislatures usually provided for gradual emancipation.
Pennsylvania in 1780 passed a law directing that black people
born after that year were to be free at the age of twenty-eight
and until then were to be treated as apprentices. In 1783, as
pointed out earlier, Massachusetts ended slavery by court de-
cree. Connecticut and Rhode Island in 1784 passed acts of
gradual emancipation, as did New York and New Jersey in 1785
and 1786, though the latter two states did not enact effective
legislation until 1799 and 1804, respectively. In the upper
South, Virginia and North Carolina passed laws encouraging
owners to emancipate their slaves. Thus in 1783 Jefferson persuaded the Virginia legislature to make it lawful for a slaveowner by will or other instrument in writing to free his slaves.
Though the law held masters responsible for the support of the
blacks they freed, a wave of manumissions followed. The high-
water mark in antislavery legislation was the Northwest Ordinance of 1787, which prohibited slavery in the Northwest Territory.

In that same year, however, the Constitution was written.
From the point of view of American Negroes, the Constitution,
coming at the close of an era of distinct improvement in their
status, must be regarded as a retrogressive document. During
the debates at the Constitutional Convention, opposition to
slavery and the slave trade was voiced; yet because of the
strength of the slave states, the framers of the Constitution gave
protection of property rights in slaves higher priority than the

protection of human rights. In three circumlocutory clauses
that avoided the direct mention of slaves or Negroes, the Constitution clearly recognized and legitimized the existence of
slavery. It provided that for purposes of direct taxes and appor-
tioning representation in the House of Representatives, each
slave would count as three fifths of a person; it prohibited Congress from stopping the slave trade before 1808; and it bound
states to assist in returning to their masters fugitive slaves who
had fled across state lines. Six years after the Constitution was
written, Congress passed its first fugitive-slave law to implement
the provisions of this clause, and Eli Whitney invented the
cotton gin. Together the Constitution and the gin were pro-
phetic symbols of a fateful reversal in the fortunes of black
Americans.

4

The late-eighteenth-century technological revolution in cotton manufacturing, which marked the opening phases of the
Industrial Revolution in England, also strengthened plantation
slavery in America. Cotton, first domesticated in Africa and an
important textile in the Middle East and India, had been known
to Europe for centuries. But it was the remarkable series of
inventions in the spinning and weaving of cotton and the application of water and, later, steam power to the production of
cotton cloth that sharply lowered the price of cotton textiles
and created a great demand for the raw lint.

Cotton had been grown in the colonies, but serious interest
in its commercial possibilities developed only after the emergence of the new English textile factories. The barrier to cotton
becoming a major staple crop was the particular variety grown
in the United States; the lint stuck tightly to its fuzzy seeds and
it could be separated only by laborious work. Planters began to
experiment with varieties of West Indian cotton, and in 1790 a
South Carolina planter harvested the first successful crop. This
long-staple "sea-island" cotton was of very high quality, in every
way superior to the short-staple upland cotton previously grown
in the United States. Moreover, it had a striking commercial

advantage because its seeds could be separated easily from the lint. But climatic conditions made it possible to grow sea-island cotton only on the low-lying coast and Sea Islands of South Carolina and Georgia. Then in 1793 Eli Whitney invented the cotton gin, a simple device for separating the seeds from the lint, making the production of the short-staple cotton highly remunerative.

Although recent research suggests that on the eve of the invention of the cotton gin plantation slavery, even in the upper South, was more vigorous than had previously been believed, certainly Whitney's work fostered immeasurably the extraordinary expansion of the slave system that followed and fastened it firmly throughout the Southern states. Almost at once cotton became the staple crop in the Georgia and Carolina piedmont between the coastal plains and the Appalachians. Cotton lent itself to cultivation on small farms, though large plantations were more profitable. Coastal plantation owners staked out new lands in the piedmont, while yeoman farmers bought slaves and tried to rise into the large-scale planter class. After 1800 cotton cultivation spread to North Carolina, southeastern Virginia, and over the mountains into Tennessee. Then planters realized that the fertile alluvial soils of Mississippi and Alabama and the bottomlands in Louisiana and Arkansas were superior to the upland soils, and they streamed southwestward.

Actually the cotton gin had been introduced into the lower Mississippi Valley in 1795. Under the French, Spanish, and British, the Gulf Coast and the lower Mississippi Valley had already developed plantation economies based on the cultivation of rice, indigo, tobacco, and Creole cotton—a long-staple variety originally from Siam. In 1795, the year that Spain ceded to the United States the territory lying east of the Mississippi and north of the 31st parallel, the planters of the Natchez area, anxious to make Creole cotton commercially profitable, eagerly adopted the cotton gin. About the same time that large-scale cotton agriculture appeared on the eastern seaboard and in the Natchez area, another major staple, sugar cane, was introduced in the delta land of southeastern Louisiana, then owned by

Spain; by 1796 it had proved a definite commercial success. A decade later there were eighty-one sugar estates, a number of them the property of refugees from the Haitian Revolution, who undoubtedly gave sugar production a real stimulus in Louisiana.

Ironically it was this Haitian Revolution that provided additional land for the expansion of slavery in the United States. The French Revolution of 1789 precipitated an uprising in Haiti in 1791, and after a bitter struggle the French recognized the freedom of the slaves. The leader of this revolution was Toussaint L'Ouverture, who was at the height of his power when Spain ceded the Louisiana Territory back to France in 1800. Napoleon, envisioning a grand empire in North America, with Haiti as its base, determined to overthrow the revolutionary government. Toussaint was captured, but this did not destroy the revolution. When yellow fever and the persistence of the Haitian black men finally defeated the French armies, Napoleon gave up his scheme, selling the Louisiana Territory to the United States in 1803.

In the early years of the nineteenth century there was a steady growth of both the slave and white populations in the Mississippi Territory, but down to the War of 1812 the chief expansion of the cotton economy was in the Carolina-Georgia piedmont. Thereafter, as small farmers and large planters alike moved steadily southwestward, they discovered in Alabama and Mississippi two especially desirable sections for cotton cultivation. One was a strip of black soil curving from south-central Alabama into northeastern Mississippi; from it came the name "Black Belt," which originally referred to the color of the soil. The other, and larger, area embraced an alluvial bottomland on both sides of the Mississippi from northern Tennessee south to the Red River. In Louisiana and Arkansas cotton agriculture was also concentrated in the rich river valleys north of Baton Rouge. After crossing the Mississippi, the cotton growers advanced into Mexico and played a crucial role in the events leading to the acquisition of Texas. This westward expansion of slavery and the cotton kingdom provided the principal focus for the sectional political controversies—the Missouri Compromise, the debate over the acquisition of Texas and the Mexican War, the Compromise of 1850, the Kansas-Nebraska Act, and the Dred Scott decision—that eventually reached a climax in the Civil War.

Although rice, tobacco, and sugar cane remained important crops in some sections of the South, cotton was indeed king. Production rose from 13,000 bales in 1792 to 461,000 in 1817, over 2 million bales in 1840, and nearly 5 million bales in 1860. The states from Alabama and Tennessee westward to Texas produced one sixteenth of this cotton in 1811; they produced one third in 1820, almost two thirds in 1840, and three fourths by 1860. By midcentury nearly three quarters of the slaves were involved in cotton agriculture. This rapid expansion of the cotton kingdom was made possible by two factors: a large supply of suitable but inexpensive land, and an increasing—though never sufficient—supply of slaves. Virgin land and slaves were the most valued possessions of the rapidly advancing cotton frontier. The speed with which the cotton kingdom spread was due in part to the planter's carelessness with the land. When fertility declined after ten or twenty years, he simply moved to another plantation, often in an adjoining state. Large plantations tended to replace small farms in the fertile Black Belt and alluvial river bottoms. Population statistics demonstrate the prevalence of large-scale plantations. In Alabama and Mississippi, slaves formed nearly half the population in the middle of the century, and among the plantation counties of the Southwest, as in the coastal areas of Georgia and South Carolina, the proportion of slaves in the population often surpassed 60 and 70 percent.

The rise of the cotton kingdom involved an enormous migration of slaves in a generally southwestward direction. In 1820 the area that was ultimately to include the states of Florida, Alabama, Mississippi, Louisiana, Arkansas, and Texas contained about sixty thousand slaves; by 1860 the region had ten times that number. Natural increase played its role, but this growth represented chiefly a vast movement of slaves from the Border

and Atlantic states to satisfy the insatiable demand of the expanding cotton kingdom. Many slaves were brought to the
Southwestern states by Eastern planters, who either established
their families on their new estates or operated them as absentee
owners. Others were moved through the interstate slave trade.
Virginia was the leading exporter of slaves—nearly 300,000
left her boundaries between 1830 and 1860. Maryland was also
an important exporting state during the early nineteenth century. After 1830 the Carolinas and then Kentucky, Tennessee,
and Missouri joined the list. In the 1850's even Georgia was
included. This geographical shift reflected not only the enormous and ever-increasing demands for slaves by the Southwestern states but also the progressive exhaustion of the soil in the
tobacco and older cotton regions. As far back as 1787, it was
openly charged on the floor of the Constitutional Convention
that Virginia's delegates favored the prohibition of the foreign
slave trade not for humanitarian reasons but because they
wanted the market value of their slaves to rise.

Slaves sold in the interstate trade were largely obtained either
from impecunious planters who disposed of them to pay off a
debt, or from executors of wills settling an estate. Such transactions sometimes involved hundreds of slaves. In the largest
sale on record from a single owner, the executors of the estate
of James Bond, the biggest cotton planter in Georgia, disposed
of his 566 slaves for a total of over $580,000 in 1860. Pierce
Butler, owner of another great Georgia estate, was forced in
1859 to sell approximately 400 slaves to pay off his debts.

Historians are now in general agreement that the deliberate
breeding of slaves for sale was only rarely practiced. Yet, among
planters everywhere, the prospect of multiplying the value of
slave property through natural increase was eyed with pleasure,
and owners often consciously took steps to encourage it by re-
warding child-bearing slaves. A slave woman's proved or anticipated fecundity was universally an important factor in determining her market value; advertisements and planters
commonly referred to fertile females as "good breeders." Some
eminent Virginia citizens openly stated the economics of the

matter. As the leading historian of the domestic slave trade, Frederic Bancroft, has said, slave rearing "became the source of the largest and often the only regular profit of nearly all slaveholding farmers and of many planters in the Upper South." He concluded that "next to the great and quick profit of bringing virgin soil under cultivation, slave-rearing was the surest, most remunerative and most approved means of increasing agricultural capital. It was advised and practised by the wisest rural slaveowners."

Usually planters who encouraged the natural increase of their slaves sincerely regretted—often for sentimental and moral as well as economic reasons—the necessity of periodically disposing of a valuable part of their "capital," but it was, of course, an everyday occurrence. Admittedly it was considered bad form to separate families, and planters who did so often sold their slaves secretly or only after first attempting to sell them together Traders playing up to this desire for respectability, even the most unscrupulous ones, advertised that they did not split families. Auction records and manifests of slaves sent to New Orleans, however, prove that separation of families was the rule rather than the exception. When families were advertised for sale, they almost always included only the mother and her younger children, and often not even all of them. Youngsters of ten or twelve were generally considered single. Since even smaller children could be marketed more profitably individually than in family groups, it was not uncommon for four- or five-year-olds to be sold that way.

Slave traders ranged from itinerants, who scoured the rural counties of the Border States, to large-scale entrepreneurs operating their businesses even in the most fashionable hotels on the main thoroughfares of the principal cities. The largest and most successful had interstate operations. Franklin & Armfield owned three vessels, which made fortnightly voyages between New Orleans and Alexandria, Virginia, during the trading season. Bolton, Dickens & Company, the largest slave traders in Memphis during the early 1850's, had branch offices in Lexington, Kentucky, and St. Louis and Vicksburg. Slave traders might be "commission agents," or "auctioneers," who sold for planters on a commission basis of usually 2.5 percent, or they might privately engage in buying slaves for speculation and re-sale. Commonly a slave trader did both. Frequently auctioneers and commission merchants were also agents for those who wished to hire out their slaves, a practice universal throughout the South. The more successful resident traders in a city oper-ated slave prisons housing their own slaves and those of other traders as well. Slaves might make the journey to the markets of the Deep South by ship or, in the 1850's, by train, but the chief method of transporting them was overland on foot. Travelers reported seeing coffles of up to two hundred and even more, the men shackled together, marching across the countryside, and it was said that such groups could cover about twenty-five miles a day.

All the Southern states enacted elaborate slave codes, care-fully defining the status of the bondsmen and enforcing their subordination in the social order. Fundamentally these codes were much alike, partly because the newer states copied their laws from the older ones and partly because the nature of the slave system determined certain types of regulations. In the years after the Revolutionary War there was a tendency toward humanizing the slave codes, but the laws became more strin-gent during the nineteenth century, particularly in the Deep South.

Basically slaves were regarded as property and as such had no rights. They could not be parties in lawsuits, except indirectly where a free person sued for a slave's freedom; nor could they offer testimony in court except against other Negroes. They could not make contracts to buy or sell goods, and, with some minor exceptions, property ownership was forbidden. Since bondsmen could not make contracts, their marriages had no legal standing. On the other hand, the Southern states carefully guaranteed the slaveowner's rights in human property. Severe penalties were set for the theft of slaves, and when a slave was executed for a capital crime, the state ordinarily compensated his master. Owners could of course sell or hire out their bondsmen. When used as security for loans, slaves could be seized for the benefit of creditors. Masters writing their wills could divide their slaves as they wished, even if it was necessary to separate families or to sell the slaves to obtain cash for the estate.

Those states where slavery flourished discouraged the manumission of slaves. The Border States erected no such barriers, other than insisting that manumitted slaves must not become public charges because of age or illness. The states of the upper South (Tennessee, Virginia, and North Carolina) insisted that manumitted slaves must leave their borders. But in the Deep South legislation on the subject became increasingly severe. Most outlawed private manumission early in the nineteenth century, the only exceptions being made by special acts of the legislature for particularly meritorious bondsmen. A master could still provide in his will that his slaves be sent to a free state and manumitted, but in the 1840's and 1850's even this practice was prohibited in several states of the Deep South. A man could always send his slaves out of the state and free them while he was still alive, but private manumissions became an increasingly rare phenomenon in the years before the Civil War.

A major part of the slave codes in all the Southern states was the provision for control and discipline. Slaves were not permitted to leave plantations without permission, and any white person finding a slave "at large" without a pass could take him to the authorities. If a slave forged a pass or free papers he was guilty of a felony. Except for a few places, bondsmen were not legally permitted to hire out their own time or to live by themselves. Slaves were not allowed to possess firearms. They could not visit whites or free blacks or receive them as visitors. Slaves could not assemble or hold a meeting unless a white man was present. A slave could not preach except to the slaves of his own master and on his master's premises with whites present. It was · also against the law to teach slaves to read or write or to give them reading matter. Slaves were not allowed to strike whites even in self-defense; to do this, or to use insulting language toward a white man, was a crime. On the other hand, for a white man to kill a slave was seldom regarded as murder. Criminal codes were more severe on slaves and free Negroes than on whites. Slaves were subject to the death penalty for rape or attempted rape of a white woman, murder or attempted murder, revolt or attempted revolt, poisoning, robbery, and arson—and, under some circumstances, striking a white person. The death penalty was usually enforced against slaves only when whites were the victims.

Slaves, though property, were thus accountable as persons for their acts. In the colonial period, they had been tried before special courts consisting of justices of the peace and, in some states, of slaveholders. During the nineteenth century, most states provided for jury trials in capital crimes, but still the accused could not expect fairness. Those convicted were most often sentenced to a whipping since jail terms or the death penalty would deprive masters of laborers.

All of the Southern states provided for a patrol system to guard against unlawful assembly, the secreting of firearms, or insurrection. All adult white males, whether slaveholders or not, were required to serve periodically. Since slaveholders preferred to evade this onerous duty by employing substitutes or paying fines, the patrols often consisted of poor whites who were jealous of the wealthy planters and vented their hostility on black people. Slaveholders constantly went to court charging that patrollers had illegally whipped their slaves. The patrol system was uneven in its implementation; in regions with many slaves and during periods of actual or rumored insurrection, it was vigorously enforced. Otherwise the system was operated more casually.

In addition to holding slaves accountable for their behavior, Southern slave codes recognized the slaves as persons in certain other respects. Some codes regulated hours of labor and fined masters for failing to provide slaves with proper food and clothes. During the colonial period penalties for killing a slave were light. Changes occurred after the Revolution and ultimately all Southern states made malicious killing punishable as murder. By midcentury branding, ear cropping, and other mutilations had pretty much disappeared as punishments for slaves, both at law and in practice. Most codes had come to regard cruelty as an offense, even if it did not lead to death. In practice, however, the courts emasculated the application of these laws, and convictions for maltreatment of slaves were extremely rare. This was inevitable, for black people could not testify against whites, white witnesses were naturally hesitant about appearing against other whites, and it was almost impossible to find a white jury that would convict. Thus, such slight protections as the law provided Negroes were, for the most part, unenforceable.

More important than some of the legal provisions in mitigating the severity of the slave code was the fact that the laws were often ignored. Not only were petty crimes handled directly on the master's estate, but even in the more serious offenses, the owners, who did not wish to lose the labor of a slave even temporarily, often failed to notify the authorities. Some masters, acting out of a sense of paternalism or from a desire to encourage good morale among their bondsmen, allowed their slaves to meet together without the presence of whites, to travel at large without passes, to trade without permits, to hunt with guns, and to hire out their own time. Nor was it rare for a master to teach a slave to read and write. A few owners even permitted their slaves to live independently, allowing them virtual freedom. Generally, in times when fears of slave revolt were in abeyance, there tended to be a certain laxity in the enforcement of the codes, and the paternalism of masters to favorite slaves led to violations of the strict letter of the law.

5

Despite the decline of slavery in the Northern states, the slave population in the whole country more than quadrupled from less than 700,000 in 1790 to about 3,200,000 in 1850 and then rose to nearly 4 million in 1860. At midcentury about 400,000 of these lived in towns and cities; the majority, about 1,800,000, were cotton producers; the rest mainly raised tobacco, hemp, rice, and sugar cane. During the 1850's, on the southwestern frontier in Texas, the majority of the early cowboys were Negro slaves.

While the great mass of slaves were field hands, others were engaged in a variety of nonfarming occupations. In addition to the house servants and the skilled artisans of the plantations, there were skilled artisans and mechanics in the towns. Slaves were also used for many kinds of heavy labor: in the turpentine industry, in sawmills and quarries, in the coal and salt mines of Virginia, in the saltpeter mines of the Mammoth Caves in Kentucky, and in the iron mines and furnaces of Virginia, Kentucky, and Tennessee. They labored as deckhands and firemen on riverboats, as dock workers, as laborers on the construction of canals and railroads. They worked in the tobacco factories of Virginia, in textile mills from Virginia to Mississippi, in cotton presses, in tanneries, in shipyards, and in laundries of many towns.

Although the typical slave was a cotton cultivator, he did not necessarily work on a large farm or plantation. Nor did the majority of white Southerners own slaves or plantations. In the South in 1860 there were only 385,000 slaveholders in a free population of 1,500,000 families, so that only one quarter of the Southern whites had a vested interest in preserving the institution of slavery. Slaveholding families were concentrated in certain states, particularly in the belt from Georgia to Louisiana, where one third or more families owned slaves. Among them were a few black slaveowning plantation families, mainly located in South Carolina and Louisiana. For example, at the end of the eighteenth century one Negro resident of St. Paul's Parish, South Carolina, held about 200 bondsmen. In 1830 members of the Meytoier family in Natchitoches Parish, Louisiana, owned a total of 212 slaves, Antoine Decuire of Pointe Coupee Parish possessed 70, and Martin Donatto of Plaquemine Brule Parish had 75. In the same year the two largest Negro slaveholders in South Carolina were listed as owning 84 slaves each, and the leading Negro slaveowner in Virginia, Benjamin O. Taylor of King George County, had 71. This class of Negro slaveholders, tiny to start with, declined sharply in the years before the Civil War.

Taking ownership of twenty slaves as the minimum for membership in the planter class, a study of the census data reveals that the great majority of Southern slaveholders could not be called planters. In 1860, 88 percent of them held fewer than twenty slaves, 72 percent held fewer than ten, and nearly 50 percent held fewer than five. Most of those in the planter class owned between twenty and fifty slaves, approximately ten thousand owned fifty or more, and only three thousand persons owned more than a hundred slaves. Yet the majority of slaves lived on plantations—over half of them on farms worked by twenty or more slaves, and a quarter of the slaves lived in units of fifty or more. At the other end of the scale, only a quarter lived on farms worked by fewer than ten slaves. Large units were more common in the lower South, and most of the large slaveholdings were concentrated in those areas best suited for staple crops, such as the alluvial river bottoms with their fertile soil and ready access to markets. These included the Louisiana sugar parishes, the Yazoo-Mississippi Delta, the Natchez region in Mississippi, the Black Belt of Alabama, and the coastal rice lands and Sea Islands of South Carolina and Georgia. In some plantation counties, slaves outnumbered whites by more than two to one, while in other counties of the South there were very few slaves and not a single plantation.

The organization of work varied according to the crop and the size of the farm. Rice planters used the task system, where individual slaves were held responsible for a given amount of daily work, which they completed at their own pace. Other staples were usually cultivated under the gang system, where slaves worked together until the task was finished. Tobacco could be grown on small farms better than the other staples. Sugar cane, which required heavy investments in refining machinery, was limited exclusively to large plantations.

On small farms, especially those with a half dozen slaves or less, there was little or no labor specialization. In the fields the master personally directed the slaves' work. On medium-sized farms, worked by from ten to twenty slaves, there was a limited amount of specialization, with perhaps a couple of slaves trained in manual skills and one or more engaged in domestic work. On such a farm the owner did not work in the fields but confined himself to the business aspects of his enterprise, typically delegating the supervision of slaves to his sons or a slave foreman. Many of these foremen were given considerable responsibility in running the farm.

Nearly half the slaves belonged to the 25,000 planters who owned thirty slaves or more. It was on such large plantations that the system achieved its highest complexity, specialization, and efficiency. Practically all plantations of this size had overseers to supervise the work of the slaves or, where the owner was an absentee, to run the entire operation. Planters constantly complained of the inefficiency and incompetency of their overseers, and few stayed on the same plantation for more than a few years. Yet the larger estates found it impossible to do without them. Overseers were usually white men, but a significant number were blacks—especially on the Atlantic Coast rice plantations—and these were highly trusted and successful managers. Beneath the overseer were typically one or more slave drivers, men who were part of the system of coercion. They kept order among the field hands and were authorized to discipline them. On the larger plantations several drivers were used and were responsible to a head driver, who acted as a suboverseer. House servants were a class apart from the field hands. So were skilled artisans—blacksmiths, carpenters, and others. Some of the plantations, with very large slave forces, had full-time workers who drove wagons, cultivated vegetable gardens, tended livestock, or performed other duties.

Because there was a decline in efficiency of operations when a plantation had over a hundred slaves, planters with large slaveholdings usually owned two or more plantations. One Louisiana owner of seven hundred slaves divided his holdings into six plantations, with six overseers, two doctors, a general agent, and a bookkeeper. Absentee ownership was naturally found among large estates such as this. A few, like the Virginia and Carolina planters who preferred to live on their ancestral estates, owned plantations great distances away in the Southwest, which they visited annually but for the most part left to the care of their overseers. Planters who divided their holdings into several contiguous or nearby plantations were similarly absent most of the time, entrusting the major responsibilities to their overseers, as did urban lawyers and businessmen who were only part-time planters.

Plantation slaves lived on a subsistence basis. Ordinarily their living quarters consisted of a single or double row of cabins near the overseer's cottage. A minority of masters attempted to provide neat, weatherproof cabins, at times with two or three rooms, a modicum of decent bedding, and perhaps some other scanty furniture. But most slaves lived in rude, drafty, leaky, clapboard shacks, with only the crudest furniture. As for clothing, a standard winter supply for a man was two shirts of coarse cotton, two woolen trousers, and a woolen jacket. In the spring he had two cotton shirts and two cotton trousers. Every year he received a pair of shoes. The standard food allowance consisted of hominy and fatback, with a basic weekly ration of a peck of cornmeal and three or four pounds of salt pork. Some masters attempted to give their slaves a varied diet and encouraged them to cultivate their own gardens. Recent research, stressing the way in which slaves supplemented their diet by hunting, fishing, and raising yams and sweet potatoes, suggests that the bondsmen's food supply was not as skimpy as most scholars previously believed.

The plantation way of life evolved a complex and often subtle system of discipline over the slave population. Treatment varied widely, from the paternalism of some slaveholders to the sadistic cruelty of others. Acts of disobedience were most commonly punished by flogging, and few adult slaves ever completely escaped the whip. Slaveowners who habitually used severe physical chastisement were common enough. Just about every farmer believed that slaves responded only to firm treatment and at least periodic whippings. Brutality was more frequent on the large plantations, particularly those in the more newly developed states of the Deep South. A few slaveholders built their own jails; others used public jails—but incarceration penalized the master as well as the slave. Chains and irons were employed to control runaways, and a strong deterrent was the threat of sale to the Deep South cotton and sugar plantations.

In addition, there were several forms of indirect controls. Slaves worked long hours—well into darkness during busy seasons, especially at harvest time—and it was necessary to reward and cajole as well as to threaten in order to get the work done. Work was stopped on Sundays and sometimes all or part of Saturday, and slaves could look forward to holidays, such as Good Friday, Independence Day, "laying-by time" after the harvest, and Christmas. On these occasions passes were granted freely by many masters. Christmas, particularly, was a time of celebration, slaves often being allowed considerable freedom and even the use of liquor. Some masters distributed gifts at the end of the year or compensated slaves with money for performing extra work or allowed them to hire out their own time. Denial of weekend passes, work on Saturdays and Sundays, and confiscation of crops in truck patches were some of the milder punishments owners used.

Other indirect controls were implicit in the social stratification system of the plantation. Because of their privileged positions, slave overseers, foremen, artisans, and domestic servants showed considerable loyalty to the planters. The identification between such slaves and their owners was sometimes so complete that in a number of instances they acted as informers concerning impending slave revolts. Moreover, despite the frequency with which masters broke up slave families through sales and the settlement of estates, they encouraged stable marital and family relationships among their bondsmen, since these improved morale and discouraged running away. Finally, masters employed religion as a form of control over the slaves. After it was understood that baptism did not confer freedom and that the Southern wings of the Methodist and Baptist Churches had no intention of applying their egalitarian concepts to the temporal status of the slaves, many planters saw advantages in having slaves attend religious services. Some owners even built chapels on their plantations. Of course, such planter-sponsored religious observances emphasized the otherworldly aspects of Christianity, rather than the impulse toward social justice in the Judaic-Christian tradition, and promised salvation to those who obeyed their masters. From the masters' perspective, therefore, Christianity functioned as an anodyne to help slaves accept their lot in this world. In fact, during the decade preceding the Civil War, white missionaries were more active among the slaves than ever before.

Historians have long engaged in a debate as to how harsh Southern servitude was. Many of the first generation of post–Civil War historians viewed the system as oppressive and cruel. This interpretation was developed further by the school of black historians that emerged with the Association for the Study of Negro Life and History, founded by Carter G. Woodson in 1915. By then, however, a Southern white perspective on slavery was moving into the ascendancy among the majority of white historians. U. B. Phillips, a Southerner writing early in the twentieth century who did the first detailed research into the plantation system, pictured United States slavery as an essentially benevolent, paternalistic institution that functioned as a civilizing force for savage Africans. A generation later, in the 1940's and 1950's, John Hope Franklin and Kenneth Stampp reversed this picture. Stampp in particular painstakingly went over the ground traversed by Phillips and, on the basis of a fresh and more comprehensive evaluation of the evidence, systematically contradicted all of Phillips's major conclusions.

Over the past decade and a half there has been an increasing effort to understand the nature of United States slavery by placing it in the broader context of New World slavery and comparing it with the institution as it developed in Latin American countries. In large part this comparative thrust stemmed from an attempt to understand how it was that despite the ubiquitousness of slavery as an institution in the

Americas, the postemancipation era in the Latin American countries proved to be one of relative egalitarianism in comparison with the racist patterns that evolved in the United States. It was Frank Tannenbaum who, nearly a generation ago—in a slim volume that for a decade was pretty much ignored by students of United States slavery—first suggested that the roots of this difference in race relations lay in fundamental differences between slavery in the United States and that which developed in the Spanish and Portuguese colonies in the New World. Developed further and given wide currency by Stanley Elkins in his controversial *Slavery*, published in 1959, the Tannenbaum-Elkins thesis, as it came to be known, maintained that the slave system of the Latin American countries was markedly less oppressive than that of the United States. Three aspects of Iberian culture were offered to account for the difference. First, there was the tradition stemming from Roman law. The Iberian Peninsula had known slavery throughout the Middle Ages, and its slave codes had been rooted in the continuing tradition of Roman civil law. This juridical tradition in its late phases, under the influence of Stoic philosophers and jurists, had done much to mitigate the evils of Roman slavery since it viewed a slave as a man with certain natural human rights and as equal spiritually with other men. The protections afforded slaves under Roman law were retained in the Iberian legal systems. Second, the Catholic Church, while recognizing the legality of slavery, insisted upon the essentially human character of slaves, their spiritual equality before God, and the importance of their religious and moral training and behavior. Third, the Iberian culture, with its lack of a middle-class or Protestant ethic rationalizing economic behavior, may have had some impact upon the character of Portuguese-Spanish slavery in the New World. The preoccupation of American slave owners with financial profits was more likely to stifle human impulses.

According to the Tannenbaum-Elkins thesis, it was argued that while slavery could be and often was as cruel in Latin American countries as in the United States, the slaves' legal and social status was quite different. A slave was permitted by law to testify against whites; he could bring his master to court for excessive cruelty; he could own property and engage in buying and selling. Slaves could hire themselves out, save the earnings, and purchase themselves. Nothing stood in the way of manumitting slaves. In fact, in the absence of evidence to the contrary, a Negro was considered free rather than a slave, and free Negroes had the rights of other citizens. Moreover, both church and state interceded to protect the well-being of slaves. In Brazil and many of the Spanish colonies there was an official protector of the slaves, and magistrates were directed to make periodic investigations of the plantations to see how the bondsmen were treated. Church officials took a similar interest. In contrast with the United States, the church required the baptism and religious training of all slaves and insisted upon the sanctity of marriage. And the church encouraged manumission as a good deed in the sight of God. Emancipating slaves was part of an "honorific tradition," fulfilled on many occasions—on the birth of a first son, on the marriage of the master's children, on a national holiday, and at other festive times. In the United States the churches acquiesced in the slave system and religion buttressed it. It took a Civil War to emancipate the slaves here, and even then they were not really accepted as citizens. None of the Latin American countries underwent such a traumatic experience, and in all of them, while discrimination did not completely disappear, the Negroes were generally accepted as part of the body politic.

Although the Tannenbaum-Elkins thesis won wide acceptance, it soon came under increasing attack from a variety of specialists, chiefly students of Latin American and Caribbean history and society. Evidence was adduced to demonstrate that laws were one thing, actual practices another; that relatively humane codes prepared in Lisbon, Madrid, and Paris were easily ignored by planters in America; and that colonies with identical laws might vary widely in practice. More significantly, it was pointed out, first by students in the behavioral sciences and then more belatedly by certain historians, that the character of slavery varied over time within a country and might vary between different parts of the same country. Thus, in Cuba, slavery prior to the nineteenth century was a relatively mild institution, with the provisions of the imperial code operative; but with the introduction of sugar cane and the rapid development of intensive cultivation of that staple, slavery there became exceedingly harsh, characterized by a high death rate and sustained by enormous human importations from Africa. Northeastern Brazil, the first area in the New World to develop a sugar-plantation regime, experienced its harshest slavery very early. By the nineteenth century, however, slavery in the declining sugar plantations there assumed a less rigorous, more paternalistic character. Meanwhile, on the new coffee plantations in southern Brazil, the institution developed all the cruelty, the overwork, and the high death rate that typified slavery at its worst. Most Caribbean countries had a similar experience. In general, slavery was harshest in recently opened areas of high agricultural productivity, where a "boom" psychology of high profits characterized the owners of large plantations. On the other hand, the institution tended to be milder on small farms, where the owners had direct and intimate daily contact with their bondsmen, or in sections where the land had declined in fertility and the planting families valued an aristocratic style of life over high financial returns. For the United States, the subject is still highly controversial and under intense investigation, but there is evidence of similar patterns. Thus very recent scholarship on early colonial Maryland and South Carolina reveals extraordinarily high death rates when intensive cultivation of tobacco and rice was first introduced, suggesting the existence of gross exploitation and callous disregard for the lives of the slaves in these periods of expansive slave agriculture. Such a high death rate does not seem to have accompanied the subsequent rise of the cotton kingdom, a situation not yet fully explained and only partly related to the fact that so much of this expansion came after the closing of the transatlantic slave trade resulted in high prices for slaves. But unquestionably, even though they never matched the pattern of the early colonies or the Caribbean, the new, large-scale plantations in states like

Mississippi, Alabama, and Louisiana, where land and labor were exploited for immediate financial return, usually had harder work conditions than the more paternalistically organized, older tidewater plantations.

As the recent assessment of Latin American and Caribbean slavery shifted, United States slavery no longer appeared to be one of unmitigated oppression, the harshest system in the history of the New World. There is evidence that, in the very period when the Southern slaveholders were tightening the slave codes so as virtually to prohibit manumission, the diet, housing, and health of the slaves in the United States was actually improving.

Accordingly, the standard of living of Southern slaves was considerably higher than that of their Latin American counterparts (although in all countries there were enormous variations over time and between different regions, and even among different plantations in the same areas). Nothing illustrates this difference in living standards more dramatically than the fact pointed out earlier that, while the United States was a very minor importer of slaves, by the nineteenth century it had become the world's major slave power. In 1825 its one and three-quarter million slaves represented over a third of all the slaves in the New World. In the Caribbean and Brazil the death rate of slaves was so high that during most of their history the slave populations did not reproduce themselves and were sustained only by large imports from Africa. In the United States after about 1720, however, natural increase rather than importations was the chief factor accounting for the striking increase in the slave population. Various factors contributed to this difference—including the greater prevalence of virulent diseases in tropical countries and the very low proportion of women in slave populations brought directly from Africa—but overall the conclusion seems warranted that the bondsmen in the United States were better treated than their Caribbean and Brazilian counterparts.

Scholars are by no means in agreement about the reasons for the relatively less oppressive treatment of slaves in the United

States. There are two major and contradictory points of view on the matter. On the one hand there is Eugene Genovese, to a large degree rehabilitating the analysis of U. B. Phillips without that historian's racist views. Genovese holds that United States slavery was essentially a "precapitalist" economic institution, with a slaveowning class that was paternalistic rather than engaged in unrestrained exploitation: a class that was guided less by pecuniary norms than by an aristocratic ethic. The economic historians Robert Fogel and Stanley Engerman, on the other hand, insist that slavery was a highly rationalized profit-making system. Planters, desiring to maintain slave morale and assure high productivity, found it necessary, not only to apply force but also to keep the slaves in good health and to place great reliance on both material rewards and opportunities for advancement within the slave hierarchy. In fact, Fogel and Engerman maintain that—as in modern industry—there is no necessary contradiction between paternalism and good old-fashioned profit making.

Such views of planter paternalism, whether they are based on the aristocratic mentality of the planter class or on rational economic calculations, romanticize the institution of slavery. Still, it is no longer possible to correlate postslavery race relations with the character of the slave system. In Latin America and the Caribbean—even in the British West Indies—white prejudice and discrimination were by no means absent, but the slaves' descendants fared far better than in the United States. A country like Brazil, for example, has simply lacked an ideology of racism such as has characterized the United States. Scholars have explained these differences by referring to demographic and economic factors. Given the very high ratio of blacks to whites in both the British West Indies and Latin America, and given the low proportion of females in the white population during the early history of these countries, there was much miscegenation. Children of such unions, as well as their mothers, were frequently given their freedom. Accordingly, a significant class of free blacks, mostly of mixed ancestry, developed. Because of the relative scarcity of white offspring, these free people of color received substantial advantages from their white fathers—a situation that occurred far more rarely in the United States. With whites few in number, the free Negro population proved essential for carrying out important economic tasks that in the United States were performed by white artisans and small farmers. Thus the free people of color established a favorable economic foothold. In other words, the evidence being accumulated by scholars would suggest that it was not the nature of the slave system but the status of the emerging class of free Negroes during the slave regimes that shaped postemancipation race relations. It is probably no accident that the United States, the one slave society that sought to systematically degrade the free Negroes and to place insuperable barriers in the way of manumission, became the most racist society in the New World.

6

The earlier historians of slavery were concerned chiefly with how plantations were run, how slaves were managed and controlled by their masters, and the degree to which the bondsmen accepted or rebelled against the regime. These scholars dealt only to a limited extent with the nature of slave life and culture. This was partly due to the biases and interests of historians; until very recently, for example, the only serious work on the slave family had been that of sociologist E. Franklin Frazier. Partly it was also due to the nature of the sources—plantation records and slaveowners' correspondence that were written from the perspective of the masters; the observations of Northern and foreign white visitors whose direct contacts were mostly with the owners rather than with the slaves; ex-slave autobiographies that were treated with skepticism because they were originally written as a form of antislavery propaganda; interviews with elderly survivors of the slave regime done three quarters of a century after emancipation and until recently not readily accessible to scholars; and stories, songs, and other surviving elements of folk culture, another form of oral tradition that historians were not inclined to utilize.

In the past decade or so, however, a veritable revolution has occurred in the way in which scholars have approached the bondsman's life under slavery. The militant black consciousness that flowered during the 1960's sensitized scholars to the importance of carefully assessing slavery from the slaves' perspective and to the likelihood that slaves possessed a rich and distinctive subculture. Simultaneously, historians were developing a new interest in the life of the inarticulate masses and new techniques to study this subject. Students of Southern slavery exploited the hitherto largely ignored slave autobiographies and reminiscences; following the lead of folklorists and anthropologists, they developed methods of utilizing oral tradition; and, in addition, they made increasingly sophisticated use of slave-owners' records.

The result has been the development of a remarkable consensus on the institutions and culture created by the slaves. Whether one views Southern servitude as harsh or as paternalistic, the older view that slavery virtually denuded Negroes of a culture of their own has now been discredited. Instead, it is universally recognized that, within the slave regime, blacks demonstrated a striking resiliency and found enough "social living space" to develop a community and subculture, which enabled them to maintain a group identity and to cope with the oppressive institution in which they found themselves. Nowhere has this new perspective of historians produced more important results than in analyses of the slave family and slave religion. White culture and the masters' actions played a role in shaping both, it is true, yet it is just as true that what emerged was as much or even more a product created by the slaves themselves.

In actual practice, of course, the policies of masters regarding slave family relations varied widely. Many treated the whole matter extremely casually, but many others encouraged at least the formalities of married life. Some carefully supervised their slaves' marital affairs, demanding fidelity and discouraging adultery and divorce. Slaves ordinarily had to secure the permission of their master before marrying. Often a simple ceremony was performed, such as jumping over a broomstick in the presence of the master; sometimes slaves, particularly skilled artisans and domestics, were married in the master's house by a slave parson with festivities following. On the other hand, much in the slave regime promoted marital and familial instability. Slave marriages were not recognized by law; slave sales were a frequent disrupter of family life; the miscegenation that resulted from the white males' sexual exploitation of female slaves, while at times involving stable and affectionate concubinage, also discouraged slave married life. In addition, evidence points to significant matrifocal tendencies. To the extent that family ties were respected by slave traders, mothers and young children were the ones most likely to be sold together. Since both sexes worked in the field at the same tasks and were supplied with food, clothing, and shelter by the master, the role of the father as provider was downgraded. Nor could the father assume the role of his family's protector. If his wife or children were beaten he was unable to do anything about it. The many instances of miscegenation in which the white father failed to take responsibility for his offspring also encouraged matrifocal tendencies.

Slaves nonetheless managed to create and sustain a stable family life, with two-parent male-headed households evidently the norm. This was especially true on paternalistically run plantations where slave sales were few. There slave families achieved marked stability and continuity through three or four generations. Evidence from postemancipation Freedmen's Bureau records recently obtained by Herbert Gutman demonstrates the universality of slave marriages across the South and how such marriages typically had been broken not through voluntary separation—though this did occur—but through separations forced by sales and estate settlements. That slaves themselves often had a good deal to say about their marital life is revealed by the many who prevailed upon their masters to permit them to marry spouses owned by others, often at a fairly considerable distance. Masters who were considerate or desirous of maintaining good slave morale frequently purchased such a spouse. Slaveowners often stressed the promiscuous nature of slave sex relations. What they failed to perceive was that slaves developed their own norms in such matters. Though premarital sex relations were accepted and children born out of wedlock suffered no indignities, once a slave woman married and settled down with one man, adultery was severely discountenanced. Fathers, within the limits of the system, played a paternal role—customarily meting out discipline and doing what they could to supplement the family diet by hunting and fishing. The eagerness with which slaves hastened to legalize their marriages after the Civil War and sought to reunite with long-separated families reveals the importance of this institution to them. It now seems abundantly clear that however much many masters might have encouraged nuclear, male-headed family life —to improve slave morale, to discourage running away, or to satisfy the owners' own sense of morality—the major thrust for the institution came from the slaves themselves.

If recent trends in historical scholarship have deemphasized the extent of matrifocality among slave families and thereby undermined the argument advanced by Herskovits regarding African survivals in black family life, the same cannot be said for the growing literature on slave religion. Yet the connection between West African culture and the sacred world view of the black bondsman is something far more subtle and complex than the distinguished anthropologist ever imagined. As we have seen, masters and churchmen encouraged the dissemination of Christian doctrine among the slaves and, aside from "conjuring," little in the way of specific Africanisms remained. But what the slaves created was neither the Christianity of their masters nor the Christianity their masters intended to create for them.

Although masters and white missionaries sought to shape and supervise the slaves' religious life, the blacks were able to retain a considerable degree of religious autonomy. This was facilitated by the development of a group of slave preachers and assistants to white missionaries. It has recently been argued that a major reason for the success that Baptists and Methodists had among the slaves was the fact that they, unlike Episcopalians and Presbyterians, encouraged the development of a black clergy. For their part, the slaves preferred to listen to their own preachers and to worship separately from the whites. Many masters gave in to this desire of the slaves and allowed them to hold their own religious and funeral services. And where masters refused permission, slaves would meet together secretly.

These slave religious services and ceremonies had important consequences. They promoted autonomy from the whites and a sense of community and solidarity among the blacks. They lessened the degree of acculturation to the white man's religion and encouraged the survival of African cultural traditions. And they facilitated the process by which slaves reinterpreted the masters' religious traditions, selecting those aspects of it that met their needs, fusing these with certain elements of West African religion, and thus creating their own Afro-American sacred world view.

Compared with Latin America, African religion survived in relatively attenuated form. In Protestant Christianity the slaves did not find saints whom they could syncretize with African deities as they did in Catholic countries; and the demography of the American South, where only rarely did the ratio of slaves to whites approach the overwhelming proportions found in the Caribbean, made slaves in the United States considerably more assimilated than those in the British West Indies. What the American bondsmen did retain was the life-affirming quality that had characterized traditional African religion and that stood in stark contrast with the sinful view of man that characterized orthodox Christianity. What the slaves found in—and adapted from—Protestant Christianity was neither St. Paul's view of man's sinfulness and his belief that masters were to be obeyed, nor the dour doctrines of predestination that were still so much in vogue, especially in the South. Rather what the slaves drew from Protestant Christianity was a stress on the spiritual equality of all people and a notion of God's love which enabled them to maintain both a sense of Christian charity toward their oppressors and a spirit of love and solidarity with their fellow bondsmen. Moreover, both the life-affirming quality of African religion and the distinctly Christian emphasis upon spiritual equality provided the slaves with a sense of self-esteem that afforded vital psychological protection against the oppressiveness of the slave regime.

Evidence for these observations is suggested in the Negro spirituals. The psychological defense of the slaves' self-esteem, for example, is indicated by the way in which they consistently pictured themselves as God's chosen people. It is no accident that the spirituals stressed so much the Old Testament heroes like Moses, Joshua, Noah, and Daniel, all of whom God delivered in this world. Actually the slaves' world view did not distinguish sharply between the sacred and the secular, between past and present events in this world and the future in the other world. What they developed was a sacred world view that fused the concept of Moses, who led a people to freedom, with that of Jesus, who redeemed suffering mankind—thus transforming the promise of individual redemption with the promise of deliverance as a people in this world.

While this religious world view was not an ideology that encouraged organized rebellion, it affirmed the human dignity of the bondsmen in their own eyes, provided the psychological basis for more quietistic forms of resistance, and, in short, was a creative adaptation of elements in African and Christian religion that enabled the slaves to cope with their hostile environment and maintain their own culture and community.

7

Modern studies in social psychology have demonstrated that members of minority groups react in various ways to their subordinate status in society. They may hate and rebel against their oppressors, or they may accept the inferiority assigned them by the dominant group. They may assert social pride and emphasize the value of their own collective action, or they may attempt to assimilate the dominant group's culture and strive for acceptance in it. They may escape into religious otherworldliness. Or individuals may exhibit a paradoxical and complex amalgam of these attitudes and reactions.

Undoubtedly, many slaves in the United States retreated into a compensatory otherworldliness. For them, Christianity served the function it had served so well for the slaves among whom it first spread in the Roman Empire. Christian doctrines exalted the meek and the lowly, making a virtue of accepting without resistance the persecution that the slaves were forced to endure. Yet, as already seen, religion also played a more complex and ambiguous role—encouraging belief in the appearance of a deliverer rather than open rebellion and simultaneously promoting a feeling of Christian charity toward the masters and a sense of self-worth that could prompt individual slaves on occasion to defy their masters' demands. Some who accommodated played the clown and told the white man what he wanted to hear. Although the slave elite—house servants, foremen, and skilled artisans—so valued their privileged status that they often identified with the master class, such people were acutely aware of their marginal position. A high proportion of runaways had been well treated by their masters; so were, not infrequently, those who became leaders of slave revolts. There has been some disagreement over the number of actual slave rebellions in American history, and this is not surprising given the limitations of the available evidence. The total of two hundred, identified by Herbert Aptheker, has been disputed by other scholars who claim that the actual number was considerably less. The most important ones were Gabriel's Revolt (1800), the Denmark Vesey Conspiracy (1822),* and the Nat Turner Insurrection (1831).

The most serious slave insurrection, which occurred in Southampton County, Virginia, in the summer of 1831, demonstrates that the slaves' religious tradition could on certain occasions provide the seedbed for armed rebellion. Nat Turner, a thirty-one-year-old Baptist slave preacher, led a band of rebels who slew about sixty whites. In the years before the rebellion, the

---

* One scholar has suggested that the Vesey plot existed only in the minds of hysterical whites. See Richard C. Wade, "The Vesey Plot: A Reconsideration," *Journal of Southern History* 30 (May 1964): 143–61.

mystical Turner, viewing himself as a divine instrument to deliver the race from bondage, had innumerable visions, one of which he described in this way: "I saw white spirits and black spirits engaged in battle, and the sun was darkened—the thunder rolled in the heavens, and blood flowed in streams. . . ." Later, he became certain that God had instructed him to "arise and prepare myself, and slay my enemies with their own weapons. . . . It was my object to carry terror and devastation wherever we went." On the morning of August 22, armed with an ax, Turner entered his master's bedroom and slew him, his wife, and three others in the household. Thereupon, he and his followers roamed the countryside and, within a matter of hours, systematically massacred the whites. He later recollected: "A general destruction of property and search for money and ammunition, always succeeded the murders." With the arrival of state and federal troops, more than a hundred slaves were indiscriminately slaughtered. At a court trial, thirteen slaves and three free blacks were convicted and hanged. Turner, who managed to escape, was captured several weeks later and also hanged.

It is one thing to delineate the types of responses made by slaves to their status; it is another to state, with any degree of precision, in what proportion each of these various reactions occurred. Historians have disagreed with one another on this matter, and the subject is now one about which swirls a major debate in black historiography. U. B. Phillips asserted that slaves were happy and revolts were few because of the benign, paternalistic nature of the system and the innately childlike character of Negroes. The black sociologists Charles S. Johnson and E. Franklin Frazier rejected the notion of inborn racial personality differences but also emphasized the accommodating nature of the Negroes' adjustment to slavery. Subsequently, historians like Kenneth Stampp and John Hope Franklin minimized the slaves' enforced accommodation and underscored instead signs of their rebelliousness. They have held that blacks, like other men, naturally resisted tyranny and oppression. Melville Herskovits, insisting that slave revolts would not have occurred if blacks had adopted the white man's views and had lost their consciousness of group identity along with their African cultural background, accented the importance of servile rebellion as reflecting the survival of Africanisms. On the other hand, the most noted scholar on the subject of slave insurrections, Herbert Aptheker, interpreted his data in the framework of his Communist ideology, holding that oppressed classes are constantly in revolt. Then, at the close of the 1950's, Stanley Elkins turned things completely upside down by asserting that insurrections, as Phillips had said, were indeed relatively rare in the United States and accommodation was the rule—not because the system was benevolent or paternalistic, but because it was extremely oppressive. Drawing upon the experiences of inmates in German concentration camps, where there was very little resistance and where many prisoners retreated into infantile behavior patterns and even admired their Nazi guards as respected and revered father figures, Elkins suggested that the picture of the "happy-go-lucky" slave, the "Sambo stereotype," contained an element of truth. He concluded that the development of such a personality type and of such patterns of adjustment underscore the horror, the dehumanizing quality of slavery in the United States, especially in the generation before the Civil War.

Thus, by the 1960's, the major lines of interpretation regarding slave resistance and accommodation crisscrossed rather than paralleled the major lines of interpretation regarding the nature of the system itself. Scholars like Aptheker, Stampp, Du Bois, and more recently John W. Blassingame, have stressed slave resistance, while Elkins, who agreed with them about the institution's oppressiveness, stressed the psychodynamics of accommodation. Conversely, one can reason in two ways from the view of those who, like Phillips, Genovese, and Fogel and Engerman, take a more benign view of the system: either that the bondsmen were so well treated that they were not disposed to resist, or that the system, by permitting the blacks to maintain their own culture and sense of identity, provided the basis for resistance and revolt. Historians, viewing the contradictions in their work, and attempting to explain why slave revolts were admittedly rather rare when compared with other slave societies in the New World, have sought insights in cross-cultural comparisons and have made a number of relevant specialized studies.

Various reasons have been offered to account for the fact that slave revolts in the Caribbean and South America were more frequent and on a larger scale and that runaways were more successful. For one, geographical factors played their part. Mountainous terrain, for example, facilitated the cause of the Haitian rebels under Toussaint L'Ouverture and the creation of settlements of escaped slaves, or maroons, in Jamaica. Demographic patterns have also been cited. In the Caribbean and South American slaveholding areas, the proportion of blacks to whites was generally far higher than in the United States, with blacks commonly forming a majority of the population. (Yet in the Mississippi Black Belt and the plantations of the Sea Islands, areas of heavy concentration of slave population, slave revolts seldom occurred.) Thirdly, given the density of the black population, African survivals were stronger in Latin American countries. Clearly these survivals contributed to some of the rebellions there. Many insurrections in Bahia, Brazil, originated in Muslim religious groups among slaves from the Hausa states. The Haitian Revolution spread rapidly as drum signals transmitted news of the first uprisings from plantation to plantation, in the same way that messages were sent over long distances in Africa. Indeed, a number of scholars, building on Herskovits's theories, have emphasized the relationship of rebelliousness and organized revolt to African survivals. Yet the most recent evidence on this is contradictory. A careful investigation of Gabriel's Revolt in Virginia found that it was the most highly assimilated slaves who were most rebellious; other studies, notably those dealing with South Carolina, have been impressed by the evident importance of African cultural traditions.

Elkins's model of a dehumanizing slave system practically stamping out resistance among slaves of the United States has now been pretty well demolished by historians, but his very correct position that revolutions do not, after all, originate among those whom conditions make hopeless still raises important questions. People in such a situation are generally characterized by passivity, resignation, and accommodation to the status quo. Some support is given to the Elkins thesis by a statistical analysis of the geographical distribution of slave revolts, which concludes that they tended to occur near cities or in rural areas of paternalistic traditions. On the large plantations of states like Mississippi, Alabama, and Louisiana, where conditions were worst, slave revolts were extremely rare. Yet no insurrections erupted in New England, the section of the country where the slave system was least repressive, and there were few instances of rebellion on the patriarchal plantations of the Sea Islands in the nineteenth century. Research on urban slavery in the United States and on servitude in the Virginia iron industry suggests that where slavery was most paternalistic and where masters skillfully manipulated the reward system, resistance and rebelliousness were likely to be minimal. On the other hand, a thorough study of conditions in eighteenth-century Virginia indicates that the most highly skilled and best treated among the plantation slaves were the ones most likely to rebel and run away. The complexity of the whole question of the connection between the degree of oppressiveness and slave insurrections is shown in a painstaking investigation of the 1739 Stono Revolt in South Carolina, which reveals that as the plantation system in that colony grew more repressive, slaves became more restive and finally revolted openly. Yet, when as a result of the rebellion the repression intensified, slave rebelliousness subsided.

In actual practice, slave-master relationships were complex and ambiguous—with cruelty mixed with sentimental attachment on the part of the masters, and deep resentment often mixed with respect and sometimes even affection on the part of the slaves. Bondsmen resisted the rigors of the slave system as much as they could on a day-to-day basis, compelling masters to respect their work rhythms, to permit them time to cultivate their own gardens, to allow them to marry spouses belonging to other masters, and to hold their own religious services. Of course, there was considerable variation in all these matters, but a growing body of evidence suggests that slavery operated less on the basis of outright repression than through a subtle and complex pattern of mutual accommodation between whites and blacks. Moreover, it is now clear that the old debate over accommodation and resistance has oversimplified the issues. Slave resistance and accommodation formed a continuum rather than a polarity; the same person might be at different times and under different circumstances both a rebel and an accommodator. Essentially, all slaves were both. A faithful house servant might easily run away when the situation offered itself; the most obsequious slave, when pressed too far, might surprise a master or overseer with an act of violent retaliation, even murder. Men like Gabriel and Nat Turner had been among the most fortunate bondsmen but developed a messianic vision of freeing their fellow slaves.

Clearly, further research is needed to isolate the crucial variables associated with servile insurrection. In view of the complicated nature of human behavior, the uneven character of the institution of slavery, and the large number of variables involved—ranging from demographic and geographic factors, through changes in the harshness of the system, to the degree of cultural assimilation to white norms—it is not going to be easy to generalize about the reasons for revolts or the lack of them. In fact, given the complexities, it is likely that we will find that not one but several different sets of circumstances provided the seedbed of resistance and revolt.

III

Negroes in the Antebellum Cities: Manumission, Alienation, and Protest

1

WHILE SLAVERY THRIVED on the plantation, it languished in the cities. From the beginning there were significant differences between urban and rural servitude. Most urban slaves were domestic servants or unskilled workers, but a high proportion were skilled artisans. Owners often derived a regular income from hiring their slaves out by the year or for shorter periods of time, skilled slaves commanding especially high wages for their masters. Most of the slaves in the Richmond ironworks and tobacco factories, where they were used for all grades of labor from the most menial to the most highly skilled, were hired bondsmen. Though the law increasingly frowned upon the practice, some masters continued to encourage a slave to find his own job and keep a portion of his earnings for himself.

In the context of city life, slaves lived under fewer restraints than in the countryside. In theory, slaves were not allowed on the city streets without passes from their masters. In practice, however, it was difficult to confine slaves to their quarters in their masters' courtyards; it was inconvenient to prepare passes every time a servant was sent on an errand about the town. Therefore, the urban slaves had considerable freedom in coming and going, simply because it was easier for their masters. Moreover, a number of slaves, especially those hiring out their own time, were permitted to live out. Their wooden shanties, ordinarily in the alleys of the commercial areas and on the edge of town, were inferior physically to the quarters in the master's yard, but the added degree of freedom was highly prized. Indeed, though the number of urban slaves declined, the number of those living out rose. Also prized was the right to worship in black churches, which were usually mixed congregations of free people and slaves. Even some prominent white ministers defended the practice of permitting separate religious institutions for Negroes. All these things allowed much informal socializing, not infrequently in illicit dramshops run by white saloonkeepers and, occasionally, by black ones as well. Although the public feared that such gatherings were seedbeds of revolt and crime, attempts to circumscribe this sort of activity largely failed. "A city slave is almost a free citizen," declared Frederick Douglass, with pardonable exaggeration, when he compared his experiences in Baltimore during the 1830's with his earlier life on Maryland's eastern shore. "He enjoys privileges altogether unknown to the whip-driven slave on the plantation."

In the two decades before the Civil War the size of the urban slave population was falling, apparently because young black males were being sold to the countryside, where prices for prime field hands were rising extravagantly. At the same time, however, the number of free Negroes increased substantially. Divided almost equally between the North and South, their numbers rose from about sixty thousand in 1790 to half a million in 1860. The chief areas of concentration were: tidewater Virginia and Maryland; the Virginia and North Carolina piedmont, where there were numbers of blacks who owned small tobacco farms; the Southern coastal cities of Baltimore, Washington, Charleston, Mobile, and New Orleans; and the Northern cities of Boston, Cincinnati, New York, and Philadelphia. Free blacks were the most highly urbanized group in the country; in 1860 over a third of those in the South resided in cities, compared to 15 percent of the Southern whites and 5 percent of the slaves.

In the Northern states emancipation laws effected the liberation of all slaves before the middle of the nineteenth century. The free black population there had been augmented through natural increase and through the arrival from the South of fugitives and slaves manumitted and sent North by their Southern masters.

In the South the free black population was descended largely from slaves emancipated by their masters because of faithful personal service or because of close kinship ties. Indeed, a relatively high proportion of the free Negroes were of mixed racial ancestry, usually the offspring of free black women cohabiting with white men, but also, more rarely, of white women cohabiting with blacks. The number of free blacks grew especially rapidly at the close of the eighteenth century. Thousands were emancipated as a result of the antislavery sentiment of the Revolutionary era; and during the 1790's substantial numbers of free mulattoes, fleeing the Haitian Revolution, migrated into Charleston, Savannah, and New Orleans. The free black population, especially in the upper South, was further augmented by runaway slaves who escaped from bondage into the relative anonymity of the cities. In the last decades of the slave regime, thousands of superannuated Negroes, who had been put off Maryland plantations, crowded into Baltimore. A number of skilled slaves, especially in the cities, purchased freedom by securing permission to hire themselves out and keep a share of the earnings. Though after 1830 it became more and more difficult—and in most states practically impossible—for slaves to obtain freedom legally as a gift from their owners or by self-purchase, the number of free blacks in the United States continued to grow by the excess of births over deaths.

Given the varied sources of the free blacks, it is not surprising that there were significant differences between those living in the upper and the lower South. Mainly because the impulse to manumission during and after the Revolution was confined to Maryland, Virginia, and North Carolina, the free people of color were heavily concentrated in the upper South. Even after the Louisiana Purchase brought the substantial free Negro population of New Orleans into the Union, only 13 percent of the free blacks resided in the lower South. Moreover, while the free blacks as a group were, compared to the slaves, disproportionately of mixed ancestry, this was truer of the lower South than of the upper South. The free blacks in the port cities of the Deep South, descended primarily from people closely related to whites and from the Haitian refugees, were predominantly light-skinned. In the upper South, where so many of the group were descended from runaways and from those freed in the widespread emancipation of the Revolutionary era, the majority were dark-skinned. Accordingly, it was in towns like Charleston, Mobile, Savannah, and New Orleans that free blacks of predominantly white ancestry most clearly developed into a self-conscious social class.

2

With the possible exception of certain New England states, the status of free blacks deteriorated in the course of the nineteenth century. At best, the antebellum free people of color could be described, in John Hope Franklin's words, as "quasi-free Negroes."

In the South, of course, free blacks had never enjoyed many rights. As time passed, legislation grew more restrictive, and their status became increasingly similar to that of the slaves. Throughout the region, laws required that the free Negro carry on his person a certificate of freedom; without this document he might be claimed as a slave. Because his movements and activities were subjected to surveillance and regulation, many local jurisdictions demanded that his name be registered with the police or court authorities. Migration to another Southern state was severely restricted, if not completely prohibited, by the 1830's. Maryland, Tennessee, and North Carolina, the only Southern states* that had accorded the franchise to free blacks, by 1835 had amended their constitutions to deprive them of the right to vote. In the courtroom the free black could neither serve on juries nor give testimony against whites. If convicted, he was liable to punishment more severe than that imposed on white men. He might be whipped prior to imprisonment or even sold into slavery.

The Southern free Negro's right of assembly was also proscribed. Evening activities were subject to a curfew in many parts of the South, and meetings of benevolent societies and churches frequently required the presence of a respectable white person. Toward the end of the antebellum period, police often forbade attendance at lodges, dramatic societies, or charitable organizations. As a potential insurrectionist, the free black was discouraged from entertaining slaves. Since his motives were questioned, he could not own a gun or a dog without a special license. As an additional safeguard, Georgia, Florida, and Alabama required him to have a white guardian. Able-bodied blacks not holding steady jobs might find themselves classed as vagrants and sold into servitude for months or even years.

In the North, there were differences in attitudes toward the free blacks between the original states of the Union and those carved out of the old Northwest Territory. Inequalities before the law existed in the Northeast, but they were far more pervasive in the Old Northwest, where many white Southerners had settled and which retained strong commercial links with the lower Mississippi Valley, especially before the building of the Erie Canal. Ironically, despite the Northwest Ordinance's

---

* In colonial South Carolina, prior to 1721, a few free blacks had occasionally voted.

prohibition of slavery, it was in this area that, next to the South, free Negroes found the most hostile reception.

The Black Laws regulating the behavior of free Negroes in the Old Northwest were in fact based upon the slave codes of the Southern states. For a period the legislatures of Illinois and Indiana evaded the antislavery prohibition of the ordinance by enacting laws placing Negro youths under long-term indentures. In modified form the measures perpetuated the practice of black slavery known in the Northwest Territory when it had been under French and British rule. The Illinois constitution of 1818 expressly provided for the hiring of slave labor at the saltworks near Shawneetown. Nowhere in the Old Northwest or in the newer Western states could blacks exercise the right to vote or serve on juries. They could not testify in cases involving whites in Ohio, Indiana, Illinois, Iowa, or California. Most of the Western states also banned intermarriage. The Northwestern and Western states attempted to discourage black settlers by requiring them to register their certificates of freedom at a county clerk's office and to present bonds of $500 or $1,000 guaranteeing that they would not disturb the peace or become public charges. Toward the end of the antebellum period, Illinois, Indiana, and Oregon excluded black migrants entirely. Only Ohio, after a long battle, repealed its restrictive immigration legislation in 1849. Though such anti-immigration statutes were only erratically enforced, nevertheless they intimidated Negroes. In 1829 an attempt to enforce an 1807 law requiring a $500 bond precipitated a race riot in Cincinnati and a mass black exodus to Canada.

In the Northeast, none of the states provided by law for discrimination in the courtroom, and Negro testimony was admissible in cases involving whites. Social custom, however, barred blacks from sitting on juries, except in Massachusetts, where a few Negroes served just prior to the Civil War. Black men enjoyed the same voting rights as whites in all the original Northern states for a generation after the American Revolution. Then, one by one, between 1807 and 1837, five of them—New Jersey, Connecticut, New York, Rhode Island, and Pennsylvania—enacted disfranchisement provisions. The laws of Connecticut and Rhode Island did not disqualify those already on the rolls, and in Rhode Island the prohibition was repealed in 1842.

The movement for disfranchisement in the Northeast was usually related to the increasing political power of urban white workingmen and the enactment of universal white manhood suffrage. Negroes tended to vote Federalist, and later for the Federalists' heirs, the National Republicans and the Whigs. This black tie with the aristocratic parties was no accident. In New York, for example, where Negroes had been servants in the homes of the wealthy, the paternalistic relationship helped to bind black men to the Federalist Party. More than this, prominent Federalists like John Jay and Alexander Hamilton were active in the antislavery movement and in charitable work among free blacks. Both *noblesse oblige* and partisan advantage prompted such men to champion the cause of Negro suffrage. In opposition was the Democratic Republican Party (by 1828 known as the Democratic Party), representing the interests of the white working classes, who viewed the blacks as economic rivals. Their prejudice was reinforced by partisan zeal, since most blacks voted for what was generally conceived to be the party of privilege. At the New York constitutional convention of 1821, the Federalists favored a franchise based on property qualifications without race discrimination, but the Democrats, who were in the majority, secured the adoption of universal white manhood suffrage; Negroes could vote only if they owned a freehold estate worth $250. In Pennsylvania the Democrats also agitated for the elimination of Negro suffrage. There race riots and other forms of intimidation practically ended black voting in Philadelphia even before the 1837–8 state constitutional convention legalized disfranchisement. In Rhode Island, those blacks still voting in 1841 were a factor in defeating a new constitution that provided for universal white manhood suffrage. The following year the victorious conservatives rewarded their black supporters by repealing the earlier racial restrictions.

The legal restrictions imposed upon blacks by the Northern

states generated a steady stream of protest and agitation. Conventions and mass meetings passed resolutions, issued addresses to the public, and sent petitions to governors and legislatures. In campaigning for the franchise, for equal treatment in the courts, for guarantees of civil liberties, and, in the Old Northwest, for the abolition of the Black Laws, Negroes emphasized that they were simply asking for basic citizenship rights. First and foremost, therefore, they appealed to the democratic principles upon which the nation was founded. They advanced other arguments as well to support their claims. They denied the existence of innate racial differences, stressed the presence of a thrifty and industrious class of Negroes, and on occasion even enumerated at length the substantial property holdings that free Negroes had acquired under unfavorable conditions. They returned again and again to the theme that blacks were native Americans, loyal to the nation that oppressed them. Fortified with these persuasive arguments, they agitated for the repeal of the Ohio Black Laws and, after achieving that goal, attempted to secure the right to vote. They unsuccessfully fought to stem the tide of disfranchisement in New York and Pennsylvania and were still propagandizing on this issue in both these and other states on the eve of the Civil War.

Most of their efforts ended in failure. It is difficult to see how it could have been otherwise. Evidences of thrift, sobriety, and economic achievements, and the hortatory phrases of even the most skillful writers, could scarcely influence a public that was fundamentally hostile, or at best indifferent, toward them. A minuscule proportion of the electorate even where enfranchised, possessing only a few champions of equal citizenship rights among their abolitionist friends, blacks lacked the power essential to convince whites of the fairness of these often humble requests. To protest against disfranchisement by refusing to pay a modest poll tax, as two black retail merchants did in San Francisco in 1857, was an act both courageous and rare. In view of their situation, black leaders could do no more than protest by respectfully petitioning for the redress of their grievances, and continue to hope that someday moral virtue and the acquisition of property would win the respect of their white fellow citizens.

Besides legal restrictions in voting rights and the courts, there were other forms of oppression. In Northern cities the most extreme of these was mob violence. During the 1830's and 1840's, riots occurred in Philadelphia, New York, Pittsburgh, Cincinnati, and other places. Most of these were pogromlike affairs in which the blacks were so thoroughly terrorized from the beginning that they failed to fight back. Yet other riots, such as the Snow Hill riot in Providence in 1831, and the Cincinnati riots ten years later, were characterized by some degree of Negro retaliatory violence in their early stages. In the Providence riot, a mob of about one hundred white sailors and citizens advanced on a small black section; a Negro shot a sailor dead, and within a half hour a large mob descended upon the neighborhood, damaging many houses. In the Cincinnati riot, a pitched battle was fought on the streets; the blacks had enough guns and ammunition to fire into the mob such a volley that it was twice repulsed. Only when the mob secured an iron six-pounder and hauled it to the place of combat and fired on the Negroes were the latter forced to retreat, permitting the rioters to hold sway for two days without interference from the authorities.

More continuous and pervasive were the patterns of segregation and employment discrimination. The Jim Crow, or segregation, laws were largely a product of the late nineteenth century. Segregation by custom, however, and even occasionally by statute, was already common during the antebellum period. In the South segregation developed as one of the devices to control the urban slaves and free Negroes. Separation in jails and hospitals was universal. Blacks were widely excluded from the public parks and burial grounds. They were relegated to the balconies of theaters and opera houses and barred from hotels and restaurants. The New Orleans street railway maintained separate cars for the two races. Sometimes these practices were codified in law: as early as 1816 New Orleans passed an ordinance segregating blacks in places of public accommodation.

The legal codes of Savannah and Charleston excluded free blacks from public parks. Charleston, Baltimore, and New Orleans were among the cities legalizing segregated jails and poorhouses.

In the North, black people were not legally segregated in places of public accommodation, nor, except for schools, in publicly owned institutions. Custom, however, barred them from hotels and restaurants, and they were segregated, if not entirely excluded, from theaters, public lyceums, hospitals, and cemeteries. Even in abolitionist Boston, the black was considered a pariah in most circles. In 1846 Frederick Douglass wrote William Lloyd Garrison from Ireland:

> I remember, about two years ago, there was in Boston . . . a menagerie [that] I had long desired to see. . . . I was met and told by the doorkeeper, in a harsh and contemptuous tone, "*We don't allow niggers in here.*" . . . Soon after my arrival in New Bedford from the South, I had a strong desire to attend the Lyceum, but was told, "*They don't allow niggers in here!*" On arriving in Boston from an anti-slavery tour, hungry and tired, I went into an eating house near my friend Mr. Campbell's, to get some refreshments. I was met by a lad in a white apron, "*We don't allow niggers in here!*" . . . On attempting to take a seat in the Omnibus [Weymouth], I was told by the driver, (and I never shall forget his fiendish hate,) "*I don't allow niggers in here!*"

Traveling by public conveyance was difficult for blacks. In Boston there were signs: "Colored people not allowed to ride in this omnibus." In New York City blacks were refused streetcar seats on certain lines, except on a segregated basis. Philadelphia Negroes were restricted to the front platform of these vehicles. Long-distance travel was even more of a problem. On stagecoaches blacks usually rode on an outside seat, and on the early railroads they often occupied filthy accommodations in a separate car. Steamboats offered the worst conditions, since blacks were almost invariably excluded from cabins and required to remain on deck even in cold weather. On the all-night trip from New York City to Newport, Rhode Island, they usually had the choice of pacing the deck or sleeping among cotton bales, horses, sheep, and pigs.

Southern blacks were unable to protest such treatment in their section of the country, nor were Negroes of the Old Northwest in a position to do much. Northeastern blacks did protest vigorously, though without much success except in Massachusetts. Some Negroes simply boycotted local omnibuses. Others—such as David Ruggles, the New York Underground Railroad leader—frequently tried to occupy seats reserved for whites but were usually thrown into the street. On one occasion in 1841 when Ruggles sought a first-class ticket on a steamer bound from New Bedford to Nantucket, he was beaten up by the ticket seller for refusing to accept deck accommodations.

When the early Massachusetts railroads provided separate racial accommodations, blacks like Frederick Douglass were forcibly dragged from the white coaches for defying segregation. Aided by leading white abolitionists, Negroes petitioned the legislature for remedial action. In 1842 Charles Lenox Remond, a noted antislavery lecturer, testified before a legislative committee of the Massachusetts House of Representatives: "The grievances of which we complain, be assured, sir, are not imaginary, but real—not local, but universal—not occasional, but continual, every day matter of fact things—and have become, to the disgrace of our common country, a matter of history. . . ." He added that a white man's "social rights" guaranteed free choice of personal friends but did not justify violating the Negro's "civil rights." Sensing a change in public opinion, the Massachusetts railroads abolished the separate coach for Negroes in 1843.

Another method of protest involved legal tests of segregation practices. In 1854 a black woman sued after being forcibly ejected from a New York City streetcar. The lawsuit was handled by the Legal Rights Association, a black group, which engaged twenty-four-year-old Chester A. Arthur as attorney. Although she was awarded damages, Negroes continued to face discrimination on the streetcars. In 1856, when a minister was removed from a vehicle, the judge upheld the transportation company on the ground that its business would suffer if Ne-

groes could sit anywhere they pleased. This decision was interpreted to apply to omnibuses, hotels, and other public facilities.
Five years later a Philadelphia court also ruled in favor of a
transportation company's right to bar blacks by force if necessary.

Recent scholarship has found residential segregation and the
origins of the modern ghetto in the antebellum city. Actually,
before the Civil War urban blacks generally resided in racially
mixed neighborhoods. The homes of the more prosperous free
black artisans and businessmen were often scattered throughout
various parts of the city, singly or in small clusters. There was a
tendency, however, for black people to be concentrated in certain neighborhoods or wards, but within close proximity to
whites. In the Southern towns the slaves who "lived out"
tended to move to the edges of the city, where they formed
neighborhoods predominantly, though not exclusively, black. In
Baltimore and Philadelphia there were blacks living in the alleys
between the main streets on which fashionable whites resided.
The most impoverished Negroes were the most segregated,
often in vice districts controlled by white overlords. New York
blacks were heavily concentrated in a few wards, where poor
whites also resided. In Philadelphia the worst slum consisted of
a few densely populated blocks inhabited by incredibly poverty-
stricken blacks living in unheated rooms, garrets, and tiny
wooden shanties lacking even the most modest comforts. In
Boston, Providence, New Haven, Cincinnati, and other seacoast
and river cities, black slum neighborhoods, with names like
"New Guinea," developed first along the wharves. Later the
Negroes tended to shift to outlying sections known by such
names as "Nigger Hill." As discrimination increased all over the
North, even the more prosperous colored men were often
drawn to predominantly black neighborhoods.

3

One reaction to the discrimination and segregation imposed
by whites was the formation in the late eighteenth and early
nineteenth century of free black community institutions. In

part this development also resulted from the growing number of free blacks in the urban centers and their tendency to concentrate in certain neighborhoods. Thus racial separation became even more deeply imbedded in American life.

The institutional organization of the black community took two forms: the church and the fraternal or mutual-benefit organization. Historically, the two were closely interrelated. The distinction between the sacred and the secular was not closely drawn. In a period when there were hardly any ordained ministers, it was natural for the mutual-aid society to perform both religious and secular functions. Moreover, leaders were few in the relatively small urban black communities, and where there were ministers it was natural that they would play an important role in all black affairs.

In Newport, Rhode Island, the mutual-benefit society preceded the church by many years. The African Union Society formed there in 1780 recorded births, marriages, and deaths and provided for decent burials. The organization also assisted members in times of distress and apprenticed Negro youths to skilled artisans. In 1807 it merged with the African Benevolent Society and established a free school. In 1824, under the auspices of the society, the first black church in Newport was formed. This pattern was not uncommon, although in some communities the mutual-benefit society and the school followed, and were outgrowths of, the church and its activities.

The independent church movement stemmed from prejudicial treatment in white-dominated churches. In Southern and Northeastern cities, free Negroes were admitted to membership in white churches but generally were seated in galleries, "nigger pews," and "African corners." Racial distinctions developed in other aspects of church life, such as separate Sunday-school classes, communion services, and baptisms. Talented blacks were sometimes invited to preach and occasionally even to be the pastor in a white church. One of the most celebrated examples is John Chavis of North Carolina, who ministered to a white Presbyterian congregation until the state prohibited blacks from preaching in 1831. Generally, however, Negroes were required to assume an inconspicuous demeanor. Deeply resenting these racial restrictions, they usually responded by attempting to form their own congregations within the predominantly white denominations or to secede completely and establish independent denominations.

Most Negroes were either Baptists or Methodists. Various reasons have been offered to explain this fact, but one factor must have been that originally, during the eighteenth century, these two churches, appealing to the poor and downtrodden, accepted both Negroes and whites on a basis of relative equality, even in the South. Here and there, blacks ministered to white or mixed Baptist congregations, and early in the nineteenth century a black Baptist minister was elected first moderator of the Louisiana Baptist Association, which, except for himself, was composed of white clergymen. By the 1790's, however, overt discrimination was becoming the more typical pattern in all of the churches.

The origins of the African Methodist Episcopal (AME) Church illustrate Negro response to this change. Its leading figure and first consecrated bishop was Richard Allen, a former Maryland slave who had been converted to Methodism. Allen in turn converted his master, who subsequently permitted Allen to purchase his freedom. Moving to Philadelphia, Allen became a circuit preacher and began attending the predominantly white St. George's Methodist Church in 1786. Allen gathered a group of Negroes for prayer meetings at the church. Realizing that blacks would not be able to achieve positions of true leadership at St. George's, he suggested establishing a separate place of worship. The response of most of the Negroes was not enthusiastic. Allen's forceful personality was drawing ever larger numbers of blacks to St. George's, however, much to the annoyance of the trustees, who stopped his prayer service and ordered black communicants to sit in the rear of the gallery. When Allen and another black leader, Absolom Jones, took places toward the front of the gallery, they were peremptorily directed to change seats in the midst of their prayers. Accordingly, Allen and Jones departed from St. George's with their followers.

Several months earlier, in April 1787, the two men had already founded the Free African Society, a mutual-aid organization which experimented with nondenominational religious exercises conducted along Quaker lines. The silent prayers and meditation, however, were satisfying to neither Jones nor Allen, who soon differed with each other on doctrinal matters. Jones led his band of followers to establish the first black Episcopal Church in America while Allen organized the Bethel African Methodist Episcopal Church in 1794. For many years Allen retained affiliation with the white Methodists, who ordained him a deacon in 1799.

Parallel developments were occurring elsewhere. In Baltimore, during the late 1780's, after both races had worked side by side in creating two interracial Methodist Churches, discriminatory practices evolved. One group of Negroes agreed to become the "African branch" within the parent body and, with financial support from the whites, opened the Sharp Street Church in 1792. For many years whites continued to pay some of the bills and supply a minister, who gave inadequate attention to the needs of the congregation. Another group of black Methodists in Baltimore seceded completely, for a while meeting in each other's homes for religious services. In the early 1800's they engaged Daniel Coker, a former slave, as their pastor. Finally, in 1816, representatives of the various African Methodist churches in Pennsylvania, New Jersey, Delaware, and Maryland met in Philadelphia to form a national body. Coker was first elected bishop, but before he could be consecrated charges of scandalous behavior were circulated and Coker withdrew in favor of Richard Allen.

If there were schisms and rivalries within the AME Church from its very beginning, there were other differences that prevented all of the Negro Methodists from joining under one roof. Some Methodists, like the members of the Sharp Street congregation in Baltimore, preferred to form separate congregations within the predominantly white denomination. Meanwhile, contemporary with the developments in Philadelphia and Baltimore, a comparable evolution was taking place in New

York, leading to the organization of the AME Zion Church in 1821. Throughout the antebellum period the New Yorkers and Philadelphians were rivals for leadership of the free black community, and this competition was apparently at the root of the failure to form a united denomination.

Black Baptists also established their own churches. The two earliest recorded instances were in Georgia and Virginia during the Revolutionary War. Virginia blacks were in fact overwhelmingly Baptists. Leading Baptist churches in Richmond, Norfolk, and Petersburg were originally mixed congregations, and blacks were regularly licensed to preach and ordained as ministers. In two rural areas during the 1790's black pastors briefly presided over white congregations. The First Baptist Church of Richmond was predominantly black, had Negro exhorters and assistant pastors to serve its large black membership, and sponsored black missionaries in Africa. Independent black churches appeared in Williamsburg in 1781, in Petersburg around 1800, in Norfolk in 1817, and in Richmond in 1842. In the latter two cases the whites withdrew and left the blacks in control of the original church building. Such black Baptist churches had a high degree of autonomy. However, as a result of the growth of repressive attitudes among the whites during the 1830's, they were required to have white pastors.

In the North, separate black Baptist churches first appeared between 1805 and 1809 in Boston, New York, and Philadelphia. In Philadelphia blacks were disturbed because the predominantly white church had employed a succession of Southern ministers who encouraged the congregation to regard the slavery issue as a political question outside the concerns of the church. The black Baptists were also sensitive to the more frequent manifestations of race prejudice that accompanied the growth of the city's nonwhite population through migration from the South. In Boston the dissatisfaction of black Baptists led the Rev. Thomas Paul, a recently ordained clergyman, to establish a congregation as a gesture to "independence and a more congenial atmosphere." He also aided a group of New Yorkers whose reasons for favoring separation included the fact that "the colored Methodists and Episcopalians had made similar propositions to their respective churches with success. . . ." For a few months Paul went to New York and filled the pulpit of what later became known as the Abyssinian Baptist Church. Other Baptist congregations followed in Northern and border cities.

Unlike the Methodists, the separate Negro Baptist churches for years remained tied to the white Baptist conventions. The first independent black Baptist conferences were the Providence Baptist Association in Ohio, formed in 1836, and the Wood River Baptist Association in Illinois, formed in 1838. Not until 1853 was a larger regional body, the Western Colored Baptist Convention, created, and not until the 1890's was a truly national Baptist organization of blacks formed.

Both the Negro Methodists and the Negro Baptists encountered considerable difficulty in pursuing their work in the South. Southern fears that gatherings of blacks were hatching places for rebellion sharply limited the work of the black denominations. Travel restrictions imposed on free Negroes prevented several clergymen from the lower South from attending the founding meeting of the AME Church, and the AME Zion Church did not establish itself in the South until 1864. The most noted AME congregation in the South was that organized in Charleston, South Carolina, by the Rev. Morris Brown. Despite police efforts to discourage the attendance of free blacks and slaves, membership tripled in the next five years, but the hysteria surrounding the Denmark Vesey Conspiracy in 1822 forced the closing of the church and Brown's flight from Charleston. From then on, the AME denomination was suppressed in most of the South.

Southern white Baptist ministers and board members closely supervised the work of the black churches and the "colored branches" of white congregations. After the Nat Turner Insurrection of 1831, laws were enacted to circumscribe the activities of black preachers and guarantee white domination of all churches. The black ministry in North Carolina was completely silenced. During 1832–3 Virginia and Alabama forbade blacks to preach except in the presence of trustworthy whites. After

1834 Georgia required black preachers to secure a certificate from ordained white ministers as a first step in applying for a license. Black Baptist congregations in the state continued at the sufferance of whites and largely became wards of the white churches. In many Southern communities curfews prevented black congregations from meeting in the late hours of the evening. Clergymen who accommodated themselves to these restrictions, however, managed to attract large congregations. In Mobile, when a trusted black preacher was found, the white elders of the First Baptist Church allowed blacks to leave the congregation and form the African Baptist Church. In a number of other communities, whites were installed as the spiritual leaders of the African Baptist churches. Apparently only in the upper South—in parts of Maryland, Virginia, and the District of Columbia—did some black Baptist congregations obtain the right to fully direct their own affairs.

Among the Presbyterians and Episcopalians, separate black congregations emerged but retained affiliation with the parent bodies. The Presbyterian officials sought to avoid conflicts in ecclesiastical government by providing that when presbyteries and synods were held, delegates from black churches should receive equal rights and privileges. In contrast, the Episcopalians maintained the attitude of a colonial power dealing with natives. In Pennsylvania diocesan conferences, Negro churches were completely denied representation. In 1852 Philadelphia's Church of the Crucifixion, a black congregation with white vestry and clergyman, asked permission to send white delegates to the Episcopal convention. Since this request might have given blacks some slight indirect influence, it was denied. In the New York Episcopal diocese, only delegations from white congregations participated in church government until shortly before the Civil War. Furthermore, Bishop Benjamin T. Onderdonk refused to admit Negroes as regular students in the General Theological Seminary. In 1834 Onderdonk forced Peter Williams, a black clergyman in the diocese, to resign his office in the newly formed American Anti-Slavery Society. The bishop suggested that affiliation with abolitionists was un-Christian. Despite these discriminatory practices, the Negro upper class of New York and Pennsylvania tended to affiliate with the Episcopal Church and, in fact, identified closely with the aristocratic white Federalist and Episcopal elite, which often took a paternalistic interest in black affairs. For example, when Bishop Onderdonk barred Alexander Crummell from the seminary, William Jay arranged for the young black to secure his training in Boston and England.

Articulate Negroes protested against church discrimination in many ways. Sarah Douglass, a Philadelphia teacher, simply ceased going to Quaker meetings, although her mother regularly attended, sitting alone on "a whole long bench." Frederick Douglass abruptly walked out of a New England Methodist church because blacks were denied participation in a communion service until all the white communicants had received bread and wine. In 1848 Douglass suggested another method of dramatizing grievances. He urged Negroes to enter white churches, take the first available seats, and remain limp while white deacons and clergymen pulled them to the street. The New York *Colored American* in 1837 told readers to combat discrimination by conducting a "stand in": "Stand in the aisles, and rather worship God upon your feet, than become a party to your own degradation. You must shame your oppressors, and wear out prejudice by this holy policy."

The most characteristic form of black protest, however, was the withdrawal from white churches and the formation of their own congregations. Only a handful of Negroes consistently opposed this kind of action. One of them was Frederick Douglass. He solemnly warned blacks that although their segregated churches were created because of exclusionary practices of whites, "complexional distinctions" in houses of worship or in other social institutions were wrong and self-defeating. The race church, said Douglass, benefited Negro haters by compounding misunderstandings between blacks and whites and therefore making racial equality harder to attain.

Like the churches, the mutual-benefit societies, whatever their possible origins in slavery and ultimately in Africa, helped the free blacks adjust to a hostile urban environment. Occupying marginal jobs, many black families lacked the financial resources to cope with periodic crises such as serious illness and death. In the late eighteenth century, leaders urged blacks to avoid reliance on charity and establish beneficial societies. They believed that the mutual-aid organizations would encourage thrift, industry, and morality; provide a method for upward mobility; and prove to whites that blacks were self-respecting citizens deserving equal treatment before the law. These societies also offered members companionship, recreation, recognition, and prestige, which to some degree compensated for the racial proscriptions facing them. The most extensive organizational development appeared in the North, at least partly because Negroes there were allowed greater freedom of movement.

The earliest recorded black mutual-aid organization was the Free African Society formed at Philadelphia by Absolom Jones and Richard Allen in 1787. Through the society, members pooled their resources to "support one another in sickness, and for the benefit of their widows and fatherless children." Shortly after its founding, the leaders persuaded influential whites like Dr. Benjamin Rush, a pioneer antislavery leader in Pennsylvania, to support an application for land in potter's field for use as a Negro cemetery. Survivors of members received financial aid, and the Free African Society educated children not admitted to a free school. Some attempts were also made to find apprenticeships for orphans. Members were required to pay one shilling monthly for distribution to the needy, "provided this necessity is not brought on them by their own imprudence." This middle-class, moralistic tone pervaded other organizational rules, such as one denying membership to those unwilling to lead "an orderly and sober life." Free African societies soon spread to Newport and Boston.

Benevolent societies multiplied all over the North. By the 1830's in Philadelphia alone there were one hundred organizations averaging about seventy-five members each. Many of course were connected with churches, and some operated on an occupational basis, such as the Coachman's Benevolent and the Humane Mechanics Societies. The Philadelphia Library Company of Colored Persons maintained a well-furnished room with several hundred volumes and scheduled public debates on moral as well as literary topics. The Phoenix Society of New York City, whose president was Bishop Christopher Rush, one of the founders of the AME Zion Church, established a library and school for Negroes and sought to encourage the study of morality, literature, and mechanic arts.

In the South blacks also formed mutual-aid associations, although their activities were limited after white fears of slave insurrections resulted in laws curtailing the assembling of blacks. In 1790 a group of light-skinned Charlestonians established the Brown Fellowship Society, specifically providing that black men were not eligible. The following year the Free Dark Men of Color organized their own association, which evidently flourished until after the 1820's when its activities were curtailed by the fear of slave insurrections. The Brown Fellowship Society, however, continued to function because of the connections its artisan members maintained with influential whites and because of the fact that the organization's bylaws prohibited discussions at meetings of such controversial issues as slavery. Baltimore was the Southern city with the largest number of benevolent societies. By 1835 there were more than thirty, with membership rolls ranging from 35 to 150. As in other communities, several associations were organized by trades, such as calkers, coachmen, and mechanics, with a number maintaining savings accounts in local banks. Many other communities had similar mutual-benefit and burial societies, which frequently had to operate clandestinely. Even in Washington, in 1855, police arrested twenty-four "genteel coloured men" during a meeting of one of these societies. When apprehended, they had in their possession a Bible, two volumes on morality, the constitution of their benevolent organization, and a document indicating their interest in buying the freedom of a female slave. The police judge ordered one prisoner, a slave, to be whipped, four free blacks to be sent to jail, and the others to be fined.

More elaborate were the secret fraternal orders. With their rituals, ceremonies, and regalia, they gave members even greater prestige and also performed some economic functions of mutual aid. The Masons and Odd Fellows were the two oldest Negro orders; both obtained their charters from England because of exclusion from white American orders. The founder of black Masonry was Prince Hall, a soap maker and a part-time Methodist preacher and active leader in the Free African Society of Boston. In 1775 Hall and other Negroes had been initiated into a military Masonic lodge by British soldiers on duty at Boston. Hall sought to establish a black lodge but was rebuffed by the white American Masons. Applying for a warrant from England, which he received in 1787, he formed an African lodge in Boston and was instrumental in bringing Negro Masonry to Philadelphia a decade later, where the organizers were Absolom Jones, Richard Allen, and James Forten, the wealthy sailmaker. About the same time a lodge was also founded in Providence, Rhode Island. The organization spread rapidly throughout the North and reached California with the Gold Rush in 1849. Restrictive legislation made it more difficult for the Masons to organize in the South. Nevertheless, as early as 1825 lodges thrived in Baltimore and in the District of Columbia. The only other Southern cities in which the Masons established a foothold were Louisville and New Orleans, where lodges were organized at midcentury.

The Negro Odd Fellows formed their first lodge in the United States in 1843, shortly after whites rejected the applications of the Philomathean Institute of New York and the Philadelphia Library Company and Debating Society. Peter Ogden, a ship steward who already held an Odd Fellows membership card from Liverpool, obtained British authorization to found the Philomathean Lodge in New York. The black Odd Fellows also organized in neighboring states, though their most flourishing period did not come until the first part of the twentieth century.

Between the founding of the Odd Fellows and the start of the Civil War, a number of other national, quasi-religious, fraternal orders came into being, but most of them had only limited influence until after the Civil War. As in the case of the smaller mutual-benefit societies, Baltimore spawned a number of these organizations, including the Galilean Fishermen, the Nazarites, the Samaritans, and the Seven Wise Men.

While the independent churches and the mutual-benefit societies contributed to the separation of the races, they were also refuges from white supremacy. While they functioned in part as an accommodation to the realities of American race prejudice and discrimination, they were also an assertion of black independence and racial self-respect. To blacks whose ambitions were crushed by caste, they offered opportunities for self-expression and the development of leadership. Prominent figures in the churches and fraternal societies were from the beginning ardent advocates of equal rights and abolition. In the generation before the Civil War they provided leadership both in the separate Negro Convention Movement and in the interracial abolitionist societies. Prior to the rise of militant antislavery they had also made a significant contribution to black education.

4

The history of black education before the Civil War can be divided into three rather distinct, though overlapping, stages: (1) white philanthropy, (2) black self-help, and (3) public support. With a few conspicuous exceptions, the general pattern was always a segregated one. During the eighteenth century, religious organizations such as the Episcopal Society for the Propagation of the Gospel, which worked in both the North and the South, and the Society of Friends undertook rudimentary education of slaves and free Negroes to enable them to read the Bible. Some antislavery societies formed during the Revolutionary era also offered free Negroes an opportunity for elementary education. The New York Manumission Society in 1787 opened the African Free School, which was so successful that six additional ones were added in the city by 1834. Ultimately they became part of the public-school system.

Under the auspices of the black churches and mutual-benefit societies emerging at the end of the eighteenth century, free blacks maintained their own schools. Even where white philanthropic support was solicited, the initiative came from blacks themselves. In Newport, Rhode Island, a white Episcopal rector established a school for blacks in 1763. In 1807, eight years after the school had closed, the leaders of the black community reopened it through their newly organized African Benevolent Society. The institution was operated with varying degrees of success until the city took over. At Boston, Prince Hall led a group of Negroes in 1787 in petitioning the Massachusetts General Court for a school, since Negroes "receive no benefit from the free schools." According to some authorities, a few black children did attend the public schools with whites at the end of the eighteenth century but most withdrew because of ridicule and mistreatment. In 1798 some black parents, supported by white friends, opened a private school in Prince Hall's home. Seven years later the institution moved to the African Meeting House. Not until 1820, however, was a black public school opened, and within a short time Negroes lost their right to use the white schools. Early in the nineteenth century several Philadelphia Negro ministers organized schools in their churches, and the Bethel AME Church founded the Society of Free People of Color for Promoting the Instruction and School Education of Children of African Descent. In 1812 the New York Society of Free People of Color established a school for orphans.

In the South during the antebellum period, Negro education never went beyond the second stage. By the beginning of the nineteenth century a substantial number of free blacks, having achieved a degree of economic security as mechanics and tradesmen, were financially underwriting their own schools. In the

Deep South the Brown Fellowship Society of Charleston as early as 1790 provided educational facilities as part of its mutual-welfare program. Two decades later the Minor Society was organized to educate indigent and orphaned children. In 1829 one of the youth trained by the Minor Society, Daniel Alexander Payne, opened a school of his own for black children. In New Orleans the Roman Catholic Church educated some Negroes, but that city's prosperous *gens de couleur* provided financial support for several schools of their own, sent their older children to France for instruction, and in 1840 established the École des Orphelins Indigents for the education of lower-class youth. As the Southern race system grew harsher in the course of the nineteenth century, the education of free blacks was restricted, though never completely eliminated. In 1823 Mississippi forbade groups of blacks larger than five to study together. In Charleston, beginning in 1834, it became legally mandatory that a white person attend each class meeting. Though Payne closed his school and moved to the North, where he became a distinguished AME bishop, some of the free black schools continued. In many other parts of the South private classes were sometimes held, even by philanthropically minded whites, often in violation of state or city regulations.

In the Border States there was no such interference by public authorities, but neither did these white educators actively assist Negro schooling. The first two schools that Negroes established in Baltimore were in existence by the beginning of the nineteenth century. One was under the auspices of the all-black Sharp Street Methodist Church and the other was conducted by Daniel Coker, the pioneer AME minister. Other black churches were soon operating educational institutions, and during the 1820's even adults received instruction at night in various subjects including Latin and French. Some white philanthropists also contributed time, money, and teachers to supplement these efforts. The first school for Negroes in Washington was formed in 1807 by three illiterate black men, two of whom worked in the navy yard. They constructed a small frame schoolhouse and employed a white teacher. Beginning with the educational institution opened in 1818 by the Resolute Beneficial Society, Washington's blacks were not without at least one well-administered school, and in their efforts they obtained the cooperation of certain dedicated whites as well. Not until 1862 did the municipal authorities undertake to create schools for blacks.

In the North free public education for all white youth was the rule by the 1830's, but the products of Horace Mann's famous crusade for the common school seldom included blacks. In Ohio, Michigan, Wisconsin, and Iowa, Negroes received no public-school funds until the middle of the nineteenth century, and in Illinois and Indiana not until the eve of the Civil War. Even where schooling was provided for Negroes, it was generally separate and unequal. Segregation was simply the custom in most places, but in some states it was legislated. A New York statute specifically gave school boards the option of establishing segregated institutions. Pennsylvania and Ohio required separate schools wherever the number of black pupils exceeded twenty. Where blacks attended integrated schools, they usually found themselves placed in special seats and subjected to other indignities. Segregated institutions ordinarily operated on as skimpy a budget as possible. An 1859 New York *Tribune* editorial noted that "the school houses for the whites are in situations where the price of rents is high, and on the buildings themselves no expenditure is spared to make them commodious and elegant. . . . The schools for the blacks, on the contrary, are nearly all, if not all, old buildings, generally in filthy and degraded neighborhoods, dark, damp, small, and cheerless, safe neither for the morals nor the health of those who are compelled to go to them, if they go anywhere, and calculated rather to repel than to attract them." In city after city, Rochester, Philadelphia, Hartford, and New Haven, the same gloomy picture was evident in segregated schools—overcrowding and limited supplies and equipment.

The tactics that Northern blacks employed in dealing with public-school discrimination in the generation before the Civil War varied with the conditions in local communities. During the years in which Illinois and Ohio refused to provide for black youth the educational opportunities offered to white children, blacks raised money among themselves and opened schools that supplemented those financed by the white abolitionists. At the same time black state conventions appealed to the legislatures to provide public education for members of the race. In certain cities, like Rochester and Hartford, where Negro children were insulted in the mixed public schools, black citizens successfully appealed for separate schools during the 1830's. Thus a segregated school system might be inaugurated by the white authorities or might be requested by blacks because it would be preferable to no schools at all or to a mixed system where black children were mistreated. In either case, once a separate system was introduced, blacks petitioned for greater financial support. Their complaints sometimes led to school improvements. For example, a memorial from Hartford blacks in 1846 resulted in the erection of a new building. New York Negroes, led by abolitionist Charles B. Ray, formed a Society for the Promotion of Education Among Colored Citizens, which in 1857 submitted a detailed analysis of the "caste" schools in the community. Subsequently one institution was renovated and another constructed to replace a school that had been torn down.

Many blacks worked to secure adequate training for their children but accepted separate schools as a necessary evil. Others insisted on a direct, frontal attack on the system of segregation. Black newspapers and conventions constantly agitated on the issue, and numerous petitions were sent to the public authorities appealing for an end to the discrimination. Robert Purvis, of Philadelphia, refused to pay the school tax in 1853, and publicly announced that school segregation violated "my rights as a citizen, and my feelings as a man." During the 1850's Frederick Douglass led a successful attack against the separate school system in Rochester.

Probably the most notable desegregation campaign occurred in Boston during the 1840's and 1850's. By then, integrated schools existed in many Massachusetts communities, among them Cambridge, New Bedford, Worcester, and Lowell. In the early 1840's black and white abolitionists of Boston sent many petitions to the primary-school committee, but these were dismissed on the grounds that neither law nor custom could efface inherent distinctions between black and white children. In 1849 Benjamin Roberts sued the committee for excluding his daughter from the school in her neighborhood and compelling her to pass five white institutions on her way to the Negro school. Roberts, who was represented by the white lawyer Charles Sumner and the black lawyer Robert Morris, lost in the courts. The state supreme court upheld the legality of segregation, justifying it with the first recorded use of the separate-but-equal doctrine. For the next several years many blacks conducted a school boycott, arranging to have their children receive an education in neighboring communities. Hundreds of Negroes and whites petitioned the Massachusetts legislature, and in 1855 it enacted a law requiring public schools to admit students without regard to color. Elsewhere, in spite of all efforts, when the Civil War began, segregation prevailed for the overwhelming majority of Negroes attending public schools. Northern white private schools that admitted blacks experienced opposition—even mob violence—from local citizens.

At the college level some private institutions accepted blacks and the first two to receive their A.B. degrees graduated from Amherst and Bowdoin Colleges in 1826. Two all-black collegiate institutions were developed during the 1850's: in 1854 Presbyterians organized Ashmun Institute in Pennsylvania, later known as Lincoln University, in order to train Negroes for missionary work in Africa; in 1855 the Methodist Episcopal Church, North, founded Wilberforce University in Ohio, transferring it in 1862 to the AME Church.

5

Because of white prejudice and discrimination the overwhelming majority of free Negroes were unskilled laborers. Black entrepreneurs found it difficult to obtain capital, since lending institutions considered them poor risks. White businessmen were reluctant to employ Negroes in skilled or white-collar work. Where employers were willing to hire a black, white laborers often refused to work with him. The black skilled artisan faced greater obstacles in the North than in the South. The New York Manumission Society complained that many students leaving the African Free School in the 1820's were idle because they could neither enter trades nor find jobs and that the educated young Negroes often had no alternative except to become sailors, cooks, waiters, coachmen, servants, and common laborers. After Frederick Douglass fled from Maryland to New Bedford, Massachusetts, in 1838, a sympathetic shipowner hired him as a calker, the trade he had learned as a slave in Baltimore. When the other calkers would not accept Douglass, he was forced into unskilled labor and took a succession of jobs sawing wood, digging cellars, collecting rubbish, and loading ships.

In the face of all these obstacles, nevertheless, a minority made a comfortable living and a few founded modest fortunes. The successful free black entrepreneurs catered principally to well-to-do whites and were concentrated in the service trades. There were many black barbers, hackmen, draymen, and owners of livery stables. Others were blacksmiths, grocers, fashionable tailors, restaurateurs and caterers, proprietors of coal and lumber yards, and occasionally hotel owners. Negroes were also engaged in the shoemaking and building trades in a number of cities, especially in the South. Baltimore had many slave and free black ship calkers. In Philadelphia sizable numbers of blacks were carpenters, tailors and dressmakers, brickmakers, shoemakers and bootmakers, and cabinetmakers. A handful of colored men created and dominated the fashionable catering business in the city until the end of the nineteenth century, making Philadelphia catering famous throughout the country. James Forten, one of the city's principal sailmakers, employed over forty white and black workers and, by the 1830's, had acquired a fortune of $100,000. William Still, the Underground Railroad leader, was the proprietor of a successful coal and lumber yard. In Charleston, as in certain other Southern cities, free Negroes monopolized barbering, practically controlled the building trades, and were prominent among the shoemakers and butchers. The more outstanding carpenters or contractors employed both white men and slaves. For a number of years, the leading hotel proprietor was a free black named Jehu Jones. In 1850, New Orleans free blacks included one architect, five jewelers, four physicians, eleven music teachers, and fifty-two merchants, exhibiting an even greater occupational diversity than in Charleston. Most of the really wealthy black artisans or retail merchants invested their money in real estate. George Thomas Downing, the prominent caterer of New York and Newport, and Thomy Lafon, the New Orleans merchant, each acquired several hundred thousand dollars in this manner.

In the course of the nineteenth century the position of the Negro artisan-entrepreneur deteriorated. As the white working class grew in numbers in the Southern cities, its members made determined efforts to exclude Negroes from the better-paying occupations. Savannah ordinances of 1822 and 1831 barred both slave and free Negroes from most of the skilled trades. In 1845 Georgia made it a misdemeanor for a black mechanic to make a contract for the repair or construction of buildings. By the 1840's the number of black draymen had declined sharply in New Orleans.

In the North there was even less opportunity for black entrepreneurs. As in the South, their status worsened as the decades passed. A detailed analysis of the unusually rich occupational and economic data available on Philadelphia free blacks reveals a sharp deterioration in their wealth and job distribution during the three decades prior to the Civil War, with the skilled artisan-entrepreneur losing out to white competitors. Moreover, the arrival of nearly five million immigrants in the antebellum generation posed an alarming threat to the Negroes' already meager economic chances. By the early 1850's Douglass observed, "Every hour sees the black man elbowed out of employment by some newly arrived emigrant whose hunger and whose color are thought to give him a better title to the place." Most of the newcomers who settled in the cities came from Ireland. Possessing no marketable skills, they became implacable competitors of the blacks for the heavy laboring and menial jobs. The Irish, who experienced discrimination from other white Americans, vented their aggression upon the "Nagurs," attacking them around docks, railyards, and coal mines. Gradually, many Negroes were displaced as laborers in these areas and in other occupations, such as hod carriers, waiters, barbers, even porters and bootblacks. Black women, who could count on a degree of economic security even when their husbands could not, began losing positions as maids, cooks, and washerwomen. On the waterfront, economic competition and hostility between the two groups was exacerbated when employers, playing one race against the other, hired black workmen as strikebreakers. In New York City this policy produced among the predominantly Irish longshoremen an intense animosity that came to a violent climax in the bloody race riots of 1863.

6

There was enough economic differentiation among the urban blacks to provide the basis for a social class system. It should be pointed out, however, that because of the limited occupational opportunities open to Negroes and the high proportion of them in the most menial job categories, their criteria for social class membership diverged sharply from those of whites. Among the slaves in the Southern cities there were distinctions based upon color, occupation, and the prominence of one's master. Among free blacks the chronically unemployed, unskilled laborers formed the lowest class. Those who had regular employment, especially if the job involved a degree of skill, formed a middle class. In the North this group included even domestic servants. Such middle-class persons were likely to be regular churchgoers and members of the mutual-benefit societies. The upper stratum included independent artisans and businessmen. While the occupational distribution among elite Negroes varied from city to city, broadly speaking it can be said that at the top were the successful entrepreneurs, particularly the barbers, restaurateurs, caterers, tailors, and contractors patronized by fashionable whites; the house servants of the most socially prominent white families in Northern cities; and the handful of well-educated professional people in law, teaching, medicine, and the ministry. In the South it included a tiny slaveowning black aristocracy.

Occupation and wealth were the most important criteria of class affiliation. There were also more subtle distinctions based on skin color, education, church membership, and family background. A long history of free ancestry was treasured, especially if one's forebears included distinguished white people. The light-skinned elites of Deep South cities like Charleston and New Orleans were particularly noted for their exclusiveness. But generally such persons, with their advantages of birth and background, were nearly everywhere disproportionately represented among the economically successful and among the race's recognized spokesmen and leaders. A recent study of Philadelphia reveals their striking preeminence among the city's black artisans and entrepreneurs, in the socially prominent churches and clubs, and in the leadership roles of protest organizations and other voluntary associations. The middle and upper classes stressed homeownership, education, thrift, hard work, and moral respectability. The upper-class black people dressed conservatively, practiced an elaborate and formal etiquette, cultivated the arts, and, in short, led lives characterized by gentility and refinement. From this elite came the majority of the race's important protest leaders.

7

The racial ideologies of the free blacks—both before and since the Civil War—can be analyzed from various points of view. One can examine how the Negroes adapted to their needs various elements in American social thought, such as belief in political democracy, advocacy of thrift and industry, and faith in the efficacy of education. One can describe how in some situations and in certain periods Negroes have protested against their status, while in others they were compelled to accommodate to it. Finally, one can discuss black social thought as ranging along a continuum of ideologies from assimilation to nationalism.

At one end of this continuum have been the advocates of complete biological amalgamation and cultural assimilation with members of the dominant society, and the complete disappearance of blacks as a racial group. At the other end have been those who advocated complete withdrawal from American society and the creation of independent Negro states. Between these two extremes have been those who held a great variety of philosophies recognizing black people as American citizens, yet emphasizing their distinctiveness as members of an ethnic group. This intermediate category has included the advocacy of attaining constitutional rights through self-help and racial solidarity, an insistence upon racial equality combined with preference for separate clubs and churches, and even the espousal of the creation of all-black communities within the United States. This ethnic dualism, this ambivalence, which is the product of the contradiction between the values of American democracy and the facts of race discrimination, was best articulated by W. E. B. Du Bois. In the essay written early in this century, he said: "One ever feels his twoness,—an American, a Negro; two souls, two thoughts, two unreconciled strivings; two warring ideals in one dark body, whose dogged strength alone keeps it from being torn asunder. . . . He simply wishes to make it possible for a man to be both a Negro and an American, without being cursed and spit upon by his fellows without having the doors of Opportunity closed roughly in his face."

In no case have blacks, even those completely favoring integration and assimilation, been able to forget their connection with an oppressed group. From this very alienation came the desire for separate institutions operated without white interference, such as the church and the mutual-benefit society. The gap between ideal and practice in American society meant that blacks not only wanted to be a part of that society but that they also found it desirable to develop their own group life within it. Thus, ironically, the establishment of the separate black church and fraternal organization was both a form of protest against American racism and yet an accommodation to it.

It should be emphasized that the whole subject of the Negro's response to discrimination and search for freedom and human dignity is a highly complex one, not easily condensed into a few pages. For one thing, the diverse ideologies delineated above have been combined in a bewildering variety of ways. Both protest and accommodating leaders have advocated thrift, industry, and economic accumulation. Usually these values have been associated with the idea of blacks gaining acceptance in American society by assimilating American middle-class ways. These economic ideas have also been combined with the advocacy of race pride and race solidarity to stimulate black support of black business and, by thus achieving material success, to gain acceptance in American society. Finally, certain highly nationalist movements, like the modern Black Muslims, have combined the Puritan ethic with complete rejection of American white society.

Negro thinking has varied under the impact of changing conditions. Gunnar Myrdal described the situation perceptively. Noting that to a large degree blacks are "denied identification with the nation or with national groups," he observed:

> to them social speculation, therefore, moves in a sphere of unreality and futility. Instead of organized popular theories or ideas, the observer finds in the Negro world, for the most part, only a *fluid and amorphous mass of all sorts of embryos of thoughts. Negroes seem to be held in a state of eternal preparedness for a great number of contradictory opinions*—ready to accept one type or another depending on how they are driven by pressures or where they see an opportunity. Under such circumstances, the masses of American Negroes might, for example, rally around a violently anti-American, anti-Western, anti-White, black chauvinism of the Garvey type, centered around the idea of Africa as the mother country. But they might just as likely, if only a slight change of stimulus is provided, join in an all-out effort to fight for their native country . . . for the Western Civilization to which they belong, and for the tenets of democracy in the entire

world. . . . Or they might develop a passive cynicism toward it all.

Keeping the foregoing observations in mind, we shall now turn to an examination of the changing programs proposed by Northern black leaders to achieve freedom for themselves and for the slaves. Having previously indicated the nature of black protest against specific kinds of discrimination, in the following pages we will focus primarily on the Negro Convention Movement and on black participation in the antislavery movement.

8

As already noted, the deteriorating status of free blacks in the North following the adoption of the Constitution was a prime factor in the formation of separate community institutions. The leaders of these organizations, despite their alienation from American society, retained their faith that in God's plan the slaves would be freed and Negroes accorded equal rights in America. Along with the more successful businessmen, they led the early Negro agitation against both slavery in the South and discrimination at home. On behalf of the bondsmen Northern blacks held meetings and passed resolutions, listened to spirited orations commemorating the legal closing of the slave trade in the United States in 1808, and sent respectfully worded petitions to Congress. There was something ritualistic about much of this activity. Whites were aware of but little of it, and most of what they perceived they ignored. Quite naturally, therefore, the black leaders tended to concern themselves mostly with something they could hope to accomplish more readily: the elevation of the Northern free people of color.

A very few exhibited an even greater degree of estrangement than had the creators of the separate community institutions, and, giving up all hope of a decent future in this country, advocated colonization or emigration to Africa. As early as 1789 the Free African Society of Newport went on record as favoring a return to Africa. In 1815 the prosperous New England black shipowner, Paul Cuffe, took thirty-eight free Negroes to Sierra Leone at his own expense. Cuffe was interested in colonization primarily as an instrument for Christianizing the Africans and destroying the slave trade. But there were indications of genuine colonizationist sentiment in a letter written by some of the migrants: "Be not fearful to come to Africa, which is your country by right. . . . Though you are free . . . Africa, not America, is your country and your home."

Actually, interest in colonization was much less common among blacks than among white antislavery advocates. The antislavery movement had flourished in the Border States after the passage of emancipation laws in the North. Colonization was espoused both by humanitarians who thought that free blacks would fare better in a land of their own and by Southern slaveholders who considered the free Negroes a dangerous element. In December 1816, a group of prominent Americans, including Henry Clay, then speaker of the House of Representatives, established the American Colonization Society. While claiming to be motivated by humanitarianism, the colonizationists not only refused to oppose racist laws and customs, but many actually supported and justified such barriers in order to make the condition of the free blacks so humiliating and debasing that, by comparison, the prospect of being transported to Africa would seem inviting. Although colonizationists stated that the establishment of an African "homeland" would ultimately encourage slaveholders to liberate their slaves in the United States, actually some founders of the society suggested that the exodus of free blacks would strengthen the institution of slavery. Nevertheless, until after 1830 most of the white antislavery advocates coupled their interest in the slave with support for colonization as a solution of the American race problem.

Before the Colonization Society was launched, those responsible for initiating it had consulted with Paul Cuffe, and there were some blacks who subscribed to its program. This was especially true in Maryland, where the largest and wealthiest of state colonization societies existed. Daniel Coker of Baltimore sailed for the society with about ninety free Negroes in 1820. As a black colonization convention in Baltimore in 1826 stated, since blacks were strangers in the United States and could never enjoy full rights there, emigration to Africa was the only way to obtain freedom.

In the main, free blacks were suspicious of the motives of the American Colonization Society and strongly opposed it. Within a few weeks after the formation of the organization, black leaders in Philadelphia—among them Bishop Richard Allen, the Rev. Absolom Jones, and James Forten—drew a large crowd to the Bethel Church for a vigorous protest against the colonizationists. The Philadelphia Negroes reminded America that in past wars black people had "ceased to remember their wrongs and rallied around the standard of their country. . . . Whereas our ancestors (not of choice) were the first successful cultivators of the wilds of America, we their descendants feel ourselves entitled to participate in the blessings of her luxuriant soil, which their blood and sweat manured; and that any measure or system of measures, having a tendency to banish us from her bosom, would not only be cruel, but in direct violation of those principles, which have been the boast of this republic. . . ." They declared that their cause could not be divorced from their brothers in bondage—with whom there were ties not only of color but "of suffering and of wrong," making it impossible to "separate ourselves voluntarily from the slave population in this country . . . and we feel that there is more virtue in suffering privations with them. . . ."

During the next years, free blacks in Northern cities for the most part were not interested in emigration to Africa and were hostile to the American Colonization Society, although several prominent leaders, including Richard Allen, enthusiastically supported an abortive Haitian colonization movement during the 1820's. In 1827 a group of New Yorkers founded the first black newspaper, *Freedom's Journal*, edited by Samuel Cornish and John Russwurm. The paper attacked the Colonization Society, declaring that the organization's true motives were not to end slavery but to rid the nation of its free Negro population.

Cornish soon resigned, and in 1829, after Russwurm joined the colonizationists, *Freedom's Journal* folded. The Boston agent for the paper had been David Walker, a clothing dealer who in 1829 published an incendiary pamphlet, *Walker's Appeal, in Four Articles.* His hatred of slavery and the American Colonization Society brought him to the conclusion that if whites refused to grant emancipation voluntarily, blacks should break the "infernal chains" by an armed rebellion.

The influence of the Colonization Society and its local branches was shown in extreme form by the Cincinnati riot of 1829. Cincinnati's black population had increased substantially since the early 1820's, causing special concern among the unskilled whites, who demanded that the new arrivals be expelled. This antiblack hostility acquired respectability through the activities of the Cincinnati Colonization Society, which, since its founding in 1826, had attracted the city's most prominent citizens. These influential leaders encouraged local newspapers and ministers to agitate against the community's free blacks, and the society's propaganda provided justification for the campaign to drive black people from the city. During the summer of 1829, Cincinnati's officials attempted to enforce the Ohio Black Laws, which required Negroes to post $500 bonds guaranteeing "good behavior." While ghetto leaders petitioned for a legislative reprieve, white mobs attacked. More than half the black population fled to Canada and other parts of the United States.

The Cincinnati riot dramatized, as had no previous single event, the exposed and defenseless position of the free Negro in American society. Fearing that it was the precursor of similar outbursts elsewhere, black leaders called a conference for September 1830, in Philadelphia, the first effort within the race to effect unified action on a national scale. Bishop Allen presided over this convention of black leaders, which was attended by representatives from Rhode Island, Connecticut, New York, Pennsylvania, Delaware, Maryland, and Virginia. Repudiating the principles of the American Colonization Society, they urged those blacks unable to endure further oppression in the United States to consider settlement only in Canada.

To the black delegates at the Philadelphia conclave, it was a source of frustration that many sincere whites in the antislavery movement supported the Colonization Society. Among these men were Gerrit Smith, one of New York State's wealthiest landowners; Arthur and Lewis Tappan, prominent New York merchants; and Benjamin Lundy, a coeditor of the *Genius of Universal Emancipation*. This antislavery newspaper had recently suspended publication because of the outspokenness of its other editor, William Lloyd Garrison. The year before the 1830 Negro convention, several Baltimore Negroes had been instrumental in converting Garrison from his former sympathy with colonization. Among them was William Watkins, "A Colored Baltimorean," who had ridiculed the organization in a letter published in the *Genius* in 1828. He and the other Negroes failed to modify Lundy's attitude toward colonization projects, but in 1829, when Garrison arrived in Baltimore, they held extended talks with him and brought him around to their point of view. In a biography of Garrison his children recalled: "Garrison was slow to discover [the society's] real animus. . . . Some of his colored friends in Baltimore were the first to point out to him its dangerous character and tendency, and its purpose to strengthen slavery by expelling the free people of color."

Garrison also read *Walker's Appeal*, with its condemnation of colonizationists, and although considering the call for a slave rebellion "injudicious," he found the pamphlet "warranted by the creed of an independent people." Impressed by the abilities of men like Walker and Watkins, Garrison became furious with the Colonization Society for seeking to convince the nation that blacks were too degenerate to profit from American civilization. Subsequently, black antislavery men in Philadelphia, such as James Forten and his son-in-law, Robert Purvis, impressed him with their refinement, their fervent belief in emancipation, and their hatred of colonization. He addressed the second national Negro convention (1831) in Philadelphia and, the following year, published *Thoughts on African Colonization*, containing a copious selection of "Resolutions, Addresses and Remonstrances of the Free People of Color," demonstrating all too clearly the long-time opposition to the Colonization Society from the race it was ostensibly aiding. Before long, other influential whites such as the Tappans and Gerrit Smith also renounced the organization. For helping to enlist these white allies, the black leaders gratefully acknowledged their debt to Garrison, but on occasion they reminded whites that, as the Rev. Charles Gardner, a Philadelphia Presbyterian minister, said at the 1837 convention of the American Anti-Slavery Society, free people of color had held numerous meetings opposing the American Colonization Society when Garrison was still a schoolboy.

9

The Negro Convention Movement, which began in 1830, continued to function until the end of the century, but its most important work was done during the antebellum period and Reconstruction. National conventions were held annually from 1830 to 1835. Subsequently, they were held irregularly, as the occasion seemed to warrant. No permanent organization was effected. Usually a concerned group would issue a call to convention, and self-constituted *ad hoc* organizations in other cities would send representatives, if they desired, to the state and national conclaves. The movement was a Northern phenomenon until after the Civil War, for the participation of Southern blacks in such gatherings would have subjected them to danger at home. The Convention Movement was important because it was led and attended by the most distinguished leaders of the race—prominent ministers, physicians, lawyers, businessmen, and, after the Civil War, politicians. More than any other source, the conventions provide illuminating insight into the thinking of articulate blacks on the problems facing the race.

The early conventions protested against slavery and, at greater length, against the indignities facing the free people of color. Besides condemning race prejudice, the convention leaders sought to convince lower-class Negroes that they could do a great deal to elevate themselves despite adverse circumstances. If blacks would only try hard enough they would attain "the standard of good society"—temperance, industry, thrift, and learning. The race was urged to stress schooling, good moral character, and economic accumulation. An important part of this economic program was a concern with training blacks for the skilled trades. For the most part shut out from apprenticeships, free blacks had little or no opportunity to learn these crafts and therefore lacked an important means of becoming independent and self-supporting entrepreneurs. Black leaders therefore eagerly seized upon the proposal, put forth by white abolitionists and reformers, that manual-labor schools would be valuable for the lower classes, both white and black. Such schools would teach not only a trade with which to earn a living, but, by paying students for their work, would inculcate the habits of thrift and industry. Negro leaders fervently believed that training for the trades would free many members of the race from menial, low-paying jobs. Unfortunately, the attempt sponsored by white and black abolitionists to establish such a manual-labor school for blacks in New Haven failed because of the hostility of local whites.

After 1835 there was no formal National Negro Convention Movement until 1843. In part it foundered on the rivalry between the New Yorkers and the Philadelphians. And in part its suspension was due to a feeling that there was a serious contradiction involved in advocating integration and equal rights by means of an all-black or "caste" convention. After the appearance of the American Anti-Slavery Society in 1833, it seemed to many that in view of substantial white interest, all-black conventions were no longer necessary or advisable.

Pennsylvania blacks like Purvis and William Whipper, a lumber merchant, admonished the race to participate with whites in all antislavery activities. Believing that the Negro Convention Movement was especially self-segregating, they sought to change its direction. In 1834 these black Garrisonians formed the American Moral Reform Society for Improving the Condition of Mankind, an organization that dominated the black conventions of 1834–5 and ultimately replaced them. The Moral Reformers, who held annual conferences until 1841, had little influence except in Philadelphia and Boston. They sought to turn blacks away from parochial racial interests to a concern for uplifting "the whole human race, without distinction as to clime, country, or complexion." In their dedication to a broad humanitarianism, Whipper and other members even scorned such terms as "Negro," "colored," and "African," urging their elimination from the names of churches, schools, and other institutions. Whipper and his associates identified themselves as "oppressed Americans" rather than "colored people." They subscribed to the view that as the entire society was regenerated, Negroes would naturally share in the moral elevation along with everyone else.

Opponents of the Moral Reformers pointedly noted that for all the talk about integration, the organization was unable to attract white members. Much of the criticism came from New York, where many gibes originated in the *Colored American*, a newspaper edited by Samuel Cornish. Commenting on their use of the term "oppressed Americans," he insinuated that the Moral Reformers lacked race pride. He contended that they were being too visionary in talking of solving the nation's problems without special attention to Negroes, the most deprived segment in the population. He insisted that discrimination forced black people to rely upon themselves to chart a program that would topple racial barriers. In pressing for a stronger racial consciousness and solidarity, the New York leaders laid the groundwork for the revival of the National Negro Convention Movement in 1843. One reason for this appeal to racial self-help and solidarity and for the renewed interest in a national convention was the growing feeling, especially strong among New Yorkers, that white abolitionists were guilty of race prejudice and of monopolizing power within the antislavery movement.

10

The American Anti-Slavery Society, founded in 1833, merged two rather distinct antislavery traditions. One was the Garrisonian wing, with its supporters largely in Puritan New England and Quaker Philadelphia. The other was centered mainly in New York State and the Old Northwest; its roots lay in the evangelical revivalism, led by the Presbyterian Charles Grandison Finney, which had swept western New York and the Old Northwest in the 1820's. Its leading apostle was the dynamic antislavery agitator Theodore Dwight Weld; its key financial supporters were the brothers Lewis and Arthur Tappan. In contrast to earlier antislavery advocates, both groups demanded "immediate abolition" of slavery, both were anticolonizationist, and both gave at least rhetorical support to the ideology of racial equality. The two groups, however, split in 1839–40. In part due to the irascible nature of Garrison's personality, the schism also involved important tactical and ideological issues. Garrison insisted on relying only on "moral suasion." He opposed political action because slavery was recognized in the Constitution, which he denounced as a "covenant with death and an agreement with Hell." Garrison also insisted on militantly championing other reform issues, including women's rights. The Weld-Tappan faction was also interested in women's rights but felt that the slavery issue was of such transcendent importance that it should take precedence over everything else. They maintained that if antislavery societies advocated other reforms, they would alienate many potential supporters. They also concluded that propaganda or moral suasion would not of itself overthrow slavery, that political action was necessary. In the split of 1839–40 most black leaders went with the Weld-Tappan group into the American and Foreign Anti-Slavery Society. A minority, chiefly in Boston and Philadelphia, remained loyal Garrisonians.

Exactly what role did the black abolitionists play in the organized antislavery movement, and what was the nature of their relationship with the white abolitionists? Historians of the black American have generally stressed the importance of the black abolitionists' role, while the historians of the antislavery movement and the biographers of its leaders have usually written as if blacks played only a minor and incidental part. Some recent scholars, quoting from speeches and letters of antislavery leaders, have engaged in a spirited debate as to whether or not the white abolitionists were genuine racial egalitarians. It would appear to us that the fundamental question to be raised is: How did blacks actually function in the abolitionist movement?

Garrison's attack on the American Colonization Society stemmed from his contacts with black leaders. Negroes were especially appreciative of the support given their cause by the new immediatist antislavery newspapers established in Boston and New York. Garrison's *Liberator*, founded in 1831, might have died without the financial help of Negroes, who constituted nearly 90 percent of the subscribers during its first year and held meetings in several cities urging support for the publication. James Forten purchased thirty-seven subscriptions before the *Liberator* was a month old. The paper's financial crises were recurrent, and three years later blacks, then constituting about 75 percent of the subscribers, helped save "our paper." In its pages Garrison published their articles, essays, letters, and reports of their meetings. They passed the paper from hand to hand and showed it to sympathetic whites. In Carlisle, Pennsylvania, a Negro barber shared his copies of the *Liberator* with J. Miller McKim, who later became a prominent abolitionist leader. Another newspaper that attracted substantial black support was the *Emancipator*, founded in 1833 by a committee of New York abolitionists. The Underground Railroad leader David Ruggles and other black agents enthusiastically built up the paper's circulation.

Although black churches and mutual-benefit societies as well as the National Negro Convention Movement had engaged in antislavery agitation over the years, it was the white leaders who seized the initiative in creating a national network of abolition societies. It was in a Boston Negro church that Garrison and a small group of white friends met to organize the New England

Anti-Slavery Society in 1832. Only after the plans had been formulated were Negroes invited to participate. When the society's constitution was approved, about one fourth of the seventy-two signers were blacks. Among the local auxiliaries was the Massachusetts General Colored Association, a fraternal and antislavery organization founded in 1826, which affiliated with the New England Anti-Slavery Society in 1833. Some blacks always attended annual conventions of the New England society, and ordinarily a few shared the platform with the white speakers.

Only three blacks were listed on the official roll of the Philadelphia conference that created the American Anti-Slavery Society in December 1833. The three men, James G. Barbadoes of Boston, and Robert Purvis and the dentist James McCrummell of Philadelphia, were also among the sixty-two signers of the society's Declaration of Sentiments—a document which Garrison drafted at McCrummell's home. Published accounts of the convention suggest that black participation in debates and motions was minimal. On one symbolic occasion Negroes had a prominent role. On a motion to praise antislavery editors, the convention resolved itself into a committee of the whole with McCrummell in the chair. Robert Purvis was among those lauding Garrison. Yet when Purvis made a forceful speech, "impassioned, full of invective, bristling with epithets," criticizing the cautious and equivocal passage on colonization that the conferees had substituted for Garrison's indictment, the convention failed to heed him. Six Negroes were appointed to the seventy-two-man Board of Managers, including the three named above. One of the others was the Episcopal minister Peter Williams of New York, who resigned before serving on it because of pressure from Bishop Onderdonk. Purvis was named to the nominating committee. Nevertheless, when it came to policy-making positions, blacks were conspicuous by their absence. There were no black officers, not even among the twenty-six vice-presidents, and none among the original nine-man Executive Committee.

In addition to its interest in abolition, the American Anti-

Slavery Society publicly opposed race prejudice and undertook
to advance the status of free Negroes in the North. The delegates asserted that since all men were "of one blood," blacks
and whites should share equally in "civil and religious privileges." To help Northern blacks achieve their potentialities, the
conference recommended a program of moral elevation similar to that adopted by the Negro Convention Movement. In
1834, the first annual report of the society declared that the way
to bear witness against race prejudice was to invite more of "our
colored brethren" into active affiliation with the organization.
Two New York Presbyterian ministers, Samuel E. Cornish and
Theodore S. Wright, received places on the twelve-man Executive Committee, and James Forten and William Watkins were
among the fifty-eight vice-presidents. Nine Negroes were named
to the Board of Managers, constituting about 10 percent of its
membership. Although Cornish and Wright remained on the
Executive Committee, after 1834 no blacks were named as vice-
president of the society for several years, and beginning in 1837
there was a sharp reduction of Negroes on the Board of Managers to half a dozen or less a year.* Throughout the decade,
only a handful of blacks attended the society's annual meetings.

The American and Foreign Anti-Slavery Society, with an executive committee twice as large as that of the American Anti-
Slavery Society, appointed a somewhat larger number of Negroes, usually four, but sometimes only two, to that body. They
included Cornish and Wright, Bishop Christopher Rush, Dr.
James McCune Smith, who had been educated at the University of Glasgow, the Congregationalist minister J. W. C. Pen-
nington, and Charles B. Ray, Presbyterian minister, noted
Underground Railroad leader, and sometime-editor of the New
York *Colored American*. During the 1850's Ray and Smith each
served as recording secretary, though the more powerful position of corresponding secretary always remained in the hands of
a white man. After the loss of Cornish and Wright, Negro

* The Board of Managers was an unwieldy and honorific group; for
example, it numbered 131 in 1839 and 63 in 1841.

participation at the top levels of the American Anti-Slavery Society declined. Robert Purvis was a perennial vice-president, however; Charles Lenox Remond served on the twelve-man Executive Committee for five or six years beginning in 1843; and between 1849 and 1852 Remond and Frederick Douglass were among the three dozen men who sat on the Board of Managers. From time to time, men like Purvis, Remond, Douglass, and William Wells Brown sat on convention committees and occasionally addressed or presided over a convention session. A similar pattern prevailed during the 1860's. No blacks appear to have had important positions in the American Anti-Slavery Society during the Civil War. Only three, including Robert Purvis, held any but honorary posts in the same organization during the period 1865–70.

Negroes occupied prominent positions in some of the state and local auxiliaries. Among the Garrisonians, Margaretta Forten was secretary of the Philadelphia Female Anti-Slavery Society and Purvis for years presided over the Pennsylvania Anti-Slavery Society. A handful of black men worked as paid agents and lecturers for the national societies. Negroes also participated as speakers at annual meetings, black delegates contributed to the discussions on the convention floor, and Purvis, Wright, and others presided over business sessions and public meetings. Yet the evidence indicates that their role in the affairs of the antislavery societies was mainly symbolic. This conclusion receives further support from the paucity of letters to and from blacks in the papers of white abolitionist leaders; only Gerrit Smith seems to have corresponded extensively with them. As Douglass said in 1855:

> Our oppressed people are wholy ignored, in one sense, in the generalship of the movement to effect our redemption. We are a poor, pitiful, dependent, and servile class of Negroes, *"unable to keep pace"* with the movement . . . not even capable of *"perceiving what are its demands, or understanding the philosophy of its operations!"* Of course . . . we cannot expect to receive from those who indulge in this *opinion practical recognition of our Equality*. This is what we . . . must receive to inspire us with

confidence in the self-appointed generals of the Anti-Slavery host, the Euclids who are *theoretically* working out the almost insoluble problems of our future destiny.

In view of the attitudes of some white abolitionists it might be deemed surprising that blacks received any positions at all in the affairs of the antislavery societies. In the early years, certain auxiliaries excluded black people entirely. Shortly after the Junior Anti-Slavery Society of Philadelphia was founded in 1836, a motion to accept members without regard to color was passed by only two votes. In the same year the New York women's antislavery society adamantly refused to admit Negroes. When the Fall River, Massachusetts, Female Anti-Slavery Society urged black women to affiliate, the organization was nearly torn apart. In 1837 the Convention of the Anti-Slavery Women of the United States took cognizance of the matter and declared, "Those Societies that reject colored members, or seek to avoid them, have never been active or efficient," but took no steps to expel such auxiliaries. Because of these attitudes, Negroes in places like Albany, Rochester, New York, Nantucket, and Lexington, Ohio, formed segregated local auxiliaries. In the published lists of auxiliaries, the American Anti-Slavery Society often designated these by the word "colored."

Although men like Weld, Garrison, and the Tappans discountenanced such exclusionist policies on the part of white auxiliaries, and the practice certainly was not typical, blacks were concerned that the white antislavery workers were not completely unprejudiced. Even the most prominent white abolitionists were criticized. For one thing, Negroes were disappointed that, in spite of the rhetoric of the 1833 Declaration of Sentiments and of the many addresses by white abolitionists, few of them actively participated in the fight against the discrimination faced by free people of color in the North. On the floor of annual conventions Negroes repeatedly tried to make the white abolitionists more conscious of this discrimination. For example, at the 1849 meeting of the American and Foreign Anti-Slavery Society, the famous abolitionist orator and Congregationalist clergyman, the Rev. Samuel Ringgold Ward, who was known as the "Black Daniel Webster," told of racial exclusion in a medical college and in churches. The following year Ray complained of discrimination in the churches and of how Negroes, "compelled by self-respect to rent or purchase churches for themselves," had encountered obstacles to making even this type of accommodation. Theodore Wright, speaking before the New York Anti-Slavery Society in 1837, expressed alarm over the "constitutions of abolition societies, where nothing was said about the improvement of the man of color! They have overlooked the giant sin of prejudice. They have passed by this foul monster, which is at once the parent and offspring of slavery."

The dissatisfaction ran deeper than this. Militant blacks made numerous references to the insincerity of "professed abolitionists." They reported that many white abolitionists refused to admit Negro children to their schools or to employ black men in their businesses other than in menial capacities. Wright, in his speech before the New York Anti-Slavery Society, denounced the sort of abolitionist who would invite a black clergyman to his home but serve him dinner in the kitchen and fail to introduce him to his family. "Our white friends are deceived," the New York *Colored American* declared in 1837, "when they imagine they are free from prejudice against color, and yet are content with a lower standard of attainments for colored youth, and inferior exhibitions of talent on the part of colored men." Eighteen years later Douglass charged that abolitionist businessmen "might employ a colored boy as a porter or packer, but would as soon put a hod-carrier to the clerk's desk as a colored boy, ever so well educated though he might be." At the 1853 convention of the American and Foreign Anti-Slavery Society white abolitionists were openly attacked for failing to employ blacks in the antislavery offices or in their places of business, and Arthur Tappan himself was criticized for using Negroes only as menials in his department store.

The blacks were right about the prejudice within the white antislavery groups. It should be emphasized that the abolitionists were a distinct improvement over their colonizationist predecessors and far in advance of the public opinion of their age. Yet at the same time they were, in fact, ambivalent in their relationships with blacks. One must therefore distinguish carefully between their egalitarian rhetoric and their paternalistic and prejudiced actions. They spoke feelingly of the "sins of caste," but they were highly sensitive to charges that they advocated social equality and intermingling. They spoke of the importance of opposing discrimination against free Negroes, but even where they fought for civil rights they often did so under prodding from their black colleagues. Much of the activity on behalf of free blacks consisted of exhorting the blacks to assume the responsibility for their own elevation by acquiring wealth and education and exhibiting good moral character. Due to black pressure, in 1838 the Executive Committee of the American Anti-Slavery Society praised Negroes for seeking advancement beyond unskilled jobs and urged abolitionists to offer employment to black people—but employers affiliated with the society were unmoved by this appeal.

The Anti-Slavery Society itself had at first bypassed Negroes when hiring lecturers. The so-called "Seventy," recruited by Weld for antislavery speaking, were all whites. Not until 1839 did Weld suggest the names of several blacks as lecturers, saying, "They would do more in three months to kill prejudice . . . than all our operations up to now." At the outset of his antislavery career Weld had helped establish schools for Cincinnati's blacks and frequently visited their homes and churches. He believed that "persons are to be treated according to their intrinsic worth irrespective of *color*" but felt that this principle sometimes required "modifications"; a sincere abolitionist must ask himself if mingling with Negroes in public would be "a *blessing* or a *curse*" to them. He regarded public association with blacks as "an ostentatious display of superiority to prejudice," which could hurt the antislavery movement as well as create mob violence against blacks. Weld even justified his own exclusion of a black delegate from an antislavery convention in Ohio on the ground that if the man sat in the convention, mobs would make renewed attacks on Ohio Negroes.

The Tappan brothers displayed a comparable attitude. As in Weld's case, it is difficult to ascertain to what degree their ambivalence and paternalism were blended with tactical considerations. Lewis Tappan, for example, was disturbed at the failure of the arrangements committee to invite Theodore Wright to speak at the 1835 convention. The committee did allow Wright's church choir to participate, but some members of the society complained about "race amalgamation" because a white chorus sang from the same platform. They charged that the "choir mingling" had later helped to incite mob rioting. Tappan believed that this accusation was merely a mask to cover race prejudice. All the same, he himself did not want to be regarded as advocating socializing with blacks; to Weld he confided that aside from the "choir mingling" incident, the only time he had ever attempted to "mix up the two colors" involved occasional dinners with a few Negro gentlemen in the course of business conferences. Like his brother, Arthur Tappan also condemned "caste usages," but yielded to social pressures. On one occasion he was severely criticized for inviting Samuel Cornish to share his pew at church. Tappan called that action the only effort at "amalgamation that I remember," and he vowed not to associate publicly with black people until white citizens became more enlightened. The influential abolitionist James G. Birney, candidate for President on the Liberty Party ticket in 1840 and 1844, argued that granting "social privileges" to blacks should be postponed until they had attained "civil privileges." In his judgment the failure to establish clearly such a system of priorities jeopardized the entire antislavery movement, since the enemies of the blacks used the social equality issue to defeat the cause of abolition.

The complexity of the attitudes of abolitionist leaders toward blacks was most evident in the case of William Lloyd Garrison. Actually Garrison could not work with anyone except on his own terms, but he portrayed himself as unselfishly seeking to encourage blacks to become independent, self-assertive citizens.

As the founder and editor of the earliest and the most celbrated of the abolitionist newspapers, financed at least in the
beginning almost entirely by Negro subscriptions, Garrison's
chief personality difficulties with Negroes quite naturally involved black editors. Although in the early 1830's he had urged
the development of a black press to vindicate the rights of the
race, when blacks decided to become editors, Garrison discouraged them. In 1837 when Samuel Cornish sought support for
his proposed *Colored American*, one of the earliest black newspapers, Garrisonians opposed the venture. After Cornish went
ahead, Garrison sometimes criticized the *Colored American*'s
policies and at other times acted as if the paper did not exist.
The editors of the *Colored American* were not intimidated. In
a pointed blast at Garrison, the paper criticized those white
abolitionists who "outwardly treat us as men, while in their
hearts they still hold us as slaves." Years later, when Cornish
died, the *Liberator* carried no obituary.

More celebrated is the experience of Frederick Douglass.
Garrison discovered Douglass's oratorical abilities at an antislavery meeting at Nantucket in 1841, when the fugitive slave
rose from the audience to tell about the world from which he
had escaped and what freedom meant to him. On the platform
Garrison was so moved that he asked the crowd, "Shall such a
man ever be sent back to slavery from the soil of old Massachusetts?" The spectators arose shouting, "No, No!" Afterward the
Massachusetts Anti-Slavery Society engaged Douglass to lecture
on his experiences as a slave. During the passing months he was
intellectually "growing and needed room," and wanted to share
with audiences the ideas of his "reading and thinking," rather
than simply mechanically perform his stage role as a slave. Officials of the antislavery society, however, discouraged his striving
toward manhood and independence. Instead of applauding his
intellectual progress as an illustration of Negro potentiality,
they preferred to exhibit him publicly in his frozen status of
fugitive slave. Garrison told him, "Tell your story, Frederick."
Others admonished, "We will take care of the philosophy. . . .
Let us have the facts." As Douglass continued to acquire self-

confidence and literary skill, members of the society complained that he seemed "too learned": "People won't believe you ever were a slave, Frederick, if you keep on this way. . . . Better have a *little* of the plantation manner of speech than not."

Douglass went his own way. Within the next four years, he published his autobiography and lectured in England. He returned to the United States, grateful for the help of abolitionists but ambitious for greater independence and the opportunity to edit his own newspaper. Over the objections of Garrison and his friends, Douglass moved to Rochester and founded the *North Star*. At the time he was still a Garrisonian in his ideology, but after coming in contact with the political abolitionists of western New York, he was gradually converted to their way of thinking. In 1851 he frankly told a meeting of the American Anti-Slavery Society of his new views, whereupon Garrison declared, "There is roguery somewhere." Later Garrison denounced Douglass as "destitute of every principle of honor, ungrateful to the last degree and malevolent in spirit."

Probably nothing could better illustrate the essentially peripheral role in which whites sought to cast blacks than the two anniversary celebrations of the American Anti-Slavery Society in 1853 and 1863. While the published proceedings of the twentieth anniversary reported in infinite detail the speeches of many white delegates, the comments of the blacks received perfunctory attention. In two instances the original remarks themselves were evidently short, but in the only other case so distinguished a person as the noted antislavery and feminist orator Sojourner Truth rated only one sentence: "Previous to the calling to order, Sojourner Truth (formerly a slave in the State of New York) sang a plaintive song, touching the wrongs of the slave, and afterwards spoke of the wrong Slavery had done to herself and others." Ten years later the American Anti-Slavery Society held its thirtieth-anniversary meeting. By then the Emancipation Proclamation had been issued, Negroes were accepted in the Union Army, and the abolitionists felt a pardonable pride in their accomplishments. Delegates like Garrison, McKim, and Lucretia Mott, who had attended the founding convention, reminisced about the early days. Several of the surviving signers of the historic Declaration of Sentiments were present, among them Robert Purvis and James McCrummell. Yet neither was invited to speak, and in fact the only black man addressing the convention was Frederick Douglass, who pointedly told the abolitionists that their task was unfinished until Negroes were accepted in American society. If, as one participant said, an abolitionist aim was to "vindicate the ability" of blacks, the fact that neither Purvis nor McCrummell was asked to speak does seem strange. Purvis especially had made significant contributions to the cause during the three decades.

Judging from these important anniversary celebrations, blacks, in the abolitionist cast of characters, were regarded as bit players or even as extras shunted off in the background, where they would not detract from the stellar performance of the whites spotlighted downstage center. The evidence suggests that this limited participation was due to the ambivalence of white abolitionists in their relationships with Negroes. The whites appeared not to have encouraged blacks to seek other than a few symbolic roles in the antislavery societies. While Negroes received token representation in the offices of both the American and the American and Foreign Anti-Slavery Societies, there is no indication that they were influential in shaping the strategy and tactics of the organizations. Despite their reiterated declaration that improvement of the black man's status in the North was "a most effectual means of promoting the abolition of slavery," the white abolitionists concentrated on the single issue of converting other whites to antislavery. Since Negroes recognized the reservations among the white leadership, they organized much of their protest activities outside of the antislavery societies. It was no wonder that in the late 1850's J. Mercer Langston felt it advisable to form a separate, black antislavery society in Ohio. And it was also no wonder that the only Negro to achieve a position of real influence in antislavery councils was Frederick Douglass, a man so Olympian in stature that he compelled recognition. To be of influence even he had to establish himself as essentially an independent force outside either of the two major antislavery organizations.

Yet Negroes did play a vital role in antislavery activities. To them must be given the chief credit for running the Underground Railroad. And from among the fugitives the antislavery societies found some of their most effective lecturers and propagandists.

11

Contrary to popular impression, and Southern fears, the Underground Railroad was not a well-organized institution and white abolitionists did not play a commanding role in it. The work of the white abolitionists of course should not be minimized—some, like Levi Coffin of Newport, Indiana, and later Cincinnati, were of great assistance to the runaways—but the most arduous and dangerous part of the fugitive's journey was in the South, where there was seldom anyone to help him. And once the fugitive did reach the North, it was usually the free Negroes who took the initiative in aiding him. Individual blacks opened their homes to runaways. Even more important was the work of the organized vigilance committees in several Northern cities, which elicited support from sympathetic whites but were founded and essentially run by black men.

Slaveholders charged that whites on the Underground Railroad were invading the South to lure away their bondsmen. Their view was distorted. John Fairfield's activities in bringing slaves out of Alabama and Kentucky and John Brown's abduction of slaves from Missouri were exceptional exploits that sprang from the urges of daring personalities. More often than not, such "conductors" were blacks who had escaped from the South and returned to take others North. Harriet Tubman, called the Moses of the race because of the large number of trips she made to bring "passengers" to the promised land, was the most celebrated of them. Her journeys from the South usually began on Saturday night, giving the fugitives more than a day before their owners discovered their departure and sounded the alarm for their return. She is reported to have thus helped three hundred slaves to their freedom. Less famous was Josiah Henson. Henson escaped from Kentucky "after a youth full of good deeds to his master." Making his way to Canada, he later returned South to help the family of another fugitive to escape, and thereafter made other trips, carrying away scores of bondsmen.

Only a small percentage of the slaves who attempted to escape actually were able to reach the North. Armed with courage and ingenuity, guided by the North Star, some began their tortuous journey by stealing supplies from their masters, "borrowing" canoes or skiffs along the way, and finding lodging with other slaves or free Negroes. William Wells Brown, later an agent for the American Anti-Slavery Society and the first American black novelist (Clotel; or the President's Daughter, 1853), escaped in 1834. He later recalled that his constant fear of recapture forced him to travel only at night and to choose between stealing food or going hungry. Although determined "not to trust myself in the hands of any man, white or colored," he did receive assistance from Ohio abolitionists and an Indiana Quaker. Finding employment as a steamboat workman in Cleveland, he aided other fugitives en route to Canada and, upon moving to Buffalo, opened his home to runaway slaves. On occasion Brown helped rescue runaways in danger of being recaptured by slave traders. Brown thus had received only minimal help from white abolitionists, extended after the major risks were taken. Frederick Douglass, like Brown, later became a leading agent in the Underground Railroad, an active participant in the Rochester depot. Unlike Brown, in the course of his own escape from Baltimore in 1838, Douglass received no help at all from whites. Using a method frequently employed by slaves escaping from Southern seaports, he borrowed a free seaman's "protection" papers. When he was unable to find a job in New York City, he finally revealed his plight to a sailor who notified David Ruggles, a black printer-bookseller and secretary of the New York Vigilance Committee. Ruggles supplied temporary lodging, later sending Douglass to New Bedford, where he stayed with a black family and started a new life "as a free man."

The vigilance committees arose in the middle 1830's. The New York Vigilance Committee—under the direction first of Ruggles and later of Charles Ray, who was also secretary of the New York State Vigilance Committee—collected pennies and nickels, mainly from Negroes, to feed, clothe, and shelter fugitives arriving from the South. Some were helped to settle in New York, while others like Frederick Douglass were sent to other cities. Even runaways who had lived in the North for years were always in danger of arrest. Because the fugitive slave laws were designed to help masters, it was even possible for free blacks to be kidnapped and taken South. The vigilance committees attempted to prevent these kidnappings and made numerous propaganda appeals to protest them. In New York, Ruggles was always on guard against slave agents and even compiled a "Slaveholders Directory" listing the names and addresses of lawyers, law enforcement officers, and others who "lend themselves to kidnapping."

In other communities, such as Boston or Philadelphia, although whites collaborated with blacks on the vigilance committees, most of the work was actually performed by Negroes. In Philadelphia Robert Purvis was president of the vigilance committee, while William Still, the corresponding secretary, was the one who coordinated the rescue work. In Syracuse, New York, the committee depended on the AME Zion minister J. W. Loguen to shelter many runaways. In Rochester Frederick Douglass and many other black men in the community assisted fugitives. Douglass, "superintendent" of the Underground Railroad station there, used his home as its headquarters and equipped his office with a trapdoor and a secret stairway for hiding fugitives. He spent many hours raising money to transport them to safety in Canada.

That the work of aiding the fugitives was largely done by blacks rather than whites was attested to by abolitionists of both races. James Birney, writing in 1837, described how slave escapes were facilitated by other Negroes: "Six weeks ago, a young married woman escaped from N. Orleans by steamboat and was successfully concealed here [Cincinnati] by her colored friends. Yesterday, her husband arrived, and at 5 o'clock in the afternoon they were both in the Stage on their way from this place to Canada. Such matters are almost uniformly managed by the colored people. I know nothing of them generally till they are passed." In the 1830's Theodore Wright complained that members of antislavery societies had not taken sufficient interest in helping fugitive slaves or protecting blacks from kidnappers. Wright, among the founders of the New York Vigilance Committee, appealed to whites to make the work of the committee a basic objective of the American Anti-Slavery Society. While limited aid was ultimately given by such leaders as the Tappans, Weld, and Gerrit Smith, fugitive rescue work did not receive the kind of support that Wright and his colleagues sought. The New York Vigilance Committee had emphasized that the institution of slavery could not be destroyed unless large-scale efforts were undertaken to alleviate the plight of its victims in the North, but the antislavery societies did not allow fugitive aid to detract from the basic goal of abolition.

After the passage of the Fugitive Slave Law of 1850, however, more whites became sufficiently aroused to help the vigilance committees or, at least, to give tacit support. In 1851 two publicized cases demonstrated how Negroes aided brethren whose liberty was threatened and how white juries were sympathetic toward such activities. In Christiana, a southern Pennsylvania town not far from the Maryland line, a slaveholder searching for runaways died in a gun battle waged against a group of free blacks who had armed to protect the home of one of their fellows. Thirty-eight were charged with treason and confined in jail to await a court trial. A jury deliberated only a few minutes before finding the first "traitor" not guilty, and the government's case collapsed completely. In Boston a black crowd entered the courthouse where a fugitive from Virginia named Shadrach was held in the custody of a United States marshal during proceedings preparatory to a return to slavery. On signal the Negroes seized Shadrach, spiriting him away to Canada. Several alleged conspirators were prosecuted, but a divided jury failed to find them guilty and the case was dismissed.

An important contribution of black people who had escaped was their work as abolitionist propagandists. It is true that during the first years of the American Anti-Slavery Society the leadership failed to make much use of black lecturers. In the 1830's the first blacks to speak before local antislavery groups were Theodore Wright, James Forten, Robert Purvis, and Charles Lenox Remond, but all of these men were free Negroes who had never been slaves. Although they eloquently discussed the peculiar institution, their presentations lacked dramatic impact. Former slaves, many of whom were fugitives, were eventually asked to lecture. By the 1840's Frederick Douglass, William Wells Brown, Samuel R. Ward, Henry Bibb, Lunsford Lane, Harriet Tubman, Sojourner Truth, and many others spoke to antislavery audiences all over the North. Their activities probably constituted the Negroes' most important contribution to the abolitionist movement. In their speeches, and also in autobiographical narratives, Negroes provided the most compelling propaganda against the institution of slavery, the fugitives serving as a constant reminder of the millions of slaves who had not been able to run away. Audiences flocked to hear these speakers describe the whippings administered by overseers, the separation from loved ones sold down the river, and the often hectic efforts to get beyond the reach of slave catchers and bloodhounds. In the most personal terms, they told exactly what slavery meant to them, and, speaking of what they had seen and experienced, they were deeply convincing.

Henry Bibb moved audiences to tears with a recital of how his wife, naked and bound, had been brutally whipped by an intoxicated slaveholder. Bibb's listeners would burst into cheers, laughter, and applause a few moments later as he described ways in which slaves outwitted their masters. Another crowd pleaser was Henry "Box" Brown, who recounted his escape from Richmond in a shipping box, which he later used as a prop on antislavery tours. Though white audiences felt entertained, they usually also came away impressed by the resourcefulness and indomitable will to freedom that these lecturers demonstrated. The sense of momentary aloneness and apprehension many runaways felt when they "crossed the line" to freedom was vividly portrayed by Harriet Tubman: "I was free, but there was no one to welcome me to the land of freedom. I was a stranger in a strange land. . . ." Recounting the tale of her escapes, she affected listeners with a profound faith in God and in herself.

For the many thousands of whites at these antislavery meetings who identified themselves with the sufferings of these speakers, there was often an opportunity to purchase their personal narratives, which were widely circulated. For example, the autobiography of Frederick Douglass received extensive distribution and the narratives of William Wells Brown and Josiah Henson sold thousands of copies. This body of literature became an important propaganda force in the struggle to win converts to the antislavery position and was supplemented by biographical and autobiographical sketches of thousands of slaves published by abolitionists. The printing presses kept turning as more fugitives arrived in the North and more whites joined the antislavery ranks.

Abolitionist writers heavily edited the bulk of these sketches, but there is no doubt that Douglass, Brown, Bibb, and others did their own writing. From the printed pages emerged black heroes whose aspirations for freedom and self-fulfillment represented a variation of the American dream, and in this sense a lesson in racial equality that aroused the interest and respect of many white Northerners. A contemporary reviewer of Douglass's *My Bondage and My Freedom* commented: "The mere fact that the member of an outcast and enslaved race should accomplish his freedom, and educate himself up to an equality of intellectual and moral vigor with the leaders of the race by which he was held in bondage, is, in itself, so remarkable that the story of the change cannot be otherwise than exciting."

12

The achievements of men like Douglass intensified black resentment of the patronizing attitude of the white abolitionists who determined organization policies and made little effort to treat Negroes as equal co-workers. Negroes were also dismayed by the deteriorating economic situation and the futility of most of their protests for equal rights. Later, they grew alarmed over the threat to their very safety raised by the stringent Fugitive Slave Law of 1850. Many concluded therefore that Negroes must band together and help themselves. Critics might blast "a caste convention to abolish caste," but advocates of a separate convention held that blacks should be less subservient to white friends and should act independently to avoid the impression that they merely echoed the words of white abolitionists. As Douglass was to say in 1855, "It is well known that we have called down upon our devoted head, the Holy (?) horror of a certain class of Abolitionists, because we have dared to maintain our Individualism." Welcoming the growing recognition of the fact that "OUR ELEVATION AS A RACE IS ALMOST WHOLLY DEPENDENT UPON OUR OWN EXERTION," Douglass maintained that while allies were useful, history had demonstrated that no oppressed group had achieved its deliverance without taking "a prominent part in the conflict," rather than being used merely to do "all the incidental drudgery of the warfare."

The new spirit was manifested in several ways. One was the revival of the Convention Movement in 1843. A second was a serious discussion of the advocacy of violence and slave rebellions. Another was an experiment with an independent black political party. There were also proposals for economic cooperation along racial lines. Finally there was a dramatic upsurge of interest in colonization.

The National Convention Movement was revived with a conference at Buffalo in 1843, and thereafter it continued an active life through the rest of the antebellum period. Those pressing for separate meetings denied any desire to eliminate joint activity with whites in the antislavery societies or in a political organization such as the Liberty Party. The 1848 National Negro Convention urged members of the race to "act with the white Abolition societies wherever you can, and where you cannot, get up societies among yourselves. . . . We shall undoubtedly for many years be compelled to have institutions of a complexional character, in order to attain this very idea of human brotherhood. We would however, advise our brethren to occupy memberships and stations among white persons, and in white institutions, just so far as our rights are secured to us."

The 1843 convention was famous for the heated controversy aroused by the Rev. Henry Highland Garnet's speech entitled "An Address to the Slaves of the United States of America." Garnet, a Presbyterian minister with a white congregation at Troy, New York, urged the bondsmen to kill any master refusing to liberate them. Douglass, Remond, and others argued that approval of Garnet's address would create further hardship for free blacks in the slave and Border States. A resolution endorsing the speech failed by only one vote as the convention declared that "a righteous government" would destroy slavery.

At the next national convention, four years later, Garnet's address was discussed again and aroused far less disapproval. Indeed, during the late 1840's, the use of violence to destroy slavery was being widely discussed by Northern black men. After the address was printed in a special volume with *Walker's Appeal* in 1848, a group of Ohio Negroes made plans to order five hundred copies. Some black delegates at a Maine convention suggested that the race was morally obliged to provide aid in a slave rebellion, and at a Negro meeting in Boston there was considerable sentiment favoring a fugitive's right to kill in order to save himself from capture. In 1849, when Douglass reminded a white Boston audience of their grandparents' militance in the American Revolution, he declared, "I should welcome the intelligence tomorrow, should it come, that the slaves had risen in the South." The following year, shortly after Congress passed the Fugitive Slave Law, Douglass suggested that "the only way to make the Fugitive Slave Law a dead letter is to make half a dozen or more dead kidnappers. . . . The man who takes the office of a bloodhound ought to be treated as a bloodhound." Blacks in several state conventions attacked the law and counseled militant resistance. Men like Henry H. Garnet carried a pistol, and Samuel R. Ward asserted that although the law might try to enslave every black in New York there was still "one Sam Ward—who will never be taken alive."

Negroes were divided as to the proper course to take in regard to political action. The 1843 convention voted overwhelmingly to endorse the Liberty Party, though it was done only over the strenuous opposition of Frederick Douglass and Charles Lenox Remond, who, as loyal Garrisonians, warned that all political parties were inherently corrupt and that only moral suasion could free the slaves from bondage. State conventions in the late 1840's and 1850's agitated more on political rights than on any other issue. In actual fact Negroes found political action particularly frustrating just because they were barred from voting in so many states. For those who were entitled to vote, the question of which political party to support was fraught with difficulties. By backing a minor abolitionist party they would be throwing their votes away, but by voting for one of the major parties they would be compromising their principles in supporting an organization that took only a mild antislavery stand. Some backed the Liberty Party in the 1840's and its offshoot, the Radical Abolitionist Party of the 1850's, but others regarded it as a tactical error to support such a weak third party. Many supported the Whigs during the 1840's, as the better of the two major parties. Others, including most of the delegates to the National Negro Convention of 1848, endorsed the Free Soil Party, despite their well-justified skepticism about the attitudes of its leaders on the question of Negro suffrage. Similarly, the Republicans, by calling merely for the exclusion of slavery from the territories and remaining silent on the matter of voting rights, placed blacks in a dilemma. Only reluctantly did most of them support the Republicans as the best practical choice. In desperation some New York State leaders turned toward independent political organizations. At a convention in

1855 they established a New York State Suffrage Association, with Frederick Douglass originally endorsing it and acting as chairman. Intended as a black political party for the state, the association hoped to serve as a balance of power in close elections. It did not run candidates of its own, but threw its weight behind the Republicans in 1856, 1858, and 1860. Nevertheless, its existence symbolized the blacks' estrangement from the mainstream of American politics.

Delegates to the black conventions of the 1840's and 1850's agreed that the race should seek respectability and wealth through mechanical trades and agricultural pursuits and through the cultivation of thrift, industry, and good moral character. Discouragement with the political scene, as well as fears aroused by the inroads of immigrants into the unskilled and menial jobs traditionally performed by Negroes, led the noted Rochester Convention of 1853 to place strong emphasis on racial solidarity and economic advancement. The delegates repeatedly asserted that as American citizens they were entitled to equality before the law, in schools, and in churches. But they also took a more nationalistic position than any of the earlier conventions by emphasizing the necessity of tightening the bonds of racial unity. The conclave created a national council to supervise a highly organized system of racial uplift. Blacks were told that survival depended on using each other's economic services whenever possible and plans were made to establish a national register of black businessmen, mechanics, and laborers. At the urging of Frederick Douglass, the convention also went on record as approving the creation of a manual-labor school. To encourage race pride, a national Negro museum and library was also envisioned. While this comprehensive program was never carried out, the 1853 convention was significant because it clearly showed increasing support for an ideology of self-help and racial solidarity in the face of the ever more critical situation in which Northern free Negroes found themselves during the decade before the Civil War.

Another manifestation of this disillusionment and frustration and consequent stress upon racial unity, or what can be called black nationalism, was the rising crescendo of support for emigration to Africa and tropical America. There was a growing interest in the subject beginning with the late 1840's. In 1854, 1856, and 1858, black colonizationists held their own national conventions. They differed among themselves as to what would be the best site. Some opted for the Caribbean area, especially for Haiti, whose ruler encouraged their aspirations. Several preferred Lower California and the Far West of the United States. But the most popular place was Africa. A few leaders even made their peace with the American Colonization Society. All agreed on the hopelessness of continued agitation for equal rights in the United States. They agreed also in articulating a nationalist ideology which insisted that Negroes had made a contribution to world civilization in the past, and that by destroying the slave trade and redeeming and Christianizing Africa, they would make one in the future. Episcopal clergyman Alexander Crummell, who had received a degree from Cambridge University before going to Africa on behalf of the American Colonization Society, summed it up best when he described Liberia as "this spot dedicated to nationality, consecrated to freedom, and sacred to religion."

The leading emigrationist during the 1850's was the Harvard-educated physician Martin Robison Delany. Delany's mind oscillated between Africa and Central America as the most appropriate place for colonization, but he consistently denounced the American Colonization Society, which he regarded as "anti-Christian in its character, and misanthropic in its pretended sympathies," its leaders "arrant hypocrites seeking every opportunity to deceive" the free Negroes. Better than anyone else during the antebellum period Delany exemplified the dual ethnic loyalties of the American Negro. On the one hand he believed, "We are Americans, having a birthright citizenship—natural claims upon this country—claims common to all others of our fellow-citizens." Yet Delany was pessimistic about the black man ever achieving the full rights he deserved as a citizen. The only real solution lay in emigrating and establishing "a national position for ourselves." In 1859 he led an exploring party up the Niger River, where he signed a treaty with the Yoruba, granting him a tract for settlement by American Negroes. As he had written to Garrison several years before, "Heathenism and Liberty before Christianity and Slavery!"

During the 1850's probably most of the black leaders at least toyed with the idea of colonization. Some, like the Ohio lawyer J. Mercer Langston, who was later a congressman from Virginia (1890–1), espoused colonization only briefly. Others, like Henry Highland Garnet, Martin R. Delany, Alexander Crummell, and Samuel Ringgold Ward, substituted a long-term advocacy of emigration for their earlier intense absorption in the campaign for equal rights. in 1858 a group of prominent New York blacks founded the African Civilization Society for missionary and colonization work. Even Frederick Douglass, discouraged by the Republican Party's moderate stand on slavery in the election of 1860 and disillusioned by Lincoln's temporizing with the white South after he entered office, became more open-minded toward colonization. He had no intention of emigrating himself, but on the eve of the Civil War he was preparing to visit Haiti in order to investigate its possibilities for settlement by those American blacks who wished to leave the United States. The Confederate attack on Fort Sumter in April 1861 dramatically altered the situation.

The outbreak of the Civil War and the momentous events of the succeeding years dissipated colonizationist sentiment. The war and emancipation were to renew the Negroes' faith in the vision of a racially egalitarian and integrated American society. But once again the American conscience, only temporarily aroused by a wartime crisis, would fail to destroy what black and white abolitionists alike described as the "sins of caste."

IV

A Dream Betrayed: Negroes During the Civil War and Reconstruction

FOR AFRO-AMERICANS the Civil War was, from its beginning, inextricably bound up with their future and their freedom. They saw it first of all as a war for the emancipation of the slaves. Beyond this, they believed that the recognition of their rights as men and citizens was at stake.

Neither the Administration at Washington nor white public opinion in 1861 generally regarded the war in this light. To them it was emphatically a war to preserve the Union, not to end slavery, much less to obtain for Negroes the rights of citizens. Yet as the hostilities dragged on, the Union was ineluctably drawn toward incorporating emancipation and the recognition of the black as man and citizen into the goals of the war and the postwar settlement.

153

1

At the outset of the war blacks and white abolitionists raised two crucial issues: the emancipation of the slaves and the right of Negroes to bear arms in defense of the Union. The free black men hoped that by fighting for the Union they would contribute to the liberation of the slaves. Indeed, in the evolution of Union policy, these two issues were closely intertwined.

When Lincoln issued his call for volunteers, blacks promptly offered their services as soldiers. A mass meeting of Boston blacks declared, "Our feelings urge us to say to our countrymen that we are ready to stand by and defend the Government . . . with 'our lives, our fortunes, and our sacred honor. . . .'" But all offers were rejected.

It was the slaves themselves who brought about the first shift in Union policy. In May 1861 three runaways appeared at Fortress Monroe in Virginia. General Benjamin Butler, upon learning that they had been helping build Confederate fortifications across the Chesapeake Bay, declared them contraband of war. News of this action spread quickly; by the end of July nine hundred Negroes had arrived at the fortress. Butler interpreted the word "contraband" loosely. In fact, no one who came was turned back. The first "contrabands" were put to work unloading vessels and storing provisions, but by July Butler decided to employ them on the erection of fortifications. Using contrabands became very popular. For Northerners, not prepared to grant slaves freedom or allow them to fight against slavery, the use of contrabands was a convenient formula for depriving the South of its labor and employing that labor itself, without any commitment to emancipation. In August, Congress passed the first Confiscation Act, providing that slaves used on Confederate fortifications were forfeited. In September, Gideon Welles, Secretary of the Navy, authorized naval officers to use fugitive slaves even in fighting, though they were to have a rating no higher than "boys" at a pay of $10 a month. But the national Administration was evasive and noncommittal on employing fugitives, and therefore the practice of field commanders varied widely. Many refused to receive the contrabands and even allowed slaveowners to reclaim those who had entered Union lines.

If the North hesitated, the South had no qualms about employing black labor. From the start Negroes were used in building fortifications. Slaves were also vital to the Southern war effort both as food producers and industrial workers, particularly in the coal and iron mines. In early 1862 the Tredegar Iron Works in Virginia advertised for a thousand slaves. In 1865 three fourths of the four hundred workmen at the naval works in Selma, Alabama, were blacks.

Some free blacks volunteered to fight in the Confederate Army. Among them were the New Orleans Native Guards, composed of proud Creole Negroes whose predecessors had served in a free black regiment during the War of 1812, winning the unstinting praise of Andrew Jackson for their role in the Battle of New Orleans.* There has been considerable speculation as to why free blacks offered their services to the Confederacy. Fear or the desire to curry favor undoubtedly played a part, and a number of free Negroes in the Charleston and New Orleans areas were substantial slaveowners themselves. In any event, the volunteers hoped to obtain better treatment by demonstrating their patriotism. Such offers were turned down, however, as they had been in the North. It was only in the final agonizing months of the war that the Confederate government in desperation finally decided to enlist black soldiers and emancipate slaves willing to fight.

Everywhere, as the Federals approached, slaves ran away from the plantations. Except in the most isolated areas, they were well posted on the progress of the war and regarded the arrival of federal troops as the harbinger of their freedom. Many a trusted servant, even some who had managed the plantations during the war, departed at the first opportunity—to the surprise of their former masters. By the end of 1861 both the

---

* During the War of 1812 black sailors had also played a major role in the Battle of Lake Erie.

Union Army and Navy were employing contraband laborers, cooks, and servants on a fairly large scale. In addition to the labor they performed, runaways were also useful to the Union forces as sources of information regarding Confederate movements, positions, and occasionally even plans. Others served as scouts and sometimes as spies. A few escaped slaves were valuable as pilots on expeditions up the narrow, treacherous, meandering channels of the coastal rivers. The most famous of these was Robert Smalls, who, one night in May 1862, as the pilot of *The Planter,* a former cotton boat converted into a Confederate armed vessel, steered her with a party of sixteen past the fortifications in Charleston Harbor to the Union naval force outside.

Despite the contributions of the fugitives, their legal status was a problem for Lincoln's Administration. To have freed them would alienate the Border States and pro-Union slaveholders in the South. It would also arouse the opposition of Northern workingmen who feared an influx of Negroes into Northern cities, where they would be serious competitors. But the abolitionists, both black and white, agitated for emancipating the slaves. In August 1861, the antislavery general John C. Frémont, facing rebel guerrillas in Missouri, declared martial law, confiscated all the property of rebels, and freed their slaves. Lincoln promptly rescinded the order.

With the President unwilling to do anything to encourage emancipation, the abolitionists shifted their goal toward securing the employment of Negroes as soldiers. Because of the suggestion of racial equality that this idea carried, it was strongly opposed. Therefore the Administration moved haltingly, and then only under considerable pressure.

Toward the end of 1861, Union forces occupied several of the South Carolina Sea Islands. The planters hurriedly departed before the arrival of the troops, and the slaves were assigned to cultivate cotton under the supervision of the United States Treasury Department. In May 1862, General David Hunter declared these slaves free and impressed the men into the Army. Hunter created a furor with his First South Carolina "Volun-

teers," both because the Administration regarded the general as
exceeding his authority and because the treasury agents and
missionaries in the Sea Islands complained that without warning the Negroes had been seized in the fields while they were
working and forced into army duty. Lincoln angrily counter-
manded Hunter's emancipation order, believing that it jeopardized his own plan of compensated emancipation in the Border
States. The general disbanded his South Carolina Volunteers
on August 10, but already one company of the unit had seen
action on the Georgia coast.

By the summer of 1862, with the war going badly, Northern
opinion veered toward accepting the idea of arming the slaves,
an idea that blacks and white abolitionists had been urging
since the beginning of the war. In March, Congress had passed
an act forbidding officers to assist in capturing runaways and
returning them to their masters. On July 17, Congress passed
the second Confiscation Act, which emancipated all slaves who
had escaped from rebel masters and gave the President dis-
cretionary power to use black troops.

Two weeks later General James H. Lane began to recruit
black companies openly in Kansas. In Louisiana, where Butler
had captured New Orleans in May 1862, caring for the large
number of contrabands proved a heavy responsibility. Since
many of the planters had taken an oath of allegiance to the
Union, Butler directed that the fugitives return to the plantations. But on August 22 he called for the recruitment of black
troops. Sensitive to the views of those who were reluctant to
arm the slaves, Butler technically simply activated the free
Louisiana Native Guards, but slave enlistments were accepted
from the beginning. Neither Lane nor Butler was acting on
authorization from Washington, and as late as August 6, Lincoln stated publicly that he did not favor the use of black
troops. Yet less than three weeks later, on August 25, Secretary
of War Stanton personally directed General Rufus Saxton to
recruit a black regiment in the Sea Islands. Undoubtedly, Lincoln had approved of this step. The First South Carolina Volunteers was reconstituted and placed under the command of

the Massachusetts abolitionist Colonel Thomas Wentworth Higginson, whose book *Army Life in a Black Regiment* later became a minor classic.

By the time Stanton authorized the First South Carolina Volunteers, Lincoln had already decided to issue the Emancipation Proclamation. On July 21 he announced that fact to his Cabinet. While it cannot be said with certainty what Lincoln's precise views were during the summer, it is quite likely that in his mind the decision to arm the slaves was closely linked with emancipation. Yet, though sentiment and pressure for freeing and arming the slaves was rising, Lincoln did not show his hand. When in a New York *Tribune* editorial in August, Horace Greeley denounced Lincoln for subserviency to the slavery interests and urged emancipating the slaves and enlisting them in the armed forces, Lincoln replied that his duty was to save the Union and that whether he freed all the slaves, or none of them, or some and not others, depended on what seemed best calculated to achieve that goal. It was the last of the alternatives mentioned in this politically shrewd document that Lincoln was going to use. The preliminary proclamation of September 1862 stated that as of January 1, 1863, slaves in areas held by rebels would be free.

Originally, Lincoln's plan for emancipation was twofold: compensation for the slaveowners and colonization for the black people. Only in this way did he feel that Union men, especially in the Border States, would accept freeing the slaves. In March 1862, he sent Congress a message urging gradual emancipation and proposing that the federal government assist states initiating such a plan. Congress concurred and passed a supporting resolution. In April 1862, Congress also abolished slavery in the District of Columbia with compensation up to $300 per slave. Lincoln advised the Border States to follow, but they ignored his warning that, if the war continued, slavery would be abolished in any case and without compensation.

Lincoln's attitude toward Negroes was essentially a conservative one, reflecting the racial biases of the vast majority of American whites. It is doubtful that Lincoln believed that the races were equally endowed; like Jefferson he thought it unlikely that Negroes and whites could live peacefully with equal rights in the same country. He had long been an admirer of colonization. Early in the war the Liberian and Haitian governments had indicated an interest in attracting American Negroes and ex-slaves to their countries and, in fact, employed agents for that purpose. Lincoln, however, cherished the notion of settlement in Colombia's Chiriquí Province (now in Panama). A speculative, fraudulent company had sold Lincoln on the idea that a black colony in Chiriquí could engage in coal mining and supply the United States Navy with fuel at half the usual price. Free Negroes attacked the proposal, and the scheme collapsed when the nature of the company's operations became clear. Later, Presidential interest in a similarly unsound colonizing venture on an island off the Haitian coast only led to tragedy for the migrants. Many of them died under the unhealthy conditions and the survivors returned to the United States.

Lincoln had hoped to sweeten emancipation with colonization, and Congress even appropriated money for it. Although his Chiriquí dream failed, the President went ahead with his plan for emancipation. Blacks and white abolitionists were jubilant when on January 1, 1863, Lincoln finally issued the Emancipation Proclamation. Abolitionists—and popular tradition since—magnified the significance of this act far beyond what it actually accomplished. Although it declared free those slaves still in rebel hands and authorized the use of black troops for certain purposes, it is hard to see that it did more for blacks than the second Confiscation Act. For the slaves still in the Confederacy, freedom of course depended upon the further progress of the Union armies. Since the proclamation did not even claim to free the slaves of the Border States or those working on plantations in areas like the Mississippi Valley (where many slaveowners had taken an oath of allegiance and pledged their "loyalty" to the national government), from a legal point of view, it was really the Thirteenth Amendment, approved by Congress in February 1865 and ratified in December, that actually emancipated all the slaves. Practically, of course, slavery as an institution disintegrated with the end of the war. Thus the importance of the Emancipation Proclamation was chiefly symbolic. It rallied the North through an idealistic appeal, encouraged the Negroes to escape and take up arms, and supported the hand of antislavery friends abroad in their efforts to prevent diplomatic recognition of the Confederacy.

After the Emancipation Proclamation the recruitment of black troops was gradually accelerated by the national government and some of the states. Massachusetts's antislavery governor was enthusiastic, but New York's Democratic governor refused to request authorization for black troops. In fact, though the use of blacks was welcomed as a relief to the battleweary white troops, sentiment in New York and many other parts of the North was still highly prejudiced.

An important source of conflict continued to be rooted in economic competition. Stevedores and longshoremen in all the major inland and coastal ports attributed the failure of strikes to black strikebreakers. In July 1862, the employment of black stevedores on Ohio riverboats precipitated the burning of Cincinnati's black section. Not until Negroes retaliated and burned several homes in the Irish neighborhood did the mayor seriously attempt to restore order in the community. Violence and race riots erupted in other Northern cities, but the worst outbreak occurred in New York in July 1863. The traditional hostility against Negroes had been further inflamed when the conscription law was passed four months earlier. On July 13, the day after announcement of the names drawn for the first draft, a crowd raided the draft headquarters, looted stores, set fire to warehouses, and clubbed and lynched black people. For four days the riot continued. People employing Negroes were attacked and their properties sacked. A mob even burned down the Colored Orphan Asylum on Fifth Avenue. After the riot subsided, businessmen raised over $40,000 as a relief fund. When the first New York black regiment departed for the front in March 1864, its members were feted by the city's most distinguished citizens. *The New York Times* congratulated the community upon a "prodigious revolution" in sentiment—though the careful student can see in this not a profound shift in public opinion but an act of atonement, or a continuing paternalistic concern for the Negroes on the part of New York's upper classes.

The black population in the North was rather small, and if any substantial black recruitment for the Union forces was to take place, it would have to be among the Southern freedmen. At the end of March 1863, Adjutant General Lorenzo Thomas was assigned the task of enlisting Negro troops in the Mississippi Valley. Thomas, in speaking to white Union troops in the course of his travels, made the project palatable to them by offering numerous commissions in the black regiments. Thus the creation of these new regiments offered enticing prospects for ambitious white soldiers of all ranks. Thomas's work was a distinct success: in March of 1865, nearly two thirds of the Union troops in the Mississippi Valley were Negroes. Altogether about 180,000 Negroes served in the Union Army, where they comprised about 9 or 10 percent of the total enlistment. Nearly 50,000 were in the navy, amounting to about one quarter of the total naval forces.

Negro servicemen faced hardships unknown to the white soldiers and sailors. One very serious problem was the Southern policy of either killing black soldiers and their white officers, even those who surrendered, or forcing the captured blacks into slavery. The most notorious instance followed the battle of Fort Pillow, on the Mississippi above Memphis, in April 1864. A rebel force captured the fort, and of the 262 Negroes stationed there, scores were massacred after surrendering. Lincoln warned of retaliation on Confederate prisoners, though the effectiveness of his threat was debatable. The conclusion of Dudley Cornish, the leading scholar on black soldiers in the Civil War, is that the main result of the barbarous Confederate policy was to make the black troops fight harder, more ruthlessly, and with more determination, since they could expect no mercy.

A black serviceman had to contend with other difficulties. Having come reluctantly to the conclusion that Negroes might serve in the armed forces, the Union military leaders saw no reason to consider black soldiers the equals of whites. In fact, one of the arguments against the use of Negro soldiers had been skepticism about their courage in battle, despite the evidence that blacks had served effectively in the American Revolution and the War of 1812. To inform the public about the bravery of earlier black servicemen, abolitionists circulated pamphlets. At the bloody battles of Port Hudson on the Mississippi below Vicksburg in May 1863, at the battle of Milliken's Bend on the Mississippi a few weeks later, and at Fort Wagner in South Carolina in July 1863, black troops again and again proved their valor. Even though the assault on Port Hudson and the attempt to take Fort Wagner were Union defeats, the steadfastness of the blacks and the high death rate sustained by them impressed many whites. Yet, for the rest of the war, black soldiers continually had to prove themselves. Always there was the lingering suspicion that they were not the equals of whites. Even some generals, like William T. Sherman, refused to the very end of the war to use Negroes in combat.

A disproportionate number of black troops were thus relegated to laboring rather than combat duties, and there were other evidences of discrimination as well. Negroes were resentful that few black men were ever commissioned. There was even reluctance to promote Negro soldiers to the grade of sergeant. The highest-ranking black officers were eight majors in the medical corps, one of whom became a lieutenant colonel, and Martin R. Delany, who was commissioned a major of infantry at the very end of the war. Aside from chaplains, the number of black commissioned officers did not exceed one hundred. Most of them served in the Louisiana Native Guards, and even there, when black officers died in battle, they were usually replaced with whites.

The pay provisions were also discriminatory. The War Department paid black privates $10 instead of the $13 a month received by whites, and of the $10, $3 were withheld for clothing, rather than permitting the Negro soldiers to purchase it as white soldiers did. Even the few Negro commissioned officers were drawing only $10 a month. The Massachusetts governor proposed that the state pay the difference for the black troops of the state, but the 54th and 55th Massachusetts Regiments rejected this compromise because on principle they believed that the federal government should end the wage discrimination. Finally, in July 1864, Congress passed a bill granting equal pay to those Negro soldiers who were free when the war began in 1861, but it was not until March 1865 that it passed an act providing for full payment for all black soldiers retroactive to the date of enlistment.

The efforts of the black and white abolitionists combined with the exigencies of war had led the Union government to free the slaves and enlist Negroes as soldiers. Thus the first steps toward freedom and toward recognition of the black as a human being had been taken.

2

Nevertheless, there were other problems clamoring for attention—economic conditions, education, civil rights, and the franchise. These were the big issues of the Reconstruction period, as far as blacks were concerned, and they were also raised during the war. The basic questions at stake were: What would be the future of Negroes in the United States? Would they be full-fledged citizens? Or would the pattern of the Revolutionary era be repeated, and would the promise of American life prove elusive once again?

Just as the black leaders had protested discrimination against free Negroes and fought against the institution of slavery during the antebellum period, so during the war they held that the emancipation of bondsmen would leave the task of the blacks and their friends only half done. Articulate blacks expressed a vision of a land of equality, and they realized that freeing the slaves would be but the beginning of their work. In this they were far ahead of most white abolitionists. Frederick Douglass set forth the situation clearly enough in addressing the Third

Decade Anniversary Celebration of the American Anti-Slavery Society in December 1863:

> I am . . . of those who believe that the work of the American Anti-Slavery Society will not have been completed until the black men of the South, and the black men of the North, shall have been admitted, fully and completely, into the body politic of America. . . . A mightier work than the abolition of slavery now looms up before the Abolitionist. This society was organized, if I remember rightly, for two distinct objects: one was the emancipation of the slave, and the other the elevation of the colored people. When we have taken the chains off the slave, as I believe we shall do, we shall find a harder resistance to the second purpose of this great association than we have found even upon slavery itself.

The views of many Northern Negroes on the future of the race were exemplified by the proceedings of the National Convention of Colored Men, held at Syracuse, New York, in October 1864. With Frederick Douglass in the chair, about 150 leading black men formulated a program of action for the months that lay ahead and organized a National Equal Rights League, selecting J. Mercer Langston for president. They were cognizant of the fact that the majority of Northern states still failed to grant blacks the ballot, and they entertained no illusions that either party—even the Republican—was unprejudiced toward Negroes. Their two chief demands were abolition and political equality. To those, including some abolitionists, who thought Negroes should be satisfied with "personal freedom"—the right to testify in courts of law, the right to own, buy, and sell real estate, the right to sue and be sued—they countered that without the right to vote, "personal freedom" was meaningless. Though Henry Highland Garnet expressed continuing support for colonization, in the light of the changed situation since 1860 most of the delegates were prepared to stake all on their American nationality. While addressing the nation on matters of abolition and citizenship, the convention exhorted the freedmen to moral, educational, and economic elevation. However, at a time when ex-slaves in the South were clamoring for land through expropriation of the plantations, this convention of Northern black men sidestepped that basic issue and confined itself to a resolution recommending that Negroes from all parts of the country settle "as far as they can, on public lands."

Subsequent conventions, both in the North and South, down to the end of the Reconstruction period, played variations upon these same themes. As in the antebellum period some leaders were disturbed by the idea of meeting in segregated "caste" conventions—and indeed with the passage of the Fourteenth Amendment and the Reconstruction acts, the frequency of state conventions declined noticeably and national conventions tended to be devoted to efforts to secure specific achievements. For example, the national convention of 1873 was called for the purpose of rallying support behind Sumner's Supplementary Civil Rights Bill. During the period of Presidential Reconstruction (1865–6), when the Southern states passed the highly discriminatory Black Codes that attempted to remand Negroes almost to a state of servitude, the black state conventions in the South took a remarkably sycophantic tone—stressing the importance of behaving well and of acquiring education and property instead of rights, even abjuring at certain conclaves any interest in the ballot. In general, however, the Southern elite Negroes, who met in state conventions from New Orleans to Richmond, expressed the same ideologies as the national conventions. In one such meeting, the black citizens of Norfolk exhibited a typical range of interests when in an "Address . . . to the People of the United States," they urged Negroes to form associations for the agitation of political rights and equality before the law, labor associations to protect colored farm workers, and land associations to aid the freedmen in buying farms.

3

The elite blacks tended to place primary emphasis on civil and political rights, but what the ex-slaves wanted most of all was land of their own to cultivate and the opportunity to secure

an education. Their interest in political activity was somewhat
less intense. The freedmen's desire for land mirrored the
American faith in property and landownership, in middle-class
virtues and pioneer independence. As was true of peasants the
world over, the slaves' whole lives had been bound up with the
soil and its cultivation; to them freedom, respectability, and
getting ahead were inextricably associated with farming their
own land. Southern planters, on the other hand, wanted to
depart as little from antebellum conditions as possible, and
Northern politicians and philanthropists were divided on the
propriety of confiscating Southern plantations and carving
homesteads out of them for the freedmen. Consequently, the
plantation system survived, though organized along new lines,
and the sharecropping and crop-lien systems developed as a
replacement for the slave-labor system.

The evolution of the sharecropping and crop-lien systems began during the Civil War itself. In 1861–2, as the Union armies
entrenched themselves on the South Carolina Sea Islands and
in the Mississippi Valley, the government was confronted with
the problem of providing for the physical needs of the blacks.
There was also the problem of cultivating and harvesting the
cotton wanted by Northern textile mills and a potential source
of revenue for the Treasury. In the ensuing years the freedmen
suffered from the lack of forethought on the part of government officials and from power rivalries between the Treasury
and Army Departments, both of whom were given imprecise
control over the affairs of freedmen and plantations. They
suffered also from differences of opinion among the missionaries
and philanthropists who were sincerely trying to assist the
blacks. Not until the creation of the Freedmen's Bureau in
March 1865 was it definitely settled that the War Department
would have the responsibility of protecting and providing for
the welfare of the freedmen. At no time was congressional approval obtained by the advocates of land expropriation and sub-
division for the sake of the freedmen. The result was confusion
in freedmen's affairs, gross exploitation of the Negroes by unscrupulous entrepreneurs and, in some cases, by dishonest mis-

sionaries and army officers, and frustration for the freedmen who had anticipated, with good reason, receiving land of their own. The disillusionment that many abolitionists, missionaries, and Radical Republicans felt with the state of black progress by the 1870's was mainly a consequence of this extraordinary mismanagement of freedmen's affairs.

After the federal authorities occupied the Sea Islands in November 1861, the Treasury Department paid the freedmen low wages to work on confiscated cotton plantations supervised by agents from the private freedmen's aid societies of the North. The missionaries disagreed among themselves: one segment favored land redistribution, while the rest, fearful that such a policy would encourage laziness, preferred the wage system, which they hoped would stimulate thrifty freedmen to purchase their own land. After the administration of freedmen's affairs on the islands was transferred from the Treasury Department to the War Department in July 1862, General Rufus Saxton encouraged economic independence among the Negroes by dividing plantations into small family units. The Treasury Department, however, decided to sell most of these plantations for unpaid taxes. Although a few blacks were able to buy some of this land, most of it fell into the hands of white entrepreneurs. The most noted of these was Edward Philbrick, who organized a company among his Boston friends with the intention of uplifting the freedmen and proving their superiority over slave labor, while personally making a financial profit. After operating a highly lucrative venture for a few years, he sold his properties. Meanwhile, when General William T. Sherman came to the Beaufort area on his sweep across the Southeastern states, he issued his famous Order No. 15 of January 1865, which definitely appeared again to guarantee Negroes the right of preemption on the plantation lands. After the war, when President Andrew Johnson restored most of the plantations to their former owners, blacks who had bought some of Philbrick's land were able to retain title, but thousands of others who had purchased directly from the government lost their holdings. Similarly, in Mississippi, the army made another unsuccessful attempt to provide Negroes with the opportunity to obtain homesteads. On the plantations of Jefferson Davis and his brother, Negroes were encouraged to run their own affairs under the leadership of Benjamin Montgomery, a freedman who had formerly been a slave overseer on one of these plantations. But this promising community disbanded when some of the land reverted to its former owners and the rest of it was sold to other whites.

Elsewhere, practically no effort was made to encourage black landownership. In the Mississippi Valley, Virginia, and North Carolina it was federal policy to permit the original owners to run their plantations or, if they had fled with the retreating Confederate forces, to lease the land to Northern entrepreneurs. Neither group had any philanthropic concern for the blacks. In Louisiana, where many planters had taken an oath of loyalty to the government, General Nathaniel P. Banks issued regulations in 1863 and 1864 requiring the freedmen to return to the plantations and work for extremely low wages. Under Banks's orders, the Negroes were forbidden to leave the plantation without a pass, and "insolence" or the absence of "perfect subordination" could result in freedmen losing pay or food rations. Black and white abolitionists condemned the Banks program of servitude; Frederick Douglass charged that "it practically enslaves the Negro and makes the Proclamation of 1863 a mockery and delusion." The New Orleans *Tribune*, a Negro-Creole publication, found little difference between the serfdom imposed by Banks and the old Louisiana slave code:

If we except the lash, which is not mentioned in these communications, one is unable to perceive any material difference between the two sets of regulations. All the important prohibitions imposed upon the slaves, are also enforced against the freedman. The free laborer, as well as the slave, has to retire into his cabin at a fixed hour in the evening; he cannot leave on Sunday, even to visit friends or simply to take a walk in the neighborhood, unless he be provided with a written authorization. . . . It is true that the law calls him a freeman; but any white man, subjected to such restrictive and humiliating prohibitions, will certainly call himself a slave. . . .

The only aspect of the Banks program that blacks applauded was the provision establishing a common school system.

Those who hoped that the government would divide the plantations and distribute the parcels among the freedmen were disappointed. The editors of the New Orleans *Tribune* in 1864—like many of the black delegates to the South Carolina constitutional convention in 1868—regarded the tillers of the land as rightfully entitled to the possession of the soil and urged the creation of a new class of small landholders as the foundation of a truly republican form of government. Washington paid no attention. The *Tribune* might optimistically assert that "revolutions never go backward," but the fact of the matter was that the policy of leasing the plantations to former Southern planters and Northern adventurers remained the general practice in Louisiana and along the Mississippi Valley from Memphis to Vicksburg and Natchez as federal forces moved South. Lessees interested in making a fast dollar could rent the plantations for ridiculously low sums, paying the black laborers very little in wages. In some arrangements, blacks were paid partly in food, clothing, and medical care, but lessees had endless opportunities to fleece the Negroes of what little they had, and medical care was practically never provided. Government agents interested in the blacks' welfare attempted to draw up regulations to mitigate the problems, but at best these were compromises with the demands of the plantation owners and the lessees. At worst they were flagrantly ignored.

Despite the government's failure and the unwillingness of whites to sell land to blacks, a significant number of ex-slaves bought farms after the war. Northern observers, Freedmen's Bureau agents, and missionaries enthused over the evidence of such progress. Examples were cited of Negroes who had pooled their resources to buy plantations, which they then divided among themselves. A Boston planter-philanthropist on the Sea

Islands reported "a black Yankee" whose industry and sharp dealing had put him ahead of the others on his plantation:

> Limus in his half-acre has quite a little farmyard besides. With poultry-houses, pig-pens, and corn-houses, the array is very imposing. He has even a stable, for he made out some title to a horse, which was allowed; and then he begged a pair of wheels and makes a cart for his work; and not to leave the luxuries behind, he next rigs up a kind of sulky and bows to the white men from his carriage. As he keeps his table in corresponding style . . . the establishment is rather expensive. So, to provide the means, he has three permanent irons in the fire, his cotton, his Hilton Head express, and his seines. . . . While other families "carry" from three to six or seven acres of cotton, Limus says he must have fourteen. . . . With a large boat which he owns, he usually makes weekly trips to Hilton Head, twenty miles distant, carrying passengers, produce and fish. . . . He is all ready to buy land, and I expect to see him in ten years a tolerable rich man.

If Northern authorities were indecisive and confused on what to do with the freedmen, Southern lawmakers were not. During 1865 and 1866 they enacted the Black Codes as a system of social control that would be a substitute for slavery, fix the Negro in a subordinate place in the social order, and provide a manageable and inexpensive labor force. Blacks who were unemployed or without a permanent residence were declared vagrants. They could be arrested and fined and, if unable to pay, be bound out for terms of labor. States enacted careful provisions governing contracts between employer and laborer—in several states the words "master" and "servant" were freely used—and particularly in South Carolina the terms of the contract were minutely defined. Stiff penalties were provided for those who did not fulfill these contracts or who encouraged blacks to evade them. These statutes generally guaranteed Negroes the right to sue and be sued and to own property, but they ordinarily could not bear firearms, could testify only in cases involving blacks, and in Mississippi could own only certain types of property. South Carolina went so far as to exclude Negroes from skilled trades and some types of businesses. Mississippi, Florida, and Texas even enacted Jim Crow transportation laws.

In the face of the Black Codes of 1865–6 and the intransigence of the planters on the one hand, and of President Andrew Johnson's pro-Southern attitude on the other, the Freedmen's Bureau found it difficult to do much for the elevation of the black men. Its efforts to distribute among the freedmen the abandoned lands that Congress placed under its jurisdiction were thwarted by Johnson's decision to return these properties to pardoned Confederates. Its desire to protect the freedmen with labor contracts was frustrated by the enormity of the task and by the resistance of the planters. The bureau drew up its own contract forms, but these bore a striking similarity to the unsatisfactory regulations arranged by the army during the war. The planters received considerable disciplinary authority over their employees, who were forbidden to break the contracts. Through special courts created by the Freedmen's Bureau, the blacks enjoyed some protection from abuse by their employers. Planters resented the bureau's interference in their affairs, its attempt to provide protections for Negroes, and the powers of its courts. Yet from the point of view of the freedmen, the bureau's contracts were coercive instruments substituting federal force for the antebellum slave codes, and many bureau officials—paternalistic where not actually prejudiced against black men—in fact viewed their basic duty as compelling Negroes to work. In Mississippi, the bureau's courts did not function and the contracts provided by state law were allowed to remain in effect. Like the bureau's contemporaries, historians have disagreed over the way in which the bureau actually operated, though recent research indicates that it was a far less radical, pro-black agency than traditionally believed.

Even more uncertainty surrounds the process by which the system of farm tenancy known as sharecropping emerged from the labor contract system that prevailed during the Civil War and early Reconstruction years. Under a sharecropping arrangement the freedman, instead of working for a wage, rented a plot of land and paid to the plantation owner a certain proportion of the cotton crop. The origins of this system are extremely obscure. There is at least occasional evidence that some wartime, army-supervised contracts provided for sharecropping as an alternative to the wage system. Planters generally would have preferred a system whereby Negroes contracted by the year to work for specified wages, but the shortage of available cash right after the war encouraged them to adopt a plan whereby they shared the crop with the black workers. A number of scholars hold that the freedmen themselves were largely responsible for the development of sharecropping, because they regarded the contract labor system, under which they worked in labor gangs, as too reminiscent of slavery times. Where they were unable to purchase their own land, as was usually the case, the Negroes preferred to be renters rather than hired laborers. Renting was desirable, even under a sharecropping rather than a cash arrangement, because tenants could organize their own time and be more independent than a hired laborer. Moreover, they could raise their own food.

Planters, however, also found advantages in the sharecropping system. Hired laborers would work no harder than forced to and, despite the law, might break their contracts. But sharecroppers had a vested interest in the crops, which they could not afford to leave standing in the field. Originally the arrangement was one that probably motivated them to work hard for their own advancement. Moreover, the evolution of the system was complicated by the fact that it was not uncommon at first for hired laborers to be paid in whole or in part with a share of the crop at the end of the year. For some years, in fact, until the courts straightened out the matter, the two types of sharecropping were not clearly distinguishable.

Whether the chief original impetus came from the planters or from the black peasants, the Freedmen's Bureau officials encouraged and often required the sharecropping contract. The practice was also stimulated by the shortage of cash resulting from poor crops in 1866 and 1867. Before the end of Reconstruction the sharecropping system appears to have been quite generally adopted. As late as the 1880's, however, the specific

terms varied from place to place, and there were still plantations with mixed systems of cultivation, encompassing hired
laborers, cash renters, and sharecroppers. Indeed cash renting
and hired-laborer work remained significant aspects of the
Southern agricultural labor system.

Typically the croppers kept one quarter to one half of the
crop, depending on what they supplied in the way of mules,
tools, and seed. Planters' evaluations of the system varied.
Complaints were made against the inefficiency of the unsuper-
vised tenant farmers, who lacked initiative to improve their
plots and maintain the capital improvements on the plantations. Yet the system had its profitable aspects for the planter,
and especially for those who, commonly enough, were not
overly scrupulous. It was the planter who weighed the cotton
and kept the accounts. Owing to the inadequate schools, the
croppers were only semiliterate, and, in view of the locus of
power in the rural South, even if they knew what was going on,
they were unable to assert their rights. This system reached its
depths in the crop lien. The croppers paid heavily for the purchases they were compelled to make at the plantation store.
Buying food and clothing on credit with the crop as lien, they
were charged high prices, outrageous interest rates, and were
forced to depend upon the planter's rendition of accounts.
After the crop was sold, they were likely to end up in debt to
the planter, particularly in a poor year. Out of this arose the
system of debt peonage, whereby insolvent croppers, unable to
repay debts from one year to another, were required by law to
work indefinitely for the same unscrupulous planter.

4

If land ownership was central to the lower-class freedmen's
wishes, close to it in importance was the desire for education.
Identifying it with the superior status of white men, the freedmen naturally shared the American passion for common school
instruction. Old and young flocked to the schools opened by the
missionaries as the federal armies moved southward.

The freedmen's aid societies that sprang up in the North in

1861–2 among both whites and blacks aimed to provide the contrabands with food, clothing, medicine, and the rudiments of an education. The activities of the white societies are better known, both because of white tendencies to ignore what Negroes were doing and because the work of the white groups had greater financial resources and was therefore more extensive. Northern blacks were active as well, under both religious and secular auspices. Among the outstanding Negro freedmen's aid societies were the Contraband Relief Association and the Union Relief Association of Israel Bethel Church (AME), in Washington; the Contraband Committee of Mother Bethel Church, in Philadelphia; and the Freedmen's Friend Society of Brooklyn. The African Civilization Society switched its activities from colonization to establishing schools among the contrabands in Washington. Between 1862 and 1868 the African Methodist Episcopal Church contributed nearly $167,000 toward freedmen's aid.

The white nonsectarian benevolent associations that dominated the work among the freedmen during the war underwent kaleidoscopic reorganization between 1862 and 1866. Sectarian missionary societies entered the field in 1864, and after the war they displaced the secular groups. Even the most important of the organizations assisting the freedmen, the American Missionary Association, which had been founded by leaders of the American and Foreign Anti-Slavery Society in 1846 as a nonsectarian antislavery missionary organization, ultimately became an arm of the Congregational Church.

While the freedmen's aid societies performed a valuable service in providing various forms of relief for the contrabands, their most permanent contribution was in education. Apparently the earliest school for contrabands was opened by Mary Chase, a free Negro of Alexandria, Virginia, on September 1, 1861. Two weeks later, Mrs. Mary Peake, a black woman, opened the first of the freedmen's aid societies' schools, under the auspices of the American Missionary Association, near Fortress Monroe in Virginia. Early in the following year Northern abolitionists energetically took up the task of education among the freedmen. As the Union armies advanced, increasing opportunities for "good work" led to a proliferation of freedmen's aid societies. The overwhelming majority of workers sent South by the white benevolent societies were Caucasians, but there were some Negroes among them. Charlotte Forten, granddaughter of James Forten, joined the teachers at Port Royal, South Carolina, in the summer of 1862. Francis L. Cardozo, a free-born Charlestonian educated at the University of Glasgow, was the first principal of the American Missionary Association's Avery Institute in his native city.

The mushrooming activities of the freedmen's aid societies would not have been possible without the endorsement of the federal government and the active cooperation of the military authorities, whatever the strains and stresses that the cooperation between these two very different groups entailed. In fact, in 1863–4 in Louisiana, it was the military authorities who created the first system of public schools for freedmen in New Orleans and its environs. This pattern of joint participation between the missionaries and the War Department was expanded under the Freedmen's Bureau, which gave hundreds of thousands of dollars to Negro education between 1866 and 1870. Under the terms of the law, the bureau supplied the buildings while the freedmen's aid societies paid the salaries of the teachers. Since in many cases the Northern philanthropic groups had difficulty in raising enough money, the bureau often rented buildings owned by the freedmen's aid societies, and with this money the latter paid their teachers.

With the financial resources at its disposal, the bureau was especially helpful in establishing some of the stronger schools that included college departments. In part because of the close relationships General O. O. Howard, commissioner of the bureau, enjoyed with his fellow Congregationalists of the American Missionary Association, and in part because of the superiority of the leadership and administration of the AMA schools, that organization benefited more than any of the others from Howard's funds. The bureau financed only one collegiate institution of its own, Howard University in Washington, but the roster of American Missionary Association schools included most of the finest institutions of black higher education: Atlanta University, Fisk University in Nashville, Talladega College in Alabama, Tougaloo in Mississippi, and, the fountainhead of industrial education in black schools, Hampton Institute in Virginia.

The response of the freedmen to instruction was enthusiastic. Missionary teachers were uniformly impressed by the ex-slaves' passion for learning. A teacher at Port Royal, South Carolina, recorded how families moved across the river so that their children could attend school; one woman "came to school daily with a baby in her arms and two boys by her side. They all stood up to read together." In 1866 the Freedmen's Bureau superintendent of education not only found that Negroes of all ages were attending school but that black children attended more regularly than white ones. Especially impressive were the numerous efforts of blacks to develop their own schools, hiring the teachers and even erecting buildings. In December 1866, South Carolina blacks raised $1,000 for their schools; in Georgia at that time there were ninety-six schools supported in whole or in part by the freedmen, who owned fifty-seven of the buildings. Such efforts ranged from the newly taught and barely educated, who were engaged in teaching those unable to read at all, to more elaborate efforts under adequately equipped teachers. At Goldsboro, North Carolina, in 1865, for example, the Freedmen's Bureau superintendent of education found that "two colored young men, who but a little time before commenced to learn themselves, had gathered one hundred and fifty pupils, all quite orderly and hard at study. A small tuition was charged, and they needed books. These teachers told me that no white man, before me, had ever come near them."

As a result of congressional action in 1867, Southern Negroes were enfranchised and new constitutions written in each of the ex-Confederate states. The new regimes, adopting a reform instituted in the North a generation earlier, provided for universal common-school education. In the constitutional conventions held in South Carolina, Louisiana, and Virginia, there was con-

siderable debate over the question of school segregation, and
South Carolina and Louisiana provided for legally unsegregated
schools. In South Carolina the black members of the convention insisted that the state constitution explicitly make schools
open to all, though they predicted that the two races would of
their own accord tend to go to separate educational institutions.
In the end only New Orleans instituted a system of mixed
elementary and high schools. South Carolina leaders made no
effort to compel acceptance of black youth in white schools,
and the university was the only integrated school in that
state. Virginia, which very shortly passed under the control
of the whites, or "Redeemers,"* quickly enacted a law requiring
school segregation. Everywhere in the South where it was not
specifically demanded by legislation, the administrative policy
of school boards was separation. Without exception the segregated schools were inferior and failed to give Negroes even the
rudiments of an adequate education.

Consequently, the real burden of training a black professional
elite and an educated leadership fell upon the missionary
schools. The Northern teachers conceived of their task in broad
terms. They aimed to give the rudiments of learning necessary
for the ex-slaves to function as free men even in a rural environment; to inculcate habits of thrift, industry, and Christian character, which would enable their students to rise to middle-class
status (hence the homilies on middle-class ethics and the interest in "industrial" classes for sewing and various trades and in
manual-labor schools like Hampton); to train teachers for the
public schools (hence the prevalence of normal schools on the
secondary level); and to provide a college education for those
intending to enter other professions. There was much conde-
scension and paternalism among the white missionaries, particularly among those advocates of industrial education who
thought higher education unsuitable for the freedmen, at least
for the present; but there was also much serious interest in

* "Redeemers" is a term used to refer to the men under whose leadership
the South was restored to white domination.

proving Negroes capable of the highest intellectual endeavor and in encouraging the full participation of the ex-slaves in American society.

In the early years the missionary schools concentrated on elementary- and normal-school training because, in the short run, this was the most essential and also because the public schools were so inadequate. In fact, until the twentieth century, private secondary institutions were the chief source of competent black public-school teachers in the South. Moreover, the missionary societies discovered that in order to obtain qualified college students, they needed to maintain their own elementary and secondary departments. For years the college departments were small. Even the very best black colleges maintained elementary- and secondary-school programs until well into the twentieth century. Leading liberal-arts institutions like Tougaloo College in Mississippi and Spelman College (founded in 1881 as Atlanta Baptist Female Seminary) were originally superior normal and industrial schools and did not offer liberal-arts college programs until around 1900.

The development of private schools on all levels, especially those aspiring to offer collegiate work, was in part a philanthropic mission and in part the result of denominational ambitions. Ordinarily each of the private colleges was connected, at least informally, with a church established to proselytize among the Southern Negroes. This was particularly true of the Methodist Episcopal Church, North, which developed a sizable Southern black membership and opened schools in most of the Southern states. Among the more important Methodist institutions whose origins go back to this period were New Orleans University (later merged with Congregationalist Straight University to form Dillard University), Clark College in Atlanta, and Claflin University in Orangeburg, South Carolina. The Episcopalians and Presbyterians established only a few schools, but the Baptists did extensive work, though only a few of their numerous institutions became really outstanding. Among the most successful ones were Shaw University in Raleigh, North

Carolina, Virginia Union University in Richmond, and More-
house College (originally Atlanta Baptist College). The Baptists and Methodists were the only denominations that founded
medical schools in connection with their colleges: Leonard
Medical School at Raleigh, Meharry in Nashville, and Flint in
New Orleans.

Of these Northern-based, predominantly white denominations, only the Baptists worked out cooperative arrangements
whereby the independent Negro connections (or organizations)
of the same faith contributed to the support of these missionary
schools and colleges. On the other hand, the various black
Methodist denominations established their own elementary,
secondary, and collegiate institutions in the South. With the
advance of the Union Army, black Baptist churches sprang up
everywhere and the AME Church spread rapidly throughout
the South. The AME Zion Church was especially successful in
North Carolina under the zealous missionary work of the Rev.
J. W. Hood, who took an active part in freedmen's educational
and political affairs and made North Carolina the new center
for his denomination. After the Civil War the black members
of several Southern white churches established their own denominations. With the religious expansion went an interest in
the education of the freedmen, though meager financial resources limited activity in this field. Both Methodist and Baptist white churches founded a number of elementary and
secondary institutions. Then in 1878 the Colored Methodist
Episcopal Church (established in 1870 as the result of a
friendly withdrawal from the Methodist Episcopal Church,
South) opened Lane College in Jackson, Tennessee. The AME
Zion Church founded its only college, Livingstone, in North
Carolina, in 1879 under the leadership of J. C. Price. When he
died in 1894, Price was an accommodationist leader of such
prominence that had he lived he might have occupied the place
later held by Booker T. Washington. Finally in 1881 and 1885,
the AME Church established its first two Southern colleges:
Allen University in Columbia, South Carolina (an outgrowth

of Payne Institute, established at Cokesbury in 1871), and Morris Brown College in Atlanta.

In the South during the three quarters of a century following Reconstruction, most of the leading professional men and many prominent businessmen were the products of the church-related colleges and Howard University, although above the Mason-Dixon line leading physicians, lawyers, and teachers were more likely to have graduated from the best Northern colleges and universities. The Southern church colleges also served as transmitters of Northern polite culture to the children of the modestly educated artisan elite of the postwar years and as a route of upward mobility for men of humbler status. However, in regard to these matters, there was a hierarchy among the colleges in each of the states and major cities. Generally the Congregationalist schools were the best and therefore the most prestigious, while the black-owned institutions were the least highly regarded. This was chiefly a response to a condition whereby the relative financial strength of their backers determined the quality of instruction offered by the schools. Congregationalist Atlanta and Fisk Universities were the fashionable institutions in their respective cities, though both Atlanta and Nashville had several black colleges, and in Nashville the Methodist Meharry Medical College attracted many upward-mobile young men. In fact Fisk and Atlanta became the most highly regarded Negro schools in the entire South, and along with Howard and Lincoln Universities produced the largest number of distinguished alumni. On the other hand, in Virginia, where the Congregationalists sponsored Hampton Normal and Agricultural Institute, Virginia Union University (Baptist) was the leading liberal-arts college. And in South Carolina, where upper-class and aspiring Charleston children attended the American Missionary Association's secondary school, Avery Institute, there was no Congregationalist college and a high proportion of the state's leaders were therefore graduates of the Methodist Church's Clafin University.

The contribution of the private colleges was made against

enormous odds. Even prior to the cessation of Freedmen's Bureau assistance in 1870, Northern philanthropy had declined precipitately. A few years later the panic of 1873 curtailed the income and operations of the schools even further. Meanwhile, beginning in the late 1860's, the violence, including murder and arson, perpetrated by Southern whites against the Northern schoolteachers and their institutions, forced a number to close their doors. Moreover, fewer whites felt a commitment to work among the freedmen, and mediocrity increased in the ranks of the white instructors. Nevertheless, despite the intimidation, despite the difficulties in obtaining financial support and qualified teachers, the schools struggled on. In the 1880's and 1890's the millionaire philanthropists began to turn their attention to black schools, but even then the assistance was directed more toward providing industrial training than college education.

5

In addition to recognizing that education and the opportunity for economic advancement were essential for full participation in American society, or in the "body politic," as the phrase of the time went, black people also focused their attention on the full attainment of constitutional rights—on full equality before the law.

During the war Negroes and white abolitionists continued their campaign of antebellum days against discrimination in the North. By 1865 Congress repealed the 1825 act prohibiting blacks from being mail carriers and provided that black witnesses were not to be excluded from federal courts. In a number of states Negroes took the initiative in fighting oppressive legislation. As a result of this pressure, in 1863 California repealed its antiblack testimony law. In 1865 and 1866 Illinois and Indiana repealed their anti-Negro testimony and anti-Negro immigration legislation, more widely known as the Black Laws. In Illinois the agitation was conducted by a Repeal Association, organized by Chicago black men under the leadership of the prosperous merchant-tailor, John Jones.

The situation in the 1860's is thus comparable to that in the 1960's: changes in white sentiment connected with the Civil War made it possible for Negroes to achieve their successes, but it seemed that black men still had to battle every step of the way for the recognition of their rights of citizenship. Even where legal impediments to civil rights were removed or did not exist, patterns of segregation retained much vitality. Under the leadership of the noted caterer and protest leader, George Thomas Downing, of New York and Newport, Negroes fought against segregated schools in Rhode Island and in 1866 succeeded with a campaign that had begun in 1857. They also protested against the continuing use of segregated streetcars. In Washington incidents occurred when streetcars refused to pick up black people. Afro-Americans protested and Senator Charles Sumner obtained a law prohibiting such discrimination in 1865. The practice continued, however. Not until Sojourner Truth secured the arrest and dismissal of a streetcar conductor who had assaulted her was the matter settled. Even more celebrated was the agitation against discrimination on horsecars in Philadelphia. Under the leadership of William Still, Negroes intensified their fight on this issue during the Civil War. Securing the support of an impressive array of white citizens, they nevertheless failed with appeals to the streetcar company and the city authorities. Finally, in 1867, the state legislature passed a law prohibiting segregation in public transportation. Only Massachusetts, however, actually outlawed discrimination in hotels, restaurants, theaters, and other amusement places.

In the South, segregation was extended as a tool of racial domination in place of slavery. Most of the segregation, however, was still customary rather than legal, and considerable historical research is needed to determine its exact extent. Also deserving of careful inquiry is the extent to which Negroes protested against the discrimination. The New Orleans black press denounced the "star" streetcars intended for Negroes, and in 1866 groups of Negroes blocked their passage in the streets. Consequently, the military authorities required the provisional governor to outlaw the separate streetcars. In both Charleston and Richmond in 1867, black men decided to defy streetcar segregation. In Richmond violence resulted, but in Charleston the military commander ordered an end to the discrimination. During the period when black men were holding elective office in South Carolina, legislation was passed penalizing discrimination in places of public accommodation, and Negroes used theaters in the leading cities and the first-class railway cars. In Louisville, in 1871, Negroes protesting against transportation segregation entered the horsecars reserved for whites until they wrested the right to ride in them without discrimination. And in Savannah, the following year, the city's black citizens conducted a successful two-month boycott against the Jim Crow horsecars.

Meanwhile, Congress had turned its attention to civil rights. In 1866 it passed over President Johnson's veto the Civil Rights Act, which defined American-born Negroes as citizens and enumerated certain rights to which they were entitled: to sue and be sued; to give evidence; and to buy, sell, and inherit property. It also provided vaguely that Negroes had the right to the full and equal benefit of all laws. The Fourteenth Amendment, proposed by Congress in June 1866, and ratified July 1868, added a similarly loosely worded constitutional guarantee against discrimination by the states. Continuing segregation indicated that the amendment did not include sufficient sanctions, and black men accordingly threw their vigorous support behind Senator Sumner's Supplementary Civil Rights Bill, which specifically offered protection against segregation in transportation, schools, and public accommodation. The largest of the Negro national conventions, held in Washington in 1873, was devoted entirely to propagandizing for this bill, which, with the clause providing for mixed schools deleted, was finally passed in 1875. When blacks tested the law in Northern and Southern cities, they discovered that there were many evasions and violations. Moreover, they soon found the machinery of enforcement so cumbersome and relief so uncertain that they ceased trying to secure the rights that it aimed to guarantee. Eventually, in 1883, the Supreme Court declared the law unconstitutional.

6

The history of the Negro's political rights followed a course roughly parallel with that of civil rights. Black leaders considered the right to vote as central to all others. They viewed it as the means to gain and protect their other rights in American society. At the same time, extending the franchise to Negroes would vindicate American institutions before the world. Time and time again during the war black leaders agitated on the question, and it became a major theme in the postwar Negro conventions. A convention of Pennsylvania leaders declared in 1868:

> The vote of one black man now—today—right here in his native land, is worth to the nation, to liberty, to the securing of our rights as citizens, and the establishing of the Republic on the eternal foundations of truth and justice, more than is involved in the theory of civilization of all other parts of the world. It is America that you have to civilize, to Christianize, and compel to accept and practically apply to all men, without distinction of color or race, the glorious principles and precepts laid down in her immortal Declaration of Independence. To build up a nation here, sacred in freedom, as an example to the world, every man equal in the law and equally exercising all rights, political and civil . . . is the surest way to civilize humanity.

Southern blacks were also evincing interest in the franchise. In November 1863, a mass meeting of New Orleans black men petitioned the state's military governor, requesting the right to vote in the election for delegates to the forthcoming state constitutional convention; and in January 1864, they petitioned President Lincoln on the same matter. Lincoln wrote to the provisional governor, suggesting privately that the constitutional convention consider granting the ballot to at least some of the antebellum free Negroes. Nothing was done about this proposal, and continued efforts to secure the vote failed until Congress acted in 1867.

The Reconstruction Act of 1867 provided that each of the Southern states was to be placed under a military governor until a convention, chosen on the basis of universal manhood suffrage, wrote a constitution that would meet the requirements set by Congress. The constitutions thus adopted did extend the suffrage to all adult male citizens. The Fifteenth Amendment, proposed by Congress in 1869 and ratified the following year, reinforced the Reconstruction Act and the new Southern state constitutions. It also secured the vote for Negroes in those Northern states where they were disfranchised. Because these states in the North failed to ratify the amendment, its ratification by the reconstructed Southern states actually enabled black men in many parts of the North to exercise the franchise.

The constitutional conventions called in accordance with the Reconstruction Act of 1867 all contained black members. Only in South Carolina, however, were they in the majority in the convention, and Louisiana was the only other state where they comprised as many as half the delegates. Nor can it be said that blacks and their white carpetbagger allies together controlled all of the conventions. In Georgia, for example, the influence of native whites was so strong that the legislative seats were apportioned to the advantage of the predominantly white counties. The first legislature elected after the constitution was adopted even ousted its Negro members. Before departing, Representative Henry M. Turner, an AME minister, delivered a sarcastic denunciation from the floor of the House. But blacks were not readmitted until the state supreme court ruled in their favor in 1869.

As a result of the new constitutions Negroes were elected to public office in all the Southern states. The highest position held was that of United States Senator. Two men, Hiram Revels and Blanche K. Bruce, represented Mississippi in the United States Senate, the former for a two-year unexpired term, the latter for a full term that began after Reconstruction had been overthrown in the state. Fourteen black men sat in the

House of Representatives between 1869 and the end of Reconstruction in 1877. The highest state office attained was lieutenant governor. Two men held this office in South Carolina,
one in Mississippi, and three in Louisiana. P. B. S. Pinchback
served as acting governor of Louisiana for over a month when
the carpetbagger chief executive was on trial for corruption.
Negroes served as secretaries of state in Florida, Louisiana,
Mississippi, and South Carolina; as superintendents of education in Arkansas, Florida, Louisiana, and Mississippi; and as
state treasurers in Florida and South Carolina. Jonathan C.
Gibbs was first secretary of state and then superintendent of
public instruction in Florida; Francis Cardozo acted first as secretary of state and then as state treasurer in South Carolina. J. J.
Wright, who had been the first black lawyer in Philadelphia,
was an associate justice of the South Carolina Supreme Court.
John R. Lynch, who was later a congressman, served as speaker
of the Mississippi House of Representatives.

An adequate analysis of black leaders and how they functioned at all political levels remains to be made. Only now are
scholars beginning to make the kinds of studies that are needed
if we are to deal with these matters. The majority of Afro-
American officeholders—especially at the local level—were
probably ex-slaves, but most of them came from relatively privileged origins: from among the skilled and better educated
bondsmen, from the antebellum Southern free people of color,
and from the North. The most careful study of the subject we
have, an analysis of New Orleans, reveals that black political
leadership there was drawn chiefly from the local antebellum
free people. This appears to have been an exceptional case,
however. Some of the black politicians like Francis Cardozo and
South Carolina's Congressman Robert Brown Elliott, both of
whom graduated from college in Great Britain, were well-
educated men whose training was far superior to practically all
of the white officeholders during Reconstruction or after. A
high proportion of the black political leaders were ministers and
teachers.

The white Southerners who overthrew Reconstruction, and

their apologists ever since, have charged Negro domination and corruption as justification for their acts. Actually, at no time can blacks be said to have been in control of any Southern state. None was ever elected or nominated for governor. Only in the lower house of the South Carolina legislature were black men ever in a majority. South Carolina was the only state with a black serving as supreme-court justice, Mississippi the only one that sent Negroes to the United States Senate. Obviously, even in these two states, where Negroes were over half the population, they never really controlled the governments since the highest state office eluded them and the majority of important offices were always in white hands. And for a state like Georgia, where there was only one black congressman and no blacks at all in high executive or judicial office, the charge of Negro domination is clearly without substance. Over time black political activists grew more assertive in demanding better representation in important offices, and in a state like South Carolina some headed important committees in the legislature. But at no time did blacks enjoy offices or influence anywhere near commensurate with the support they gave the Republican Party, even though the party's tenure in office in the Southern states was made possible only by the black vote.

Nor can it be said that Negroes were consistently identified with the corrupt elements among the carpetbaggers and scalawags. Actually, the highest costs of state government arose from the corruption associated with railroad construction and railroad subsidies. Democrats participated in these as much as Republicans, and the post-Reconstruction regimes as much as or more than the Radical Republican regimes. Mississippi, with more black officials than most Southern states, had no graft on the state level and very little lower down in the political hierarchy during Reconstruction but a considerable amount of it under the Redeemers afterward. In Louisiana and South Carolina, where corruption seemed especially flamboyant, certain prominent black politicians supported conservative coalitions that attacked the corrupt elements in the Republican Party. In Louisiana, Pinchback appears to have been an opportunist, but

Lieutenant Governor Oscar J. Dunn fought the corrupt group. In South Carolina, Martin R. Delany and R. H. Cain, a two-term congressman and later bishop in the AME Church, for a while at least supported the Democrats in preference to the graft-ridden elements in their own party.

Most historians have concluded that, as a group, black politicians accomplished little. The exact way in which black politicians functioned during Reconstruction, however, has never been analyzed. Negroes were ranged on all sides of the complex factional politics that characterized the Reconstruction regimes. Coming from diverse social backgrounds, they cannot be said to have demonstrated overwhelming unity even on key issues like the land question. Their support was courted by white political leaders; those in high offices and on committee posts often had an important voice. Yet it seems likely that just as the white Republicans failed to accord blacks a proportionate share of high offices and legislative seats, so in the decision-making process they tended to ignore their black colleagues. The two senators from Mississippi, for example, were rather conservative men who were useful as symbols for the black voters. Neither they nor the more militant protest leaders were ordinarily included in the inner circles of Republican Party decision makers.

7

In any event, whether black politicians were powerless or influential, corrupt or incorruptible, Southern whites resented them. In the 1860's, as in the 1960's, the Southern white man perceived the black man as a threat to his security, his status, his dominance. During the 1870's white Southerners used a variety of methods to reassert their control. In states where Negroes were in a minority or where, as in Georgia and Florida, the apportionment of legislative seats favored the whites, it was a relatively simple matter to overturn the radical regimes. In some cases, notably Virginia, Negroes for many reasons sided with the upper-class white conservatives. Even in South Carolina many blacks believed Wade Hampton's promises when he ran as the Democratic candidate for governor in 1876; and he in

turn kept his word to the extent that for years those Negroes
who had voted for him remained on the suffrage rolls. White
Southerners also terrorized Negroes and their white sympathizers from the North. Techniques of intimidation included
economic pressures against recalcitrant Negroes and violence in
the form of beatings, murders, and even race riots.

Between 1866 and 1898 there were scores of race riots in the
South. Although the peak of organized social violence occurred
in the two years before the election of 1876, Southern riots
continued into the twentieth century, with outbreaks of major
proportions erupting at Wilmington, North Carolina, and
Greenwood County, South Carolina, in 1898, and Atlanta in
1906. Most of these conflagrations were inspired by the desire of
whites to remove blacks from participation in the functions of
government, as officeholders and as voters, and generally they
were expressions of a fear of black domination. The great wave
of riots of 1874–6 accompanied the white Democratic drive to
"redeem" the South of Radical Republican control. The turn-of-
the-century outbreaks were designed to deprive blacks of the
limited political rights they still enjoyed. Whites viewed these
events as such sharp wrenches of the social order that they
sometimes referred to a riot as a "rebellion" or a "race revolution," demonstrating, as contemporaries put it, "the determination of leading white citizens to liberate the city from black
tyranny."

Almost any attempt of blacks to realize their hope for a racially egalitarian society could call forth violent repression from
whites. Thus the New Orleans riot of July 1866, whose death
toll was officially listed as forty-eight, occurred after Negroes
generated pressure to call a convention to amend the state constitution and obtain the suffrage. The Memphis riot of the
same year erupted when black soldiers took a Negro prisoner
from the custody of the Memphis police, who had a reputation
for brutality in the black community. When the police later
arrested two soldiers, shots were exchanged, killing one white
policeman and one Negro soldier. The whites interpreted these
incidents as evidence that "the niggers . . . are going to take

Memphis." The Savannah riot of July 1872 broke out when
Negroes challenged the segregated seating pattern on streetcars;
after a Republican meeting in which blacks demanded streetcar
integration, large numbers of whites and blacks attacked one
another along the car tracks. The precipitating incident for the
Hamburg, South Carolina, riot of July 1872 occurred when the
all-black militia company commanded by a former Georgia politician, Doc Adams, refused to interrupt their military drill to
allow two whites in a buggy to pass.

Most of the Reconstruction riots were actually pogroms, with
blacks being attacked and killed by whites. The whites received
relatively few injuries. This was true even of the riots that were
precipitated by an act of Negro resistance or retaliatory violence. Thus the Meridian, Mississippi, riot of 1871, which
erupted in a town controlled by a coalition of white and black
Republicans, grew out of an altercation during a court trial of
three black politicians charged with "incendiary speechmak-
ing." One defendant interrupted a white witness to declare
heatedly, "I want three colored men summoned to impeach
your testimony." After the witness moved toward him with a
stick, the defendant allegedly pulled a gun and accidentally
killed the judge. In the ensuing riot as many as twenty-five or
thirty blacks were murdered, marking "the end of Republican
control in the area surrounding Meridian." At Memphis, in
1866, many blacks were frightened into inactivity, while others
fought off the attackers as best they could. At Fort Pickering,
located in the city, black soldiers pleaded for their guns but
were peremptorily refused by the military authorities. In desperation a group of twelve to fifteen black soldiers "made a
rush" on the arsenal, but before they could secure the weapons,
the Negroes were stopped by a warning volley from the guards.
Memphis whites, led by police and firemen, invaded a black
residential area, killing forty-six Negroes, according to official
count. They also put the torch to ninety-one houses, twelve
schools, and four churches. The chairman of the congressional
committee that investigated this riot compared it to the massa-
cre of black prisoners at Fort Pillow during the Civil War.

Black resistance was greater at Hamburg, South Carolina, in 1876. There more than two hundred heavily armed whites surrounded an armory in which Captain Adams and his men had taken refuge. For more than two hours the Negroes exchanged gunfire with the mob outside, and fled through the rear only when the whites mounted a cannon in front. The pursuers searched the homes of the blacks, flushed out about thirty men from their hiding places, and forced them to kneel in the middle of a street. Several prisoners were slaughtered as an example to the rest, who were then set free while the whites amused themselves firing at the figures fleeing in terror down the road.

In the aftermath of the Hamburg riots came one of the exceptional cases of extensive black aggressive violence during the Reconstruction period. Congressman R. H. Cain presided at an indignation meeting in Charleston, where the Negroes threatened massive retaliation in the event of another outbreak: "There are 80,000 black men in this state who can bear Winchester rifles, and know how to use them, and there are 200,000 women who can light a torch and use the knife." The furious overflow crowd spilled into the street, blocking a streetcar from passing. When a policeman made an arrest after ordering them to move, the crowd freed the prisoner, shouting, "This is no Hamburg." Several weeks later, a major riot was precipitated when a crowd of black Republicans fought with a group of black Democrats being escorted home from a meeting by the latter's white political associates. The blacks refused to report their injuries, fearing implication in the riot, but when the police finally separated the combatants, an emergency hospital was set up to care for the injuries of over fifty whites. The Negroes' fury was unabated, and from midnight through the early hours of the morning, they attacked any whites they saw. Along King Street, the major business thoroughfare, they smashed windows and looted stores. For several days thereafter, the rioters continued their attacks on the side streets, defying the authorities, while terrified whites dared not leave their homes.

The Charleston riot, though not unique in the annals of Reconstruction, was unusual. For the most part, Negroes were the victims and whites the successful aggressors in the inter-racial violence of the Reconstruction period.

8

Southern whites were not entirely responsible for the success of their methods. The fact was that the North had changed its mind. Most Northerners had never been racial egalitarians, and they had had to be pushed and shoved to accord equal constitutional rights to Negroes. When it came to essential economic reform in the South, the North failed entirely. The economic interests that had looked to the Republican Party and its continued hegemony as the basis for advancing their own interests eventually formed an alliance with substantial Southern business elements that had complementary needs. They arranged for the Compromise of 1877, whereby Southern Democrats acquiesced in the elevation of the Republican Rutherford B. Hayes to the Presidency in the disputed election with the Democrat Samuel J. Tilden. Even those individuals who had been most sincerely interested in the Negro became tired, disillusioned with the freedmen, and enamored of the idea of sectional reconciliation. They had anticipated great things of the black man. When, very largely because of the confusion and halfheartedness of the policies of their supposed benefactors, the freedmen did not live up to these high expectations, those very benefactors concluded that the ex-slaves were not ready for self-government. Corruption in high circles did not disqualify whites for self-government, but somehow it did seem to disqualify the Negroes, who had been notably less corrupt. Thus, even the Northern humanitarians deserted the freedmen and left them under the control of their former masters and the even more hostile working-class whites.

All in all, the Northern whites—including many former abolitionists—found it relatively easy to pay the price of sectional reconciliation. That price was the rejection of the idea of a racially egalitarian society—and even the desertion of the blacks' fundamental constitutional rights. The Negroes' vision of a just and democratic society seemed doomed to frustration. A hundred years after Emancipation, Martin Luther King could still best express the extent of black participation in American society by saying, "I have a dream. . . ."

V

"Up from Slavery": The Age of Accommodation

1

DURING THE GENERATION following the Compromise of 1877 Negroes throughout the country found themselves increasingly the victims of discrimination, proscription, and mob violence. This was particularly true in the South, where the withdrawal of federal military support from the last of the "radical" governments and the acceptance of white and Democratic hegemony in the South by the officials at Washington left Southern Negroes without any effective defense. The result was the unimpeded development of a race system that supplanted the old institution of slavery as a mechanism of social control.

Black voting fell off precipitately with the restoration of the Southern state governments to the control of the Redeemers.

194

First by violence, primarily, and then by ballot-box stuffing, false returns, and complicated registration and voting procedures, black political influence was effectively curtailed. It was not at once completely eliminated, however. Democratic votes were cast by some Southern Negroes, who were mainly of the old servant class, or successful, conservative farmers and businessmen, with close ties to the antebellum Southern white aristocracy. A Mississippi black owner of five hundred or six hundred acres of land and more than one hundred head of cattle, all acquired since the war, told a Senate committee in 1879 he voted Democratic "because I sympathize with my own self, knowing that I expected to stay with them [the Southern white Democrats] to make property if I could, and the South has always been kind to me. My master that I lived with I nursed him and slept at his mother's feet and nursed at her breast, so I thought my interest was to stay with the majority of the country who I expected to prosper with." Moreover, in the predominantly black counties of both Mississippi and South Carolina, during the 1880's and early 1890's, the practice known as "fusion" appeared—the dividing up of offices between black Republicans and white Democrats so that the former held a seat or so in the legislature and a share of the less important local positions. Indeed, there was something of a revival of black voting as alliances with independent parties like the Virginia Readjusters, the Greenbackers, and the Populists helped stave off complete political effacement for a while; but this trend only culminated in the final wave of race riots and constitutional disfranchisement.

Mississippi in 1890 and South Carolina in 1895 were the first states to amend their constitutions effectively to disfranchise practically all Negroes; between 1898 and 1903 Louisiana, North Carolina, Alabama, and Virginia imitated them, followed by Oklahoma and Georgia in 1907 and 1908. Generally these revised constitutions required poll taxes and literacy and/or property qualifications, which could be applied discriminatorily by voting registrars, especially in the case of literacy qualifications. Some constitutions provided an obvious escape hatch for Southern whites by the device of a "grandfather clause," which waived these requirements for those whose ancestors had voted in 1860. Florida, Arkansas, Tennessee, and Texas employed poll taxes and other devices short of constitutional change. Between 1896 and 1915 all Southern states passed legislation that permitted the Democratic Party, nomination by which was nearly always tantamount to election, to declare only whites eligible for voting in primary elections. The United States Supreme Court consistently refused to intervene in these disfranchisement regulations, until in 1915, it declared the Oklahoma grandfather clause unconstitutional. In view of these facts, and in the face of the riots in Wilmington, North Carolina, in 1898, and Atlanta, Georgia, in 1906, which capped the disfranchisement campaigns in those states, Southern Negroes became increasingly disillusioned with political activity.

The wave of disfranchisement legislation after 1890 was contemporaneous with the Populist movement and the rise of the so-called poor whites to political consciousness and power. The agrarian protest of the Populist Party was rooted in the work of the Northern and Southern Farmers' Alliances that developed during the 1880's. Seemingly allied with the Southern Farmers' Alliance was the Colored Alliance, formed in Texas in 1886 under the leadership of a white preacher who became its general superintendent. The Colored Farmers' Alliance and Cooperative Union spread over the South and at its peak claimed a membership of over one million. This figure would make the Alliance one of the very largest black organizations in American history. Unfortunately, only fragmentary evidence of its activities survives, and so little is known about it. One would like to ascertain, for example, whether the Colored Alliance was developed by blacks because they were excluded from the white Southern Alliance, or whether the Southern Alliance's leaders encouraged its development in the hope that they could control it. That the latter may have originally been the case is suggested by the existence of a rival National Colored Alliance, claiming 250,000 members, which did not merge with the larger group until 1890. Like the white organization the Colored Alliance sponsored farmers' cooperatives. On many matters the platforms of the two organizations were quite similar. Yet there were differences. The Colored Alliance favored the Lodge Federal Elections Bill, designed to guarantee the voting rights of Southern blacks in national elections through the use of federal troops; the Southern Alliance opposed it. Publications of the Southern Alliance often expressed antiblack views. In Mississippi it was an important force behind the constitutional convention of 1890, which disfranchised blacks, and in Georgia the Alliance-dominated legislature in 1891 passed a Jim Crow railroad-car law. In 1889 a group of North Carolina black men accused the Southern Alliance of setting low wages for black farmers and of influencing the state legislature to pass discriminatory laws. Two years later disagreement arose over a cotton pickers' strike fostered by leaders of the Colored Alliance; it was opposed by the Southern Alliance, many of whose members employed black cotton pickers.

The Colored Alliance also suffered from internal tensions. At times the black members and officers resented the actions of the handful of whites who held administrative positions in the organization—the general superintendent, people in comparable positions at the state level, and managers of some of the cooperative stores. Moreover, most of the members were actually opposed to calling the cotton pickers' strike; some because they were themselves farmowners and employers of labor, the majority because they regarded such a tactic as futile and suicidal. In most parts of the South, in fact, the strike proved abortive, and where a strike did occur it was quickly and ruthlessly crushed. As a consequence, by the end of 1891, the Colored Alliance had collapsed.

The paucity of data leaves unanswered a number of intriguing questions. To what extent was the Colored Alliance, at least in its early years, under the influence, guidance, even control of the white Southern Alliance? To what extent did the Colored Alliance engage in large-scale cooperative enterprise? And to what extent did its members share in a conscious feeling of class solidarity against the Redeemers and capitalists? If genuine solidarity along class lines was evident in the Alliance, as claimed by romantic writers seeking to establish a historical base for united action of poor whites and blacks, why were blacks organized into a separate Alliance? And how was it that the Alliance men and Populists were later so easily led into extreme antiblack actions? In spite of various gestures to obtain black support, attitudes such as those exhibited in North Carolina and on the Lodge bill would support the conclusion that whatever interracial solidarity existed, it was not firmly rooted.

Confusing and paradoxical are the only terms to describe the radical agrarian movement when it entered politics in the 1890's. In South Carolina, Benjamin Tillman captured the Democratic Party in the name of the radical agrarians, partly by appealing to race prejudice. Under his leadership South Carolina became the second state to enact constitutional disfranchisement. Yet in other situations, the agrarians did make substantial efforts to obtain the support of Negroes, who responded to a considerable degree. Even though the backcountry whites were traditionally hostile to Negroes, and even though the Lodge Federal Elections Bill alarmed Southern white farmers and played into the hands of the Democrats, part of the Populist political strategy was a coalition with black farmers. A few Negroes were delegates to the St. Louis conference of Farmers' Alliances and other organizations in 1892, which in effect launched the Populist Party in national politics. One black served as assistant secretary at the conference. His election was made all but unanimous on the motion of a white Georgian, who said, "We can stand that down in Georgia." A Negro's name appeared on a call for the national nominating convention held at Omaha by the Populist Party in July 1892.

In some states at least, black participation in the Populist Party was significant. As early as 1890 the Kansas Alliance Party nominated a Negro for state auditor, and at least a sizable minority of black voters supported Populists in that state in 1892. In the same year, the Arkansas Populist platform contained a resolution proposed by a black delegate, "that it is the object of the People's Party to elevate the downtrodden, irrespective of race or color." In Louisiana among the delegates to the first convention of the party in that state were twenty-four Negroes, one of whom was nominated for state treasurer but withdrew. In Texas two blacks were named to the party's executive committee in 1891, and there were always colored members of that body until 1900. In Georgia perhaps the most spectacular effort to enlist black support occurred when Tom Watson, the white Populist leader, openly espoused the cause of Negroes and defended his black backers against violence. Generally, Populist platforms in the Southern states denounced the convict-lease system* and lynching and supported political rights for blacks.

The evidence concerning political coalitions between Republicans and Populists on state and local candidates is difficult to evaluate. In a number of states in 1892, 1894, and 1896, fusion was attempted—sometimes formally, sometimes informally. But Populist fusion with Republicans did not necessarily mean with blacks. In Georgia, for example, in 1896, the white Republican leaders, whom Negroes accused of racism, supported the Populists. On the other hand, prominent black members of the state Republican executive committee maintained close connections with upper-class white Democrats and urged black men not to back the Populists. It was generally agreed by Negroes in a position to know that in Alabama and Georgia black men supported the Democrats rather than the Populists on the whole, though of course this was accomplished largely by intimidation, fraud, and other pressures. Broadly speaking, fusion tended to be between the Populists and the Lily-white Republican faction rather than between Populists and the Black-and-Tan faction of

---

* Under the convict-lease system, state and county governments leased prisoners to plantation owners and industrialists for a small fee. An incredibly brutal system of labor exploitation developed on plantations, in mines, turpentine camps, and railroad construction. Black people who had been convicted of committing petty crimes were the chief victims of this system.

the party.* On the other hand, the election of 1896 in North Carolina was a notably successful example of fusion between Populists and black Republicans.

Of all Southern states North Carolina was the least discriminatory in its racial practices. For example, it sent a Negro to Congress during most of the 1880's and 1890's. In 1894 fusion was not officially adopted, but Republicans nominated the same slate of state officials as the Populists. Populists failed to endorse the black candidates of the Republicans, but remained silent rather than attacking them, and as a result the two parties together acquired a majority in the legislature and elected other state officials. Although certain eminent black Republicans had been active in the arrangements, six of the black counties were found in the Democratic column. In 1896 the Republicans fused successfully with the Populists on most state and congressional offices, electing white Republicans to the offices of governor and senator and one black, George H. White, to the U.S. House of Representatives. The campaign of 1898, however, was marked by a vituperative and successful use of the race issue on the part of the Democrats, resulting in the defeat of the fusionists and its dreadful aftermath—the Wilmington, North Carolina, race riot. Disfranchisement followed as a matter of course. The charge of black domination used by Democrats to wean upland whites from the policy of fusion was, of course, a myth. But it appears that the fusion arrangements here—and in other states—were chiefly a marriage of political convenience rather than a coalition signifying any genuine consciousness of common class interest between blacks and lower-class whites. Similarly, in Kansas, where black support for the Populists was unusually strong, endorsement was based, not on any ideological affinity with the views of the white agrarians, but on a temporary alliance born of pragmatic politics.

All in all, it is difficult to say just how many Negroes espoused

* In the Southern states the Lily-whites were the white Republican faction that sought to purge Negroes from leadership positions in the party. The Black-and-Tan Republican faction was the one that included Negroes and their white allies.

the Populist cause. Democrats were usually able to secure blacks to speak and organize clubs against the Populists. Furthermore, as in North Carolina, those Negroes who did support the Populists usually remained Republicans. Frequently they were registering a negative vote against the Democrats rather than for any positive policy. The election returns showing heavy black support for the Democrats in the Black Belt are, of course, open to question. Many planters saw to it that their black tenants voted for the Democrats, and the party also used intimidation and fraud to obtain large majorities for its candidates. It was this situation that caused Populists like Watson to turn against black people and become extreme purveyors of racial hatred. In general, Southerners' deeply held prejudices could not be easily eradicated, and most rank-and-file Populists never held any real conviction of racial equality. The tendency to segregate Negroes in Populist Party units and at Populist rallies bears eloquent testimony to this fact. The Democrats found it all too easy to destroy the party on the basis of an appeal of white supremacy.

The net result of the Populist movement, then, seemed to be increased racial hatred and the embitterment of race relations. In the disfranchisement campaigns at the turn of the century, the conservative Democrats and the radical agrarians each variously favored and opposed black suffrage according to what seemed politically advantageous. At the Alabama state constitutional convention, for example, the small amount of support for permitting Negroes the franchise was chiefly found among a handful of conservative Democrats who had earlier benefited from black votes and the endorsement of black Republicans. One ambitious study, recently published, concludes that the chief thrust for disfranchisement came from Black Belt plantation Democrats. Nevertheless, in view of the shifting positions that both white factions took on the issue, the most valid conclusion seems to be that each faction was motivated less by ideological considerations than by the fluctuating tactical considerations of practical politics.

Like disfranchisement, the great wave of segregation laws came with the entrance of the agrarians into politics. The occasional laws and customary de facto segregation of the ante-bellum period and Reconstruction received new impetus after Redemption. Statutes requiring segregation appeared first in the field of education. By 1878 the majority of the Southern and Border states placed legal sanction behind what was already universal practice, and the rest of the states followed in the 1880's and 1890's. There was also growing discrimination in the appropriation of school monies. By the end of the century, funds for black schools were in many localities actually being reduced; and, overall, while the average per capita expenditure for Negro children rose slightly, the divergence in per capita appropriations for the two races widened rapidly. One observer reported in 1910 that in most of the Southern states at least twice as much was spent per pupil on whites as on blacks. The consequences in regard to attendance, length of school terms, quality of buildings, and teacher pay and qualifications were all too evident. Conservatives acceded to the desirability of indus-trial education for the uplift of a "backward race," but extrem-ists like Governor J. K. Vardaman of Mississippi, who voiced the hatreds of the lower classes, objected to any sort of educa-tion for blacks.

During the post-Reconstruction years, segregation in trans-portation was less uniformly practiced, and laws on the subject came later than on the schools. The earliest Jim Crow railroad-car law was enacted by Tennessee in 1881. There were increas-ing incidents involving Negroes with first-class tickets who were ejected from first-class or "ladies" coaches and Pullman cars, though for financial reasons most Negroes of both sexes ordi-narily bought second-class tickets and rode in the smoking car. As late as 1887, W. H. Councill, president of a black state college in Alabama, who customarily purchased a first-class ticket, was surprised to find himself directed to the smoking or Jim Crow coach. He filed suit with the newly established Inter-state Commerce Commission, charging discrimination in rail-road rates since his ticket had not been honored in the first-class coaches. Ruling on his and other similar complaints, the com-mission held that equal facilities must be provided for members of both races. This decision prompted a rush of "separate-but-equal" railroad legislation in the Southern states, all but three of which passed such laws between 1887 and 1891. In practice, first-class accommodations were not made available even to the most refined Negro ladies, who were relegated to the coarse and dirty environment of the smoking cars, used also by white male passengers with their cigars and profanity. The Supreme Court nevertheless upheld the validity of the separate-but-equal transportation laws in the famous *Plessy* v. *Ferguson* case of 1896. On the other hand, transportation segregation was not yet uniformly applied throughout the South. Blacks could still ride with whites in the first-class coaches in Virginia and the Carolinas until those states passed Jim Crow car laws at the very end of the century. Legislation requiring separate Pullman cars and waiting rooms did not come in most states until after 1900, though custom often supplied what the law left unsaid.

Thereafter the Jim Crow principle was applied with inexorable logic. For years streetcar segregation had been practiced unevenly by Southern traction companies. Georgia enacted a law on the matter in 1891, and after 1900 nearly all of the Southern states passed such legislation. Segregation had prevailed at an early date in state penal and welfare institutions and now became the universal practice in parks and other recreational facilities. As the textile industry moved into the piedmont, certain states protected the underpaid white workers against black competition by requiring segregation in the factories. In 1913 there was even agitation in North Carolina for restricting black farm ownership to certain areas. Beginning in 1910 a number of cities, including Baltimore, New Orleans, Louisville, Atlanta, Augusta, and Richmond, passed residential segregation ordinances, a practice that was declared unconstitutional by the Supreme Court in 1917.

The Southern race system also involved inequities in the administration of justice. Although the Supreme Court insisted that blacks had the right to sit on juries, they were, in fact, almost completely excluded. The convict-lease system, with its many abuses, had been instituted in Louisiana before the Civil

War and elsewhere in the South during Reconstruction, but under the Redeemers it expanded rapidly, to the profit of planters and industrialists and the misery of the prisoners. Lynching was another important instrument for maintaining the racial system. The number of black persons lynched, most of them in the South, reached its height in the 1880's and early 1890's, averaging about 100 a year during the two decades and climbing to a peak of 161 in 1892.* Thereafter lynchings declined somewhat, though they grew in barbarity as the number of those burned at the stake increased. Lynching was mainly a rural phenomenon; in the growing Southern cities mob violence became more common, exploding in the race riots at Wilmington, North Carolina, in 1898 and in Atlanta in 1906. Popular opinion held that Negroes were lynched for raping white women, and the hysteria arising from newspaper propaganda about such attacks precipitated the Atlanta race riot. Actually, in less than a third of the lynchings was the crime of rape even alleged, much less proved. Underlying both the Wilmington and Atlanta outbreaks was the hatred whipped up during the disfranchisement campaigns in North Carolina and Georgia.

Thus, piece by piece, the patterns of disfranchisement, segregation, and racial subordination were brought to completion during the early part of the twentieth century. It is important to emphasize that this racial system evolved over a long period of years. On the one hand, its roots went back to the antebellum period; much de facto segregation had existed during the height of Reconstruction; and mob violence was an essential element in the strategy of the Redeemers who overthrew the radical state governments in the 1870's. On the other hand, as late as the 1880's distinguished Southerners were accepting Negro voting as an accomplished fact, and in certain places blacks were still being called "mister," being buried in the same cemeteries as whites, and being served in white restaurants. Black expectations revealed the extent to which nonsegregated patterns per-

* The figure of 235 for 1892 is often given, but it includes whites as well as blacks.

sisted. W. H. Councill, even though dependent on the favor of state officials, did not become an "Uncle Tom" until after the railroad-car incident mentioned earlier. In 1894 even the accommodator Booker T. Washington noted with approval that by boycotting the Atlanta streetcars Negroes had recently secured the abrogation of a newly instituted segregation policy. As late as the period between 1898 and 1906, black citizens in about thirty Southern cities unsuccessfully employed the same technique when Jim Crow trolley cars were introduced in their communities. In Houston, Chattanooga, Nashville, and Savannah, the blacks even organized their own short-lived transportation companies. In 1905 Jacksonville, Florida, residents temporarily held the line by securing a court decision declaring the city's segregation ordinance unconstitutional. In the end, all the efforts proved unavailing, and the wave of segregation swept relentlessly on.

Southern Negroes might have continued the battle for their constitutional rights, but by the opening of the century it was clear that even the Supreme Court would permit only a very narrow definition of those rights. In 1883 the Court voided the Civil Rights Act of 1875 on the grounds that discrimination by individual citizens was not prohibited by the Fourteenth Amendment. The Court in 1896 went further and sanctioned segregation laws, enforced by the police power of the states, on the basis of the separate-but-equal doctrine. Then in 1898 it upheld literacy and poll-tax qualifications for voting. Five years later it refused to interfere with franchise restrictions that did not explicitly disqualify people because of race, color, or previous condition of servitude. Thus, the Court's actions emasculated the Fourteenth and Fifteenth Amendments and cloaked with respectability the subterfuges enacted by the Southern states.

One reason why the South was able to flout the Constitution was that by the end of the century Northerners were becoming more hostile toward blacks. This is revealed by the actions of the state governments, the attitudes of trade unions, and the policies of the national administrations in Washington. Protective state legislation, black officeholding, and the racially egalitarian policies of the Knights of Labor marked the 1880's as a period of rising status for Northern Negroes. But evasion of state civil-rights laws was easy, the progress in politics and labor proved temporary, and in retrospect it is clear that by the 1890's the Republican Presidents had all but deserted the Negro's cause.

During the 1880's blacks came to occupy positions in the legislatures and city councils and in a few cases on the bench in several areas of the North. Officeholding, which reached a high point around 1890, thereafter declined. To be sure, in Illinois there continued to be one or two Negroes in the legislature. But in Massachusetts, for example, though blacks still received appointive offices, the lawyer W. H. Lewis was the last one to sit in the legislature (1902); and in Boston, where there had been three blacks on the Common Council in 1894–5, only one served in 1909.

As for civil rights, Northern states generally gave legislative support to the Fourteenth Amendment. In 1874 Kansas and New York followed Massachusetts's earlier example in prohibiting segregation in places of public accommodation, and by 1880 blacks in the North secured recognition of their right to an education, albeit usually a segregated one. After the Supreme Court declared the federal Civil Rights Act unconstitutional in 1883, blacks and their friends agitated for state guarantees against discrimination. California and almost all of the Northern states east of the Mississippi River passed public accommodation laws. The typical statute forbade discrimination in restaurants, hotels, barbershops, theaters, public conveyances, and places of amusement. California and the majority of Northeastern states also abolished their separate schools.

Such laws, however, were of little value in the face of hostile public opinion. Relatively few cases came to the attention of the courts, the fines meted out to guilty parties were small, and local custom, particularly in areas· contiguous to the South, often acted as an effective deterrent to the exercise of rights protected by legislation. Moreover, school integration was commonly accomplished at the expense of black teachers who were excluded from jobs in the mixed systems. A student of conditions in southern Ohio in 1913 found that despite strong civil-rights legislation Negroes were excluded from restaurants, hotels, and some stores and were educated in separate schools. About the same time another investigator reported that in Pennsylvania "this disposition to discriminate against Negroes has greatly increased within the past decade." In Cleveland and Boston, where abolitionist traditions lingered longest, where schools were still integrated, and where a few Negroes achieved significant successes in the white business and professional world, even the old humanitarian supporters of the race were becoming indifferent. Nothing illustrated the trend of the times more dramatically than the race riots that occurred in New York City in 1900 and in Springfield, Illinois, in 1908. In fact, the New York riot was the first major racial clash in a Northern city since the draft riots of 1863.

Two thirds of the Northern blacks at the turn of the century were city dwellers, and like the 20 percent of Southern blacks who also lived in cities, most of them still had to work at menial occupations and at unskilled labor in heavy industry. In the North employers continued to find Negroes useful as strike-breakers. It was mainly discrimination on the part of organized labor that led Negroes to play this role in industrial conflict, a situation that in turn further exacerbated the antipathy between black and white workers.

Before the Civil War the weak trade-union movement had been highly discriminatory, and during Reconstruction the efforts of the leaders in the National Labor Union to include blacks foundered on the hostility of the skilled white workers who composed the membership of the organizations affiliated with it. In the 1880's, however, the Knights of Labor seriously sought to recruit black members, even in the South, and for a brief period a genuinely interracial trade-union movement seemed possible. In 1886 it was estimated that the Knights had 60,000 Negroes in a total membership of 700,000. In all sections of the country they formed both mixed and all-black assemblies.

A few of the latter admitted white members and became inter-racial. In the Southern cities craft unions had black locals; in Savannah, New Orleans, and Galveston, Negroes were integrated in longshoremen's units; and in New Orleans organized labor called a sympathy strike in support of a union of black draymen, who thereby won their demands. The Knights even organized Southern Negro farmers. Among the cotton pickers in Pulaski County, Arkansas, a group of perhaps a hundred black Knights unsuccessfully struck for twelve days in 1886. In the fall of 1887, nine thousand blacks and one thousand whites, in a mixed union, struck against the Louisiana sugar planters for higher wages. Except on a few plantations, the effort failed after a long and bitter conflict.

By the end of the decade, the American Federation of Labor, established in 1881, was superseding the declining Knights. At first the AFL took a stand against discriminatory practices on the part of its affiliated unions. In 1888 the International Association of Machinists, a largely Southern organization, applied for membership but was rejected because its constitution excluded blacks. In 1890 the federation went on record as opposing unions that barred black men and urged the machinists to remove their restriction. Finally in 1895 the union dropped the color provisions in its constitution and was accepted by the federation. But the machinists eliminated the color line in name only, as they maintained exclusion in the initiation ritual. Similarly, the International Brotherhood of Blacksmiths was barred from the federation in 1893 but admitted in 1897 after removing the offending clause from its constitution only. By the end of the century the AFL was even admitting unions with exclusion clauses in their constitutions. Federation leadership, although fearing the use of blacks as strikebreakers, was brought to accept, even condone, the practice of barring Negroes from a union or organizing them into powerless Jim Crow locals. A few AFL unions—the cigarmakers, the coal miners, the garment workers, and the longshoremen—did accept Negroes without discrimination. Some others, fearful of black competition in the skilled trades, admitted them with varying restrictions. Thus several building-trades unions barred Negroes in the North but admitted them in the South, where there were still substantial numbers of black craftsmen. In Nashville, where blacks outnumbered whites as artisans in 1880, whites joined the unions, often learned the skills from the black members, and then, having achieved a commanding majority, voted to eliminate the Negroes from membership as rapidly as possible. By 1910 control of the crafts in the city had passed to the whites.

By the turn of the century most unions excluded blacks to a greater or lesser extent—a dozen openly, the majority by subterfuges. Some unions, most notably perhaps the railroad brotherhoods, eliminated Negroes from certain types of work by striking against their employers. Yet on the railroads and elsewhere there were occasional strikes notable for their expression of interracial labor solidarity, as in the case of the Alabama coalmine strike of 1908. In fact, of the AFL unions, it was the United Mine Workers, with its thousands of black members in the coalfields from Pennsylvania and Ohio to Alabama, that was the most racially egalitarian. In that labor organization, despite considerable ambivalence toward blacks on the part of the white workers, blacks held office in the locals and, during the 1890's, one served two terms on the union's national executive board. Of the labor federations, however, only the syndicalist Industrial Workers of the World (organized in 1905) had an explicit philosophy of interracial unity which it applied even in the Deep South.

The policies of the Republican Party mirrored the changing attitudes of its Northern constituents. From championing the black cause it shifted first to compromise and then to acceptance of the Southern race system. The Compromise of 1877 revealed that the Republicans were unwilling to enforce the Reconstruction legislation in the South. During the 1880's President Chester A. Arthur courted antiblack "independent" political organizations in the South in an effort to increase Republican strength. Not only did the party fail to halt mob vio-

lence and disfranchisement, but it was a Republican Supreme
Court that found the Civil Rights Act unconstitutional; and it
was a Republican Congress that in 1890 repudiated campaign
pledges by failing to pass the Lodge Federal Elections Bill.
Then, during the 1890's, the Lily-white faction made its appearance, while Republican Presidents grew increasingly silent on
the question of black rights.

The impetuous Theodore Roosevelt alternately pleased and
angered Negroes by his actions. He won their approval by inviting Booker T. Washington to dinner at the White House, by
closing the Indianola, Mississippi, post office rather than acced-
ing to white demands that he dismiss the black postmistress
there, and by insisting on appointing a black as collector of the
Port of Charleston despite powerful Southern and senatorial
opposition. At the same time, he was playing a shifty game with
the antiblack Lily-white Republicans. He spoke favorably of
Southern traditions and falsely asserted that most lynchings
were caused by sexual assaults on white women. In 1906 he
summarily discharged three companies of the black 25th Regiment on unproved charges of rioting in Brownsville, Texas. No
action of the President hurt and angered Negroes more than
this one. William Howard Taft's pronouncements, while he
was still Secretary of War under Roosevelt, were also unaccept-
able to Negroes, for he endorsed ballot restrictions and criticized higher education for blacks. The race had been pleased by
Roosevelt's well-publicized appointments (though his policy
put fewer black men in office than his predecessors had), but
Negroes deplored President Taft's open policy of not appointing
Southern black men to office where whites objected. The Lily-
whites made even more progress under Taft than they had
under Roosevelt. He permitted segregation to be introduced in
a few of the federal office buildings. By the election of 1912
Negroes faced a choice among the Democratic candidate, Wilson, born in the South, who would make only the vaguest
promises to Negroes; the Republican candidate, Taft, who had
completely alienated the race; and the Progressive Party candidate, Roosevelt, who appealed to black voters in the North but

refused to seat Negro delegates from the South at the Progressive Party convention. Under the circumstances most blacks probably voted for Roosevelt. Those who supported Wilson soon discovered that he ignored Negroes when it came to making appointments and that he permitted even greater segregation in the federal office buildings.

By the opening of the twentieth century, Southern extremists were influencing public opinion in the North and West more than before. A spate of ultraracist books appeared with such titles as *The Negro a Beast* and *The Negro: A Menace to Civilization*. Southern polemicists held not only that blacks were an innately inferior, immoral, and criminal race that could never catch up with the whites in civilization, but that in fact freedom had caused a reversion to barbarism. Many of the Southern propagandists believed colonization the only alternative to violent extermination. There were differences in degree, but scarcely in basic outlook, between conservatives like Thomas Nelson Page, who glorified the aristocratic plantation tradition, and extremists like Governors Vardaman of Mississippi and Hoke Smith of Georgia, who voiced the hatreds of the lower classes. In the North weighty scholarly opinion in the biological and social sciences supported Southern racist doctrines. Distinguished anthropologists and anatomists regarded blacks as a separate species next to the ape, and eminent historians and political scientists reinterpreted Reconstruction in a manner favorable to the white South. Almost alone among the prominent social scientists, the anthropologist Franz Boas maintained that innate racial differences were inconsequential. Like the Southerners, Northerners widely believed that blacks were less industrious, less thrifty, less trustworthy, and less self-controlled than their own ancestors. These views were reinforced by the ideology of American overseas imperialism that justified white racial superiority and the "white man's burden." Probably nothing symbolized so clearly the thinking of the American public about Negroes at the eve of the First World War as the enormously popular racist melodrama, the movie *Birth of a Nation*.

2

In the face of the deteriorating conditions of the late nineteenth century, the dominant trends in Negro thinking shifted gradually from protest to accommodation, especially in the South. There was first of all a growing tendency to minimize the value of political participation. A few leaders, especially during the 1880's, openly advocated supporting the Democratic Party. More widespread was the belief that the race should accept the disfranchisement constitutions. When Isaiah Montgomery, the lone black member of the Mississippi constitutional convention of 1890, advocated this, his remarks were greeted with shock and dismay. "Judas" and "traitor" were words commonly used to describe him. Yet five years later, when the black delegates to the South Carolina constitutional convention proposed the acceptance of literacy and/or property qualifications, as long as they were equitably applied to both races, it did not seem so extraordinary. This formula was acceptable to the more conservative blacks. Even if honestly applied, it would have disfranchised a greater proportion of blacks than whites. In actual practice, of course, these qualifications were administered dishonestly, drastically reducing the remaining number of black voters. Nevertheless, the ideas provided a face-saving device for Negroes by holding out the hope that as they acquired property and education they could gain the franchise.

If politics was closing as an avenue of racial advancement, if segregation was growing apace, and if whites were becoming more inimical, what route lay open for the ambitious blacks who were striving to rise up from the disabilities of slavery? Most Southern and many Northern leaders felt it lay in the economic realm, and most articulate Negroes throughout the country stressed the ideals of self-help and racial solidarity.

Protest organizations like the Afro-American Council, founded in 1890, acted on the principle that since whites had lost interest in blacks, black men would have to stick together and help themselves. In extreme form the ideologies of withdrawal were manifested in the continuing interest in African colonization on the part of a few of the articulate and in efforts to establish all-black communities.

Usually, however, self-help and racial solidarity were still combined with an economic ideology that preached the acquisition of middle-class virtues and black support of black business. Advocates of this economic philosophy looked in two directions. They insisted upon the necessity of Negroes "buying black" if black business was to develop in the face of declining white support for black barbers, artisans, and retail merchants. They also held that if Negroes acquired wealth and middle-class respectability, the race would thus earn acceptance from whites and the walls of prejudice would crumble. On the one hand, this cluster of ideologies functioned as an accommodation to the system of segregation and discrimination; in fact, in contrast with the 1850's when this viewpoint was held by militant protest leaders like Frederick Douglass, in the expression of Southern leaders it now became explicitly identified with a program of conciliation and accommodation. On the other hand, this way of thinking also functioned as a means of inculcating group pride and self-respect.

This cluster of ideologies became dominant not only because of the declining status of Negroes in American society but also because there was a fundamental shift in the character of black business and the Negro class structure. During the last third of the nineteenth century, the entrepreneurial class in the black community continued to depend in considerable part upon the support of white customers. As before the Civil War, this group was composed primarily of barbers, skilled artisans, hackmen and draymen, grocers, and caterers. In certain Southern cities the more prominent carpenters and masons had become contractors who built residences for whites. The more successful among these entrepreneurs, along with the better-educated ministers, still formed an important part of the black upper class, but the inclusion of civil servants, postal workers, college-trained teachers, Pullman porters of good family background, the growing number of physicians, and an occasional lawyer reflected the occupational diversification that had taken place. Accordingly, by the end of the century the domestic servants in wealthy families, the headwaiters and bell captains in fashionable restaurants and hotels, and the stewards at exclusive country clubs were beginning to decline in social status.

By about 1900 these economic and social changes were well under way. A growing antipathy on the part of whites toward trading with Negro businessmen and changes in technology and business organization forced many of the small entrepreneurs out of business. At the same time the urbanization of blacks and the increasing tendency to live in ghetto neighborhoods supplied a base for professionals and businessmen dependent on the black market. Of course certain business people, such as newspaper editors, undertakers, some barbers, and storekeepers, had always relied on the Negro market, and these now grew in number. The most important new enterprises catering to blacks were banks (the first two founded in 1888), cemetery and realty associations, and insurance companies.

Examples of what contemporaries referred to as "cooperative" businesses were not lacking in previous years, but their number rose sharply in the last decade of the nineteenth and early years of the twentieth century. The most celebrated of the earlier enterprises had been the Chesapeake and Marine Railroad and Dry Dock Company, formed by the Baltimore ship calkers after a strike against black mechanics and longshoremen resulted in the dismissal of a thousand Negroes from the city's shipyards in 1863. The company operated successfully for eighteen years. During the 1880's and 1890's exclusion from white cemeteries and difficulties in borrowing money from white lending agencies played an important role in the creation of cemetery and building-and-loan associations. In Philadelphia, for example, the first building-and-loan association was founded in 1886; twenty years later the number in that city reached ten. Successful realty companies also appeared, like one in New York which, employing over two hundred persons, was the largest black enterprise in the city before the company collapsed around 1910.

Especially significant was the growth of Negro insurance, today the most important of black business enterprises. This development was closely related to the mutual-benefit fraternal organizations, which enjoyed a great boom beginning in the 1890's. The 1880's had been the heyday of the local, usually church-oriented mutual-benefit and burial societies. Though such organizations are to be found in the rural South to this day, and though a few of them, like the Afro-American Industrial Insurance Society of Jacksonville, developed into full-fledged insurance companies, by the end of the century they were eclipsed by the fraternal orders. Among the secret orders the Odd Fellows forged into the lead, growing from eighty-nine lodges to a thousand lodges in the eighteen years between 1868 and 1886, and then more than quadrupling the number of its lodges in the next eighteen years, 1886–1904. By 1906 the organization had investments of $3 million. The Masons and the black Knights of Pythias (formed in 1880) also experienced significant expansion. Among the nonsecret, quasi-religious fraternal orders, the Galilean Fishermen and the Independent Order of St. Luke (founded in Richmond in 1865) were among those enjoying phenomenal growth, but the most celebrated was the Grand Fountain of the United Order of True Reformers founded in Virginia in 1881. Before it failed in 1911 it had become a mutual-benefit stock company with a membership of 100,000, operating a bank, five department stores, and a weekly newspaper in addition to its insurance department. Inspired by the success of these associations, the secret orders improved their insurance features. Meanwhile, regularly chartered mutual-aid and beneficial societies, specializing in weekly sickness and health insurance, had appeared (the first one in Baltimore in 1885). The final step in the evolution of Negro insurance was the appearance of the regularly chartered legal-reserve company, the first one being organized in Mississippi in 1909.

In the life of John Merrick, the man chiefly responsible for North Carolina Mutual, one of the two largest black life-insurance companies, one observes the evolution of black insurance from the quasi-religious fraternal society through the chartered mutual-aid organization to the legal-reserve company. Merrick was a Durham barber who catered to upper-class whites. In 1883 he and some friends obtained control of a quasi-religious fraternal order, the Royal Knights of King David. Then in 1898 the business was twice reorganized, first as the North Carolina Mutual and Provident Association, and then as an insurance company. Alonzo Herndon, who in 1905 founded the Atlanta Life Insurance Company, today the chief rival of North Carolina Mutual, had a similar personal career, though his company began as a frankly commercial venture rather than as a mutual-benefit society.

Related also to the fraternal organizations was the development of Negro banking. After the failure of the federally owned Freedmen's Bank following the panic of 1873, the first two black banks were the True Reformers' Bank in Richmond and the Capital Savings Bank of Washington, both founded in 1888. By 1900 there were four black banks. Thereafter the number increased rapidly, reaching fifty-six by 1911. Most of these, however, went under in subsequent financial depressions. The great majority of the banks originated as depositories for the fraternal orders. The importance of the fraternities in the development of black banking is suggested by the fact that in 1907 the first and third largest in capitalization and deposits were the True Reformers' Bank and the Mechanics Savings Bank, the latter established in Richmond by the grand chancellor of the Virginia Knights of Pythias.

It is also noteworthy that although the secret fraternal organizations like the Masons and the Odd Fellows had lost the close connections with the churches that had existed before the Civil War, the relationships between the ministers and the mutual-benefit societies survived to a considerable extent in the prominent role clergymen played in organizing the insurance societies and banking enterprises. The True Reformers' Bank, the Galilean Fishermen's Bank, and the St. Luke's Bank were all either founded by ministers or closely connected with the churches. Again, in Philadelphia the pastor of the Berean Presbyterian Church organized the largest building-and-loan association in the state as a service provided by his "institutional" church. By the end of the century, however, this ministerial influence was declining, and it waned even more during the twentieth century as the black community leadership and class structure became more highly differentiated.

The impact of the newer type of business enterprise and the expansion of the black entrepreneurial and professional group were evident in the changing nature of the Negro class structure. In general, between about 1890 and the 1920's the forces of segregation and discrimination were instrumental in creating a *petite bourgeoisie* of professionals and businessmen almost completely dependent for their livelihood on the black masses. The majority were self-made men, of humble origin, on the whole a darker-skinned group than the older upper class, less likely to be descended from antebellum house slaves or from free people of color. They formed an ambitious, striving middle class, and the more successful among them were achieving upper-class status before the First World War. The process occurred at different rates and times in different cities, most markedly in those communities where the largest in-migration and residential segregation were taking place.

It was chiefly from the members of this rising middle class, and from men of the older upper class who, like Merrick and Herndon, turned from serving white customers to serving the black community, that the main impetus for the philosophy of Negro support for black business emanated. The whole process is dramatically symbolized by a comparison of the sources of two of the largest fortunes made by Negroes before the First World War. R. R. Church of Memphis, the son of a wealthy white man, was reputed to have amassed over a million dollars, first as a saloonkeeper, and later out of speculation and investment in white real estate between Reconstruction and the time of his death in 1912. A few hundred miles north on the Mississippi River, with a business started in the 1890's, a St. Louis laundress, Madam C. J. Walker, reportedly made a million dollars as a result of her invention of the first commercially successful hair-straightening process. Madam Walker was never accepted by "the cream of colored society," but in the 1920's her daughter became a noted social leader among the literary and artistic elite in Harlem.

3

Interwoven with these changes in economic life and outlook and in the class structure was the educational system. The public schools remained inferior. Even after the revised land-grant college act of 1890 compelled each of the Southern states to establish a black land-grant college, the only adequate higher education could be obtained in the private schools. These institutions, especially the better ones, continued to be identified with middle- and upper-class blacks and were the source of the great majority of black leaders, particularly in Southern communities. This was especially true of the Congregationalist colleges in the South and the Presbyterian Church's Lincoln University in Pennsylvania, in spite of their paternalistic reluctance to employ blacks as teachers and administrators. (The Methodists and Baptists, on the other hand, were more sensitive to black opinion on this matter, for the Methodists had many Southern Negro members and the Baptist schools were aided financially by the black Baptist conventions. Both denominations were using blacks to staff their schools well before the end of the nineteenth century.)

In the 1890's the liberal-arts colleges were being temporarily eclipsed in popular esteem and financial resources by the rise of industrial education. "Industrial education" was a catchall term that included manual training, home economics, and preparation for farming and for trades such as shoemaking, printing, carpentry, and bricklaying. A number of abolitionists and antebellum Negro conventions had been interested in manual-labor schools; during Reconstruction many of the freedmen's schools boasted of "industrial work," which usually consisted merely of home economics and odd jobs for the men. At several places, however, most notably Hampton Institute in Virginia, successful manual-labor and vocational institutes were established.

In the 1880's industrial education was widely adopted in the curricula of white high schools, and, under the aegis of the John F. Slater Fund, industrial and agricultural education on the secondary level became popular among a large number of black institutions, even among many known for their college departments. Both Hampton Institute's founder, Samuel Chapman Armstrong, and the Slater Fund trustees viewed industrial education as particularly adapted to fitting Negroes for the environment in which they were to live. At the same time it would uplift them by creating a class of self-sufficient artisan-entrepreneurs in farming and the skilled trades. Throughout the writings of the advocates of industrial education there was a stress upon the moral virtues which it allegedly implanted and which were regarded as essential to the Negro's progress as a man and a citizen. But in the view of these educators and philanthropists it would be years—even centuries—before blacks would be prepared to enjoy the rights of citizenship equally with whites.

Industrial education was widely adopted because philanthropists encouraged it and because Southern whites saw it as keeping blacks in the subordinate position of working with their hands rather than preparing them for professional careers. Industrial training was a particularly expensive form of education. Therefore, in view of the inadequate funds received by black schools, they had inferior, inadequate programs, except for a few like Tougaloo and Spelman, Tuskegee and Hampton. Ironically, the vogue of industrial education came when white artisans were forcing Negroes out of the skilled trades. For both these reasons the black graduates of industrial schools were usually unable to practice their skills, and most of them became teachers of the trades rather than the independent artisans the propagandists for industrial education dreamed of creating. Nevertheless, many black leaders found industrial education appealing, partly because philanthropy subsidized it, and even more because it fitted the moral-economic ideology of advancement that was in the ascendancy. And though clothed in a philosophy of racial advancement, its advocates—from Samuel

Chapman Armstrong to Booker T. Washington—saw it as a platform of compromise and accommodation between the North, the South, and the Negro. It satisfied those philanthropists and leading Southerners who opposed race equality, yet liked to think that they were in favor of black uplift. Finally it enabled many Negroes to convince themselves that it was a way not only of obtaining money for black schools, but also of indirectly and ultimately elevating the race to the point where it would be accorded its citizenship rights.

Although the major thrust of educational philanthropy in the Southern states at the turn of the century was to improve the quality of white public schools, black institutions received some assistance in addition to that accorded to industrial education. The Rockefeller interests, working through the General Education Board (founded in 1902), made some contributions to black institutions and began the financial aid that was to make Spelman College one of the two best-endowed colleges for women in the South. Andrew Carnegie contributed libraries to a number of black institutions, ranging from Booker T. Washington's Tuskegee Normal and Industrial Institute to Fisk University. During the early years of the twentieth century other funds for black education were established, most notably the Anna T. Jeanes Fund (1905), which paid the salaries of supervising teachers in order to raise standards in rural schools, and the Julius Rosenwald Fund (1913), which contributed money for the erection of school buildings.

4

Epitomizing these varied strands—accommodation, self-help, racial solidarity, acceptance of disfranchisement, economic accumulation and middle-class virtues, and industrial education—and doing more than anyone else to popularize this particular complex of ideas, was Hampton Institute's most distinguished alumnus, Booker T. Washington, who was catapulted into world fame in 1895 by a speech he made at the Cotton States and International Exposition in Atlanta.

Washington declared his belief that the solution of the race problem would come through an application of the gospel of wealth. He urged Negroes to stay in the South, since it was in the South that the black was given a man's chance in business. Whites were urged to help uplift blacks and thereby further the prosperity and well-being of the region. Coupled with this appeal to the white South's self-interest was conciliatory phraseology and a criticism of Negroes. Washington deprecated politics and the Reconstruction experience. He criticized blacks for forgetting that the masses of the race were to live by working with their hands and for permitting their grievances to overshadow their opportunities. He reminded whites of the loyalty and fidelity of blacks, "the most patient, faithful, law-abiding, and unresentful people that the world has seen." He denied any interest in social intermingling when he said, "In all things that are purely social we can be as separate as the fingers, yet one as the hand in all matters essential to mutual progress." He asked only for "justice" and an end to sectional differences and racial animosities. These, combined with material prosperity, would usher in a new era for "our beloved South."

Washington advocated a conciliatory and gradualist philosophy. He minimized the extent of race prejudice or discrimination and referred to Southern whites as the black man's best friends. He held that discrimination and prejudice were basically the Negroes' own fault. Poor and ignorant as most of them were, blacks naturally alienated white people. They must, therefore, take the chief responsibility for their own advancement. Whites could help, but basically blacks would have to come up from slavery by themselves. Accordingly, Washington accepted segregation and criticized political activity. He believed that economic accumulation and the cultivation of morality were the methods best calculated to raise the black people's status in American society. Agricultural and industrial training was far more appropriate for the mass of blacks, just then, than education for the professions.

Not perceiving the inexorable trends toward urbanization and technological change, his program stressed farming and animal husbandry and training in the handcrafts. He constantly deplored the tendency of black farmers to move to the cities, and though his message was most successfully communicated to the black urban businessmen, Washington's vision was fundamentally of virtuous, landowning peasants proving their worth in their native Southland. He even approved literacy and property qualifications for voting; they would stimulate Negroes to obtain education and wealth. Yet, while stressing the need for Negro self-improvement, Washington insisted that blacks should be proud of their race and should loyally support it. Especially should blacks support black businessmen, in order to advance the race economically. With such solid economic foundations, blacks would receive their constitutional rights and the respect of whites. But Washington was basically tactful, vague, and even ambiguous, so that most whites confused his means for his ends and assumed that for an indefinite period he anticipated that Negroes would continue to occupy a subordinate place in American society.

Booker T. Washington's public image as an accommodator was one thing; his covert behind-the-scenes activity was another. Privately he appeared to contradict his public stance. He might denounce higher education as a "bacillus," but his own children received not only training in the trades but a thorough grounding in the liberal arts. Overtly he might urge blacks to acquiesce in the separate-but-equal doctrine; privately he had entrée to white social circles in the North and abroad that few Southern whites could enter, and secretly he aided the fight against railroad segregation. On one occasion, working through intermediaries, he hired a lobbyist to defeat legislation that, if passed, would have encouraged segregation on interstate trains in the North. Overtly he denied any interest in politics and urged blacks to soft-pedal the desire for the franchise; behind the scenes he was the most influential politician in the history of American Negroes and surreptitiously fought the disfranchisement laws. He served as political adviser on Negro affairs to Presidents Roosevelt and Taft. All black men who were appointed to office by Roosevelt, and most appointed by Taft, were recommended by Booker T. Washington. Among his most notable recommendations were: Robert H. Terrell, who served as judge of the municipal court in Washington, 1901–21; Charles W. Anderson, collector of internal revenue in New York, 1905–15; and William H. Lewis, assistant attorney general, 1911–13. These were the highest federal judicial and executive appointments of Negroes thus far made; and they were not to be equaled or surpassed until after the Second World War. Even more revealing of Washington's private ideological ambivalences was the way in which he clandestinely spent thousands of dollars financing the fruitless test cases taken to the Supreme Court against the Southern disfranchisement amendments.

Washington wielded more power within the black community than anyone else had ever done. This authority derived from his political influence and from his popularity with the philanthropists. No black schools received contributions from Carnegie, Rockefeller, and lesser donors without Washington's approval. In short, ambitious men and institutions found it difficult to get ahead without the Tuskegeean's support. Washington also assiduously cultivated influential leaders in the black community; for over a decade it was impossible to achieve a major position in the Negro churches if one attacked him, and judicious advertisements and contributions kept the Negro press in line.

Booker T. Washington's career was truly a remarkable one. Born an obscure slave in western Virginia, he rose to a pinnacle of international fame. He appropriately entitled his autobiography *Up from Slavery*, and indeed his life epitomized what thrift and industry—combined with talent and diplomacy—might accomplish in an age of accommodation.

5

Despite Washington's prominence, black protest never entirely disappeared. The Afro-American Council, which lasted, with periods of inactivity, from 1890 to 1908, had been founded as a militant protest organization and always retained something of a protest outlook. Its sessions at the close of the century were enlivened in fact by attacks on Washington by such people as the noted antilynching crusader Ida Wells-Barnett. By then, however, the Council was coming under Washington's influence, and after 1900 its annual conventions expressed a rather mild point of view until Washington's critics obtained control in 1906–7. Even in the South, as our previous discussion of streetcar boycotts illustrates, protest activity had not completely vanished, but the chief opposition to accommodation came from a small group of Northern intellectuals. For the most part they were an upper-class elite of editors, lawyers, ministers, and teachers. The majority of them had attended prestigious Northern universities. From Harvard came the two best-known critics of Washington's policies: William Monroe Trotter and W. E. B. Du Bois.

Trotter in 1901 founded the militant Boston *Guardian*, the most caustic of the handful of newspapers that opposed Washington. It epitomized the anti-Bookerite sentiment of "Radical"* New England blacks. In July 1903, Trotter and his associates unsuccessfully challenged the Tuskegeean for control of the Afro-American Council. The following month the embittered Radicals precipitated disorder and pandemonium when they heckled Washington at a public meeting in Boston. This "Boston Riot" widened the cleavage between the two groups, especially after Trotter was jailed and his antagonists financed a libel suit against the *Guardian*.

A few months prior to this event, W. E. B. Du Bois had published a volume of essays, *The Souls of Black Folk*, which contained an incisive and critical analysis of Washington's leadership. James Weldon Johnson, the noted author and later executive secretary of the National Association for the Advancement of Colored People (NAACP), credited Du Bois's analysis of racial leadership with effecting "a coalescence of the more radical elements . . . thereby creating a split of the race into two contending camps." During the 1890's Du Bois, who

---

* "Radical" Negroes in this period were anti-Washington advocates of militant protest.

held a doctorate from Harvard and was a professor at Atlanta University, had supported most of Booker T. Washington's program. He had been a strong advocate of self-help and of Negro support of black business, and in 1890 had even opposed the Lodge Federal Elections Bill on the grounds that many blacks were "not fit for the responsibility of republican government. When you have the right sort of black voters you will need no election laws." The chief differences between the two men had been that Du Bois never flattered the white South as Washington did and that Du Bois saw a place for higher education as well as industrial training. Now, in 1903, in *Souls of Black Folk*, Du Bois, though he continued to share Washington's interest in racial solidarity and self-help, denounced the Tuskegeean for condoning the caste system and for shifting to blacks the major responsibility for their elevation. Du Bois held that Washington's accommodating ideology had brought together the South, the North, and the Negro in a monumental compromise that "practically accepted the alleged inferiority of the Negro." He observed that in the period of Washington's ascendancy segregation and disfranchisement laws had risen in number, while philanthropic support for higher education had declined, and he held Washington accountable for the acceleration of these trends. Because Washington's popularity with whites had led blacks to accept his leadership, criticism of him had virtually disappeared. Du Bois hoped, however, that prominent blacks would now speak out, for it had become obvious that justice could not be achieved through "indiscriminate flattery"; that Negroes could not gain their rights by voluntarily throwing them away or obtain respect by constantly belittling themselves; that, on the contrary, black citizens must speak out constantly against oppression and discrimination.

In Du Bois's view, the Negro race could be saved only by the "Talented Tenth"—i.e., the minority who had received a liberal-arts education and thus were in a position to elevate blacks both culturally and economically. In his words, "Progress in human affairs is more often a pull than a push, a surging forward of the exceptional man, and the lifting of his duller brethren." Du

Bois was disturbed by Washington's exclusive preoccupation with industrial education and the financial support whites gave it at the expense of black colleges. Du Bois did not deprecate industrial education and in fact agreed that it made a significant contribution in teaching the masses of the race to work, but he reminded Washington that many of the teachers of the industrial and elementary schools had attended liberal-arts institutions, and that until many more did so, black leadership and the Negro race would be seriously retarded.

In order to inaugurate an organized program of public agitation for the Negro's constitutional rights, Du Bois in 1905 founded the Niagara Movement. In sharp vigorous language the Niagara declarations placed the responsibility for the race problem squarely on the shoulders of whites. White America was crisply told that blacks were dissatisfied and would continue to be until they had obtained voting rights and "the abolition of all caste distinctions based simply on race and color." In Philadelphia and Chicago its members actively opposed school segregation. The movement's legal redress committee won a railroad segregation suit, receiving a judgment of one penny in damages. Although the concrete achievements of the Niagara Movement were indeed few, it clearly articulated the black protest, contrasting the Washingtonian assertions that Negroes were content to make the climb from slavery by "natural and gradual processes." The Niagara men told whites that they should not be lulled into thinking that "the Negro-American assents to inferiority, is submissive under oppression and apologetic before insult. . . . We do not hesitate to complain, and to complain loudly and insistently."

Washington used all reservoirs of power at his disposal to silence his critics. He placed spies in radical organizations, attempted to deprive opponents of their government jobs, subsidized the black press to ignore or attack "the opposition," successfully exerted pressure to prevent the election of radicals to high office in the black churches, and used his enormous influence with the philanthropists to divert funds away from educators who were inimical to him. Washington's control over the advancement of blacks in government, education, and the church probably discouraged many ambitious men from affiliating with the Niagara Movement.

The Niagara Movement was thus no match for Washington. It was further weakened by a rupture between Du Bois and Trotter in 1907. After that the organization merely limped along. Nevertheless, particularly in view of the Tuskegeean's opposition, it was significant because, as the journalist Ray Stannard Baker reported, "It represents, genuinely, a more or less prevalent point of view among many coloured people."

While the Niagara Movement was losing its momentum, liberal whites who had previously supported Washington were becoming increasingly impatient with his tactics and with his efforts to monopolize black leadership. Outstanding among this group was Oswald Garrison Villard, the grandson of William Lloyd Garrison and publisher of the New York *Evening Post*. The tide of segregation, disfranchisement, and racial violence seemed irresistible and in 1908, in a letter to Washington, Villard concluded that only "a strong central defense committee" could effectively advance Negro interests. In 1909, in response to a call issued by Villard, a National Negro Conference was held in New York which led to the formation of the National Association for the Advancement of Colored People. Those present included prominent members of the Niagara Movement and eminent white Progressives and Christian Socialists. A number of the black radicals who attended, most notably Du Bois, also considered themselves Socialists. It should be emphasized, however, that only a small minority of white Progressives were supporters of the NAACP. Most Progressives were either supporters of Washington, like Roosevelt, or were, like Wilson, quite indifferent to the Negro. In fact Washington's *petit bourgeois* philosophy of thrift and industry and self-help reflected the basic values of most American leaders at that period, whether conservative or progressive.

In their speeches at the conference radical leaders like Ida Wells-Barnett and Du Bois stressed the importance of the ballot. The conferees denounced mob violence and segregation, demanded academic training for the gifted, and above all insisted on the right to vote. The NAACP did not actually unite with the Niagara Movement, but most of its members joined the new organization. The interracial character of the NAACP was essential to the success of its early work. The prestige of the names of well-known white Progressives like Villard, Lillian Wald, Jane Addams, John Haynes Holmes, Moorfield Storey, and Clarence Darrow gave the agitation for Negro rights better financial support and, more important, a wider audience. Except for Du Bois, who became director of publicity and editor of the Association's organ, the *Crisis*, all of the chief officials were at first white. Several of these white leaders seemed somewhat paternalistic in their dealings with black associates in the NAACP. Nevertheless, as Du Bois observed, the interracial tensions during the early days of the organization were mild when compared to those in the abolitionist movement. In any case, from the first the real backbone of the Association consisted of an elite, college-educated black membership. By 1914 the Association had six thousand members in fifty branches. Mainly a legal-action organization from the very beginning, the NAACP achieved its first important victory just a few months before Washington's death in 1915 when the United States Supreme Court declared the Oklahoma grandfather clause unconstitutional.

Beginning in 1909 Booker T. Washington took steps to limit the effectiveness of the new organization, and the old pattern of various forms of pressure was repeated. For their part Du Bois and his black associates openly attacked Washington, though Villard insisted that this was not the official policy of the NAACP and encouraged the efforts of R. R. Moton of Hampton Institute, later Washington's successor at Tuskegee, to effect an understanding between the two groups.

For the first decade of the century at least, the majority of articulate Negroes had supported Washington. This was even true of many of the Northern intellectuals, for originally only a small minority of them had deemed it desirable to battle the Tuskegeean. Many of them, it is true, did not endorse his entire program wholeheartedly, and others changed their attitudes toward Washington over the years. Yet he enjoyed enormous support in the black community. What were the reasons for this?

First, there was the discouraging trend of the times. Protest, agitation, political action had failed. There had been a definite trend in the direction of accommodation in the 1880's and 1890's, and at the turn of the century certain prominent protest leaders, who would later be among Washington's most prominent critics, in their despair thought that his method might be of some help. Even Du Bois had expressed an ideology remarkably similar to Washington's. Only when it became evident that the worsening situation persisted in the face of Washington's program did many who had supported him change their minds.

Second, Washington's emphasis upon economic development and black support of Negro business undoubtedly attracted the majority of the rising bourgeoisie, whose income was based on the Negro market. And in the South those who still depended on white customers were drawn to that side of his philosophy that insisted upon the value of conciliating Southern whites, whose respect for business acumen would, Washington believed, lead them to patronize energetic black entrepreneurs.

Nor can one neglect Washington's power over political appointments and philanthropy as a third factor in shaping ideological expression during his ascendancy, making the combination of ideas he represented more palatable than they otherwise would have been. There is a fascinating irony in noting, for example, that the *sine qua non* in receiving Washington's endorsement for political office was to declare constantly that, for blacks, officeholding was unwise or unimportant. School officials, finding Washington's blessing essential for securing the funds from the philanthropists, cultivated Washington and endorsed his leadership and ideology. With ample backing from Andrew Carnegie, Washington in 1900 founded the National Negro Business League, which provided him with an influential platform for propagandizing the values of thrift, industry, self-help, and black support of Negro business, as well as for down-grading the values of agitation and the franchise. Washington's income from speaking and philanthropy enabled him to use advertisements and, in half a dozen cases, actual subsidies to encourage newspaper editors to support him and his program.

Finally, Washington's very prominence in the eyes of white America drew black support for his program, his fame making the complex of ideas that he represented far more acceptable than it otherwise would have been. Beyond this, his achieve-ment made him the very image of success for countless thou-sands in the black community, a model to be not only admired but emulated as well.

Space here will not allow exploration of the complexities of thought in the age of Booker T. Washington. A number of men shifted from one point of view to another. Some, especially in the North, saw no contradiction in endorsing Washington's leadership while engaging in protest themselves; an overwhelm-ing majority of articulate Northerners supported both protest and economic accumulation, both citizenship rights and racial solidarity, and many tried to maintain friendship with both the Bookerites and the Radicals during the bitter struggle. Du Bois himself consistently encouraged the building of Negro enter-prise and enthused over black support of black business, or what he described as a "group economy," which he viewed as the only way to advance the race economically, given the cir-cumstances under which blacks lived.

Though the Niagara Movement was disappearing by 1909, black protest grew stronger with the founding of the NAACP. At the very time that the NAACP, with its prominent backers, was making black protest more respectable, Washington's power was declining. He had less political influence with Taft than with Roosevelt and none at all with Wilson. Meanwhile, it was clear that even if, as has been claimed, his conciliatory program perhaps had slowed down the pace of deterioration in the Negro's status, it certainly had not halted the process. Given this combination of circumstances, a revival of black protest was almost inevitable. By the time Washington died, even some of his closest friends found it wise to identify themselves with the NAACP. And a year after his death, the NAACP played an ironic master stroke by inviting James Weldon Johnson, one of the most versatile figures in the Washington camp, to join its staff as national organizer.

VI

Black Men in the Urban Age:
The Rise of the Ghetto

AFTER THE CIVIL WAR and Emancipation, the major
watershed in American black history was the Great Migration
to Northern cities that began during the First World War.
According to the census of 1910, blacks were overwhelmingly
rural and Southern; approximately three out of four lived in
rural areas and nine out of ten lived in the South. A half century later Negroes were mainly an urban population, almost
three fourths of them being city dwellers. About half lived outside of the old slave states. The changes in the texture of Afro-
American life that have resulted are enormous, though unfortunately the subject is one that has yet to be systematically
studied.

232

1

Migration of Southern black people searching for better conditions was not new. In the years since the Civil War there had been a steady drift of blacks to Southern urban centers, along with a trickle to the North. Negroes left the land at about the same rate as Southern whites and for the same economic reasons. Moreover, there was a considerable interstate and intrastate movement of black farmers into newly developed agricultural lands, particularly in Florida, parts of Georgia and Alabama, the Yazoo-Mississippi delta of northwestern Mississippi, and Arkansas and Texas, resulting in a net southwestward movement of the center of Negro population. At certain dramatic times, such as during the Kansas Exodus of 1879, black migrants, and more especially their supporters among the better-educated classes, expressed an ideology that protested against all aspects of race discrimination. But the main push seems to have been economic. Negroes left worn-out land and moved toward more fertile fields in an effort to raise themselves from day laborers or sharecroppers to cash renters and even farm owners. In fact, as the sociologist Charles S. Johnson has demonstrated, often the largest black migration was into counties with the highest incidences of mob violence and lynchings. Though the evidence is sketchy, it appears that the peaks of black movement were during periods of acute economic crisis—toward the close of the depression of the 1870's, at the height of the Populist-agrarian agitation around 1890, and perhaps again during the minor depression that hit the United States on the eve of the First World War.

In 1912 the year-old National Urban League, the major social-welfare agency working among blacks, reported that "the migration of Negroes to the cities, as a part of the general movement . . . to the cities, is a fact of common observation." Between 1890 and 1910 the proportion of Negroes classified as urban by the United States census rose from about 20 to 27 percent. In the latter year there were a dozen cities that had over forty thousand Negroes. Between 1900 and 1910 large percentage increases in the black population occurred in New South cities like Birmingham (215 percent) and Atlanta (45 percent). New York City had a gain of 51 percent, while Philadelphia and Chicago each reported increases of more than 30 percent. The growing northward movement was noted by Du Bois as early as 1903 when he asserted that "the most significant economic change among Negroes in the last ten or twenty years has been their influx into northern cities." About that time New York had three fourths as many blacks as New Orleans, Philadelphia had almost twice as many as Atlanta, and Chicago had more than Savannah. During the next years the population movement produced even more striking consequences. According to the census of 1910, two cities, Washington and New York, had over ninety thousand Negroes. Three others, New Orleans, Baltimore, and Philadelphia had over eighty thousand. Of these five cities, only one was in the Deep South.

Those blacks who moved to the cities in the decades preceding the First World War entered an environment in which racial lines were being more and more tightly drawn. One manifestation of this trend was the expansion of residential segregation. The pattern of Negroes living in scattered enclaves about the town, with some individuals here and there living in white neighborhoods, was giving way to larger concentrations of blacks limited to one or two sections of a city. Mixed neighborhoods survived in the older sections of Southern seaports like Charleston and New Orleans, but the New South mercantile and industrial centers like Atlanta and Birmingham had known only residential segregation. In the major cities of the Border and Northern states the growth of ghettos was greatly accentuated. As the Fisk University sociologist and National Urban League official George Edmund Haynes observed in 1913, "New York has its 'San Juan Hill' in the West Sixties, and its Harlem district of over 35,000 [concentrated] within about eighteen city blocks; Philadelphia has its Seventh Ward; Chicago has its State Street, Washington its Northwest Neighborhood, and Baltimore its Druid Hill Avenue. Louisville has its

Chestnut Street and its Smoketown: Atlanta its West End and Auburn Avenue." The rapidity and intensity of the process varied from city to city. Chicago blacks were the most highly segregated in the nation, while those in Detroit, though concentrated on the city's east side, mostly still resided in mixed neighborhoods.

The Great Migration of the World War I era stimulated trends already under way. While blacks were clearly dissatisfied with the whole pattern of race relations in the South, it was an economic crisis arising from several converging factors that precipitated the population movement. Cotton agriculture was suffering from the ravages of the boll weevil, which had entered the United States from Mexico and gradually moved eastward through Texas. Then in 1915 disastrous floods in Alabama and Mississippi increased the misery of hundreds of thousands of rural blacks. At the same time, Northern industry, fed by demands from the Allies in Europe, greatly needed unskilled and semiskilled labor. Since the world war cut off immigration from Europe, some Northern manufacturers encouraged the poverty-stricken Negroes to leave the South. Their efforts were greatly aided by several Northern black newspapers, particularly the Chicago *Defender*, which painted a glowing picture of Northern living conditions and denounced Southern racism. Indeed, as in earlier periods, much of the explanation given by contemporaries emphasized disfranchisement, Jim Crow, and mob violence.

The result of all these forces was a clear-cut reversal of the main tendencies in the black population movement since Emancipation. The principal direction of black migration shifted away from the undeveloped Southern rural areas toward the cities, particularly of the North. Nearly a half million left the South during and shortly after World War I and observers found the effects startling. For example, Chicago's black population jumped from 44,000 to 110,000 between 1910 and 1920, while Cleveland's more than quadrupled, rising from 8,000 to 34,000. There were accounts of Southern towns practically depopulated of Negro residents, of black preachers, physicians, and morticians moving North because of the departure of the people whom they served. Southern states and communities, alarmed by the loss of cheap labor, blamed Northern labor agents for enticing unwilling Negroes to make secret nighttime departures. This wartime Great Migration intensified the gradual changes in the pattern of life of Northern urban Negroes and set in motion a population stream that was to continue, in war and peace, prosperity and depression, until the present day.

2

What were the conditions that the migrants met in the "promised land"? There was the animosity of white workers, even though black men obtained mostly the heavy, laborious, unskilled jobs. In 1917 the fears and suspicions of whites erupted into race riots in Philadelphia and Chester, Pennsylvania, and at East St. Louis, Illinois, where the most serious racial outbreak in the twentieth century cost the lives of at least thirty-nine blacks. Friction also resulted from the competition between Negroes and whites for limited housing. Yet, despite resistance both during and after the war, the ghettos expanded irrepressibly, block by block.

White attitudes of racial animosity, which demanded the exclusion of blacks from white residential areas, was the basic factor responsible for the creation and expansion of the ghettos. During the early decades of the northward migration, it was not infrequent for Negroes who "invaded" white areas to suffer personal beatings and stoning or bombing of their homes. Most white realtors refused to sell black people homes in white neighborhoods, and white property owners formed so-called neighborhood improvement associations for the purpose of keeping Negroes out. Typically they stressed their members' fear of depreciated property values, a fear exploited by certain real-estate agents—usually white—who engaged in the practice of "blockbusting"—forcing panic selling on the part of whites by moving in a Negro family. The dealers benefited handsomely by the resulting rapid turnover of properties. After the U.S.

Supreme Court declared municipal residential segregation ordinances unconstitutional in 1917, many white improvement
associations resorted mainly to the restrictive covenant—an
agreement among the property owners of an area that they
would not sell to blacks. Until 1948 the courts upheld these
covenants; although in the face of inexorable pressures stemming from the growth of the black population they frequently
proved unenforceable in the long run, they were an important
instrument in impeding the expansion of black residential areas
and thus contributed to extraordinary overcrowding in the
ghettos.

In addition to these external pressures from whites, there
were also internal forces among blacks that contributed to the
increasing ghettoization of Negro life. Motivated by pride,
habit, and the need for mutual protection from rejection, Negroes found a refuge within their own community. Furthermore, the institutional structure of the black community—the
churches, clubs, fraternal orders—were centered in the ghettos,
thus discouraging many from moving into distant white neighborhoods. And the concentration of blacks in specific parts of a
city proved beneficial to black politicians and businessmen who
based their careers on the support and patronage of the Negro
masses. Thus it is not surprising that, during the late 1950's and
1960's, fair-housing groups found relatively few black people
anxious to move into the white suburbs that were far from the
institutions and life of the black community.

In addition to promoting the growth of residential segregation, World War I and postwar migration brought greater discrimination and segregation in other aspects of everyday life.
Jim Crow schools arose in many Northern communities that
had never known them—partly as a result of the changing ethnic character of residential neighborhoods, but also because of
deliberate gerrymandering and transfer policies on the part of
boards of education. Even in cities like Chicago or Boston,
hotels and restaurants that had previously served Negroes now
barred them. As conditions worsened, earlier black settlers
blamed the mass of Southern newcomers, with their awkward

and unrefined ways, for the more intense prejudice that all blacks in the North now faced.

During World War I this pervasive pattern of discrimination extended even to the treatment of black men as members of the armed forces. Negroes were allowed to serve in the navy only as messboys and were barred entirely from the marines. The army accepted enlisted men, but planned originally not to commission Negroes. The highest-ranking black officer, Colonel Charles Young, was retired, allegedly on grounds of ill health. Only after agitation by black college students, NAACP officials, and a committee of prominent white citizens did the War Department finally establish a Negro officers' training camp at Des Moines, Iowa. Many criticized the NAACP leaders for endorsing a segregated camp, but their position was that without accepting such arrangements no Negroes would have been trained as officers. In October 1917, 639 men were commissioned with the ranks of captain and first and second lieutenant; later other Negroes became officers at unsegregated officer-training camps and in the field. All served only as officers of black units.

YMCA recreation units at army camps made no provisions for Negroes. Conditions in the South were especially difficult because of the actions of white civilians. At Houston in late summer of 1917 black soldiers who had been insulted and beaten by whites broke into an army ammunition storage room and marched on the city's police station. A riot followed that cost many lives. After a perfunctory trial, thirteen soldiers were hanged on charges of murder and mutiny, and forty-one others received life sentences. A similar occurrence at Spartanburg, South Carolina, in October was only narrowly averted by hastily sending the black regiment overseas. The army in these situations did nothing to protect its men against civilian attack; it either disarmed the blacks or shipped them to Europe. The War Department, however, did appoint Emmett J. Scott as a special assistant to the Secretary of War on matters affecting Negroes. Scott attempted to deal with Negro complaints, but it seems that he functioned principally as a device that the War

Department used to divert dissatisfaction, at least temporarily, from the responsible authorities. It was a symbolic role that Emmett Scott, Booker T. Washington's former private secretary, must have understood very well.

Despite discrimination at home and attempts by American troops—even high army authorities—to inculcate race prejudice among the French abroad, black soldiers performed honorably and courageously in battle. Most black newspapers supported the war effort, and even the militant Du Bois wrote a famous editorial in the *Crisis* urging blacks to "close ranks" with white Americans in defeating the nation's enemies. "If this is our country, then this is our war," he declared. He hoped that, by proving their patriotism, Negroes would receive greater recognition of their manhood and their citizenship rights in the postwar era. Some black editors, however, were critical of Du Bois's stand, believing that he had conceded too much in asking Negroes "to forget our present grievances" until war's end.

Du Bois's hopes for the postwar reconstruction were completely frustrated. Returning soldiers in 1919 found themselves in a situation that if anything was worse than the one before they left: a revived Ku Klux Klan, loss of job opportunities due to demobilization, and an extraordinary outbreak of race riots— over twenty in that "Red Summer" of 1919. They ranged from Washington, D.C., to Elaine, Arkansas, from Longview, Texas, to Chicago. The basic cause of most of these riots lay in white fears of economic competition and voting power of urban black migrants. The mobs harassed and murdered black victims without hindrance because of police prejudice and ineptitude. In some communities state militia reinforcements were called in too late, and even when deployed they often proved no better than the police. Generally all that blacks could do was attempt to flee.

Yet there was unmistakable evidence of increasing black militancy, and it is likely that the riots reflected to some degree white fear of this militancy. In 1919 the NAACP was disturbed by carefully verified reports from many places, even in Mississippi—where one would have thought that the oppressive race system had snuffed out all significant protest—of Negroes planning to meet fire with fire, to fight back. Moreover, acts of retaliatory violence on the part of Negroes actually triggered some of the major race riots of the war and postwar years.

In these cases blacks, goaded and angered by increasing numbers of white assaults during the months of rising racial tension that always precede a riot, struck back. The East St. Louis race riot of 1917 was precipitated when blacks, having been beaten repeatedly by white gangs, shot into a police car. In the dusk they mistook it for another Ford automobile containing white joyriders who had shot up black homes earlier in the evening. Two detectives were killed and white reaction led to the bloodiest race riot of the twentieth century. A similar sequence of events occurred at the Houston riot a few weeks later and in Chicago in 1919. In the same year the Longview, Texas, riot occurred after blacks shot whites who entered the ghetto seeking a teacher who had reported a recent lynching to the Chicago *Defender*. The event that triggered the Elaine, Arkansas, riot of 1919 was the shooting into a black church by two white law-enforcement officers. The Negroes returned the fire, causing one death. The white planters in the area, already angered because black cotton pickers had banded together to compel fairer treatment from the landlords, embarked upon a massive Negro hunt to put the black men "in their place." Two years later, in 1921, a riot in Tulsa, Oklahoma, originated when a crowd of armed Negroes assembled before the courthouse to prevent the possibility of a lynching of a Negro arrested for allegedly attacking a white girl. The blacks shot at the white police and civilians who attempted to disperse them.

In each of these conflagrations, the typical pattern was black retaliation to white acts of persecution and violence, and white perception of this resistance as an organized, premeditated conspiracy to "take over," which unleashed the armed power of white mobs and police. In the face of overwhelming white numerical superiority, black resistance ordinarily collapsed fairly early during the riots, especially in the South. Generally, white mobs would attack individual Negroes who happened to be passing through white areas and those whose homes were on the borders of white neighborhoods or in small enclaves surrounded by white residences or businesses. Often armed, but terrified, Negroes fled their homes, leaving guns and ammunition behind. Occasionally, however, black retaliation occurred toward the close rather than at the start of a riot. This happened in the unusual, if not unique, Washington riot of 1919, when blacks attacked white passengers on trolley cars passing through black areas.* Nevertheless, Negroes were generally defenseless in the face of superior numbers and force and police support for the rioters. While some whites were killed in the riots by blacks who did retaliate, by far the greater number of victims were black men, unable to do anything effective to protect themselves or their families.

The idea of retaliatory violence was occasionally reflected in the utterances of leading intellectuals during the war and post-war years. In 1916, inspired by the Irish rebellion, Du Bois had admonished black youth to stop spouting platitudes of accommodation and remember that no people ever achieved their liberation without armed struggle. In 1920, embittered at the wave of racial proscription that followed the war and reiterating a thought he had expressed as early as 1905, the year in which he founded the Niagara Movement, Du Bois predicted a race war in which Negroes, allied with Asians, would overwhelm the white race. In 1919, A. Philip Randolph, editor of the militant Socialist monthly, the *Messenger*, advocated physical resistance to white mobs. He observed that Anglo-Saxon jurisprudence recognized the law of self-defense and that Negroes should use armed force against their attackers. Half a dozen years later, in the noted *Sweet* case of 1925,† the NAACP also espoused the idea of the legality of retaliatory violence in self-defense and won. The open expression of such doctrines was thus a signifi-

---

* The Atlanta riot of 1906 was another example where black retaliatory violence occurred toward the end of the riot. There white mobs and police were shot at when they invaded the heart of a Negro ghetto, rather than remaining on the periphery.

† For the *Sweet* case, see p. 243.

cant, though rare, theme in the statements of black leaders and intellectuals.

3

What programs did the established black leadership organizations have to offer in the face of these trying conditions? Actually, they could do little for the masses of people; middle class in their orientation, they had little to offer the urban slum dweller. The National Urban League, founded in 1911 by a group of conservative blacks and white philanthropists and social workers, all allied with Booker Washington, took as its special province improving the employment opportunities of urban Negroes. Basically, the Urban League approach was a gradualist and conciliatory one of attempting to convince employers of the moral righteousness and economic value of hiring Negroes—to persuade them that black men were efficient workers. Attempts at negotiation with the discriminatory AFL unions got nowhere, and, indeed, if concessions were to be gained, they were certainly to come from philanthropic, if paternalistic, businessmen rather than from workers who regarded Negroes as economic rivals. The unionization of industrial plants often led to the expulsion of black employees. On the other hand, many employers wanted to use blacks to destroy or suppress union activity, which of course only antagonized white workers even more.

In the wave of labor difficulties and mass unemployment after World War I, the Urban League wrestled with this predicament. At a Detroit conference of Urban League officials in 1919, a resolution was passed that declared that directors of local leagues should be guided by their particular situations. If the opportunity existed, black workers should be urged to join labor unions, but where there were barriers, it might be appropriate to supply strikebreakers to employers during labor disputes. Some local leagues did indeed send black strikebreakers, but the results seldom if ever led to any permanent rise in black employment. Jobs or promotions obtained during strikes usually proved only temporary; once the labor disputes ended, no matter which side won, white workers generally took the jobs. The antiunion attitudes of many Urban League officials have been attributed to their middle-class background and outlook, and this is in part undoubtedly the case. In the context of trade-union discrimination, however, it is hard to see how Urban League executives could have acted much differently. Yet even their appeal to businessmen in economic and moral terms gained little. League reports magnified minor accomplishments into major achievements. The Atlanta league even boasted about training blacks to be better janitors. Whatever gains the Urban League did make during the prosperous 1920's were wiped out by the Depression. It was honestly trying to improve black employment opportunities, and in view of trade-union attitudes it is difficult to see that any approach would have been more successful. It is only a sign of the bitter context in which it operated that the Urban League's efforts were futile.

The NAACP concerned itself only slightly with discrimination in employment, leaving the job situation chiefly with the Urban League in a division of function that was not really disturbed until the rise of the NAACP's labor department around the middle of the century. It did extraordinary service, however, in legal defense of victims of race riots and unjust judicial proceedings. It secured the release of the imprisoned Houston soldiers; it successfully defended the Negroes charged with insurrection in the Elaine riot; and in numerous cases it worked to prevent miscarriages of justice against innocent black people. One of the most celebrated cases was its defense of Dr. Ossian Sweet and his family. The Sweets had moved into a white neighborhood in Detroit, and in self-defense shot at a mob that came to attack the home, killing one man. The NAACP employed Clarence Darrow to defend the Sweets, who were eventually acquitted. A major effort of the NAACP during the 1920's was to secure passage of an antilynching bill. Though the law was not enacted, the NAACP rallied a great deal of public support, and the number of lynchings gradually declined in the nation.

In the long run the most important of the NAACP's activities was the litigation designed to secure the enforcement of the Fourteenth and Fifteenth Amendments. In two landmark cases almost at the outset of its career, the NAACP began the long uphill fight against disfranchisement and segregation. In 1915 the Supreme Court declared grandfather clauses unconstitutional limitations on the right to vote. Two years later it outlawed municipal residential segregation ordinances. White property owners and realtors then retreated behind other subterfuges, particularly restrictive covenants, and the decade of the 1920's saw the beginning of the lengthy legal battle against this form of Jim Crow. At the same time the NAACP embarked upon the almost endless fight against the white primaries. The Association, despite its immediatist philosophy, was compelled to use an essentially gradualist approach, attacking one small aspect of discrimination at a time, hacking away piece by piece at the structure of discrimination. Though recognition of the Negroes' constitutional rights was still a long way off, the NAACP could at least point to a corpus of definite accomplishment. Less successful, however, were the attempts to prevent the development of school segregation in Northern cities. Gerrymanders of school boundaries and other devices initiated by boards of education were fought with written petitions, verbal protests to school officials, legal suits, and in several cities school boycotts, but in the end all proved to be of no avail.

The NAACP appealed to the "New Negro," to the business and professional people of the ghettos—North and even South. The Association in part depended on the new militance of the war and postwar years and in part was responsible for it. Originally a small interracial body, the Association's first real growth came during the war when, having employed the noted black writer James Weldon Johnson as field secretary, it consciously built its membership base in the black community. Johnson's work gave the organization a foothold in the South, and, as he crisscrossed the country organizing branches, he also cemented close relations between the Association and the black churches and fraternal orders. When, in 1920, he became the first Negro to occupy the top executive post of Secretary, the NAACP's ties to the black community were strengthened even more. Over the following years, as a result of the effective teamwork of Johnson and Assistant Secretary Walter F. White, control of the Association and its policies gradually passed from the prominent white liberals on its board of directors into the hands of the organization's black secretariat. Meanwhile, for the black upper and middle classes, Du Bois, as editor of the *Crisis*, symbolized that militance and exerted an enormous influence on their thinking. When R. R. Moton, principal of Tuskegee Institute, though still a conciliator and gradualist, spoke out in unmistakable terms against racial injustice in *What the Negro Thinks* (1929), it was clear that the protest ideology represented by the NAACP was generally accepted.

The Association, considering itself heir to the abolitionist tradition, and regarded as radical during the ascendancy of Booker T. Washington, now found itself in the curious position of being lumped together with Tuskegee, Hampton, and the Urban League as a conservative institution. Or so it was regarded by that economic and social radical, the *enfant terrible* of Negro journalism, A. Philip Randolph. His editorials in the *Messenger* even roasted and satirized Du Bois as a renegade Socialist, a political opportunist, and a "handkerchief head . . . hat-in-hand" Negro. The *Messenger's* point of view was that the NAACP was basically a middle-class organization unconcerned about the pressing economic problems of the masses. The *Messenger* took an outright Marxist position regarding the causes of prejudice and discrimination. It attributed these to capitalism, which kept white and black workers apart and exploited both by an appeal to race hatred. To Randolph and his colleagues the postwar era called for a New Negro, a radical black demanding the Negro's rights, concerned with the problems of the working class, and dedicated to the theory that only by united action of white and black workers against the capitalist class would social justice be achieved. Randolph appealed to Negroes to join trade unions, and he called upon trade unions to admit them. In practice his theory worked no better than the strategy of the Urban League in solving the economic problems of the race. Randolph did chalk up one accomplishment: the organization of the Brotherhood of Sleeping Car Porters in the mid-1920's. This was achieved against the determined opposition not only of the Pullman Company but also of much of the black leadership class—ranging from the conservative Chicago Urban League to the militant Chicago *Defender*. In 1937, after years of struggle, the brotherhood benefited from the changes in labor-management relations that accompanied the New Deal and finally achieved recognition as the porters' bargaining agent.

Although Randolph addressed himself to the urban working masses, few of them knew or understood the intellectual theories of the *Messenger*. The magazine circulated chiefly among elite black people. Its scintillating wit and mordant satire made it a conversation piece in middle-class homes, and for several years in the early 1920's its pages were devoted very largely to singing the praises of black business enterprise. The one man who really reached the frustrated and disillusioned masses in the ghettos was a Jamaican citizen, Marcus Garvey.

Garvey, founder in 1914 of the Universal Negro Improvement Association (UNIA), which after the war had branches in many cities in the United States and in several foreign countries, aimed to liberate both Africans and American blacks from their oppressors. His utopian means of accomplishing both goals was the wholesale migration of American Negroes to Africa. He contended that whites would always be racist and insisted that the Negro must develop "a distinct racial type of civilization of his own and . . . work out his salvation in his motherland, all to be accomplished under the stimulus and influence of the slogan, 'Africa for the Africans, at home and abroad.' " On a more practical level he urged Negroes to support black businesses, and the UNIA itself organized a chain of groceries, restaurants, laundries, a hotel, a doll factory, and a printing plant. Thousands bought stock in the UNIA's Black Star Steamship Line, which proposed to establish a commercial link between the United States, the West Indies, and Africa. Tens of thousands of Negroes swelled with pride at the parades of massed units of the African Legion in blue-and-red uniforms and the white-attired contingents of the Black Cross Nurses. Garvey's followers proudly waved the Association's flag (black for Negro skin, green for Negro hopes, and red for Negro blood) and sang the UNIA anthem, "Ethiopia, Thou Land of Our Fathers." Stressing race pride, Garvey gloried in the African past and taught that God and Christ were black.

He denounced the light-skinned, integrationist, upper-class Negroes active in the NAACP for being ashamed of their black ancestry and desiring to amalgamate with the white race. Garvey insisted that the UNIA was the only agency able to protect the darker-skinned black masses against the Du Bois–led "caste aristocracy" of college graduates. Thus while the *Messenger* denounced Du Bois as a cowardly renegade Socialist, Garvey charged him with preferring white men to black.* In turn both the *Messenger* and the *Crisis* joined in condemning Garvey. The established Negro leaders resented and feared the "Provisional President of the African Republic" and several of them called the attention of the United States government to irregularities in the management of the Black Star Line. Once Garvey had been jailed and then deported on charges of using

* Ironically, at this very time Du Bois was busily engaged in projecting his own program for African and Afro-American unity—the anti-imperialist Pan-African congresses of 1919–27. As early as the 1890's Du Bois embraced "Pan-Negroism" and hoped to create among Negroes everywhere an emotional commitment to one another. He believed that regardless of where Negroes lived, they owed a special attachment to Africa as the race's "greater fatherland." Upon the initiative of a group of West Indian intellectuals, the first Pan-African Conference was held in London in 1900. Du Bois wrote the "Address to the Nations of the World," urging self-government for Africans and West Indians and the creation in Africa of "a great central Negro State of the world." Although he envisioned no back-to-Africa movement, Du Bois believed that the formation and growth of such an African state would raise the status of blacks in all countries. Between 1919 and 1927 Du Bois convened four Pan-African congresses in Europe and the United States. Like the original London conference, these conclaves were dominated by the personality of Du Bois and ceaselessly condemned both beliefs in racial inequality and the imperialist exploitation of Africa.

the mails to defraud, the movement collapsed. But Garvey dramatized as no one before had done the bitterness and alienation of the black masses.

Thus the Garvey movement provided a compensatory escape for Negroes to whom the urban promised land had turned out to be a hopeless ghetto. It is significant, however, that the relationship between black migration and nationalist ideologies was not a new one. The peaks of interest in African colonization among blacks in the half century after the Civil War coincided with the peaks of domestic migration—in the late 1870's, around 1890, and again on the eve of the First World War. In many cases, in fact, spokesmen for the migrants regarded African colonization as an alternative to seeking better opportunities elsewhere in the United States. Ordinarily, colonization attempts had a strong nationalist emphasis, even though economic misery seems to have been the chief stimulus. Moreover, some of the migration movements within the United States were associated with strongly ethnocentric ideologies. Thus there were a number of attempts to establish all-black towns, especially within the South and in the Far West. The best known of these was Mound Bayou, Mississippi, founded in 1887 by Isaiah Montgomery, whose father had been the leader of the Davis Bend agricultural community during the Civil War. Mound Bayou expressed a nationalistic ideology of Negroes working out their own destiny without white assistance. More significant for our discussion at this point was the attempt to erect an all-black state in Oklahoma, an effort initiated by E. P. McCabe, formerly state auditor of Kansas. Disillusioned when the Republicans failed to renominate him, McCabe urged blacks to migrate to the Oklahoma Territory when it was opened for settlement. He painted a vision of a black-governed commonwealth, sending representatives and senators to the United States Congress. Between 1891 and 1910 about twenty-five towns were established. The migration aroused fears in the whites and eventuated not in political power but in disfranchisement. Then the economic dreams of the all-black towns in Oklahoma completely collapsed during the cotton depression of

1913–14. As a result, many Negroes of Oklahoma and surrounding states became intensely interested in the prospects of large-scale African migration. Tremendous excitement was generated in 1914–15 by an apparently fraudulent venture whose promoter, "Chief Sam," an alleged Ashanti chieftain, claimed that he had land in Africa on which American Negroes could settle. A few hundred actually sailed on an ill-fated expedition for the African homeland.

Thus, though it existed in a ghetto setting, the Garvey ideology and movement were part of a larger pattern associated with migration tendencies among Southern Negroes. Except for a few prominent leaders like Bishop Henry M. Turner, who for half a century after the close of Reconstruction denounced American hypocrisy and advocated migration to Africa, colonization in the late nineteenth and early twentieth centuries was almost entirely an ideology of the lower classes. This fact is in marked contrast to the antebellum period, when many prominent, articulate blacks were its advocates at one time or another.

That these colonization efforts manifested themselves as nationalist movements does not contradict the thesis that their motivation was largely economic. Mob rule and other forms of oppression played their roles, but just as the highly nationalistic Fascist organizations of Italy and Germany did not become mass movements until a period of acute depression, so ideologies of the sort represented by "Chief Sam" and Garvey flowered at times of great economic discontent.

4

The patterns of adjustment of rural Southern blacks to the urban environment and the institutional adaptations made by the black community have not been seriously studied. The paucity of data may make it difficult, if not impossible, ever to analyze the process adequately. Yet a few observations can be made.

In the black church the migrants carried with them an institution that helped them adjust to the dismal realities of urban life. The church, as it had in the South, remained the center of black community life. Migrants sought to reconstruct the institutions they had known in their Southern homes. Indeed, throughout the North and West one could identify church congregations composed of people from specific locales in the South. The traditional denominations—especially the Baptist and the Methodist connections—expanded rapidly. To a considerable extent, moreover, the rural black Baptist Church became transformed in the cities into the storefront evangelical churches and sects, and the religious frenzy of Sunday worship allowed communicants to forget briefly the realities of daily life. These numerous churches were forums for ambitious men of humble origins wishing to develop their leadership talents. They were also the root from which the larger-scale sects that flowered during the 1930's and 1940's grew—those led by Father Divine, Daddy Grace, and Elder Lightfoot Micheaux. These organizations gave their members a sense of self-esteem. Daddy Grace's House of Prayer for All People, for example, by its very title indicated that everyone was welcome and important. To the poor his sermons held out the possibility of self-improvement, upward social mobility, and respectability. The sect's organizational structure created offices for about 25 percent of its followers, thus giving them a feeling of importance and identity. Emotional release was provided through brass bands, syncopated music, ecstatic dancing, seizures and swoonings, and "speaking with tongues." In Daddy Grace, members perceived a charismatic figure who offered security—"sweet Daddy Grace," healer and miracle worker, and to many, even God incarnate, the second Christ. The dollars which Grace received from the poor who flocked to his services, and which made him a wealthy man, were for the people themselves a small price to pay for the void he filled in their lives.

These storefront churches and cult groups, creating a life meaning out of meaninglessness, self-respect out of poverty, functioned for the slum-shocked urban blacks in much the same way that Garvey did. The promise of self-esteem, rather than nationalism, was the significant ingredient of the Garvey movement. This is demonstrated by the fact that many followers of the nationalist Garvey ended up in the ostentatiously interracial cult of Father Divine, whose "Heavens" did not really multiply until the economic depression of the 1930's. Undoubtedly these religious cults provided an alternative for what might otherwise have been a highly explosive nationalist movement. The more recent Black Muslims have combined nationalist and religious escape ideologies.

In regard to another institution, the black family, there has been considerable debate. Not only does recent scholarship minimize the prevalence of matrifocal families under plantation slavery, but there is also disagreement on what happened in the cities. Theodore Hershberg's researches in Philadelphia indicate that the hostile urban environment of the antebellum years produced not only, as indicated earlier, a loss in economic status but a significant growth in female-headed households among lower-class blacks as well. On the other hand, Herbert Gutman, analyzing data from a number of cities, North and South, maintains that the matrifocal family was essentially a twentieth-century phenomenon.

Whatever the final conclusions that will emerge from this scholarly debate, it seems clear that the conditions of life in the twentieth-century urban ghettos encouraged matrifocal family patterns. When the migrants moved into the cities, they found that women could obtain and hold jobs more easily than men; women became domestic servants and their work was steadier and commonly more remunerative than that of men. In a society where the man is regarded as responsible for the support of his family, black men often felt inadequate. The results were frequent separations and many households where the mother or grandmother was the central figure. While it is customary to look upon the high incidence of such households as a sign of social disorganization among lower-class Negroes, there is another way to view the matter. The matrifocal family pattern can be regarded as a stabilizing influence in the lives of its members, as a creative response to the circumstances under which black people found themselves in the urban ghetto. Economic factors are not wholly responsible for the matrifocal family, for once established, such forms of institutional life tend to perpetuate themselves.*

Along with the lower-class migrants from Southern towns came a professional and business elite, whose numbers were increased by aspiring members from the lower classes. Bred in the ideology of self-help and racial solidarity and black support of black business, which had become current during the age of Booker T. Washington, this group, as the saying of the time put it, clearly took "advantage of the disadvantages" inherent in segregation and achieved economic success in the rapidly expanding urban ghettos. In some cities, as in Atlanta, the upwardly mobile men of wealth merged with members of the older pre-World War I upper class. In others, as in Chicago, they largely displaced the "old settlers" as the top stratum in black society.

Such men came to have a vested interest in the ghetto, for it was the source of their wealth, power, and social prestige. In the North this was also true of aspiring politicians. The "Dream of Black Metropolis," as St. Clair Drake and Horace Cayton termed it, was most forcefully advanced in Chicago, and there more than anywhere else the political aspect of the dream found fulfillment. In 1928 Chicago elected the first Negro to sit in Congress since the turn of the century. Chicago also boasted the biggest aggregation of black banks and insurance companies north of the Mason-Dixon line. The Black Metropolis ideal also had its development in the South, especially in Atlanta and Durham, where the three largest Negro insurance companies were located. In fact, E. Franklin Frazier in 1925 called Durham the "capital of the Black Middle Class."

To many, this vision of creating a business, professional, and political elite on the basis of a concentrated Negro market and on black votes was viewed as a temporary expedient, at best only an indirect way of achieving full participation in American

---

* In view of current misconceptions about black family life, it should be emphasized that matrifocal families, while common among lower-class Negroes, are not in the majority.

life. To them it was clearly no solution to the problems of the race because the political and economic dominance still remained in white hands. Yet to some black people the dream was inspiring in and of itself, and they believed that a well-organized community supporting black "captains of industry," professional people, financiers, and politicians was a satisfactory alternative to the destruction of segregation. As Gunnar Myrdal was to observe, the black middle class was in a cruel and tragic dilemma: earning their bread from at least an implicit appeal to race loyalty and segregation, they were also the backbone of organizations like the NAACP, dedicated to moving Negroes into the mainstream of American life. Thus, in contrast to the turn of the century, the Black Metropolis ideal was now usually coupled, not with a philosophy of accommodation, but with one of protest. Then the dream, however psychologically satisfying, however materially advantageous to a few, collapsed in the face of the Depression of the 1930's, when the flimsy foundation of the black business world became evident. Nevertheless black business and professional men still appealed for support on the basis of race pride. They did so, however, not with the vision of creating a self-sufficient black community, but as a device to ensure their own economic survival.

5

The sense of community and racial solidarity characteristic of the Garvey movement and the dream of a Black Metropolis had its intellectual counterpart in the "Harlem Renaissance," the literary and artistic movement summed up by the term, the "New Negro." In 1925, when *Survey Graphic* published its special Harlem issue edited by Alain Locke, a Harvard Ph.D. and the first black Rhodes scholar, it suddenly became apparent to the educated public that a cultural renaissance was under way. The New Negro was militant and proud of his race, desired to perpetuate the group identity and yet participate fully in American society. The New Negro protested and demanded his rights of citizenship and insisted upon the value of a black subculture. Intellectually and artistically, he believed that Negroes should have pride in their past and their traditions; and by using the themes from Negro life and Negro history as an inspiration for his literary work, the New Negro intended to enrich the culture of America.

The ethnic dualism and cultural pluralism of the New Negro movement or Harlem Renaissance had diverse origins. Interest in the race's past had been rapidly growing since the beginning of the century. The first courses in black history were introduced in a few black colleges about the time of the First World War. The Association for the Study of Negro Life and History, founded in 1915 by Carter G. Woodson, placed on scholarly foundations the investigation of both the African and American past.

At about the same time, many white authors were exploring in their novels the rich regional diversity of American culture. During the 1920's DuBose Heyward enlarged this interest to include Negro life. His novel *Porgy*, the inspiration for George Gershwin's famous musical *Porgy and Bess*, was set in the coastal area of South Carolina, where African survivals were strong. Many white literati, who during the heyday of Greenwich Village made a cult of primitivism, regarded the Negro and Africa as possessing intriguing qualities of savagery, occultism, and uninhibited sexuality. Indeed, the 1920's was the period, as Langston Hughes has said, when "Harlem was in vogue." Whites, attracted by jazz and the alleged exotic way of life among Harlem's citizens, flocked to the Harlem speakeasies and to such spots as the Cotton Club, where entertainment was supplied by a chorus line of light-skinned Negroes. But blacks themselves could enter only as performers and employees, not as paying guests.

The result of these and other converging currents was a remarkable outpouring of literature, painting, and sculpture. It was a movement with many midwives, among whom were the aesthete and scholar Alain Locke, Charles S. Johnson, editor of the magazine *Opportunity*, W. E. B. Du Bois, and white sponsors such as author Carl Van Vechten. The *Crisis* and *Opportunity*, published by the National Urban League, printed much of the new writing and awarded prizes for the most creative work.

Some of the whites connected with the Urban League were originally responsible for the publication of the *Survey Graphic*'s Harlem number. The white reading public made it profitable for book firms to publish volumes written by blacks. Whites, ranging from the equalitarian Amy and Joel Spingarn of the NAACP to the paternalistic Park Avenue matron who subsidized Langston Hughes's career for a time, encouraged the young black writers. They provided money for prizes, grants, and scholarships. Paradoxically, therefore, the race-proud Harlem Renaissance was largely made possible by white interest. Paradoxically also, the race-proud New Negro writers and artists, associating with white literati like Carl Van Vechten and the Greenwich Village aesthetes and gathering at places like A'Leila Walker's Dark Towers on 136th Street, where celebrities of both races jammed the fabulous parties, were almost certainly the best-integrated group among American blacks. Stylistically they were strongly influenced by current white literary vogues.

The white support and financing of the renaissance created some serious problems. Themes that concerned the writers were often seen differently by their white patrons and the white reading public. Tensions arising over the color line within black society and the problem of "passing" were genuine concerns for the middle-class and upper-class Negroes. Yet they were also subjects of incredible fascination for whites who thought in terms of stock characters, such as the "tragic mulatto," and assumed that black people really wanted to be white. So also the unique aspects of the life of the folk Negro was a genuine subject for artistic representation, but whites found the material interesting mostly if it was exotic and played up lower-class sexuality. Thus the conflict between artistic integrity and commercial success assumed a particularly aggravated form among the blacks of the renaissance. Langston Hughes, for example, recounts the painful experience he had when the woman who was financing his work, and whom he deeply admired, insisted that his writing was not "primitive" enough. Hughes had the integrity to break the tie, though it was economically difficult and psychologically traumatic to do so.

The artistic outpouring of the 1920's was, it should be pointed out, rooted in the past. Since the 1890's there had been an incipient interest in folk materials, in the richness of life on the Sea Islands, in the African background, in the mystique of cultural nationalism, and in the insistence on the racial experience as a source of artistic inspiration. Black theater had been flourishing on Broadway since the 1890's; the productions were mostly stereotyped musicals and included the dialect comedy team of Bert Williams and George Walker, who made the cakewalk fashionable. During the prewar years there had also been a rise in literary works by Negroes. Much of this literature had tended either to be imitative of conventional Victorian poetry and melodramatic novels or to be written in stereotyped dialect, such as many of the poems and short stories of Paul Laurence Dunbar. On the other hand, Charles Chesnutt in his short stories had started to explore folk culture in a serious way, while his novels were vigorous protests against American racism. And in 1912 there appeared anonymously James Weldon Johnson's volume, *The Autobiography of an Ex-Coloured Man*, the first and most successful novel about passing, but more significant for its glorification of ragtime, a black folk-music idiom then considered unrespectable, and for its portrayal of the somewhat unconventional life among the theatrical and sporting elements in black society.

During the 1920's blacks were allowed for the first time to pursue serious careers in the theater and the concert hall. The great nineteenth-century American Negro Shakespearean actor, Ira Aldridge, had forged his remarkable career in England and Europe, not in the United States. In the 1920's dramatic roles still tended to be somewhat stereotyped, it is true, but Paul Robeson first achieved fame not in some forgotten musical but in a serious play by one of the great writers for the American stage, Eugene O'Neill. The concert stage remained closed to black instrumentalists. But working against incredible odds, the tenor Roland Hayes became the first black to be accepted as a concert artist.

The writers of the renaissance articulated the various ideologies of the 1920's. The interest in the race's past was reflected in such poems as Langston Hughes's "The Negro Speaks of Rivers"; in the rather ambivalent poem of Countee Cullen "Heritage," which appears to accept white stereotypes about the sensuous, exotic, and primitive quality of African life and the difficulty of even educated Negroes assimilating Anglo-Saxon culture; and in novels such as Arna Bontemps's *Black Thunder,* based on Gabriel's Revolt. Overlapping this historical concern was the exploration of traditions in the black subculture. In *Cane,* a series of poems, short stories, and vignettes, Jean Toomer, the most sophisticated literary genius of the renaissance, recaptured the life of the black folk who worked in the lumber camps of Georgia in the 1880's. James Weldon Johnson in *God's Trombones,* subtitled *Some Negro Folk Sermons in Verse,* employed the cadence and imagery of the black rural preacher. Langston Hughes in numerous poems used the rhythms and moods of jazz and the blues as an inspiration for his poetry. Claude McKay in his novel *Home to Harlem,* Zora Neale Hurston in her renditions of Negro folk materials, and Sterling Brown in his poems about Slim Greer were among those who found in the common folk a subject for literary treatment. Thus, in "Memphis Blues," using the dialect of the black working class, Sterling Brown expresses the resignation of the poor. Langston Hughes combined the themes of working-class-black life with an underlying spirit of protest in such poems as his "Brass Spittoons," an evocation of a hotel bellhop's daily life, and "To the Negro Washerwoman," whom he idealized for her self-sacrifice in supporting and educating her family.

Others portrayed black middle-class life, emphasizing its gentility and respectability, and often employed plots based on passing and on the color line within the black community. Two examples are Walter White's *Flight* and the novels of Jessie Fauset. White also wrote a protest novel, *Fire in the Flint*, based upon his investigations of lynchings.

Protest was evident in some of the ironic poems of Countee Cullen, such as "Yet Do I Marvel," in which after pondering on the ways of an inscrutable, omnipotent, but undoubtedly just God, Cullen concludes, "Yet do I marvel at this curious thing: / To make a poet black, and bid him sing!"; or in some of Claude McKay's poems like "The Lynching" and "If We Must Die": "If we must die—let it not be like hogs / Hunted and penned in an inglorious spot . . . If we must die—oh, let us nobly die . . . dying, but fighting back!" After the renaissance, during the 1930's, protest replaced folk culture as the dominant theme of black writing. In those years Langston Hughes penned his "Let America Be America Again," a protest against oppression of all the subordinated groups and a vision of an equalitarian society. The dominant literary figure of the 1930's and 1940's was Richard Wright, whose *Uncle Tom's Children* and *Native Son* portrayed with bitter sociological and psychological realism the plight of the oppressed working-class Negroes. Wright treated the same subject even more searingly in his autobiographical *Black Boy*. His achievement as one of the major writers of the twentieth century in the United States has been eclipsed among black authors only by the post–World War II novelist Ralph Ellison, whose heavily symbolic *Invisible Man* draws upon material from Negro life to pose the fundamental problem of freedom in modern impersonal society.

6

In *Native Son* Wright described black people of the Depression years, victimized and hardened by life in the urban ghetto. Despite the misery, squalor, and limited opportunity in the cities, the New Deal era witnessed a continued, though reduced, migration to urban centers. In effect, New Deal programs actually encouraged this population movement, both by the policies of the Agricultural Adjustment Administration as applied to the Southern plantations and by providing public aid to unemployed Negroes in the cities, particularly in the North.

The New Deal, though in certain particulars regressive for the status of black people, marked a real turning point in the trends of American race relations. Despite the work of the NAACP and the interest of philanthropic whites in the Urban League and the Harlem Renaissance, it was only during the 1930's that a clear-cut reversal in the attitudes of white Americans started to become evident. Of paramount importance was the genuine interest of prominent New Dealers in the status of American blacks. Their concern was part of the larger humanitarian interest in the welfare of all the underprivileged in American society. At the same time, the black vote had reached sizable proportions in a number of Northern cities, creating an additional motivation for the attention to Negro welfare among New Deal politicians. Of top prominence among those promoting the Negro cause was the wife of the President, Eleanor Roosevelt, who more than any other person during this era symbolized genuine humanitarian concern in race relations. To the dismay and consternation of Southern supporters of the President, she was openly friendly with blacks. The most dramatic incident illustrating her attitude came in 1939, when the Daughters of the American Revolution refused to permit Constitution Hall, Washington's only concert stage, to be used for a recital by the contralto Marian Anderson. Mrs. Roosevelt thereupon resigned from the DAR. Harold Ickes, Secretary of the Interior and a former president of the Chicago NAACP, arranged for Miss Anderson to give a concert from the steps of the Lincoln Memorial. On Easter Sunday, over 75,000 people attended this memorable program.

Black leaders wanted more than symbolism. They protested against the exclusion of Negroes from large, federally financed construction projects. In 1933, under NAACP initiative, various race-advancement organizations established the Joint Committee on National Recovery to fight discriminatory policies in the federal agencies. The JCNR was especially effective in exposing the unequal wage rates provided in the National Industrial Recovery Act codes. Meanwhile, the Roosevelt Administration had decided to appoint race-relations advisers in the major federal departments. At first Roosevelt appointed Southern whites, only some of whom were genuinely concerned about improving the Negro's status. Blacks protested, and soon the Administration began using highly talented and well-educated black people in these posts. Among the more noted of these were Mary McLeod Bethune, director of the Division of Negro Affairs of the National Youth Administration, Robert C. Weaver, adviser to the Department of the Interior, and William H. Hastie, judge of the district court in the Virgin Islands, the first black federal judge in the nation's history. These new positions were the highest held by blacks in the federal government since Taft's Administration. Their importance, however, was chiefly symbolic.

The New Deal's real impact upon Negroes came not from such well-publicized appointments but from more tangible benefits. Negroes were the ones hardest hit by the Depression, being the last hired and first fired. Compared with unemployed whites, a smaller percentage of the unemployed Negroes benefited from relief and public-works programs. Despite this discrimination, a higher proportion of the black population than of the white population received government unemployment aid, since black unemployment was so much greater. Negroes felt singularly indebted to the New Deal and the Roosevelt Administration, and have felt so ever since (as testified to by John F. Kennedy's effective use of the Roosevelt mantle in black newspaper advertisements during the 1960 campaign). By 1936 the black vote dramatically shifted from Republican to Democratic. The New Deal welfare programs, which were administered with less discrimination in the North than in the South, encouraged black migration to the North and, therefore, also increased the number of Negroes who would vote Democratic in subsequent elections.

Although the New Deal helped create a new climate of opinion and supplied material benefits to the unemployed, in certain ways its policies were less helpful and even negative in their impact. This was especially true in the fields of housing and agriculture. The federal housing agencies definitely supported and strengthened the trend toward residential segregation. In agreements with banks and other lending institutions, the Federal Housing Administration refused to guarantee mortgages on homes purchased by blacks in white communities. The United States Housing Authority, while providing public housing for many black families, financed separate projects for the two races. In addition, the policies of the Agricultural Adjustment Administration were clearly discriminatory in their application. Cotton agriculture had been experiencing competition from synthetic fibers as far back as the 1920's. The Depression intensified the decrease in the demand for cotton and prices tumbled. The Southeastern states suffered the most, for they were faced with the continued ravages of the boll weevil at the same time that Texas and Oklahoma were recovering from the worst effects of the boll-weevil infestation and, therefore, becoming more effective competitors to the older cotton states. As part of its general program for raising farm prices, the AAA paid farmers to restrict their acreage. Supposedly, tenant farmers were to receive a share of this money, but in practice they usually did not. In fact, because of acreage reduction, plantation owners had less need for workers. Many sharecroppers were forced off the land and they moved to the urban ghettos. The final collapse of the cotton tenant-farm system in most of the Southeast occurred in the post–World War II years, due to the mechanization of cotton agriculture, the erosion and depletion of many older cotton lands, and the spread of cotton agriculture to mechanized plantations in the West, especially California.

Patterns of race relations in the South remained essentially unchanged during the Depression. When the predominantly black but interracial Southern Tenant Farmers Union, formed in Arkansas with Socialist assistance in 1934, attempted to organize the sharecroppers, it met terrorism and violence; and a cottonpickers' strike that it organized in 1935 was defeated by harassment and intimidation. More celebrated was the Scottsboro, Alabama, case, which was tried in the spring of 1931, when nine black youthful hoboes, ranging in age from twelve to nineteen, were convicted on false charges of having raped two white girls riding on the same freight train. Scottsboro became a *cause célèbre*, one of the leading civil-liberties cases of the decade, that twice reached the United States Supreme Court. Not until 1950 were all of the defendants out of jail.

On the other hand, there were evidences of more progressive forces in the white South, most notably in the work of two interracial organizations—the Commission on Interracial Cooperation and the Southern Conference for Human Welfare. The former, established in 1919 and most noted for antilynching work, continued its educational activities. In 1944 it was transformed into the Southern Regional Council. The Southern Conference for Human Welfare, a coalition, established in 1938, of radicals and liberals in the region, was more outspoken than the commission and concentrated its efforts largely on a campaign against the poll tax. Later charged with Communist infiltration, it disintegrated after the war. An offshoot, the Southern Conference Educational Fund, still survives.

During the New Deal period, the rise of industrial unionism and the formation of the Congress of Industrial Organizations, which broke with the AFL, proved of immense value to the urban black. Led by John L. Lewis of the racially integrated United Mine Workers, the CIO's policy not only reflected the idealism of the period but also recognized that in a time of labor surplus it was hardly possible to organize workers effectively by excluding Negroes and thereby forcing them into the ranks of strikebreakers. Of course, perfect racial egalitarianism did not ensue. In the South especially, the CIO felt it necessary to permit separate locals and the relegation of Negroes to inferior jobs. Not until the 1960's did even the very liberal United Automobile Workers elect a black to its international executive board, and even that development occurred only after a well-organized black caucus compelled it. Nevertheless, the CIO's contribution to the changing patterns of race relations has been incalculable. It made interracial trade unionism truly respectable. It gave black and white workers a sense of common interest, of solidarity, that transcended racial lines. Although prejudice was not eliminated, it was certainly lessened among laborers who worked together in jobs of equal status and equal pay.

The interracial industrial trade unions had an important impact on the Negro protest movement. Black labor leaders like Willard Townsend of the Red Caps and A. Philip Randolph, and some of the other young intellectuals like Ralph Bunche went so far as to predict that the solution to the whole problem of discrimination would be through an alliance of black and white workers in industrial unions that would fight to bring social justice for all. Many of the middle- and upper-class leaders in the established race-advancement organizations were initially skeptical, though the Urban League took concrete steps to educate Negro workers on the value of joining labor unions. NAACP leadership was divided for several years. The turning point came in 1941 when the United Automobile Workers requested NAACP assistance in getting Negro scabs out of the Ford automobile factories. After securing assurances that the union would cease discriminatory policies against black members, the NAACP Secretary, Walter White, personally went to Detroit and circled the strikebound River Rouge plant in a car with a loudspeaker, urging black strikebreakers to leave. A large number did so. Negro–labor union solidarity was a cornerstone of NAACP policy for nearly twenty years thereafter, until disillusionment with the discrimination of many unions in the reunited AFL–CIO led to renewed criticism of the racial practices in organized labor.

Even before the CIO appeared, the economic catastrophe of the 1930's and the outlook and program of the New Deal had stimulated changes in the orientation of black protest thinking. Specific concern with economic problems became much more the order of the day. During the early 1930's this took a nationalist turn. In an effort to obtain retail sales positions for Negroes in white-owned stores, "Don't Buy Where You Can't Work" campaigns were conducted in a number of urban ghetto business districts.

The employment situation and the general radicalization of American thinking during the 1930's led to intensified criticism of the NAACP's program. Du Bois resigned as editor of the *Crisis* in 1934 largely because he was convinced that the NAACP emphasis on attacking disfranchisement and segregation without seriously pursuing an economic program proved its identification only with the bourgeoisie. Du Bois, furthermore, never had given up completely his belief in the value of collective racial economic endeavor. His ardent advocacy of a separate black cooperative economy as a solution to the problems posed by the Depression led to a clash with White and others who supported the NAACP's traditional position of opposing any form of segregation, and resulted, not only in his withdrawal from his position with the NAACP, but also in his demise as a black leader. Younger critics of the NAACP, like Ralph Bunche, who was then a professor at Howard University, also attacked the Association for what they conceived to be its gradualist approach and its lack of attention to economic problems. From the beginning of the Roosevelt Administration, the NAACP as well as the Urban League protested against discrimination in the New Deal agencies, and as we have seen, eventually the NAACP modified its platform and endorsed the new interracial industrial unions.

The organization also broadened the scope of its legal work. No longer largely depending on the voluntary work of prestigious white attorneys, as it had once done, the NAACP in 1935 established the salaried post of special counsel. The first man to fill this position was the brilliant black lawyer and dean of Howard University Law School, Charles H. Houston, who as a student at Harvard had been the first black to make the *Harvard Law Review*. He was later succeeded at the NAACP by his former law student Thurgood Marshall. Under the leadership of these two men, the Association continued its attack on the white primaries, and eventually, in 1944, the Supreme Court handed down a decision ending Southern subterfuge on that particular issue. The heart of NAACP litigation in the 1930's was the beginning of a long-range battle against segregation. For tactical purposes, the main emphasis was placed on educational discrimination. The NAACP adopted the strategy of attacking the most obvious inequities in the Southern school systems: the lack of professional and graduate schools and the low salaries received by black teachers. The Association hoped that by this indirect method segregation would become so expensive that it would fall of its own weight. Not until about 1950 did the organization make a direct assault against school segregation on the legal grounds that separate facilities were inherently unequal.

7

A significant aspect in the history of the black protest movement during the New Deal was the role of the Communist Party. Because the great majority of Negroes belong to the working class, and because blacks have been discriminated against and oppressed, the Communists considered American Negroes to be ideal material for a revolutionary movement. During the 1920's and early 1930's, the Communists attempted to appeal directly to the black masses and attacked the black bourgeoisie, black advancement organizations, and black intellectuals. Though the Communists did much to publicize the injustices against blacks and did significant organization work among Southern sharecroppers, black people at no time constituted more than about 10 percent of Communist Party membership. In other words, blacks did not join the party any more readily than did whites.

Around 1935, with the rise of Hitler in Germany and the Nazi threat to Soviet Russia, Communist international policy shifted to courting Socialists, liberals, and middle-class groups in Europe and America and to forming so-called popular fronts with them. A number of these groups eventually found themselves taken over and dominated by their Communist members. In the case of American Negroes, too, the Communists did an about-face and now wooed the NAACP, the Urban League, and the black middle class in general. Walter White was no longer a lickspittle of the capitalists; Lester Granger of the Urban League was no longer a Judas of the race. Neither the League nor the NAACP, however, favored close cooperation with Communists, and generally the latter were obliged to look elsewhere to make significant gains among black Americans.

Representative of the nature of Communist activity in the late 1930's was the career of the National Negro Congress. It was organized in 1936 under the auspices of a group of Negroes, chiefly younger intellectuals, who were critical of the conservatism of the NAACP and the Urban League and especially of the reluctance of these two organizations to engage in a program that would be meaningful to the economically depressed black masses. Taking active parts were men like Ralph Bunche and A. Philip Randolph, the National Negro Congress's first president. A few Communists were also active; the executive secretary was sympathetic with the Communist point of view; and Communist cooperation seemed natural in the days of the popular front. The congress was actually an organization of organizations; as such, its work was largely in the area of propaganda and publicity. Its program was similar to that of civil-rights groups in that period, except for its strong pro-union orientation. It received a great deal of publicity, and at the second conference in 1937 the National Negro Congress was addressed by a brilliant galaxy of Negro leaders, practically a *Who's Who* of the leadership elite among the black bourgeoisie.

Then in 1939, as a result of the Soviet-Nazi nonaggression pact, there was a reversal of Communist tactics. The popular-front strategy was shelved. Erstwhile friends now became enemies, tools of imperialist warmongers. Even A. Philip Randolph came under attack. The party packed the congress's third convention in 1940. Speakers who did not agree with Communist-inspired resolutions were booed and hooted. Fully one fourth of the delegates were white representatives from pro-Communist trade unions, and when Randolph was delivering his speech, these delegates and a number of their sympathizers walked out. Disillusioned, Randolph, Bunche, and other prominent leaders withdrew their support from the organization, which declined rapidly into a small and impotent group consisting principally of Communists and their "fellow travelers."

When Hitler attacked Russia, the Communists again reversed themselves. Now everything was to be sacrificed to winning the war and aiding Russia. The attack on discrimination in the armed forces and in the war industries was to be soft-pedaled because, the Communists held, such protests interfered with the effectiveness of the war effort. Randolph, the NAACP, and the Urban League replied that the full and unsegregated use of black manpower would actually bring victory closer.

8

The ambivalent legacy of the New Deal to the cause of black people was very evident in the role that Negroes played during the war. On the one hand, conditions were markedly better than they had been in the First World War; on the other hand, the New Deal administration temporized, compromised, and moved only under pressure. As in the First World War, the major problems for blacks were employment, racial tensions in the cities and at army camps, and the treatment of black soldiers. Although Negroes were sent to integrated army officers' training camps, in other respects they were segregated in the armed forces. There was segregation also in the blood banks, although, ironically, the process of storing blood plasma had been invented by a black physician, Dr. Charles Drew of Howard University Medical School. Precedents were shattered by the admission of Negroes into the Army Air Corps and the Marines, and for the first time since early in the century Negroes were accepted in naval grades above messmen. The first black naval officers and the first black brigadier general were commissioned. Yet at army posts Negroes were segregated in inadequate recreational facilities; there were reports from Italy of low morale because of prejudiced treatment by white army officers; in the South black soldiers were often insulted by white citizens; and William H. Hastie, supported by the NAACP, angrily resigned as civilian aide to the Secretary of War when, over his opposition, a segregated training base for Negro pilots was established at Tuskegee Institute. The fact that it was conservative Tuskegee which encouraged this offer, while the

NAACP opposed it, is symbolic of the degree of improvement that had taken place since World War I, when the Association's leaders had welcomed a segregated officers' training camp. So also was the greater degree of freedom with which black leaders and editors criticized discriminatory policies on the part of industry and public officials.

As industry retooled for war production in 1940 and 1941 and absorbed many of the unemployed, Negroes at first were ignored or used only for menial employment. They protested vigorously, and after A. Philip Randolph threatened a march on Washington of 50,000 to 100,000 black men, President Roosevelt issued his famous Executive Order 8802 establishing a Fair Employment Practices Committee. Although the committee lacked enforcement powers and was stripped of any real influence when it became too controversial, it did perform some useful work in advancing the employment of blacks in war industries; and the federal employment service in many communities encouraged the hiring of Negroes. In most cases they entered factories organized by CIO affiliates. The beneficial results of the racial policies of the industrial unions were thus further enhanced and carried over into the postwar era. Nevertheless, discrimination was still flagrant. Tensions among workers erupted into a series of race riots, most notably at Detroit, where in June 1943 the most serious racial outbreak occurred. In contrast to the Red Summer of 1919, however, there was no postwar racial violence when the soldiers were demobilized.

Indeed, the Truman Administration in some ways opened a new era in the history of American race relations. The political impact of the heavy black migration to Northern and Western cities and the shift in allegiance from the Republicans to the Democrats now became evident. As the number of migrants rose to new heights during the war, the West Coast for the first time attracting a substantial segment of them, the expansion of the urban ghettos accelerated. Representing these enlarged black ghettos, new and more black politicians came to power. With the election of Adam Clayton Powell in 1944, New York became the second Northern city to send a Negro to Congress. Two decades later there were six blacks in the House of Representatives, two from Detroit, and one each from Philadelphia, New York, Chicago, and Los Angeles.

In early 1948 the NAACP's public-relations director, Henry Lee Moon, published the book *Balance of Power*, in which he held that the black vote in certain pivotal states was enough to swing close national elections. The Presidential election of 1948 vindicated his thesis. President Truman, regarded as a certain loser by practically all observers, realized that to keep his office he would need the black vote. It was the first election since Reconstruction in which the Negro's status was a major issue and in which his political power was a critical factor in the outcome. Because the Democratic National Convention adopted a strong civil-rights plank, Southern elements walked out and backed their own "Dixiecrat" candidate, who captured four of the traditionally Democratic states in the election. The left-wing Progressive Party took a vigorous stand on Negro rights and siphoned off enough voters from the Democrats to throw New York into the Republican column. Nevertheless, Truman, with the overwhelming support of the black electorate, squeaked through to victory.

Though the Democratic Congress failed to enact a civil-rights act as the party's platform had promised, the Truman Administration was marked by some advances. The President appointed William H. Hastie to the Third U.S. Circuit Court, making him the highest black judicial appointee up to then in American history. Truman issued the directive that ended segregation in the armed services, settling an issue about which blacks had agitated constantly since Randolph listed it among his original demands when he proposed the march on Washington in 1941. This change of policy had an incalculable effect in shifting white attitudes, for as a result of it millions of young men of both races lived and worked together, and fought together in Korea, and white men often served under black officers, especially noncommissioned ones. The President also ordered that firms doing business with the federal government pursue a nondiscriminatory employment policy. The committee appointed by Truman and his successor, Dwight D. Eisenhower, was ineffectual in enforcing this directive, however. Truman also appointed a commission to study race relations in the United States. Its report, *To Secure These Rights*, called for the full integration of Negroes in all aspects of the society. The principal value of both these commissions, largely symbolic and educational, was propagandistic, for they helped pave the way for new norms in American race relations. The shift in public opinion, abetted by the new power of black voters, was reflected in a trend toward enacting fair-employment-practice and public-accommodations laws in Northern and Far Western states and municipalities.

Thus, at midcentury the Great Migration to the industrial centers since the First World War was about to usher in the most momentous changes in black-white relationships since the Civil War. The context and texture of Negro life had changed, and the process of future racial adjustment would take place in a chiefly urban environment. The urban ghetto was at one and the same time the force that constricted Negro life and aspirations and yet formed the base for black political power and the activities of civil-rights organizations. Because the black vote was often closely tied to Democratic city machines, it was not as effective a voice of protest as some believe it could have been; nevertheless, by 1950 it had already determined a Presidential election, elicited several important actions on the part of the Chief Executive, and secured the passage of some state and municipal antidiscrimination laws. Without the urban base, the Negro protest movement would have remained small, and without the political leverage the urban masses provided, it would have remained impotent. Though no one realized it at the time, and though other factors were also essential in bringing about the events that were to follow, by midcentury the vote of the black ghetto in the North had reached the proportions that made possible the civil-rights revolution.

VII

The Black Revolt of the 1960's

"THE NEGRO SCHOOLS OF THOUGHT," A. Philip Randolph, patriarch of the black protest movement said, "are torn with dissension, giving birth to many insurgent factions. . . . All are engaged in a war of bitter recriminations . . . while the long-suffering masses . . . [are] victims of the vanities, foibles, indiscretions and vaulting ambitions . . . of various leaderships." This was written in about 1920, when there was a conservative group best represented by Tuskegee Institute and the National Urban League, a radical left wing of Marxists connected with the *Messenger*, a radical nationalist back-to-Africa movement, and, in the middle of the road, the NAACP. Randolph's words so aptly describe the situation throughout the twentieth century that they might just as easily have applied to the period a dozen years earlier when the conflict between the

271

"conservative" Booker T. Washington and the "radical" NAACP was raging, or to the 1960's, when the "conservative" NAACP was criticized first by the more "radical" activist civil-rights organizations, and then by the Black Nationalists.

1

What happened to the civil-rights movement to produce a situation where a platform, that early in the century was censured for its militancy, sixty years later was being condemned for its gradualism? Externally there was a significant shift in white public opinion in the direction of racial equalitarianism. Internally, what was once a liberal white and Negro upper-class movement became a completely black-led and almost entirely black, largely working-class movement. There was a shift in strategy from agitation, legislation, and court litigation aimed at securing the black person's constitutional rights to emphasis on direct-action techniques, and finally to mobilizing the potential power of the masses in the ghettos along political and economic lines. When, in the 1960's, the nation moved closer toward protecting the rights guaranteed by the Constitution, goals were redefined, and the Negro protest organizations went beyond constitutional rights to demand special efforts to overcome the poverty of the black masses. In some cases, they rejected the platform of integration for one of militant ethnic separatism.

The goals, tactics, and strategy of the mid-twentieth-century civil-rights movement were clearly foreshadowed during the Second World War by Randolph's March on Washington Movement and the founding of the Congress of Racial Equality (CORE). Though its career was brief, the former organization prefigured things to come in three ways: (1) it was an avowedly all-Negro movement; (2) it was deliberately based upon action on the part of the black masses; and (3) it concerned itself with the economic problems of the urban slum dwellers. Moreover, the wartime Fair Employment Practices Committee that President Roosevelt created in response to Randolph's threat was itself important, for it established a precedent suggesting that the right to fair employment might be regarded as a civil right.

Randolph's March on Washington Movement was greatly influenced by the tactics of Gandhi's movement of nonviolent resistance in India, but it was the Congress of Racial Equality that was chiefly responsible for projecting the use of nonviolent direct action as a civil-rights strategy. CORE's origins lay in the activities of the Fellowship of Reconciliation, a Christian pacifist organization founded during the First World War. Certain leaders of the FOR, interested in the use of nonviolent direct action to fight racial discrimination, founded CORE in 1942 with the hope of enlisting persons whose major concern was in race relations instead of pacifism. CORE combined Gandhi's techniques with the sit-in, derived from the sit-down strikes of the 1930's. Until about 1959, CORE's main activity was attacking discrimination in places of public accommodation in the cities of the Northern and Border states. A cornerstone of its philosophy was that American racism could be destroyed only through an interracial movement. It was thoroughly interracial—even "color-blind" in its internal operations; as late as 1961, two thirds of its membership and the majority of its national officers were white.

The drift in public opinion toward a more liberal racial attitude, which had begun during the New Deal, accelerated during the war and the postwar years. Thoughtful whites became painfully aware of the contradiction in fighting the Nazis with their racist philosophy while permitting race discrimination at home. After the war the revolution against Western imperialism, first in Asia and then in Africa, engendered a new respect for the nonwhite peoples of the world and a new importance for them in international councils. Ironically, nothing was more helpful to the Negroes' cause than the Cold War, with the Communist powers holding American democratic pretensions up to ridicule before the uncommitted peoples of the world.

In this context of changing international trends and shifting American opinion, the campaign for black rights broadened. The growing size of the Northern black vote had already made civil rights a major issue in national elections, and eventually, in

1957, led to the establishment of a federal Civil Rights Commission with the power to investigate discriminatory conditions throughout the country and to recommend corrective measures to the President. Under pressure from the NAACP and other organizations, both black and white, more and more Northern and Western states outlawed discrimination in employment, housing, and public accommodations. The NAACP, piling up victory upon victory in the courts, successfully attacked racially restrictive covenants in housing, segregation in interstate transportation, and discrimination in publicly owned recreational facilities. Finally, with the Supreme Court ruling of 1954 it brought its legal campaign against educational segregation in the South to a triumphant climax.

Over the years Negroes had gradually taken over most of the offices in the NAACP. In 1920 James Weldon Johnson had become the Association's first black executive secretary. In 1935 the NAACP legal work had come under black direction when Charles Houston was hired as special counsel. In 1965 only two white people were on its national staff, and less than one fourth of the national board was white. During and after the Second World War the backbone of the NAACP's expanding membership came to rest among the working-class urban blacks. In the postwar era, it continued to conduct voter-registration drives and established housing and labor departments to improve its program in these two areas. Thus, in the 1950's, the NAACP was strengthening its work along the legal-legislative lines it had employed in earlier years.

CORE by midcentury was embarking upon demonstrations in the Border states. Public accommodations were still its major focus, but it also began experimenting with direct-action techniques to open employment opportunities. In 1947 CORE, in cooperation with the Fellowship of Reconciliation, conducted a "Journey of Reconciliation"—or what would later be called a "Freedom Ride"—in the states of the upper South. Their purpose was to test compliance with the *Morgan* v. *Virginia* decision of the preceding year, in which the Supreme Court had declared that for states to require segregation on interstate buses was an undue burden on interstate commerce. The riders met resistance in some areas, and the pacifist Bayard Rustin, who was to become one of the prominent civil-rights leaders of the 1960's, was one of those who was sentenced to a thirty-day jail term on a North Carolina road gang.

It was not CORE, however, but the Montgomery, Alabama, bus boycott of 1955–6 that captured the imagination of the nation and of the Negro community in particular and was chiefly responsible for the rising use of direct action in the late 1950's. In large measure this happened because the boycott, a local action, catapulted into national prominence the one person in the civil-rights movement who most nearly achieved charismatic leadership, the Rev. Martin Luther King, Jr. Like the founders of CORE—but unlike the great majority of the civil-rights activists, who regarded nonviolence as a convenient tactic—King professed a Gandhian belief in the principles of pacifism. In King's view, the civil-rights demonstrators who were beaten and jailed by hostile whites educated and transformed their oppressors through the redemptive character of their unmerited suffering.

Even before a court decision obtained by NAACP attorneys in November 1956 desegregated the Montgomery buses and gave victory to the Montgomery Improvement Association, a similar movement had started in Tallahassee, Florida, and afterward one developed in Birmingham, Alabama. In June 1957, the Tuskegee Civic Association undertook a three-year boycott of local merchants after the state legislature gerrymandered nearly all the black voters outside of the town's boundaries. This campaign was crowned with success when, in response to a suit filed by the NAACP Legal Defense Fund, the Supreme Court ruled the gerrymander illegal. Today blacks control the public offices in the community where Booker T. Washington used to preach that Negroes had erred by starting in politics instead of at the plow. Events in Montgomery, Tallahassee, Birmingham, and Tuskegee were widely heralded as indicating the emergence of the "New Negro" in the South— militant, no longer fearful of white hoodlums, police, or jails, and ready to use his collective weight to achieve his ends. Seizing upon this new mood, King in 1957 established the Southern Christian Leadership Conference (SCLC), designed to coordinate direct-action activities in Southern cities. Black protest now moved in a vigorous fashion into the South; like the Northern protest activities, it was concentrated in the urban ghetto.

2

The effectiveness of King's leadership was not the only reason for the popularity of nonviolent direct action. The fact was that the older techniques of legal and legislative action had proved themselves limited instruments. Impressive as it was to cite the advances in the fifteen years after the end of World War II, particularly the new state laws and Supreme Court decisions, something was clearly wrong. Though in the dozen years following the outlawing of the white primary in 1944 the NAACP and other groups had raised the total number of Negroes registered in Southern states from about 250,000 to nearly a million and a quarter, Negroes were still disfranchised in most of the South. Supreme Court decisions desegregating transportation facilities were still largely ignored there. Discrimination in employment and housing abounded, even in Northern states with model civil-rights laws. Beginning in 1954, the black unemployment rate steadily moved upward. There was the Southern diehard reaction following the Supreme Court's 1954 decision on school desegregation with attempts to outlaw the NAACP, intimidation of civil-rights leaders, "the massive resistance" to the Court's decision, the forcible curtailment of black voter registration, and the rise of the White Citizens' Councils.

At the very time that legalism was thus proving to be of limited usefulness, other events were bringing about a change in black attitudes. Negroes were gaining a new self-image as a result of the rise of the new African nations; King and others were demonstrating that nonviolent direct action could succeed in the South; and the new laws and court decisions, the international situation, and the evident drift of white public opinion developed in American blacks a new confidence in the future. In short, there occurred what has appropriately been described as a "revolution in expectations." Negroes no longer felt that they had to accept the humiliations of second-class citizenship, and consequently these humiliations—somewhat fewer though they now were—appeared to be more intolerable than ever. Ironically, it was the NAACP's very successes in the legislatures and the courts that more than any other single factor led to this revolution in expectations and the resultant dissatisfaction with the limitations of the NAACP's program. This increasing impatience accounted for the rising tempo of nonviolent direct action in the late 1950's, culminating in the student sit-ins of 1960 and the inauguration of what is popularly known as the "civil rights revolution," or the "Negro revolt."

Many believe that the Montgomery boycott ushered in this Negro revolt, and the importance of that event in projecting the images of both King and nonviolent direct action cannot be overestimated. But the really decisive break with the preeminence of legalistic techniques came with the college student sit-ins that swept the South in the spring of 1960. In scores of communities in the upper South, the Atlantic coastal states, and Texas, student demonstrations secured the desegregation of lunch counters in drug and variety stores. Arrests were numbered in the thousands, and police brutality was only too evident in scores of communities. In the Deep South the campaign ended in failure, even in instances where hundreds were arrested, as at Montgomery, Alabama, Orangeburg, South Carolina, and Baton Rouge, Louisiana. But the youths captured the imagination of the black community and, to a considerable extent, of whites as well.

The civil-rights movement would never be the same again. The Southern college-student sit-ins set in motion waves of events that shook the power structure of the black community. They made direct action temporarily preeminent as a civil-rights technique, ended NAACP hegemony in the civil-rights movement, speeded up incalculably the whole process of social change in race relations, all but destroyed the barriers standing against the recognition of the Negro's constitutional rights, and ultimately turned the black protest organizations toward a deep concern with the economic and social problems of the masses. Involved was a steady radicalization of tactics and goals: from legalism to direct action and ultimately to Black Power; from participation by the middle and upper classes to mass action by all classes; from guaranteeing the protection of the Negro's constitutional rights to securing economic policies that would ensure the welfare of the culturally deprived in a technologically changing society; from appeal to the white American's sense of fair play to demands based upon the power in the black ghetto. Most of these things had been adumbrated by the March on Washington Movement of the early 1940's; but it was the train of events set in motion by the college generation of 1960 that made Randolph's vision of civil-rights tactics and objectives a reality.

The election of John F. Kennedy in 1960 symbolized another set of factors that were to have importance for the course of the black revolution. Kennedy campaigned vigorously for the black vote, and his narrow victory would not have been possible without it. At the same time he was heavily indebted to some segregationists who kept their states in the Democratic column, and he did not wish to jeopardize other parts of his legislative program by pushing for a civil-rights bill to strengthen those passed in 1957 and 1960, which had provided mainly for a fact-finding but powerless Civil Rights Commission. He attempted therefore to placate Southern states by following their recommendations in making appointments to the federal district courts. This policy led to the selection of certain extremely segregationist judges and thus removed effective judicial assistance for blacks in the Deep South to the more distant circuit and supreme courts. On the other hand, Kennedy privately encouraged the Taconic and Field Foundations to finance a voter-registration campaign among Southern blacks being conducted by the various civil-rights organizations. Despite resistance in many areas, particularly in the Deep South, black registration in the South as a whole roughly doubled to a total of about two million between 1962 and 1964.

Basically Kennedy hoped to satisfy blacks by strategic use of executive authority. After much delay Kennedy in late 1962 ordered the federal housing authorities to cease discrimination connected with the financing of private homes. For the first time the Presidential committee charged with securing fair-employment policies from firms with government contracts seriously attempted to put some pressure on the offending corporations. But the most effective response Kennedy gave to his black supporters was in his appointments policy. For the first time Negroes received a significant number of positions at the middle and higher levels in the government departments, the most notable being the appointment in 1961 of Robert C. Weaver to head the Housing and Home Finance Agency. Although in retrospect Kennedy's program seems mild, one thing is clear: where President Eisenhower had proved vulnerable only to international pressures (as when he finally sent troops to Little Rock, Arkansas, to enforce the Supreme Court's decision integrating the white high school there), Kennedy was susceptible to pressures from Negro public opinion as well. He needed the vote and, as subsequent events showed, both he and his successor could be pushed into progressively stronger action on behalf of the race.

3

The successes of the student movement brought a decisive break with the preeminence of legalistic techniques and threatened the existing leadership arrangements in the black community far more profoundly than had the Montgomery boycott and the rise of King and SCLC. What ensued was a spirited rivalry among all civil-rights organizations. Both the NAACP and SCLC attempted to identify themselves with the student movement. The organizing meeting of the Student Nonviolent Coordinating Committee (SNCC) at Raleigh, North Carolina, in April 1960 was called by Martin Luther King. The SNCC platform expressed the same ideas of religious pacifism as did King himself. But within a year the youth had come to consider King as too cautious, not dedicated enough to the cause, and had broken with him and SCLC. The NAACP, which had previously engaged in demonstrations only in a peripheral way, now decided to make direct action a major part of its strategy. Its youth secretary organized and reactivated college and youth chapters in the Southern and Border states with the specific intention of promoting direct-action campaigns. Other staff members at regional conferences that spring urged the adult branches to support this kind of activity. In many cases eager youths pushed reluctant adults into backing direct action. Much as the latter might have initially opposed a demonstration, once dozens or hundreds of young people had been arrested, their elders could do nothing but rally to them. The young people, especially in NAACP branches, depended heavily on the legal and financial aid that adult citizens supplied. Yet the dynamics, if not the full reality, of the situation were summed up by a college student at the 1961 NAACP convention who remarked, "We don't need the adults, but they need us." CORE, which was still unknown to the general public, installed James Farmer as national director in January 1961 and moved to the front rank of civil-rights organizations with the famous Freedom Ride to Alabama and Mississippi that spring. Designed to dramatize the lack of transportation desegregation in those states, the Freedom Ride eventuated in a bus burning in Alabama, hundreds spending a month or more in Mississippi prisons, and partial compliance with a new order from the Interstate Commerce Commission desegregating all facilities used in interstate transportation.

Disagreements over strategy and tactics inevitably became intertwined with rivalries between personalities and organizations. Each civil-rights agency felt the need for proper credit if it was to obtain the prestige and financial contributions necessary to maintain and expand its own program. The clashes between individuals and organizations, both nationally and locally, were often very severe, and the lack of unity was often deplored. Actually, down to 1964, the overall effect of the competition was to stimulate more and more activity as organizations attempted to outdo each other, and thus to accelerate the pace of social change in city after city. On the other hand, even among the strictly direct-action organizations, there developed differences in style. SCLC appeared to be the most deliberate and to engage chiefly in a few major projects. From the beginning SNCC staff workers lived on subsistence allowances and almost made going to jail a way of life. More than any of the other groups, SNCC workers were "true believers."

Direct actionists often criticized the NAACP for being dominated by a conservative black bourgeoisie wedded to a program of legal action and gradualism. Actually, in the 1960's the NAACP's program became the most highly varied of all the civil-rights organizations. It retained a strong emphasis on court litigation. Acting in part through the Civil Rights Leadership Conference, consisting of many Negro and interracial organizations interested in promoting civil-rights legislation, it maintained an effective lobby at the national capital. And it also engaged in many direct-action campaigns. Some branches disdained direct action, but others enthusiastically adopted the tactic. In a few cases NAACP branch presidents even served as heads of SCLC affiliates.

In the absence of carefully collected empirical data, it is impossible to speak with precision about the sources of membership and leadership in either the NAACP or the other groups. Individuals of middle- and upper-class background or attainments predominated in the leadership of all organizations, for they alone were likely to possess the necessary skills of administration and communication. This was true even though SNCC and CORE consciously worked to create indigenous grass-roots leadership, and many purely local groups that arose in the late 1960's also developed leaders from among the poor themselves. The college students who founded SNCC and formed the backbone of the demonstrations in 1960–1 tended to be mainly from an upwardly mobile lower-middle-class background, or what they themselves often described as "striving lower class." By 1962, however, SNCC had ceased to be a coordinator of college groups but had become a staff of activists whose field-workers stimulated direct action in Southern communities. Both SNCC community projects and SCLC affiliates appealed mostly to working-class people rather than to the bourgeoisie. The NAACP since the 1940's had also drawn most of its members from the working class, although certain branches with a mass-membership base, like the one in Chicago, were closely allied with urban political machines, which had used the organization to siphon off protest rather than to articulate it. CORE, by 1962 and 1963, when it was turning its attention to employment problems in the Northern cities, attracted a number of blue-collar workers and even some people from the chronically unemployed lower class. During 1963–5 its Southern staff created and closely cooperated with working-class community organizations. But frequently CORE chapters, most of which were located in the North and West, had leaders and members who were mainly middle class. In fact, in many localities the range of membership and leaders in the NAACP, in CORE, and even in the SCLC affiliates made it hard to distinguish among them on the basis of social class. Rather, the NAACP and the more activist groups often seemed to attract different personality types from roughly the same social classes.

4

Meanwhile the role of whites in the movement was changing. Instead of occupying positions of leadership, they found themselves relegated to the role of foot soldiers and followers, although white contributors and foundations continued to supply the principal financial support for the Urban League and the three direct-action organizations. Blacks in the movement came to feel less dependent on whites, more confident of their own power, and demanded that their leaders be black. The NAACP had acquired black leadership some years before; and both SCLC and SNCC were from the start Negro-led and Negro-dominated. CORE, having acquired a new image in 1961 after the Freedom Ride, became predominantly black as it expanded in 1962–4. Its 1965 convention adopted a constitutional amendment that officially limited white leadership in the chapters; by 1967 all of its national executives were blacks, and a year later whites were totally excluded from active membership in the organization.

White liberals, Socialists, and pacifists found themselves increasingly under suspicion in the activist organizations, especially if they did not endorse the most militant steps. Many of them must have felt rather like the Girondists did when overtaken by the Jacobins. In the labor movement, black workers grew restive over the failure of even the most liberal unions to place Negroes on their international boards or to eliminate discrimination in Southern locals. Consequently, the Negro-labor alliance forged during the 1930's disintegrated. "Farewell to Liberals," an article in *The Nation* by an NAACP vice-president, expressed the idea well enough.

Thus, by 1962, "white liberal" joined "black bourgeoisie" and "Uncle Tom" as an epithet of opprobrium in the vocabulary of many black militants. The phrase "white liberal" was also employed by white revolutionary Marxists who had·jumped on the direct-action bandwagon. But beginning about 1963 they, too, found themselves in the ranks of those being "race-baited" by their Negro colleagues in the movement.

Nevertheless, whites continued to play an essential supporting role. Involved were many individuals, hitherto not sensitive to the civil-rights issue, whom we can call the "white moderates." Such whites, most notably leaders of the three major religious faiths, were of critical importance in the coalition of forces that were represented in the March on Washington in 1963, and it was this coalition that made possible the Civil Rights Act of 1964 and the Voting Rights Act of 1965. Subsequently, in the wake of the waves of summer rioting that began in 1964 and the emergence of the black-power movement in 1966, some elements in the white business community came to play an increasingly important supportive role.

5

The white radicals were attracted to the activist cause because they regarded it as the key to a socialized America. Yet the precise role of the white—and black—revolutionary leftists is difficult to ascertain. Actually, purely as a result of its own dynamics, the Negro protest movement of the 1960's underwent a continuous radicalization in tactics and ideology. As already noted, it was disappointment with the results of the NAACP's legal-legislative strategy that led to the triumph of direct action as a technique. Then, as lunch counters were desegregated, sit-ins and boycotts were used to attack exclusion from other places of public accommodation in the South, racist housing developments in the North, and, most important of all, discrimination in employment. The rivalries among the various groups accelerated the process. As progress was made in one area, organizations looked for other forms of discrimination to attack—in part to further the battle against racism and in part to justify their own continued existence.

Large sections of the NAACP enthusiastically embraced direct action. The National Urban League, under the leadership of Whitney M. Young, Jr., appointed executive director in 1961, became outspoken and militant. The League began to talk much more firmly to businessmen whom it had previously treated with the utmost tact and caution. It was principally the new climate provided by the activists that made this change in Urban League strategy possible. As businessmen came to fear demonstrations at their doorsteps or factory gates, they listened more carefully to requests and suggestions from the Urban League.

Meanwhile, as the excitement created by the earlier demonstrations dissipated, and as it became evident that many places of public accommodation remained firmly segregated, more dramatic forms of direct action became essential. A few arrests were no longer newsworthy. To desegregate the more intransigent Southern communities, it was necessary to persuade dozens and even hundreds of people to go to jail and stay there. It became quite obvious that the unmerited suffering of the direct actionists did not bring a change in the hearts of the oppressors. Rather it was the economic pinch created by sit-ins and boycotts, the publicity obtained through mass arrests, and the national and international pressure generated by the violence of white hoodlums and police that forced political and social change. There followed a secularization of those Southern Negro activists who remained in the movement for any length of time. Few of them had ever been pacifists in the first place, but an important reason for the initial attraction of nonviolent direct action had been its consonance with their Christian faith. Now, instead of speaking of love and Christianity, activists began to talk of power. They thought less of convincing the white man of the moral righteousness of their aspirations and more of forcing him to change his policies through the power of black bodies to create social dislocation.

A major factor leading to the radicalization of the civil-rights movement was unemployment and poverty—and an important force awakening the civil-rights organizations to this problem was the meteoric rise of the Black Muslims to national prominence. Paradoxically, this nationalist sect, established around 1930, reached the peak of its influence at a time when more progress toward equal rights was being made than ever before in American history. But this was also a time of deteriorating economic opportunity for the lower classes in the urban ghettos. In 1952 the median black-family income was 57 percent of white-family income; ten years later, despite the highly publicized occupational breakthroughs of a minority of blacks, the average income of black families had fallen to 53 percent of that of whites. The first real spurt in the membership rolls of the Black Muslims seems to have occurred during the recession of 1953–4. Due to automation and other forms of technological change, black unemployment rose steadily after 1958. By 1962 it was two and a half times that of whites, and in some industrial cities the differential was even greater.

More than anything else this increasing unemployment, combined with the revolution in expectations, created a climate in

which the Black Muslims thrived. They preached an eschato-
logical vision of the doom of the white "devils" and the coming
dominance of the black person, promised a utopian paradise of
a separate territory within the United States in which black
people would establish their own state, and offered a more immediate practical program of building up black business
through hard work, thrift, and racial unity. To those willing to
submit to the rigid personal discipline of the movement, the
Black Muslim organization gave a sense of purpose and destiny.
Its program offered them four things: an explanation of their
plight (white devils); a sense of pride and self-esteem (black
superiority); a vision of a glorious future (black ascendancy);
and a practical, immediate program of uplift (working hard and
uniting to create black enterprise and prosperity). With this
Puritan ethic the Muslims appealed chiefly to an upwardly
mobile group of the lowest social class of Negroes. Basically, like
the integrationist Negro revolt, the Black Muslims were a manifestation of the Negroes' quest for recognition of their human
dignity and their rejection of the philosophy of gradualism. In
the same way that the Garvey movement was a lower-class
counterpart of the New Negro of the 1920's, so the Black Muslims were a counterpart of the *new* "New Negro" of the early
1960's. Ironically, until split by internal dissension, the Black
Muslims distinctly assisted the civil-rights organizations, for
their talk of violence and their hatred of blue-eyed devils frightened white people into becoming more amenable to the demands of the integrationists. The Black Muslims sounded so
extreme to many whites that integration appeared to be a conservative program; the same thing was to happen later with
respect to the black-power movement.

Paradoxically, the trials and successes of the integrationist
protest movement after 1960, by producing heightened self-
esteem among black people, also encouraged nationalist tendencies. For one thing, as blacks grew in racial pride, they displayed a sharply rising interest in black history. Another
manifestation of black consciousness was the call for black
leadership within the civil-rights movement, based upon the

growing belief that Negroes, through their own power, could bring about dramatic changes in American society. As early as 1963 there were proposals for the formation of an all-black political party. At the same time other proposals along the lines of self-help and racial cooperation were suggested to attack the economic needs of the rural and urban poor. Finally, a group of writers expressed their alienation by questioning the values of middle-class white America and militantly calling for preservation of the unique aspects of the black subculture. After 1965, this cultural pluralism became a widely held ideology, described by the phrase "black consciousness."

As the direct-action tactics took more dramatic form, as the civil-rights groups began to articulate the needs of the masses and draw some of them to their demonstrations, the protest movement in 1963 assumed a new note of urgency and immediatism, a demand for complete "Freedom Now!" Moreover, direct action returned to the Northern cities, taking the form of massive protests against economic, housing, and educational inequities. The new mood of militance suffused the events of 1963: the fresh wave of demonstrations that swept the South from Cambridge, Maryland, to Birmingham, Alabama, and Jackson, Mississippi; the NAACP national convention, which passed a resolution calling for more direct action; the fruitless Northern street demonstrations against the discriminatory building-trades unions; and, the following winter, the equally fruitless school boycotts against de facto segregation. The frustration of the expectations of 1963 largely accounted for the further radicalization of the most militant activists beginning in 1964.

At first the new militance of the early 1960's tended to propel the more "conservative" black community leaders, whether prominent in the NAACP or not, into a more radical tactical position. It was notable that in crisis situations engendered by mass arrests, especially if these were accompanied by obvious police brutality, temporary unity was achieved between organizations and classes—generally on the militants' terms. On such occasions only rarely did even a conservative NAACP chapter refuse aid and support. The most prominent citizens were likely to mortgage their property for bail money and, in a few cases, went to jail themselves. For example, before the Birmingham demonstration conducted by SCLC in the spring of 1963, the wealthy upper-class black citizens had opposed King's decision to use that citadel of segregation as the site of a major direct-action campaign aimed at securing equal job opportunities and the desegregation of lunch counters in downtown stores. For a month following the opening demonstrations in April, King found no appreciable support locally or nationally. Conditions changed after King's lieutenants began using hundreds of black schoolchildren as demonstrators, some as young as six or seven. Their arrests caused the jails to overflow. Before the campaign ended more than two thousand persons were arrested. In the presence of newspaper and TV cameras, police used high-pressure firehoses and snarling dogs, arousing millions of Americans who witnessed such brutal scenes as a black woman pinned to the ground by burly policemen, one of whom dug his knee into her throat. Tensions mounted even more a few days later when bombs exploded at the motel that served as King's headquarters and at his brother's home. The blasts infuriated angry blacks who rioted with rocks and bottles. By this time even the early opponents of direct action had rushed to SCLC's support.

Though a superb example of how to run a direct-action demonstration, the Birmingham project resulted in a compromise that brought the city's Negroes not "Freedom Now" but token concessions that later were not carried out. Nevertheless, the demonstration was enormously important because it compelled the United States to face the problem of Southern discrimination in a way it had never done before. For the first time in American history the President appeared before the nation and declared that race discrimination was a moral issue. Moreover, the Birmingham campaign forced President Kennedy to cease depending on mild executive manipulations as a way of advancing Negro welfare and to ask Congress for a major civil-rights bill that would not only solve the public accommodations problem but would attempt to protect the Southern blacks' political rights and provide national legislative sanction for fair-employment practices. The bill was stalled, and after Kennedy's death, President Lyndon B. Johnson proved even more vigorous in pressing Congress to enact a meaningful civil-rights bill. The Civil Rights Act of 1964, in contrast to the token and symbolic civil-rights acts of 1957 and 1960, clearly declared discrimination in places of public accommodation to be illegal, instituted a modest program for protecting Southern Negroes' right to vote, created a federal fair-employment-practices agency with mild enforcement powers, and gave the national Executive the power to withdraw federal funds from state and local agencies that discriminated against Negroes.

6

Although the demonstrations in Birmingham and other numerous cities during that spring of 1963 precipitated the shift in Presidential strategy, the Civil Rights Act of 1964 would not have been passed were it not for a series of developments that converged at the March on Washington in August 1963. Early in the year, at the suggestion of Bayard Rustin, the long-time civil-rights activist, pacifist, and Socialist, A. Philip Randolph issued a call for a March on Washington in the fall in order to dramatize the need for jobs and to press for federal action. At about the same time, the Protestant, Jewish, and Catholic churches held a conference on religion and race. Though individual Jewish and Protestant clergymen had been jailed in Southern demonstrations in 1961–2, not until 1963 did the churches officially encourage such activity. After the Birmingham demonstration, at the request of SCLC, the date for the march was advanced to the summer, and the emphasis was shifted to passage of the civil-rights bill. Then the churches sought and obtained representation on the march committee. Finally, though the AFL–CIO national council refused to endorse the march, thus adding to the estrangement that had been growing between the civil-rights groups and organized labor, a few labor leaders and international unions did participate, and Walter Reuther of the UAW was given a place on the march committee.

With this impressive support, the march became fashionable. The President, reversing an earlier stand, welcomed the march, though he refused to appear on the platform. A quarter of a million people, about 20 percent of them white, participated. From the steps of the Lincoln Memorial, where slightly less than a quarter-century earlier Marian Anderson had sung on Easter morning, the leaders of the civil-rights organizations addressed the throng. For Randolph the occasion was the culmination of a vision he had held for over two decades. Roy Wilkins, executive secretary of the NAACP, recalled the contribution of W. E. B. Du Bois. The night before, at the age of ninety-five, Du Bois had died in Ghana, a Communist, completely alienated from his native land, whose citizenship he had renounced. Martin Luther King articulated in the cadences of the old-fashioned Baptist preacher the dream of inclusion in American society that Negroes had held for centuries. It was the dream that Du Bois had had for most of his life; and before that it had been the dream of Booker T. Washington and Frederick Douglass, of Nat Turner and Harriet Tubman, of the runaway slaves and contrabands, of the bondsmen who had worked to buy their freedom, and the black peasants who had sought land and education after their emancipation. After King's address, an old-line civil-rights leader commented with some acerbity: "Martin had no right to say 'I have a dream'; why, we have all had that dream for generations."

The march was more than a summation of the past years of struggle and aspiration. It also symbolized certain new directions: a deeper concern for the economic problems of the masses; more involvement of white moderates; and a new radicalism among the most militant, as suggested by the address of the SNCC chairman, John Lewis, who implied that only a revolutionary change in American institutions would permit blacks to achieve the dignity of human beings and citizens.

7

The black revolt produced an acrid controversy over the relative merits of legal action and direct action. Historical analysis reveals that in actual fact the two approaches complemented and reinforced each other. Legal action may be said to include not only litigation in the courts but also propagandizing and lobbying for new laws. Subsidiary to the legal-legislative approach were *nonpartisan* voter-registration campaigns designed to impress politicians with the potential power of the black vote. Nonviolent direct-action techniques included picketing, boycotts, sit-ins, courting arrest by disobeying unjust laws and police regulations, and filling the jails.

In the North and Far West, the post–World War II nonviolent demonstrations were one of several factors leading to the enactment of antidiscrimination legislation. Although certain of these laws—those dealing with employment and housing—to a considerable extent were disobeyed, in general the new legislation not only broke down discrimination in places of public accommodation but also helped establish new patterns of socially accepted behavior. So also did the court victories being obtained by the NAACP at the same time. These new norms of behavior reduced Northern white resistance to further black demands, while among Negroes they created higher expectations and thereby encouraged further direct action. Neither the Northern fair-employment-practice laws nor the Presidential fair-employment committees accomplished anything very striking, even among those businessmen who claimed that they followed a technically nondiscriminatory policy. Later, however, in 1963 and 1964, when direct actionists staged major demonstrations to break down employment barriers, their successes were greatly facilitated by the degree to which employers, especially those who had signed President Kennedy's "Plans for Progress," felt morally vulnerable because they had accepted the idea of equal employment practices. Black buying power, which had been demonstrated by boycotts, was another potent influence in these campaigns, but even firms that did not manufacture or sell consumer goods began to hire blacks, suggesting that a change in racial attitudes had been taking place.

In regard to the South we have already noted the role of litigation in securing victory for the direct-action work in Montgomery and Tuskegee. As a result of the Supreme Court ruling in the Montgomery case, several other cities quietly desegregated their buses. The public, both white and black, remembered not the abstruse language of the courts but the vivid language of a Negro mass movement; and, as one might have expected, direct action, not legalism, received the credit. In 1961 the Freedom Rides tested compliance with the High Court's opinions in other transportation cases. Though the Court's views were largely respected on the main roads in the Atlantic coastal states, Alabama and Mississippi had had no intention of complying until the Freedom Riders brought the glare of national publicity and an ICC order that did much to diminish segregation in interstate bus travel. Lawyers and judges had paved the way and effected some progress; the Freedom Riders built on the foundation they had laid.

The growing number of black voters, an important factor in the enactment of national and state civil-rights laws, was also of distinct value to the direct-action campaigns. Where blacks voted in substantial numbers, public authorities were likely to urge compliance with black demands. This was true not only in the North but in the South as well. The sit-in demonstrations of the early 1960's were successful principally in places like Atlanta, Nashville, Durham, Winston-Salem, Louisville, Savannah, New Orleans, Charleston, and Dallas—cities where Negroes voted and could swing elections. Ironically, the great majority of these voters had been placed on the rolls in registration campaigns sparked by the NAACP and local affiliated groups after the white-primary decision secured by the Association's legal department in 1944.

In the mid-1960's, major demonstrations in the South were successful where employed to compel Presidential action, now that the Chief Executives had become sensitive both to the aroused conscience of many white people and to the justice of the blacks' claims and their vote. The relationship between Birmingham and the Civil Rights Act of 1964 is a case in point. The moral indignation aroused across the nation by police brutality during that momentous week rallied white moderates as well as Negroes behind meaningful civil-rights legislation—a fact dramatized by the March on Washington. But it was the tireless lobbying of that unofficial arm of the NAACP, the interracial Civil Rights Leadership Conference—along with the efforts of President Johnson—which finally led to enactment of the bill.

The Civil Rights Act of 1964 settled the public accommodations issue in the South's major cities. Its voting section, however, promised more than it accomplished. Again Martin Luther King and SCLC dramatized the issue, this time at Selma, Alabama, in the spring of 1965. Again the national government was forced to intervene, and a new and more effective voting law was passed. On this occasion even the President wrapped himself in the mantle of the civil-rights movement by quoting its anthem: "We shall overcome" he promised, addressing Congress and a nationwide TV audience. Yet as Lyndon Johnson himself pointed out in that speech, beyond the protection of constitutional rights (for which Congress was now providing, a century after emancipation) lay the as yet unsolved problems of the poor.

8

Where Birmingham had made direct action respectable, the Selma demonstration, drawing thousands of white moderates from the North, made direct action fashionable. Nevertheless, as early as 1964 it was becoming evident that like legalism, direct action was but a limited instrument. This was the result of two converging developments.

One of these was the failure of the sit-ins of 1960–1 to desegregate public accommodations in Deep South states like Mississippi and Alabama, and the realization, first grasped by Robert Moses of SNCC, that, without the leverage of the vote, demonstrations there would be failures. Beginning in 1961, Moses established SNCC projects in the cities and county seats of Mississippi. He succeeded in registering only a handful, but by 1964 had generated enough support throughout the country to enable the Mississippi Freedom Democratic Party, which he had created, to challenge dramatically the seating of the official white delegates from the state at the Democratic National Convention.

Direct action had also failed when applied to the difficult economic and social problems facing the Negroes in the ghettos of the North. Separate and inferior schools, rat-infested slum housing, and police brutality did not prove vulnerable to an attack of this kind. Street demonstrations did compel employers, ranging from banks to supermarkets, to add many Negroes to their work force in Northern and Western cities, and even in some Southern towns where conditions were propitious and the blacks had considerable buying power. By these successful demonstrations, and by other fruitless ones against the building-trades unions, the black protest movement probably did more than anything else to make the nation aware of its poor. (Indeed, the civil-rights organizations deserve much of the credit for the inauguration of the federal antipoverty program.) But technological innovation was leading to a steady decline in the number of unskilled jobs available, and the black masses, half of whom had not gone beyond the eighth grade, were unable to qualify for positions requiring higher skill and education. As a result, while the black "job mix" changed because of new hiring policies on the part of business, the basic pattern of mass unemployment remained.

Faced with the intransigence of the Deep South and the inadequacy of direct action to solve the problems of the slum dwellers, the programs of the civil-rights organizations diverged. The tendency toward a unity of strategy, if not between personalities, that was emerging during 1963 was dissipated by the middle of 1964. At the very time that white support for the movement was actually rising, its most militant members felt increasingly isolated from the American scene. People in the radical left wing of the movement were growing disdainful of American society and the middle-class way of life and cynical about liberals and the leaders of organized labor. Any compromise, even if a temporary tactical device, had become anathema to them. They talked more and more of the necessity for "revolutionary" changes in the social structure, even of violence. They became increasingly skeptical of the value of white participation in the movement and insisted that black power alone could compel concessions from the "power structure" of capitalists, politicians, and bureaucratic labor leaders. The black nationalist, Malcolm X, after his assassination in 1965, became the symbolic hero for the militants. At the extreme left wing of the movement Marxism and nationalism coalesced into a truly revolutionary ideology.

In contrast, the "conservative" wing, mostly an older group of individuals, appreciated the legislation of 1964 and 1965, the public stands taken by Presidents Kennedy and Johnson, and other signs of racial progress. They were keenly aware of the new opportunities in business, in government, and in the academic world for those with training to fill them. Civil-rights activity in general, and the NAACP in particular, had become so respectable that even famous protest leaders achieved high public office. The most notable example was Lyndon Johnson's elevation of the brilliant NAACP chief counsel, Thurgood Marshall, to the Supreme Court. Those NAACP leaders who could be described as "conservative" did not believe that the millennium had arrived, but changed conditions prompted a reorientation of their strategy. Impressed by the degree of social change, many of them came to view their role as exercising influence within established institutions rather than fighting such institutions from the outside. Overt protest was not, it should be emphasized, ruled out in the views of these moderates. In fact, effective publicity of Negro grievances was often the best means of compelling reluctant public officials to take action. But the typical conservative now thought of direct action as a tactic of last resort only.

Between the two poles of thought there existed a group who

recognized the new willingness of the nation's decision makers to move toward greater racial justice but perceived also that powerful pressure would be needed to push them in that direction. This group held that blacks, as a dispossessed minority, could not hope to achieve their goals purely through their own actions. They based their strategy on a coalition of blacks with white liberals, organized labor, and white clergy, such as the one that had developed during the plans for the March on Washington. Though this theory was not officially a part of the NAACP platform, the Association, through the Civil Rights Leadership Conference, actually based part of its strategy upon it. Ultimately, the centrists hoped that a Negro-liberal-church-labor alliance, acting as a political force, would compel the national government to eliminate poverty in America for whites and blacks alike. But they still favored direct action—even mass civil disobedience—where it was needed to create the kind of social dislocation that would bring remedial action from political authorities. Birmingham and Selma were prototypes of this kind of strategy.

While it would be a gross oversimplification to pigeonhole black protest leaders and organizations, broadly speaking it can be said that the militant left wing was composed of SNCC and many people in CORE. The conservative right wing included Urban League officials and a substantial group in the NAACP. Varieties of the centrist position were held by many in CORE and the NAACP, best articulated by Bayard Rustin, A. Philip Randolph, and Martin Luther King, Jr.

Although by the middle of 1965 all segments of the movement were agreed that future protest activity would focus on the problems of the ghettos, and that rather than direct action the major weapon would be the political potential of the black masses, there were wide differences in programs. The centrist group had developed its theory of "coalition politics." With the black vote looming so large in many cities and playing such a strategic role in Presidential elections, it appeared logical for the right wing to believe that the greatest progress could be achieved by pushing from within the Democratic Party on both national and local issues. In contrast, the most radical bloc advocated the creation of Negro political organizations like the Black Panther Party of Lowndes County, Alabama. It was evident, however, that the future of collective political action would lie with the urban ghettos. There the main emphasis was on organizing the masses to challenge the Democratic machines from within the party and elect officials who really represented the interests of the poor.

The success of the coalition strategy from 1963 to 1965 was due in no small part to the role of Martin Luther King, Jr. At least on specific issues he was able to piece together an effective coalition. To critics on the left King appeared cautious, hesitant to go to jail or lead a demonstration in the streets, altogether too willing to listen to the pleas of Presidents and their emissaries. Yet to others, both black and white, he seemed a militant, though responsible, agitator. In his very willingness to make tactical compromises with the political establishment, in his very combination of militance with conservatism and caution, of righteousness with respectability, lay the secret of his success.

King articulated the dreams and aspirations of American blacks as no other leader did. At the same time he was by far the most effective interpreter of these aspirations to white America. His use of religious phraseology and the Judeo-Christian symbols of love and nonresistance were partly responsible for this, because they were reassuring to the mind and emotions of white America. But his appeal to whites went deeper. For one thing, he unerringly knew how to exploit to maximum effectiveness the white people's growing feelings of guilt. In this he was not unique. The novelist and essayist James Baldwin is the most conspicuous example of a man who achieved success with this formula—but unlike Baldwin and other angry young writers, King explicitly believed in the white man's salvation. Not only would the nonviolent crusade fulfill the blacks' dream, it would help whites live up to their Judeo-Christian and democratic values. If King's approach was reminiscent of Booker T. Washington, it was because, like the Tuskegeean, he had faith in the white man and believed that it was for the good of the white man as well as the Negro that justice be done to the black man. But Washington's career did little to influence the mainstream of historical events, whereas King's contribution was incalculable. His occupation as a minister, his manner of speaking, and his style of operation made him a sort of "conservative militant" able to attract an enormous range of people among both races. Without King as its symbolic leader, it is difficult to perceive how the civil-rights movement would have achieved half as much as it did. It is doubtful, for example, that there would now be on the books the major civil-rights legislation that nonviolent direct action brought about in 1964 and 1965.

King also occupied a position of strategic importance as "the vital center" within the civil-rights movement. Identified as militant and activist, his SCLC was the most deliberate of the direct-action groups. This not only gave King respectability in the eyes of whites but also enabled him to serve as a bridge between the militant and conservative wings of the movement. For example, it appears unlikely that the Urban League and the NAACP would have joined the 1963 March on Washington if King had not done so. Because King participated, the march drew not only enormous support from white ministers and other middle-class white moderates but also the numbers and money that the NAACP could bring and the respectability that accompanied Urban League endorsement.

Yet between 1964 and 1966 the black protest movement became increasingly fragmented and ineffective. King found it more difficult, and finally impossible, to continue his unifying role. Fundamentally the growing disunity in the protest movement was rooted in the frustration of radically heightened expectations and in the extraordinary problems involved in achieving genuine equality for the black poor. In these circumstances, the various segments of the movement became increasingly divided on how to tackle the situation.

The 1964 Democratic Party Convention foreshadowed this trend. Events there, in the eyes of the militants, thoroughly discredited both the Democratic Party establishment and the white liberal elements in the interracial coalition backing the national civil-rights legislative program. As an outgrowth of the voter-registration campaign in Mississippi, begun in 1961 and conducted under the sponsorship of a joint CORE–SNCC–NAACP coalition known as COFO, or the Council of Federated Organizations, the Freedom Democratic Party was created. This organization came to the 1964 Democratic Convention challenging the seating of the regular Mississippi delegation on the grounds that blacks were unconstitutionally disfranchised in Mississippi. The black militants not only rejected the party's compromise offer of two delegates-at-large but their growing distrust of the white liberals became complete when many of the latter, having originally supported the challenge, in the end advocated accepting the compromise. Finally, the Negroes themselves were deeply divided, with SNCC and CORE refusing to approve the compromise, while NAACP elements in the Freedom Democratic Party and men like Rustin and King argued for its acceptance.

The war in Vietnam exacerbated the growing cleavages. Some believed that the war diverted attention and funds from solving the country's leading domestic problem. Others went further and regarded the war as cut of the same cloth as domestic racism, charging that both involved the attempt of the American "white power structure" to keep a colored race in a colonial status. A number of people, heretofore devoting their full energies to fighting racial discrimination, were diverted to working against the war in Vietnam. At the opposite pole were those who held that the Vietnam issue was irrelevant as far as the black protest was concerned, and that to mix the two issues was tactically dangerous, since it would lose some support for the blacks' cause. The Urban League and the NAACP refused to identify themselves with the Vietnam issue. King, previously a key figure in the coalition strategy, openly attacked United States policy in Vietnam, as did SNCC and CORE. The white supporters of the coalition were similarly split, with organized labor particularly endorsing the war program.

Meanwhile, by 1965, white funding of the direct-action organizations was drying up. All along, the NAACP had been financed primarily by blacks, and the Urban League continued to receive money from white businessmen. Various factors accounted for the financial problems of CORE, SCLC, and SNCC—the riots, annoyance with the refusal of SNCC and CORE to accept the compromise offered at the 1964 Democratic Convention, and the position of all three organizations on the Vietnam War. Even King, who had urged the Mississippi Freedom Democratic Party (MFDP) to accept the compromise at the 1964 Democratic Convention, found that his opposition to the war produced a sharp drop in SCLC's income. The financial situation exacerbated the distrust for the white liberals and moderates and accelerated the decline in the activities of CORE and SNCC. Then, too, many civil-rights workers turned to peace activities; equally important, others, including many among the most effective local leaders, were siphoned off into well-paying administrative positions in the War on Poverty.

The antipoverty act, passed in 1964, had several effects on the protest movement. It accelerated the shift, already evident, from an emphasis on a national legislative program to local community action led by grass-roots people from among the poor themselves. The struggle within the black community over who would administer the community-action programs exacerbated the polarization between the more moderate middle-class leaders, often identified with the NAACP and Urban League, and the more radical types. Finally, the antipoverty program unintentionally served to increase the frustration and discontent among the black poor by further escalating their expectations but failing to deliver anything substantial. Yet one legacy of the War on Poverty was the feeling that the government should allocate resources to the ghetto, to be spent for programs initiated and administered by the ghetto dwellers themselves. Thus, paradoxically, the Office of Economic Opportunity projects, while not solving the problems of the poor, led to a heightened militance among them.

9

Lower-income Negroes were on a dreary treadmill. Without much education, they found it difficult to obtain decent jobs; without adequate work and something for their children to aspire to, it was not likely that they would have the motivation to seek an adequate education even if it were available. The feeling of frustration, of hopelessness, was reflected in the riots at Los Angeles, Newark, Detroit, and in the more than four hundred disorders of varying degrees of seriousness between 1964 and 1969. Paradoxically, these outbreaks were born of a sense of powerlessness and at the same time a sense of power derived from the knowledge that "whitey" now felt afraid or guilty and was unlikely to fight back.

The riots of the 1960's were clearly different from those of the nineteenth and the first part of the twentieth centuries. What we may call the "new-style" riot first appeared in Harlem in 1935 and in 1943, where Negro attacks were mainly directed against white property rather than white people. The Detroit race riot of 1943, one of the more serious racial conflicts in American history, which brought death to nine whites and twenty-five blacks, had affinities with both the older and more recent varieties of race warfare. As in the Chicago and certain other conflagrations of the World War I period, the 1943 Detroit riot was precipitated by black retaliation against mounting white hostility. White mobs kicked, beat, and shot Negroes to death, and though members of both races lost their lives, the majority of the dead and injured were Negroes. On the other hand, because the black mobs' major attention was directed toward destroying and looting white-owned businesses in the black ghetto, and because most of the Negroes who were killed were shot by white policemen, this riot bore certain striking similarities to the riots in Detroit and other cities in the period since 1964. This symbolic destruction of "whitey" through his property, characterizing the new-style riot, did not truly fulfill James Baldwin's prediction of "the fire next time," since it did not mark a direct reversal of those conflagrations nearly half a century ago when white mobs literally hunted and killed dozens of blacks. The modern riot involved hardly any white civilians at all, and policemen or National Guardsmen constituted the relatively small number of white casualties.

One can identify perhaps two major factors responsible for this contrast between the old-style and the new-style riot. In the first place, there was the relatively marked shift in the climate of race relations in this country over the preceding generation. On the one hand, whites had become, on the whole, more sensitive to the blacks' plight, more receptive to black demands, and less punitive in their response to Negro aggression. The black masses, on the other hand, had raised their expectations markedly and, disillusioned by the relatively slow pace of social change that had left the underprivileged urban Negroes of the North scarcely, if at all, better off than they were ten or fifteen years before, had become more restless and militant.

In the second place, there was an ecological factor. From South to North, the migration of the World War I period was a mere trickle compared to what it became later. The migration to the North in each decade since 1940 has been equal to or greater than the migration of the whole thirty-year period, 1910 to 1940. At the same time, owing to the Supreme Court's outlawing of the restrictive-housing covenant in 1948 and the tearing down of the older slums through urban renewal, the black population has been dispersed over a wider area, thus accentuating the trend toward the development of vast ghettos. Indeed, compared to the enormous ghettos of today, the black residential areas of the World War I period were mere enclaves. By the 1960's Negroes were close to becoming a majority in several of the major American cities.

The character of American race riots was markedly affected by these demographic changes. Even if white mobs had formed, they would have been unable to attack and burn down the black residential areas; even in the nineteenth- and early-twentieth-century riots, white mobs did not usually dare invade the larger black sections, and they destroyed only the smaller areas of Negro concentration. Since black people were now such a large share of the population of the central-city areas, white mobs were no longer in a position to chase, beat, and kill isolated blacks on downtown streets. More important, from the Negroes' point of view, the large-scale ghettos provided a relatively safe place for the destruction and looting of white-owned property. It was impossible for local police forces to guard business property in the far-flung ghettos; even state police and federal troops found themselves in hostile territory where it was difficult to chase down rioters beyond the principal thoroughfares.

Beyond the seething discontent among the masses in the urban ghettos which during the long, hot summers, tended to erupt into overt racial warfare, the theme of retaliatory violence was evident in various forms in the thinking of the most militant elements in the black protest movement of recent years. The Black Muslims suggested that blacks should fight back against the vicious "slavemasters," and their eschatology included a violent end to white domination. A small number of Marxist-nationalists appeared at the fringes of the black protest movement in the early 1960's, the most vocal of whom was Robert F. Williams, dismissed as president of the Monroe, North Carolina, branch of the NAACP in 1959 for his open advocacy of violence against the oppressive white community. From his place of exile in Havana, Cuba, and later in China, Williams issued a monthly bulletin not only advocating violent revolution but specifically urging blacks "to wage an urban guerrilla war of self-defense" by throwing from rooftops Molotov cocktails and lye or acid bombs (made by injecting lye or acid in the metal end of light bulbs). Subsequently, Williams was named chairman in exile of an organization known as the Revolutionary Action Movement (RAM), a tiny group of college-educated people in a few major Northern cities, two of whose members were sentenced to prison in 1968 for conspiring to murder Roy Wilkins and Whitney Young. Later, Williams was named chairman of another revolutionary nationalist group, the Republic of New Africa.*

Williams, RAM, and the better-known Black Muslims were on the fringes of the Negro protest movement of the early 1960's. Subsequently, violence and the propaganda for violence moved closer to the center of the race-relations stage. There was an increasing use of revolutionary vocabulary and a rising skepticism about the value of nonviolence among many of the more militant people in the nonviolent direct-action organizations. By 1964 and 1965 at least some of them, especially in SNCC and to a lesser extent in CORE, were toying with the idea that revolutionary violence might be necessary. The view that "no people ever gained its freedom without some bloodshed" became widely voiced. In 1964 and 1965 there was considerable publicity about the Deacons for Defense, organized in Louisiana to protect blacks and civil-rights demonstrators from white attackers. In that period, CORE, without departing from its advocacy of nonviolent direct-action methods, welcomed the protection offered by the Deacons, who did not engage in talk of general revolutionary violence but asserted the necessity of defending black people and white civil-rights workers if they were attacked.

Beyond the wave of race riots following the summer of 1964, the incendiary statements of the militant SNCC spokesmen, Rap Brown and Stokely Carmichael, became familiar TV and newspaper fare. The Black Panther Party, founded by a group of young California militants and espousing a nationalist and revolutionary rhetoric, thrived and received national publicity. As has often been pointed out, there is no evidence that the race riots of the 1960's had any direct relation to the teachings of Williams, of these various groups, even of the SNCC advocates of armed rebellion and guerrilla warfare. But the statements of these ideologists and the spontaneous actions of the masses had much in common. For both were the product of the frustrations resulting from the growing disparity between the

* He returned to the United States in 1969.

Negroes' status in American society and the rapidly rising expectations induced by the civil-rights revolution and its earlier successes.

It should be stressed that the theme of retaliatory violence has never been entirely absent from black thinking. This sentiment has taken various forms. Some have advocated self-defense against a specific attack—a type of action legal under the Anglo-American system of jurisprudence. Some have called for revolutionary violence. Others have predicted an apocalyptic race war from which blacks would emerge victorious. Though seldom articulated for white ears, and only rarely appearing in print, such thoughts have been quite common. Ralph Bunche, in preparing a memorandum for Gunnar Myrdal's *An American Dilemma* in 1940, noted, "There are Negroes, too, who, fed up with frustration of their life here, see no hope and express an angry desire 'to shoot their way out of it.' I have on many occasions heard Negroes exclaim: 'Just give us machine guns and we'll blow the lid off the whole damn business.' " Thus, it would appear that the idea of violence has been a continuing, if unpublicized, undercurrent accompanying other forms of protest.

While in no period has retaliatory violence been a central thrust in black protest, advocacy of violence has often been expressed more explicitly in periods of intense black protest activity. David Walker's and Henry Highland Garnet's calls for slave rebellions coincided with marked revivals of other kinds of militant Negro protest. A thorough study of race violence during Reconstruction remains to be made, but it is clear that in some cases, blacks employed physical resistance in that period. As already noted, a major twentieth-century protest leader like Du Bois did not foreclose the possibility of revolutionary violence if and when conditions made it practicable. It is notable that in the twentieth century overt discussion about the advisability of violent retaliation and actual incidents of this type of violence were most prominent during the periods of heightened militancy just after World War I and again during the 1960's. In both eras a major factor leading Negroes to advocate or to adopt such a tactic was the discrepancy between the blacks' expectations and their objective status. We have already alluded to the rapid escalation of the expectations of the black masses who shared Martin Luther King's dream and identified vicariously with the successes of the civil-rights revolution, while their own opportunities and economic situation did not improve. A comparable situation existed during and after the First World War. The agitation of the recently founded NAACP, which more than doubled its membership between 1918 and 1919; the propaganda of fighting a war to make the world safe for democracy; and especially the Great Migration to the Northern cities, which were viewed by those who moved out of the South as a promised land—all created new hopes for the fulfillment of age-old dreams. But the blacks' new hopes collided with increasing white hostility, with overcrowded ghettos and unfriendly white workers who feared black competition for their jobs, with the disastrous drop in job openings following the return of peace, and with the revival of the Ku Klux Klan.

One period of marked and rising Negro militance, however, was not accompanied by a significant increase in manifestations of black retaliatory violence. This was the one following the Second World War. Indeed, the Second World War itself witnessed far less black violence than did the First World War. The reason for this would appear to be that the 1940's and early 1950's were years of gradually improving Negro status and a period in which the expectations of the masses did not greatly outrun the actual improvements being made. In fact, from 1941 until the mid-1950's, the relative position of the black workers, as compared to the white wage earners, was generally improving, and as already noted, it was not until the recession of 1954–5 that the Black Muslims, with their rhetoric of race hatred and retaliatory violence, began to expand rapidly.

It would appear that throughout the history of black Americans there has been a strong element of fantasy in discussion and efforts concerning violent retaliation. Robert Williams talked of Molotov cocktails and snarling up traffic as devices for a largely poverty-stricken ethnic minority to engineer a revolution. The Black Muslims spoke of retaliatory violence, but the talk seemed to function as a psychological safety valve; by preaching separation, they in effect accommodated to the American social order and placed racial warfare off in the future when Allah in his time would destroy the whites and usher in an era of black domination. Similarly, in view of population statistics and power distribution in American society, Du Bois and others who have spoken of the inevitability of racial warfare and Negro victory in such a struggle were engaging in wishful prophesies. And blacks have been nothing if not realistic. The patterns of black behavior in riots demonstrate this. In earlier times, as already indicated, those who bought guns in anticipation of the day when self-defense would be necessary usually did not retaliate. And black attacks on whites occurred mainly in the early stages of the riots before the full extent of the anger and power and sadism of the white mobs became evident.

Blacks of the World War I era resisted white insults and attacks only as long as they had hopes of being successful in the resistance. It should be emphasized that one of the remarkable things about the riots after 1964, in spite of their having been marked by particular resentment at police brutality, is the fact that Negro destruction was aimed at white-owned property, not white lives, even after National Guardsmen and policemen killed scores of blacks. And in those cases where retaliatory violence was attempted, Negroes retreated in the face of massive white armed force. Economically impoverished Negroes press as far as they realistically can; and one reason for the explosions of the 1960's was the awareness that whites were to some degree in retreat, that white mobs in the North no longer organized to attack, and that to an extent the frustrated Negroes in slums like Watts, Detroit, Washington, or Newark could get away with acts of destruction.

When it became evident that the destruction in black neighborhoods hurt blacks as well as whites, that mostly blacks rather than whites were killed, and that violence did not bring appreciable improvement in the life of the urban slum dwellers, the civil disorders of the late 1960's ceased. Despite all the rhetoric of engineering a social revolution through armed rebellion and guerrilla warfare, of planned invasions of downtown business districts and white suburbs, after 1968 the number and seriousness of the riots fell off sharply. While both black spokesmen and certain elements among white elites perceived the civil disorders as evidence for the necessity of taking serious steps to solve the problems of the black poor, the advocacy and use of violence as a deliberate program for attacking these problems remained in the realm of fantasy.

10

The disillusionment with the Johnson Administration and the white liberals, the fragmentation of the black protest movement, the enormous difficulties that stood in the way of overcoming the problems of the black masses, and the riots that erupted spontaneously in 1964 and 1965 as a consequence of the anger and frustration of the urban slum dweller all set the stage for the dramatic appearance of the black-power slogan in the summer of 1966.

Black power first articulated a mood rather than a program—disillusionment and alienation from white America, race pride, and self-respect or "black consciousness." The precipitating occasion was the June 1966 freedom march of James Meredith, whose enrollment at the University of Mississippi in 1962 had triggered a riot that brought two deaths, hundreds of injuries, federal intervention, and the presence of thousands of troops. Four years later Meredith decided that a dramatic way to interest more Mississippi Negroes in voter registration was to demonstrate that it would be possible for him to walk unharmed through Mississippi to Jackson during primary election week. Hardly had he begun when a would-be assassin's bullet wounded him. National civil-rights leaders rushed to Memphis, and Martin Luther King and Stokely Carmichael, chairman of SNCC, resumed the march amid harassments and taunts from jeering whites. The two men soon revealed to the world a leadership schism of major proportions. While King continued to preach nonviolence and racial integration to Mississippi blacks, Carmichael electrified the crowds with cries of "Black Power": "The only way we gonna stop them white men from whuppin' us is to take over. We been saying freedom for six years and we ain't got nothin'. What we gonna start saying now is black power. . . . Ain't nothin' wrong with anything all black 'cause I'm all black and I'm all good. Now don't you be afraid. And from now on when they ask you what you want, you know what to tell them." The crowd replied in unison, "Black power! Black power! Black power!"

The slogan expressed tendencies that had been present for some time and had been gaining strength in the black community. Having become a household phrase, the term generated intense discussion of its real meaning, and a broad spectrum of ideologies and programmatic proposals emerged. In politics, black power meant independent action—Negro control of the political power of the rural Southern Black Belt counties and of the black ghettos and the use of this control to improve the conditions of the farm laborers and the slum dwellers. It could take the form of organizing a black political party or controlling the political machinery inside the ghetto without the guidance or support of white politicians. Where predominantly black areas lacked Negroes in elective office, whether in the rural Black Belt of the South or in the urban centers, black-power advocates sought the election of blacks by voter-registration campaigns and by working for the redrawing of electoral districts. The basic belief was that only a well-organized and cohesive bloc of black voters could provide for the needs of the black masses. Even some black politicians allied to the major political parties adopted the term "black power" to describe their interest in the Negro vote. In economic terms, black power meant creating independent, self-sufficient black business enterprise, not only by encouraging black entrepreneurs, but also by forming Negro cooperatives in the ghettos and in the predominantly black rural counties of the South. In the area of education, black power called for local community control of the public schools in the black ghettos. Throughout, the emphasis was on self-help, racial unity, and, among the most militant, retaliatory violence, the latter ranging from the legal right of self-defense to attempts to justify looting and arson in ghetto riots to guerrilla warfare and armed rebellion.

Phrases like "black power," "black consciousness," and "black is beautiful" enjoyed an extensive currency in the Negro community, even within the NAACP and among relatively conservative politicians. Expressed in its most extreme form by small, often local, fringe groups, among the national organizations the black-power ideology became most closely associated with SNCC and CORE.

Generally regarded as the most militant among the leading black protest organizations, CORE and SNCC had different interpretations of the black-power doctrine. Though neither group was monolithic in its viewpoint, broadly speaking it can be said that SNCC called for totally independent political action outside the established political parties, as with the Black Panther Party in Lowndes County, Alabama; questioned the value of political alliance with other groups until Negroes themselves built a substantial base of independent political power; applauded the idea of guerrilla warfare; and regarded riots as rebellions. CORE, while not disapproving of the SNCC strategy, advocated working within the Democratic Party to overthrow the established machine leadership and forming alliances with other groups. It sought to justify riots as the natural explosion of an oppressed people against intolerable conditions, but it sanctioned violence only in self-defense. While favorable toward cooperatives, it was more inclined toward job-training programs and developing a black entrepreneurial class based upon the market within the black ghetto.

Paradoxically, the popularity of the term "black power" represented both a sense of power produced by the earlier successes of the movement and an escape into the rhetoric of power caused by the powerlessness of the masses to achieve more rapid progress toward full equality. The slogan emerged when the black-protest movement was slowing down, when it was finding increased resistance to changing goals, when it discovered that nonviolent direct action was no more a panacea than legal action, when CORE and SNCC were declining in activity, membership, and financial support. Unable to make fundamental changes in the life of the masses, the advocates of black power substituted a separatist program for the platform of integration. Ironically, although the goal of equality was still far off, this occurred at the very time that Negroes were closer to the goal of integration than ever before. Whereas sixty years earlier the themes of racial unity and separatism had functioned primarily as part of an ideology of accommodation and the black radicals had demanded immediate integration, now the latest generation of black radicals rejected integration as a white man's strategy of tokenism aimed at holding Negroes in a subordinate position. Racial separatism became part of a platform of radicalism and militance, while the old radical program of integration was denounced as conservative and sometimes as downright racist.

With CORE and particularly SNCC greatly weakened, the banner of black power and black nationalism passed to other groups, mostly locally based. Black caucuses appeared in the predominantly white professional and church organizations. There was a general surge of community organization—of a spirit of self-help and racial solidarity, of uniting ghetto residents for concerted action, culturally, economically, and politically. Better known—because far more dramatic and extreme—were such Marxist-oriented revolutionary movements as the Black Panthers, founded in Oakland, California, in 1966, and the Republic of New Africa, founded in Detroit the following year. Both advocated forms of territorial separatism. The Black Panthers, who took their name from the abortive SNCC-sponsored Lowndes County, Alabama, Black Panther Party of 1965-6, espoused black control of the central cities. The Republic of New Africa proposed a separate all-black sovereign state in the Deep South. More significant was the rapid proliferation of Afro-American societies and black student unions on the predominantly white college and university campuses, with their demands for greater black representation in the student body, in the faculty, and in the curriculum on the one hand, and for separate dormitories, recreational centers, courses, and even separate colleges within the universities on the other. These groups, which often espoused revolutionary violence, were frequently led by middle-class student intellectuals. But they flourished largely because the black students from the ghettos, who were entering the major colleges and universities under liberalized and compensatory admissions policies, faced serious problems in adjusting to the academic and social norms of a middle-class or upper-middle-class environment, for which neither their background nor their schooling had prepared them. Most pervasive was the widespread revival of cultural nationalism, which enjoyed an enormous popularity among all social classes. There was more interest in black history than ever before; countless local groups devoted to black art, literature, and drama sprang up; and a national magazine like *Ebony*, heretofore devoted largely to chronicling the achievements and social life of the black bourgeoisie, became a leading popularizer of "black consciousness." And at the same time an unprecedented renaissance in art, literature, and the theater occurred.

Black nationalism, black separatism, and black revolutionary rhetoric seized the headlines at the end of the 1960's. Yet, though nationalist sentiment was growing, the thrust for integration was far from dead. Neither SCLC nor the NAACP adopted a nationalist program or ideology. Martin Luther King's last months before his assassination in 1968 were spent in developing a major project intended to show the continuing viability of the nonviolent direct-action strategy—the Poor People's Campaign that brought thousands to Washington during the summer of 1968 to demonstrate for greater justice to the economically deprived—and, in what was probably his last published article, Dr. King still articulated the dream of "black and white together." The NAACP counterattacked against the separatists, especially those in universities, denouncing them as segregationists who undermined the very things the black-protest movement had sought for so many years to accomplish. Important as the enthusiasm for various forms of black nationalism became after 1966, however much people in all sectors of the black community resonated to Stokely Carmichael's call for black pride, it must nevertheless be stressed that, as the public-opinion polls demonstrated, full participation in American society on an integrated basis remained the goal of the great majority of black Americans.

VIII

The Legacy of the Black Revolt

WHAT HAVE BEEN THE FRUITS of the black revolt of the 1960's? What is the status of blacks today in American society as a result of the surge of Negro protest? And what has happened to this black activism in the 1970's?

Afro-Americans have not yet achieved equality, and the dream of which Martin Luther King spoke so eloquently is far from realized. As Vernon Jordan, National Urban League executive director, has said, "Far-reaching changes have come to this nation . . . as a direct result of the civil rights movement" of the 1960's. But, as he went on to emphasize, much remained to be done: "From securing the tools of change in the form of laws, court orders and executive orders, we have moved to trying to use those tools to bring real changes in the daily lives of millions of citizens." Most notably, the Voting Rights Act of

1965 and the equal-economic-opportunity section of the Civil Rights Act of 1964 have proved to be useful levers for promoting improvements in the status of blacks.

The momentum behind these social changes has been fueled by two phenomena, themselves the legacy of the black revolt of the 1960's. In the first place, that revolt legitimized for many whites the black man's insistence on his constitutional rights and his quest for equality in American society. This legitimization has been especially evident among key sectors of white elites in business, politics, the courts, the mass media, and the academic community. Second, black activism, though transformed, has continued to be a vital force. Direct action, it is true, has practically disappeared, and the militant nationalist and often revolutionary mood that became so prominent at the end of the 1960's has also waned. The scene of action has shifted back to the courts and, more importantly, to the political arena. This political activism has achieved results partly because of the greater legitimacy that black demands now have among many white Americans and partly because of the growing power of the highly cohesive black vote, newly enfranchised in the South and concentrated primarily in the urban ghettos around the country.

1

Black Americans continued to move out of the South and into the cities. During the 1960's the high level of migration to the North and West had been sustained as another one and a half million left the South. Yet, because of the high growth rate among the black population, slightly over half the American Negroes were still residing in the South in 1970. Moreover, Census Bureau samplings suggest that during the early 1970's the northward movement was slowing down and that the new climate of race relations, produced by the Southern activism of the 1960's combined with the improving economic opportunities associated with growing industrialization, had even stimulated a small reverse flow of blacks going back South.

More striking than ever has been the continuing concentration of blacks in the nation's largest cities. During the 1960's, New York's black population increased by 580,000, Chicago's by 290,000, Detroit's by 178,000, Washington's by 126,000, Houston's by 102,000, and Atlanta's by 69,000. By 1970 less than half the whites but about two thirds of the blacks lived in the sixty-seven largest metropolitan areas. And within these metropolitan areas the black population has been concentrated in the central cities, while whites have been fleeing to the suburbs. Thus these central cities during the 1960's lost 2.5 million whites and gained 3.4 million blacks. By 1970, only 42 percent of the whites but fully 84 percent of the blacks in these major metropolitan areas lived in the central cities. As a result there was a striking tendency for a number of major cities to become predominantly black in population. By 1970, cities with black majorities or approaching black majorities included Washington, Newark, Baltimore, Atlanta, New Orleans, and Detroit. The dramatic changes that had occurred can be seen, for example, in Baltimore, whose population was 24 percent black in 1950 and 46 percent black in 1970; in Detroit, whose population shifted from 16 percent black to 44 percent black, and in Newark, where Negroes rose from 17 percent to 54 percent of the city's residents in the same twenty-year period; and in Atlanta, whose population in the single decade of the 1960's shifted from 38 percent to 51 percent black. There was, it is true, an increase in the black population of suburban areas, most notably around Los Angeles, Washington, and New York. Yet because of the enormous dimensions of the white flight from the deterioriating central cities and the economic and social impediments on black movement to the suburbs, Negroes still constituted only a tiny proportion of this suburban population—rising very slightly from 4.2 percent to 4.5 percent between 1960 and 1970.

While preliminary analyses of 1970 census data suggest that there was a slight increase in the proportion of people living in mixed neighborhoods, in absolute numbers more and more blacks were living in overwhelmingly black areas of the central cities, and stabilized mixed neighborhoods remained rare. Nor did the movement to the suburbs produce much residential integration. Typically this growth consisted of an extension of the inner-city ghetto, with upper- and middle-class blacks—in a pattern that paralleled the earlier history of urban ghetto expansion—forming the vanguard of the outward movement. In Cleveland, as the ghetto continued its movement eastward, working-class blacks spilled over the city line into the formerly white working-class town of East Cleveland, where during the 1960's the population changed from 2 percent black to nearly 60 percent black. Simultaneously, well-to-do Cleveland Negroes moved farther out to wealthy suburbs like Shaker Heights.

This phenomenon of continued residential segregation persisted despite efforts of private groups to foster mixed neighborhoods and despite some changes in the policies of the federal government. By act of Congress in 1968, racial discrimination is now forbidden in the sale of most of the nation's housing. Although the federal courts have handed down some rulings enforcing this act, and although there has been some effort on the part of federal agencies to develop low-income scatter-site housing that would move poorer blacks into white suburbs, the substantial white opposition to more than a token movement of blacks into white neighborhoods, the tactics of realtors, the Nixon Administration's moratorium on publicly assisted housing, and the federal bureaucracy's reluctance to cut off financial grants to discriminatory localities have all discouraged the development of mixed neighborhoods. While the hostility is now less severe than in previous decades, most white Americans nonetheless accord less legitimacy to fair housing than to voting rights or equal-employment opportunity. At the same time most blacks, while seeking better housing and insisting on the right to buy any home they can afford, are not particularly interested in promoting integrated housing per se. Not only fears of unfriendliness in white neighborhoods, but the attraction of the black churches and other Negro community institutions, ties with old friends and social clubs, the black clientele of most Negro professionals and businessmen, and the political base that black politicians built in the ghettos, have also served to encourage the maintenance of residential separation. The result of all these factors is that, despite a growing sprinkling of prosperous blacks in affluent white suburbs, the phenomenon of the black ghetto is likely to be a durable feature of American society.

2

This persistent pattern of residential segregation has served to inhibit the desegregation of the public schools. Moreover, where urban education facilities have been integrated, the trend toward residential segregation and toward black majorities in the central cities has been accentuated as whites moved to the suburbs to escape the newly mixed schools. As a result, the recent history of the school desegregation issue has been characterized by certain ironies. In 1954, the Supreme Court handed the NAACP a stunning victory. *Brown* v. *Board of Education* declared that any enforced, educational separation was unconstitutional and explicitly overturned the separate-but-equal doctrine embodied in *Plessy* v. *Ferguson*. Ten years later, the wave of direct action that began at Montgomery in 1955 and culminated in the Civil Rights Act of 1964 had virtually eliminated Jim Crow from transportation, public accommodations, and publicly owned recreational facilities. But in that momentous decade efforts to desegregate Southern schools had only token success. On the other hand, significant progress was made in the following decade. Then, when the South reached the point where most of its children were in mixed schools, Northern city schools were found to have remained as segregated as they were before. Changes have come about chiefly through pressure from the federal courts. As these have turned to ordering cross-city busing and, most recently, have begun to order the desegregation of Northern city school systems, the distinction previously made between de jure and de facto segregation has tended to disappear.

In the years following the *Brown* decision, Southern boards of education, acting with deliberateness rather than speed, used whatever delaying tactics they could. They clearly were moving at a snail's pace. In 1964, only 1.2 percent of all the black pupils in the eleven Southern states attended mixed schools: in Alabama, only twenty-one children; in South Carolina, only ten; and in Mississippi, absolutely no black pupils were in schools with whites. Although the Civil Rights Act of 1964 strengthened the hand of the federal government by giving HEW power to withhold funds from school districts that flouted the *Brown* decision, that department still sought to secure "voluntary compliance" and encouraged "freedom of choice" plans under which black students upon request were allowed to transfer into white schools. Hostility, even violence, directed toward these youngsters, and economic reprisals against their parents, inhibited use of these plans. As late as 1968, only about one fifth of the black pupils were in predominantly white schools, the overwhelming majority still being in all-black schools.

In that year, impatient with the evident effort of Southern boards of education to maintain dual school systems, the Supreme Court ruled that if "freedom of choice" plans did not achieve desegregation, other devices must be employed. HEW, finally threatening to withdraw federal funds from recalcitrant schools, set the school year 1969–70 as the deadline for complete desegregation. Although under the Nixon Administration HEW retreated from this vigorous position, in a small percentage of districts funds were actually withheld, the pressure of the courts was sustained, and as a result desegregation actually proceeded more rapidly. Meanwhile the federal judiciary was also taking up the controversial issue of using busing to destroy dual school systems. In 1971 the Supreme Court unanimously upheld a lower-court decision requiring the Charlotte–Mecklenburg County, North Carolina, school district to achieve racial balance throughout the system by busing both black and white children. By then, in the eleven Southern states, nearly one half of the black pupils were attending majority-white schools. Only 9 percent still went to all-black ones.

In the North, meanwhile, a few medium-sized cities, like Berkeley, Evanston, and Harrisburg, had completely desegregated their schools; but overall only about one quarter of the black pupils were in majority-white schools and more than half were attending schools that were over 80 percent black. This de facto segregation, rooted primarily in residential segregation, had been exacerbated by deliberate practices of school officials in such matters as selecting sites for new schools, assigning teachers, setting student transfer policies, and gerrymandering attendance zones. Because during the 1960's the federal courts refused to rule de facto segregation in Northern schools unconstitutional under the *Brown* decision, NAACP attorneys decided to argue that since this racial segregation resulted partly from official policy it was accordingly de jure in character and thus unconstitutional. In 1973 the Supreme Court accepted this argument in a Denver case, thus compelling the board of education to establish racially balanced schools through the city. Such court-decreed desegregation and busing were not popular with most whites, and in certain cities, like Pontiac, Michigan, and Boston, determined opposition and even mob violence erupted.

The continuing white exodus into the suburbs intensified the prevalence of de facto school segregation throughout the country and actually led to the resegregation of schools in a number of border and Southern cities. This produced a situation where, in places like Detroit, Baltimore, Washington, New Orleans, Atlanta, Richmond, and Newark, more than two thirds of the public-school population became black. In such cases, it became evident that meaningful desegregation could be achieved only by combining the urban school districts with those in the suburbs and busing pupils across municipal boundaries. Accordingly, civil-rights attorneys urged the courts to promote such consolidation. In 1971, in litigation involving Richmond and Detroit, federal district courts ruled that the *Brown* decision required combining city and suburban districts with appropriate busing to secure desegregation. The Supreme Court did not sustain these district-court decisions, since the lawyers for the blacks had not demonstrated that deliberate action on the part of the suburbs was responsible for the de facto segregation. Yet the high tribunal clearly left the door open for further litigation on the matter.

Black opinion has not been unified on the value of school desegregation. For one thing, the desegregation of Southern schools had its negative aspects. Large numbers of Southern black principals were demoted, as whites were selected to run the newly mixed schools and thousands of black teachers were dismissed, allegedly on the grounds of inadequate training at marginal Jim Crow colleges (something white school authorities had not cared about when these teachers were instructing only black children). Black schoolchildren who transferred to white schools frequently found themselves in an unfriendly milieu, excluded from many activities and penalized for deficiencies in the training they had received in inferior Jim Crow schools. As schools were desegregated, blacks lost positions on student councils and in other school offices.

Some Southern blacks felt that desegregation, or at least the way it was carried out, degraded them and robbed them of their identity. Although many black parents continued to believe that desegregation meant more responsive school boards and better instruction, some came to sharply question its value, especially if it meant closing neighborhood schools and busing their children to outlying white areas. Ironically, in 1974, when school officials in Topeka, Kansas—the city where the *Brown* case originated—were under court order to further improve racial balance by busing, Linda Brown Smith, the plaintiff of twenty years before and now the mother of two grade-school children, said, "I would accept busing only if they forced me to. There has to be a better solution."

Another source of black opposition to school desegregation came from people who were ideologically committed to separatism. During the late 1960's the widespread demand that blacks be accorded autonomy in running their own local communities spawned proposals for decentralization of large urban school systems. The advocates of such "community control" included disillusioned activists who had organized the boycotts for integrated schools in 1963–4. CORE even proposed creating a dual system of independent black and white school districts within major cities as a way of getting around the *Brown* decision. Such proposals did not get very far; even in the highly publicized case of New York City, the controversial experiment in the Ocean Hill–Brownsville section of Brooklyn with its numerous problems led not to neighborhood control but to a compromise enacted by the state legislature providing for only a limited degree of decentralization. Yet this separatist sentiment among blacks was fairly widespread. At the 1972 Black Political Convention in Gary, Indiana, nationalist forces pushed through a resolution condemning busing for school integration.

Thus, in the more than twenty years since *Brown*, the challenge of securing desegregation of schools has moved from the South to the North. At the same time, the struggle has shifted from attacking segregation imposed by law to assaulting separation arising from residential patterns and informal community pressures on school authorities. In short, whereas in 1954 school authorities were directed to cease overt acts of segregation, two decades later they were being directed to take affirmative action to counteract all the forces in American society that fostered the creation of separate schools. The country is now at a crossroads on this issue. While organized black opposition to school desegregation has waned, many whites are overtly resistant, and it is scarcely certain that the Supreme Court will order far-reaching metropolitan desegregation requiring the cross busing of blacks into white suburbs and of whites to the inner-city schools. Accordingly, how much further desegregation of the schools is likely to go is not clear.

Change has come not only to the elementary and secondary schools but to the colleges and universities as well. The proportion of blacks in the country's college-student population increased from around 4 percent in the early 1960's to about 8 percent in the early 1970's. Well over half these black students are now in predominantly white institutions. Propelled by the black-student revolts of the late 1960's and the increasing sensitivity in academic circles to the aspirations of black Americans, predominantly white colleges and universities enrolled increasing numbers of blacks, often with special financial aid. Similarly, the professional schools have significantly increased their admissions of black students. For example, the number of blacks enrolled in law schools has risen from about seven hundred in the mid-1960's to five thousand by 1974. In implementing their policy of affirmative action, many institutions, especially professional schools, made racial background a consideration for admission, treating applications of blacks separately from whites. Many white students came to resent this policy and charged "reverse discrimination." In 1974 the Supreme Court heard a case involving a white man who was denied entrance to the University of Washington law school while minority students with lower grades and test scores were accepted. On a technicality the Court refused to make a ruling and the issue remains to be resolved. In any event, the increasing number of black college and professional-school graduates has been an important factor in black economic advancement, since they have been the ones best situated to take advantage of opportunities opening in government and industry.

3

The momentum generated by the employment campaigns of the 1960's, the changing climate of American race relations, and the affirmative action policies of the federal bureaucracy have produced improvements in the economic status of black Americans. Nonetheless, Negroes are still overrepresented in the low-income group, among the unemployed, and in the unskilled sectors of the population; black entrepreneurs are very few in number; and economic equality remains a distant goal. The economic progress that has been achieved was facilitated by the prosperity that characterized most of the period after 1960. Although black unemployment rose substantially in the steep recession of the mid-1970's, it is likely that permanent improvements have resulted.

There were clear-cut gains during the decade of 1963–73, although the unemployment rate among blacks remained double that for whites, and Negroes were still disproportionately concentrated in lower-skilled, lower-paying jobs. The proportion of black males who were employed in white-collar jobs rose from 15 to 23 percent, and the proportion employed as craftworkers rose from 11 to 15 percent. For example, during the 1960's, the number of nonwhite elementary- and high-school teachers increased from 143,000 to 223,000; social workers rose from 16,000 to 41,000; plumbers and pipe fitters from 12,600 to 18,000; machinists from 15,000 to 23,000; welders from 24,700 to 44,200. Between 1958 and 1973 the number of blacks classified as managers and administrators, professional and technical workers, and craftsmen—the three highest-paying among the job categories listed in the census—nearly doubled. And in the same fifteen-year period the number of blacks in the three lowest-paying occupations—service workers, farm workers, and nonfarm laborers—fell by one third.

Viewed from another perspective, blacks were still far behind. Forming about 10 percent of the labor force in 1973, they made up 22 percent of those in domestic service and the personal-service fields and 14 percent of those in health services (chiefly as low-skilled hospital workers). At the same time blacks represented only about 3 percent of the managers and administrators and about 6 percent of the professional and technical workers and the craftsmen. Moreover, within these categories, blacks were seriously underrepresented in the elite occupations. Thus, in the professional and technical category, a majority of the Negroes were either elementary and secondary teachers, nurses, medical technicians, or engaged in social, personnel, or labor-relations work. Blacks constituted less than 3 percent of the accountants, architects, physicians, and newspaper editors and less than 2 percent of the lawyers, authors, and engineers. In the managerial ranks of major corporate enterprises blacks were likely to find themselves in personnel and public-relations jobs rather than in positions of real authority. Moreover, there are few blacks on the boards of major corporations. Although in recent years companies like General Motors, Standard Oil, and IBM have appointed an occasional black to their boards, in 1973, only seventy-two of the fourteen thousand directors in the major corporations were black.

In the public sector, the situation was similar. Between 1960 and 1970 the number of blacks employed by local, state, and federal government agencies nearly doubled to a total of 1.6 million. In the federal government, Negroes, not surprisingly, were overrepresented in agencies responsible for delivering welfare and other services to the black community. Moreover, in 1972, although 15 percent of all employees in the federal bureaucracy were blacks, Negroes held only 3 percent of the higher-status, higher-paying positions at the GS-12 level and above. But at the bottom of the scale, grades GS-5 and below, blacks represented 19 percent of federal workers.

A comparable situation existed in another sector of the federal government, the armed services, which many blacks regarded as a place that offered economic opportunity. Here the percentage of Negroes steadily increased for about fifteen years, though disproportionately at the lower ranks. Blacks still complain of continued inequalities in the armed services, and there was considerable overt racial friction between black and white enlisted men in the late 1960's and early 1970's. Nevertheless, in the view of many lower-income black males, the services, particularly the army and the marines, provided a better living than did civilian life.

In all the branches combined, blacks rose from about 9 percent in 1960 to 11 percent in 1970 and to 16 percent in 1974. During the 1960's this resulted partly from the fact that a disproportionate number of blacks were drafted, since more whites were able to qualify for deferments. Yet the advantages of a career in the armed services were such that the black reenlistment rate was at least twice as high as that of whites. This black reenlistment rate remained high in the 1970's, and beginning in 1973, with the scrapping of the draft, the proportion of blacks among those volunteering rose sharply. This was most vividly evident in the marines, where blacks constituted 18 percent of the enlisted men by the end of 1974, and in the army, where the proportion of enlisted men who were black had jumped from 14 percent in 1970 to about 22 percent four years later. Thus the armed forces were becoming increasingly black, especially in the combat units. By 1975, in fact, a new controversy had arisen over what some called "overrepresentation" of blacks in the military services.

In contrast, the ranks of the commissioned officers, especially at the higher levels, have remained overwhelmingly white. In 1962 the proportion of commissioned officers who were black in all the services combined was only 1.7 percent. These were almost entirely at the lower levels. At the time there was only one black general in all the services, Lieutenant General Benjamin O. Davis, Jr., of the air force; there were only twelve black colonels in the entire army and air force; and there was not one of equivalent rank in the marines or the navy. The proportion rose gradually over the next decade, so that by early 1974, blacks constituted 2.5 percent of the commissioned officers. Yet, as late as 1970, only one additional black general had been appointed. Promotion of blacks to the top ranks came only in the 1970's. The first admiral was appointed in 1971 and by 1975 there were twelve army generals, two air force generals, and two admirals. The marines appointed their first black colonel in 1974. These breakthroughs symbolized both the progress blacks had achieved and the distance yet to be covered before the legacy of past discrimination would be overcome.

Also indicative of both the gains blacks made and of the limited nature of those gains has been the growth in black business enterprise. The overwhelming majority of these businesses (totaling 163,000 in 1969 and 195,000 in 1972) are still tiny "Mom and Pop" operations—retail and service establishments such as grocery stores, barbershops, beauty parlors, dry cleaners, and owner-operated trucking and taxi outfits. The small number of real success stories included a few older firms like the North Carolina Mutual Life Insurance Company and the Atlanta Life Insurance Company, the H. G. Park Sausage Company of Baltimore, Johnson Publications (*Ebony* and other magazines), and the cosmetic manufacturer, Johnson Products. But most were newer enterprises. Of the one hundred largest black-owned firms in 1973, seventy had been founded in the preceding decade. The largest black enterprise in the country—Motown Records—had started on a shoestring in Detroit just fourteen years earlier. The number of black-owned banks nearly tripled from thirteen in 1963 to thirty-seven ten years later. One company, Daniels and Bell, became the first black-owned firm to have a seat on the New York Stock Exchange.

To some extent, black business enterprise has benefited from the federal government's encouragement. Nixon in his 1968 Presidential campaign called for the development of "black capitalism" to attack the economic problems of the black community. As President he established an Office of Minority Business Enterprise to stimulate blacks and other minorities to start their own businesses; his Administration also increased government purchases from black-owned firms; working with the government, a Manhattan group called Capital Formation persuaded major corporations to deposit over $200 million in nonwhite banks; and the Small Business Administration expanded its loans to Negro businesses. Among the most celebrated results of these efforts was the Watts Industrial Park in Los Angeles, which owed its existence to government loans, housed twenty-two black-owned firms, and provided employment for 1,200 workers. Actually, the impact of these government programs has been slight. Most of the hundred largest black businesses, half of which were established after Nixon's election, received no government aid, but developed through the determination and shrewdness of their owners.

Compared with all American businesses, the advance in black enterprise does not appear very consequential. The proportion of American businesses that are black-owned has not changed significantly, still remaining around 2 percent and taking in about one half of one percent of all gross receipts. Of the hundred top black corporations in 1973, only twenty-six had annual sales of over $5 million, and the income of all hundred firms combined would have ranked 284 on *Fortune*'s list of the five hundred largest American businesses. The Small Business Administration's loans to whites increased even faster than those made to blacks; moreover, the average loan to blacks was less than half the size of the average loan made to whites. In addition, most black businesses continued to operate under

many of the disadvantages historically confronting Negro entrepreneurs. Small businesses—in which blacks are concentrated—
have always had a high rate of failure. For black enterprises,
typically located in ghetto neighborhoods where theft and fire
insurance are costly and where the market is constricted by the
poverty of the people, the failure rate is even higher. For example, 80 percent of the black-owned businesses founded in
Chicago during the prosperity of 1972 had failed within a year.
Such problems have been intensified by the severe recession of
1974–5. Though there was significant progress in the expanding
economy of the early 1970's, success stories like Park Sausage,
Johnson Publications, and Motown are still notable exceptions.
Thus the future of black capitalism remains marginal.

Whatever the future of black capitalism, employment opportunities for the masses of Afro-Americans lie with government
and with white-owned industry. And in pressing for occupational advances in the private economic sector, Negroes must
deal not only with the policies of employers but with those of
organized labor as well. Basing their strategy for job equality in
American industry on the Civil Rights Act of 1964, blacks
utilized the leverage of the courts and the federal bureaucracy
and agitated within the trade-union movement. Therefore, the
changing role of blacks in private industry is directly related to
the practices of both unions and employers, the tactics of black
trade unionists and black protest organizations, and the role of
the federal government.

Trade unions varied widely—from the old-line AFL craft
unions, which had long sought to exclude blacks, to a handful
of militantly egalitarian unions, which have consciously tried to
organize occupations in which unskilled black workers pre-
dominate.

Not surprisingly, the least amount of progress had been made
in the skilled building trades, which have remained overwhelmingly white in the face of a degree of pressure from federal
government agencies, litigation mounted by the NAACP, and
the friendly persuasion of both the AFL–CIO Civil Rights Department and the A. Philip Randolph Institute headed by

Bayard Rustin. It is true that growing numbers of blacks are entering these unions through apprenticeship-training programs. But all this effort notwithstanding, and despite the optimistic estimates offered by spokesmen for organized labor, the actual proportion of blacks in the skilled building-trades unions remains very small.

During the 1930's the emergence of industrial unionism had seemed, to many black intellectuals and black workers alike, to inaugurate a new era in the relations between blacks and organized labor. Black workers who joined the CIO unions did indeed benefit substantially. Not only were their wages and working conditions improved along with those of all union members, but racial differentials in wages paid for identical work, prevalent in the South, were wiped out, and black union officers, previously a rarity, became fairly common. Even in the South, where some unions began to hold integrated meetings in defiance of local custom, by the early 1940's blacks were appearing on state executive boards. Mixed Southern locals in unions like the United Steelworkers of America adopted a formula developed earlier by the United Mine Workers under which whites served as president, secretary, and treasurer, and blacks occupied the office of vice-president and other minor positions. On the other hand, leadership in these CIO unions, faced with the prejudices and the vested interests of white workers, was either unable or unwilling to completely eliminate inequities, nor did it in most cases seek to undo discriminatory patterns stemming from the policies of white employers.

By the late 1950's and 1960's there were two major issues to which blacks were increasingly objecting: their virtual absence from the top offices in the unions, and the promotion policies that excluded them from the most highly paid skilled jobs in the plants. The question of black representation stemmed from the fact that Negroes were everywhere a minority of a union's total membership, with whites generally unwilling to elect blacks to high office. The concentration of blacks in the lower-paying, lower-skilled, and hottest, heaviest, and dirtiest jobs reflected both the hiring policies of employers and often also union-backed seniority systems. Typically such seniority systems provided for "separate lines of progression" under which promotions were made on the basis of seniority within a department rather than years of service in a plant. Thus if someone transferred to a different department, that person would lose any seniority already accumulated. With blacks relegated to the lowest-paying departments, the maximum wages they could achieve, even with promotions, were limited. And when, in the 1960's, opportunities for blacks in the lucrative skilled departments expanded, they were discouraged from transferring because they would forfeit seniority, a fact that effectively inhibited the breakdown of the historic legacy of job discrimination. In the South, job separation was so complete that certain unions, like the tobacco workers, established separate locals for whites and blacks, and in many cases labor leaders, fearful of antagonizing white workers, accepted segregated lunchrooms and lavatories. The merger in 1955 of the CIO and the AFL, dominated as the latter was by the exclusionary craft unions, further weakened the racially egalitarian tendencies in the CIO—a development that came at a time when the militance of black workers was on the rise.

The shifting status of blacks in major industry and the complex relations with the former CIO industrial unions are illustrated by the developments in steel and auto manufacturing, two of the largest industries. In steel, where blacks in the mid-1960's formed about one sixth of the work force, they held few paid staff positions in the national union, the United Steelworkers, and none at all on its executive board. At the same time, blacks in the plants were disproportionately among the unskilled laborers—comprising 28 percent of all unskilled steelworkers but only 6 percent of the skilled workers. Thus, at the huge Baltimore Sparrows Point Plant of Bethlehem Steel, most of the blacks were employed in all-black or overwhelmingly black departments. Construction, refuse disposal, and maintenance workers ranged between 94 percent and 100 percent black; employees in the unpleasant blast-furnace department were 81 percent black. But skilled job categories, such as lubrication, pattern shop, machine shop, and the tin and strip mills, were between 99 percent and 100 percent white. Conditions at this plant were so discriminatory that as late as 1967 the U.S. government ordered the integration of locker rooms and restrooms there.

In 1964 a committee of dissatisfied black unionists demanded more employment of blacks at all levels in the steel union's district and national offices, the election of a black to the executive board, and, subsequently, a Negro vice-president. By supporting I. W. Abel in his successful bid for the union presidency in 1965, they secured the appointment of a Negro to head the union's civil-rights department and the addition of several others to important staff positions. But despite their pressure, there is as yet no Negro on the executive board and no black vice-president. Seeking to satisfy Negro demands without alienating much of the white membership, President Abel attempted to secure black representation at the top policy levels by backing Leander Sims in his bid to become director of the Baltimore district when the post became vacant. Unfortunately, black steelworkers failed to turn out in large numbers and Sims lost the election, though he was subsequently appointed assistant director. Black pressures had thus brought some gains within the union during the 1960's; but it was the leverage afforded by the federal government rather than the union that resolved the seniority problem. In 1971 the NAACP secured in the federal courts modification of the separate lines of progression at Bethlehem Steel's Lackawanna, New York, plant; three years later, in a sweeping agreement arranged by federal agencies, the industry and the union acceded to the dismantling of the discriminatory provision of the seniority system. Although black protest leaders in and out of the union have asserted that the agreement did not go far enough toward redressing inequities and that its provisions have not been fully implemented, it nevertheless marked an important precedent.

In the automobile industry, the situation, in many ways similar to the steel industry, was less severe. The black workers tended to exhibit more militancy and were able to secure more concessions than their counterparts in steel. Moreover, the changes that came about were not only more substantial but were secured without government intervention. As in steel, black workers were found in the least desirable jobs. In the late 1950's, 40 percent of the foundry workers were blacks, but less than 3 percent of the tool-and-die division was black. Blacks were well represented as officers in a number of auto locals, but there was none on the United Auto Workers national executive board. The leadership was explicitly committed to racial egalitarianism. No union leader was more identified with the civil-rights movement than was UAW president Walter Reuther— board member of the NAACP, supporter of CORE, and friend of Martin Luther King and the SCLC. Yet he was also faced with the prejudices of many white workers, not all of whom were from the South. The UAW had stood firm in the face of wildcat strikes against the employment or upgrading of blacks, but it had failed to combat the discriminatory practices of both employers and the skilled workers who resisted the entry of blacks into the trades. Given the periodic threats from skilled workers to secede from the union, Reuther feared to discipline them on this issue.

As far back as 1957, black officials in the UAW had formed the Trade Union Leadership Conference (TULC) to press for greater union recognition of the needs of the black workers. Five years later their pressure resulted in a black vice-president —the first Negro to serve on the UAW executive board. But further progress was slow. As late as 1968, at a time when blacks formed about one fourth the union's membership, protesting black auto workers complained that out of one thousand UAW international representatives only seventy-five were black, and only seven of the hundred key staff jobs in the union were held by Negroes. Meanwhile, during the middle 1960's, several factors combined to produce heightened demands from black trade unionists: a sharp increase in the number of blacks employed in Detroit's automobile factories (actually giving the labor force in certain plants a black majority); the upsurge in black militance that came to a climax with the call for black

power and the Detroit riot of 1967; and the fact that Detroit
was a leading center of black radicalism and nationalism. At the
1968 UAW convention, a group of militant black unionists
asked for a "fair share" of the top leadership positions in the
union, including a second black vice-president, directorships of
the UAW's Ford and Chrysler departments, and two regional
directorships.

In the course of the following months two distinct groups
emerged as spokesmen for blacks—the Ad Hoc Committee of
Concerned Negro Auto Workers, a moderate group representing the middle-aged workers headed by TULC's president
Robert Battle, and the Marxist-nationalist League of Revolutionary Black Workers, composed of young radical workers.
The latter group, using revolutionary rhetoric, engaged in wildcat work stoppages in the plants to dramatize their demands for
upgrading blacks and for an international union staff that
would be half black, headed by a black union president who
would replace Walter Reuther. The pressures from both these
groups, combined with the growing proportion of blacks in the
Detroit auto factories, produced some significant changes. A
second black was soon added to the international executive
board, and growing numbers of blacks joined the ranks of local
union officeholders, with a substantial increase, for example, in
the number of shop stewards. By 1972, there were eleven black
presidents of locals in the Detroit area. At the same time, the
auto companies promoted increasing numbers of blacks to foremen, a job category from which blacks had been virtually absent. By then the League of Revolutionary Black Workers was
virtually dead, the victim of several phenomena: intense internal factionalism; its shrill attack on the UAW's leadership,
which had made the union look like a greater enemy than the
employers; and, not least, the gains that the pressures generated
by both the league and the ad hoc committee had secured.

Among the older unions, the United Packinghouse Workers
had long been known for its commitment to egalitarian practices. Recently, the organizing drives of the American Federation of State, County and Municipal Employees as well as the

Drug and Hospital Employees Local 1199 of the Retail, Wholesale, and Department Store Clerks Union exhibited a concern reminiscent of the early days of the CIO for the unskilled, poorly paid, and unorganized mass of black workers. During the late 1960's, in fact, these two unions became closely tied to the black protest movement, as was vividly demonstrated in a garbage-workers strike in Memphis in 1968 and a hospital-workers strike in Charleston the following year. The AFSCME, in attempting to organize the overwhelmingly black Memphis garbage collectors, obtained the assistance of Martin Luther King. King was killed while leading mass protest demonstrations on behalf of the strikers, and in the wake of his tragic death the garbage workers won recognition of their union, a pay raise, and an agreement that promised to end racial discrimination against them. Soon afterward SCLC joined hands with Local 1199—a union which over the preceding decade had successfully organized black and Puerto Rican hospital workers in the Northeast—in a bitterly fought strike against a major Charleston hospital. Again the combined forces of the civil-rights activists and organized labor secured a dramatic victory in an area notoriously hostile to labor unions as well as blacks.

The stance of the skilled building-trades unions on the one hand, and of the AFSCME and Local 1199 on the other, illustrate the variety and complexity involved in any analysis of the relationship of blacks and organized labor. Nevertheless, it is clear that organized labor has become more responsive to the problems of the black workers. This has been largely due to direct pressures from blacks themselves: from the NAACP's labor department, utilizing the leverage of publicity and legal action, pressing from outside the trade-union movement, and from the increasingly militant black workers acting within the ranks of organized labor.

The role of these black unionists in securing these changes cannot be overestimated. During the early 1960's the Negro American Labor Council (NALC), a federation of black union leaders and caucuses headed by A. Philip Randolph, maintained a constant pressure on the leadership of the AFL–CIO unions. By 1965, Randolph, impressed with the steps that the top leaders in the AFL–CIO were starting to take, came to a rapprochement with President George Meany. Meany, who was himself a member of a building-trades union, and who, unlike Reuther, had opposed labor support for the 1963 March on Washington, now secured trade-union funding for the new A. Philip Randolph Institute, dedicated to advancing the cause of black workers through close cooperation with organized labor. The institute has, for example, recruited and trained Negroes for admission to building-trades apprenticeship programs. While the aging Randolph no longer continued to agitate against discrimination within organized labor, the NALC kept up the attack under its new president, Cleveland Robinson, head of the predominantly black District 65 of the Retail, Wholesale, and Department Store Clerks Union. Further pressure has more recently come from the Coalition of Black Trade Unionists formed in 1972 under the leadership of men like Robinson and William Lucy, secretary-treasurer of AFSCME.

At least as important as the direct pressures from black protest organizations and trade unionists in promoting changes in the policies of both employers and trade unions have been the actions of the federal government. Uneven, frequently inconsistent, and often reluctantly undertaken, these actions, representing both a response to black pressures and the growing power of the black vote and the increasing legitimacy that black aspirations now possess for many white Americans, have had an important cumulative impact. With the Civil Rights Act of 1964, Congress for the first time gave legislative sanction to the principle of fair-employment practices. In the decade that followed, the federal government has intervened with increasing vigor to secure equal-employment opportunity. At the same time, flowing from demands for compensatory employment, which were first articulated by the civil-rights movement as early as 1962, the concept of fair-employment practices came to include the doctrine of affirmative action, under which employers were required to move beyond a "color-blind" hiring and promotion policy. In order to produce "equality of results," they must take positive steps to correct the effects of past discrimination.

The 1964 act established an Equal Employment Opportunity Commission (EEOC). Lacking effective enforcement powers at first, the EEOC during its early years resolved complaints of discrimination through the procedures of conciliation that earlier state and federal equal-employment agencies had utilized since the 1940's. The results of EEOC's work during the 1960's were, therefore, relatively meager. More effective, because it had specific enforcement powers, was the Office of Federal Contract Compliance (OFCC) in the Department of Labor, created by executive order of President Lyndon Johnson in 1965. While the 1964 Civil Rights Act simply obliged employers to refrain from overt acts of discrimination, Johnson's order directed that holders of government contracts take "affirmative action" to ensure that minorities were employed. During the next few years this concept was developed to require employers to establish job goals, and timetables for their fulfillment, so that the number of minority workers hired in various job categories would be substantially increased. In 1969, a precedent-setting directive known as the Philadelphia Plan required federal construction contractors in that city to make a real effort to increase their minority craftsmen from the current 2 percent to about 20 percent in four years. The following year the federal government in another important action ordered a major defense contractor, the McDonnell Douglas Corporation of St. Louis, to implement a five-year affirmative-action program. The firm agreed to establish a million-dollar training program for upgrading black employees and to set numerical goals for hiring and promotion in order to assure that the percentage of black employees would approximate the proportion of blacks in the local labor pool.

Although OFCC rarely used its power to actually cancel contracts, and although the enforcement and implementation of the Philadelphia Plan and similar programs in other cities left much to be desired, important precedents had been established.

And the principle of affirmative action became an integral part of civil-rights law when the Supreme Court in 1971 allowed a lower court decision sustaining the Philadelphia Plan to stand. In the same year, the Supreme Court also advanced the cause of equal employment and affirmative action by outlawing the use of educational requirements and achievement tests that were not relevant to the duties to be performed on the job.

In 1972 Congress amended the Civil Rights Act, giving the EEOC the authority to file lawsuits against violators in the federal courts. With its powers thus substantially enhanced, and with a series of court decisions quite clearly upholding affirmative action, EEOC mounted court cases against large corporations and labor unions. In this context of enforcement, an increasing number of firms entered into agreements with EEOC that set specific goals and timetables.* AT&T, under threat of an EEOC effort to block its application for a tele-phone-rate increase, reached a court-supervised agreement in 1973 with that agency and the Department of Labor providing goals and timetables for hiring more blacks and promoting substantial numbers into technical and managerial jobs.

Especially important was the steel settlement that the EEOC and other federal agencies secured in 1974. For half a dozen years the EEOC, the Labor Department's OFCC, and the Department of Justice had been involved in the issue of discrimination in the steel industry. There had been investigations and drawn-out negotiations, a Justice Department lawsuit against United States Steel and the United Steelworkers in Alabama, and an order handed down—and then suspended—by the Secretary of Labor against Bethlehem Steel in Maryland. Progress seemed token at best. But then in 1974, by threatening federal court proceedings, the EEOC, the Department of Justice, and the Labor Department jointly secured an agreement from nine steel companies and the union to change the seniority and promotion system throughout the country. The agreement called

---

* Typically these agreements involved other racial minorities and women as well as blacks.

for specific goals and timetables. For example, during the first year half the openings in craft jobs were to be filled by minority workers; promotions and layoffs would be determined by length of service in each plant rather than in a specific department; and minority workers would be permitted to transfer into departments previously reserved for whites without losing seniority or pay. The agreement also provided a token amount of compensatory back pay for the victims of the discriminatory policies.

Meanwhile, a series of court decisions, requiring state and city police forces to hire blacks in proportion to their numbers in the local population, was beginning to raise black representation in a job category that was, given the nature of police–black community relations, a highly sensitive one. Moreover, HEW, beginning in the late 1960's, was pressing colleges and universities to set and implement affirmative-action goals, under threat of cancellation of federal contracts. Finally, the continuing role of the federal judiciary can be seen in two 1975 circuit court decisions ruling that labor unions are obligated to work against discriminatory policies on the part of management and that, in fact, the National Labor Relations Board may not certify a union that discriminates as a collective bargaining agent.

Cumulatively, the persistent protests by black workers and advancement organizations, the growing scope of court decisions, and the more vigorous implementation of the law by the federal bureaucracy had wrought significant changes in the decade following passage of the Civil Rights Act of 1964. Yet the thrust for affirmative action has met with considerable resistance. Critics maintain that in meeting numerical goals and timetables, whites with greater qualifications are frequently passed over and thus experience what they call "reverse discrimination." How much closer blacks will be able to move toward a fair share in employment remains to be seen. Much will depend on the state of the economy, on how effectively the agreements reached are actually carried out and policed, and on the extent to which the recent developments, having secured a degree of legitimacy, will go forward on their own momentum.

The improvements in employment that occurred during the 1960's were reflected in changes in income. In 1959 the median black family income had been 52 percent of white family income. Ten years later it was 61 percent. Black families with earnings of $10,000 or more (in terms of 1971 dollars) rose from 3 percent in 1951, to 13 percent a decade later, and to 30 percent in 1971. Meanwhile, the proportion of black families who were below the official poverty line decreased from slightly over half in 1959 to about one third in 1973. Particularly striking, the income of young married couples, where both spouses were working, reached equality with their white counterparts in the North and West. However, in the early 1970's, black income gains slowed down. Indeed, with white earnings now growing faster than those of blacks, the median black family income by 1973 was only 58 percent of white family income. Blacks were more severely affected by the recession at the opening of the decade than were whites. The percentage of black families headed by females on welfare increased, and although the growing number of college-educated blacks still found economic opportunity, clearly the gap between them and the unskilled and poorly educated was widening. Even the newly successful blacks have felt vulnerable, realizing that the economic gains, while fueled by black activism and affirmative-action policies, would not have occurred without an extraordinary period of national prosperity. As a matter of fact, the proportion of black families with incomes over $10,000 a year increased very slightly in the 1970's. While the impact of the serious economic downturn of 1974 and 1975 cannot yet be fully evaluated, it is clear that the crisis of the mid-1970's poses a severe threat to the gains made in the 1960's.

4

Comparable to the changes in the economic sphere have been those in the political realm. The 1965 Voting Rights Act, the continued expansion of large-scale black urban ghettos, and the reapportionment of congressional and legislative districts in accordance with the requirements laid down by the Supreme

Court have together brought greater political recognition for black Americans.

In the South the long-range results of the civil-rights activism of the 1960's have become increasingly evident. The percentage of the black voting-age population that was registered rose from 20 in 1960 to 38 in 1964, and, in the aftermath of the Voting Rights Act, jumped to 62 by 1971. During the ten years after Martin Luther King highlighted the problem of disfranchisement in the demonstrations at Selma, Alabama, in 1965, the proportion of eligible Negroes registered in that town rose dramatically from 2 percent to 60 percent. During the same period in Mississippi, the number of registered blacks, out of a voting-age population of about 450,000, changed from 22,000 to 300,000.

Moreover, in the decade following passage of the Voting Rights Act, black officeholding in the South reached proportions higher than at any time since Reconstruction. In 1965 there were just seventy-two black elected officials in the states of the old Confederacy; ten years later there were nearly sixteen hundred. As late as 1962 there had been no blacks in the legislatures of any of these states; by 1975 there were ninety-five. Each of these eleven states had at least one representative, and seven had at least one state senator. The first two blacks from the South to sit in Congress since 1901 were elected from Atlanta and Houston in 1972; a third was elected from Memphis two years later. By 1975 there were eighty-two black mayors scattered across the South, chiefly in small towns like Fayette, Mississippi, and Tallulah, Louisiana, but also including a medium-sized city like Raleigh and the major metropolis of Atlanta. There were several police chiefs and sheriffs, a sprinkling of members on county governing boards, and, most numerous, city councilmen and members of boards of education. In a few Black Belt counties—four in Alabama alone— black control of electoral offices was virtually complete.

On the other hand, Southern Negroes had not achieved elective office even remotely commensurate with their share of the population. Technicalities in registration procedures, threats of economic intimidation, and the low degree of voter turnout often characteristic of poorer people all served to inhibit black political advancement. In 1974 in the seven Deep South states —those with the largest proportions of blacks in their populations—only 36 of the 1,174 legislators were Negros. Most of the Black Belt counties where Afro-Americans were in a majority— some where Negroes are as much as two thirds or more of the population—have no black elected officials whatsoever. Race advancement organizations, fearful of actual retrogression if the federal government should withdraw from active support of Southern black voting rights and alarmed at efforts to circumvent the Voting Rights Act in places like Mississippi, pressed successfully in 1970, and again in 1975, for a renewal of the law, with its guarantees of Justice Department intervention in areas where black voting had previously been particularly low.

The number of black elected officials in the North also rose substantially. Nationally the total climbed from a paltry 480 in 1967 to 3,503 by May 1975. About half of these were in the North and West. Although blacks formed only .7 percent of all elected officials in the country, some were holding significant offices. There were seventeen congressmen in the House of Representatives, up from six in 1967; the first two lieutenant governors since Reconstruction (California and Colorado); one state treasurer (Connecticut); two secretaries of state (Michigan and Pennsylvania); and a state superintendent of education (California). The number of black mayors in the country grew from 29 in 1968 to 135 by 1975, about two fifths of them in the North and West. Although most were in very small communities, the list included ten major cities. The first large cities to elect black mayors were Cleveland and Gary in 1967. Newark followed in 1970, and three years later Los Angeles, Atlanta, and Detroit joined the list. Today three of the ten biggest communities in the country have Negro mayors—Washington,* Detroit, and Los Angeles.

* Walter Washington, Washington's black mayor, was originally appointed to that office by President Johnson; the post became elective in 1974.

This record is essentially the fruit of black political activism, although many of the major officeholders are from biracial constituencies. Almost 70 percent of the black mayors serve communities that are more than half black. These predominantly black towns are typically small and Southern. On the other hand, most of the medium and large-sized cities that elected black mayors are Northern and have voting populations that are majority white or very closely divided between the races. Black mayors in these cities generally would not have been elected without white support. In Detroit, Gary, Cleveland, Atlanta, and Newark, a small minority of the white voters provided the margin of victory for the black candidates. And in Los Angeles, Thomas Bradley, who for years had represented a predominantly white district in the city council, was elected mayor of a community where blacks constituted less than one fifth of the population. Similarly, most if not all of the new black congressmen elected in the 1970's came from constituencies where blacks were about 40 percent of the voters. Massachusetts's Senator Brooke had only a tiny minority of black voters in his state. People like Senator Brooke, Mayor Bradley, the two lieutenant governors, and California State Superintendent of Education Wilson Riles, elected by overwhelming white majorities, are of course atypical. The bulk of the voters for most of the black mayors and for all of the black congressmen are black. Clearly, on the whole, black officeholding has been possible only on the basis of a substantial and unified black vote. Yet, at the same time, the access of Negroes to high political office has been accentuated by the willingness of a minority of the white electorate to vote for black candidates.

The number of officeholders is one thing; the actual wielding of decisive political influence another. With black elected officials well under 1 percent of the total, Negroes do not yet have an impact proportionate to their numbers in the electorate. Yet in certain Northern and Western states, particularly Michigan and California, blacks have moved into positions where, as holders of cabinet-level posts and as chairmen of legislative committees, they possess real levers of power. Thus in California, Mervyn Dymally, now the lieutenant governor, previously served as chairman of the Democratic caucus in the Senate. More significantly, for four years Representative Willie Brown, Jr., as chairman of the Committee on Ways and Means, held the third most influential political office in California, with power over nearly all aspects of the state's multibillion-dollar budget. Although Brown was very narrowly defeated in his bid to become Speaker of the House and lost his important chairmanship in 1974, blacks broadened their political power when the new Speaker appointed four of them to head other key committees.

In the South, although black politicians have nowhere achieved such positions of influence, the black vote has not been without effect. The election of blacks in every Southern state was a dramatic break with past tradition, and across the South race is no longer such an explosive issue among white voters. Racist rhetoric has sharply declined. Southern white moderates, openly bidding for black support, have won elections, including gubernatorial contests, in such states as South Carolina, Georgia, Florida, and Arkansas. Even leading politicians formerly identified with virulent racism have been forced to moderate their stance. Republican Senator Strom Thurmond of South Carolina, the Dixiecrat candidate for President in 1948 and a key architect of Nixon's Southern strategy, having promoted the unsuccessful candidacy of a racist in the gubernatorial campaign of 1970, found it essential to refurbish his own image prior to his campaign for reelection to the Senate in 1972. Accordingly, Thurmond appointed a black man to his staff and used his influence to channel federal money into black community projects. Similarly, Governor George Wallace of Alabama, the most infamous of Southern governors in the view of Afro-Americans, sought to improve his standing among blacks by appointing a Negro to a cabinet-level position and funneling millions of dollars into predominantly black communities.

High expectations have accompanied the election of black mayors in predominantly black towns and cities. However, the economic problems of these cities and the realities inherent in the structure of American politics place serious constraints upon the mayors and limit what they can deliver. In addition to providing a psychological lift for the black community, Negro mayors are able to arrange some contracts for black entrepreneurs, provide jobs in municipal posts not restricted by civil-service regulations, and make very visible appointments to key positions at the top levels of the city administration and on public bodies like boards of education. However, black mayors of big cities have typically inherited a decaying metropolis with a predominantly poor population much in need of social services. Faced with a declining tax base, the continued movement of middle-class whites and blacks to the suburbs, an entrenched white civil-service bureaucracy, and often a hostile, white-dominated city council, black mayors find it extremely difficult significantly to alleviate the problems of the poor. The necessary resources have to come from the state and federal governments.

Under these circumstances the black mayors find it necessary to take a moderate stance as they seek to coax tax funds from officials and to cajole white homeowners and businessmen to remain in the cities. In Los Angeles, Thomas Bradley was elected without the support of important militant black activists. In Newark, Mayor Kenneth Gibson, who originally ran for office with the active help of the black-nationalist Imamu Amiri Baraka (LeRoi Jones), eventually broke with Baraka. And in Alabama, black mayors acting in pragmatic fashion have secured cooperation from Governor Wallace in their quest for state funds. In short, black mayors have pursued not a "politics of confrontation," but a "politics of delivery" as they have tried to alleviate the problems of the black masses. Within these circumscribed limits, many have been able to bring about some improvement. For example, during Richard Hatcher's first two terms in office in Gary, Indiana, he obtained $200 million in federal funds for programs that included constructing 2,200 units of low- and middle-income housing; and in Tuskegee, Alabama, through the judicious cultivation of Governor Wallace and President Nixon, Mayor Johnny Ford obtained a $5.3 million federal grant for a new sewage system and $9 million in state funds to bring new industry into the area. Generally, however, black mayors have had only a very limited impact on the housing and economic problems of the slum dwellers. This is true not only of the large decaying metropolises in the North but also of the small, predominantly black towns of the South that are often so poor they cannot even raise the matching funds necessary to obtain federal grants.

With few exceptions—Senator Brooke being the most conspicuous—black political activism has taken place within the Democratic Party. This is scarcely surprising, given the fact that the black vote has been heavily Democratic since the 1930's. Only occasionally have Republican politicians really courted the Negro electorate. President Nixon fashioned his electoral victory in 1968 by appealing to white suburban and Southern voters, and he repeated this strategy in 1972. In both elections blacks, perceiving Nixon as neglectful of their concerns, gave him only one tenth of their vote. Once in the White House, Nixon, who publicly opposed busing for school integration, faced a unanimous decision by the Supreme Court that reversed his directive that the Justice Department delay desegregation in Mississippi. The President also tried unsuccessfully to water down the Voting Rights Act when it came up for renewal. Nixon dismantled the antipoverty program and suspended federal funds for low-cost public housing. He appointed no black to a cabinet post, although he did name Benjamin Hooks to the Federal Communications Commission. Hooks was the second Negro to be named to a federal regulatory agency. The first, Andrew Brimmer, had been appointed to the Federal Reserve Board by President Johnson. On the other hand, Nixon named five blacks to the federal district courts, thus building on the record of Lyndon Johnson, who had added eight blacks as federal district and circuit court judges in addition to elevating Thurgood Marshall to the Supreme Court.*

It is still too early to evaluate the policies of Gerald Ford's Administration, but unlike Nixon he did not fear dialogue with black congressmen, he endorsed extension of the Voting Rights Act, and he appointed the second black cabinet member in history, William T. Coleman, Jr., Secretary of Transportation. Through both Republican Administrations, the momentum of social change inaugurated during the Johnson years was sustained by segments of the federal bureaucracy, most notably in the encouragement of affirmative action in employment on the part of the Department of Labor and HEW. Yet it is evident that the principal federal agency for promoting change during the years of Republican occupancy of the White House has been the judiciary. Most of the positive actions taken by the federal bureaucracy to further economic opportunity and school desegregation were undoubtedly a reflection of what was happening in the federal courts.

The Democratic Party affords a contrast to the Republicans. Nearly all elected black officeholders are Democrats, including all Negroes in the House of Representatives. And with blacks supplying about 20 percent of the Democratic votes in national elections, they have, not surprisingly, been able to exercise greater influence in that party. The nature of this influence and the way in which blacks have increasingly sought to wield power within Democratic Party councils can be seen by examining the issue of black representation at the Democratic National Conventions. This matter was first raised by the Freedom Democratic Party in its challenge at the 1964 Convention. Although the FDP distrusted the Democratic Party pledges to prevent racial discrimination in the selection of future delegations, the

* The recent rise in the number of black judges is noticeable because twelve years elapsed between Truman's appointment of Judge Hastie in 1949 and Kennedy's selection of three blacks as federal district judges in 1961. In 1975, the total number of Negroes on the federal bench in the continental United States was eighteen, including the one judge appointed by Ford.

The Legacy of the Black Revolt 347

Democrats, under black pressures, have gone further than anything that FDP in 1964 had demanded. Not only does the
interracial "loyalist" Democratic faction now represent Mississippi at national conventions instead of the "regulars," but the
proportion of convention delegates who are black has risen from
about 2 percent in 1964 to 5 percent in 1968 to about 15 percent in 1972. Since blacks supplied the party with an important
bloc of votes, by the 1970's there developed a thrust to guarantee them a proportional share of the delegates to the qua-
drennial conventions. The reforms associated with Senator
McGovern's campaign for the party's nomination during 1971
and 1972 provided that state delegations must demonstrate that
they had taken affirmative action to secure adequate representation of blacks as well as other minorities, the young, and
women. Acrimonious debates followed. In 1974 blacks, appre-
hensive that the affirmative-action program was being emasculated, threatened a walkout from the national meeting called to
draft new rules for the Democratic Party. In the resultant compromise, the blacks essentially won their point. Their importance in party affairs was also symbolized by the selection of
Basil Paterson as the Democrats' national vice-chairman in 1972
and by the fact that blacks now form 12 percent of the Democratic National Committee.

Clearly blacks are a long way from achieving a proportional
share of political offices and from wielding a proportional share
of influence within the party for which most of them vote. Nor
has the enhanced black political activity succeeded where legalism and direct action failed in bringing about full equality in
American society. Yet it is evident that blacks are likely to
achieve more access to positions of real political power and that
they will use their increasing leverage to claim a greater share of
the nation's resources and to secure a more influential role in
the mainstream of American life.

5

The organizations identified with nonviolent direct action in
the 1960's have declined, but as the heightened political activity

suggests, black activism has by no means disappeared. It has taken new forms instead. Not only are the kinds of energies that were once channeled into street demonstrations and voter-registration campaigns now evident in political involvement, but a significant minority of the protest leaders of the 1960's have become officeholders. It is true that former SNCC and CORE activists, with their dislike of anything smacking of compromise, have mostly avoided partisan politics, and that the national NAACP is unhappy about those who, having achieved civic prominence through the Association's branches, want to use the local branch members as a continuing political base. Yet, while aspirants and officeholders of the 1970's are mainly new faces, a number of former civil-rights leaders are now active in politics. Congressman William Clay had once been promi-nent in the NAACP and CORE in St. Louis. Congressman Andrew Young had been executive vice-president of SCLC. Secretary of Transportation William T. Coleman had a long record of civil-rights litigation in the courts and had been presi-dent of the NAACP Legal Defense and Educational Fund. Georgia Senator Julian Bond had been public-relations director of SNCC. Charles Evers, mayor of Fayette, Mississippi, was an NAACP field secretary. Aaron Henry, president of COFO and longtime state president of the Mississippi NAACP, heads the "loyalist" faction of the state's Democratic Party and is a mem-ber of the Democratic National Committee. Individuals formerly active in SNCC and SCLC campaigns are prominent among the black leaders who have taken control of Lowndes and Greene Counties, Alabama. Elsewhere a number of state and local officials, North as well as South, were similarly re-cruited to political activism as a result of their participation in the civil-rights movement of the 1960's.

Of the major protest organizations of the 1960's, SNCC has disappeared while CORE and SCLC have suffered sharp de-cline. Despite the black-nationalist surge of the late 1960's and early 1970's, both SNCC and the Black Panthers, with their revolutionary stance, proved unable to formulate viable pro-grams. Although the Panthers briefly obtained enormous publicity in the mass media and, like Malcolm X earlier, symbolized for many blacks courageous resistance to white domination, their membership always remained small. By the early 1970's, widespread police repression had all but destroyed the movement. Nor was CORE with its reformist black-capitalist orientation able to maintain itself as a major black-protest organization. Actually, the latter's greatest continuing influence was to be found in the new organizations established by former CORE leaders who did not espouse its separatist ideology. Particularly important was the work of George Wiley's National Welfare Rights Organization. An aggressive group of welfare mothers which included whites among its black majority, this organization used both direct action and litigation to increase the number of people on welfare rolls and secure improvements in benefits being paid.

SCLC, following King's death, foundered, partly because of the waning of direct action and partly because of internal leadership problems. The most successful aspect of its work consisted of the direct-action campaign for better economic opportunities known as "Operation Breadbasket." In Chicago this campaign came under the direction of the most charismatic of King's aides, Jesse Jackson. Pressing against consumer-goods manufacturers and retail chains, Jackson secured agreements with firms ranging from Avon cosmetic products to the A&P, providing both jobs for Negro workers and market outlets for black manufacturers. Jackson left SCLC in 1971 as a result of clashes with other SCLC leaders and established People United to Save Humanity (PUSH). The new organization not only continued Breadbasket activities but also served as a base from which Jackson propelled himself into a position of national prominence.

In contrast, both the NAACP and the Urban League have remained very active. The NAACP, though down from its peak membership of half a million at the height of the "Freedom Now" fervor of 1963, has stabilized at over 400,000. At a time when the federal courts are proving to be, in all likelihood, the most important single mechanism for obtaining continued social change, the NAACP's tactic of legalism has experienced a resurgence. The Association has pressed particularly hard for school desegregation and affirmative action in employment. For example, the steel-industry agreement was in large part due to NAACP pressures, and the struggle over desegregation of the big-city school systems has been spearheaded by the NAACP. The Urban League, with a multimillion-dollar budget, obtained through federal grants and contributions from major business corporations, has funded a wide range of programs from health care through low-income housing to apprenticeship job training aimed at increasing the number of blacks in these building trades. As earlier, its central mission is to increase employment opportunities. Both from the public platform and in his intimate contacts with the nation's biggest business leaders, the league's new executive director, Vernon Jordan, has warmly supported affirmative action.

Both the NAACP and the Urban League have maintained undiminished their belief in an open, integrated, pluralistic society where the same opportunities are available to every person regardless of race. In pursuit of this goal, the race-advancement organizations have moved in the past fifteen years from simply seeking equality of opportunity to seeking compensatory action that would bring equality of results. In short, the drive for the greater inclusion of blacks in the mainstream of American life is now characterized by a quest for parity, under which blacks would achieve an economic and political status that would be commensurate with their proportion in the total population.

The intense nationalist and separatist impulses expressed by the "black power" slogan of the late 1960's did not become the dominant thrust of black thought. Black separatism probably reached its climax at the Black Political Convention held in Gary in 1972; subsequently it declined. As earlier discussions of black ideologies have suggested, the ethnic identity of black Americans has been too ambiguous and too complex for an unalloyed separatist or nationalist ideology to become firmly rooted in the thinking of American blacks. There is an increasing pride of race, but this is combined with a drive to take advantage of the new opportunities to participate in the main-stream of American society. Black caucuses in unions and pro-fessional associations and black student organizations at pre-dominantly white universities and colleges often employed a highly nationalist style; yet their activities proved paradoxical. They stressed not only black unity, separate black curricular and extracurricular programs at the colleges, and black consciousness but were also concerned with obtaining for blacks "a bigger piece of the action"—with achieving greater recognition for blacks and giving them more status and influence within the institutions under attack. Many blacks, in fact, interpreted "black power" to mean what blacks, by their united action, had been doing all along to advance themselves within American society. Thus the ethnic dualism that has characterized the thinking of most Afro-Americans throughout their history is still a basic element in their sense of identity and plays a vital role in shaping the strategies they select to solve their problems.

The complexities and ambiguities of black ethnic identity and the persisting variety of black strategies for survival and advancement in American society were evident at the Black Political Convention. Officially called by the Congressional Black Caucus, it was the result of two parallel developments. On the one hand, the congressmen sought to put pressure on the Republicans and, especially, the Democrats to make both of them more sensitive to the needs of black Americans. The pur-pose of the convention, declared the congressmen in their call issued late in 1971, would be to develop "a national black agency and the crystallization of a national black strategy for the 1972 elections and beyond." On the other hand, ideological nationalists outside the ranks of the two major parties, unhappy with the fruits of black political activism thus far and critical of elected officials for having played the game of political compro-mise and done nothing fundamental to alleviate the glaring problems of the black masses, had been considering the idea of independent black political action—possibly creating a black political party. For the congressmen and the nationalists alike, it seemed clear that a show of black unity would be a useful form of pressure. To some extent, the congressmen felt the heat of nationalist criticism, but in addition they sought to use the pressures generated by the nationalists to further their own programs. What developed was a joint movement of both elected officeholders and ideological nationalists. The conveners of the conclave were Congressman Charles Diggs of Michigan, Mayor Richard Hatcher of Gary, and the noted black nationalist author, Imamu Amiri Baraka. The invitation went out to all black elected officials, community organizations, and nationalist movements.

The Congressional Black Caucus, formed in 1969 in order to provide a unified and therefore more effective voice for Negro congressmen, was composed of a broad spectrum of individuals, ranging from old-style, low-keyed politicians to outspoken militants. And so it was not surprising that a division of opinion developed among them as to the wisdom of cosponsoring the convention. In the end the caucus decided not to participate as a body, though it encouraged its members to attend the convention as individuals. About half the congressmen were among the six thousand who converged on Gary. These participants ranged from integrationists to revolutionary nationalists. Figures as diverse as Mrs. Martin Luther King and Black Panther leader Bobby Seale sat on the same platform. Coming together at the cresting of the tide of black-nationalist sentiment, the conferees sought to weld blacks into a cohesive bloc under the banner of "unity without uniformity." At one dramatic high point almost the entire audience rose to its feet, clenched fists aloft, chanting "Nationtime! Nationtime! Nationtime!"

Yet the gathering was marked by serious cleavages. Though there was substantial representation from separatist groups like the Black Muslims and Baraka's organization, and although the nationalists dominated the proceedings, a large number of veteran NAACP members were also present, as well as emerging local leaders from the rural South who were uncomfortable with the rhetoric about an independent black nation. The NAACP national office, alarmed by the separatist tone of the conference and the nationalist and revolutionary spirit of the preamble that had been drafted for the convention's platform, seeming to call as it did for the withdrawal of blacks from the American political process, firmly reaffirmed the Association's integrationist goals. Rejecting the concept of "separate nationhood for black Americans," the NAACP defended its commitment "to a practical policy of accomplishment, utilizing the system as we find it in the conviction that its own processes provide the mechanism for needed changes" to "achieve equality and to make a reality of the doctrine of 'all men are created equal' enunciated in the Declaration of Independence."

More significantly, there was a sharp difference of opinion between the nationalist-minded groups who were pushing for an independent black political party and the elected officeholders, chiefly Democratic, who saw the convention as part of a strategy for pressing black demands through the existing political system. Although black nationalist delegates were in a minority at the convention, in the enthusiasm of the moment the conferees adopted a Black Political Agenda whose language expressed extreme alienation and a separatist rhetoric. Its preamble called upon the "Brothers and Sisters of our developing Black nation," to turn their backs "on the dying weight of a bloated inwardly decaying white civilization. . . . White politics has not and cannot bring the changes we need. . . . We lift up a Black Agenda recognizing that white America moves toward the abyss created by its own racial arrogance, misplaced priorities, rampant materialism, and ethical bankruptcy." The document demanded "radical fundamental change" in American society as the only way to provide justice for black Americans. Yet specific resolutions called for representation in Congress proportionate to the numbers of blacks in the total population and asked for billions in reparations, with the black community having complete control over how this money would be spent. Thus the demands made were for a greater black share in the economic and political life of the country, rather than a fundamental restructuring of the basic nature of society. The convention created a permanent Black Political Assembly that would endorse candidates, conduct voter-registration drives, and, in the words of one black leader, serve "as the chief brokerage operation for dealing with the white-power political institutions." On the other hand, the push for a separate black political party was thwarted, though Mayor Hatcher seemed to threaten this as a distinct possibility when he warned, "We say to the two American political parties, this is their last chance."

Subsequently, it became clear that the Democratic politicians, while employing this demonstration of black unity and the threat of the Negro vote to gain further concessions, were unwilling to endorse a truly separatist program. Many openly rejected sections of the agenda, claiming that the Gary convention did not accurately represent the black community. Members of the Congressional Black Caucus produced their own "Black Bill of Rights" and repudiated the CORE-sponsored resolution that had termed busing for school integration "bankrupt" and "suicidal." Instead, the Caucus endorsed busing as "one of the many ways to implement the Constitutional requirement of equal educational opportunities." Democratic politicians, threatening a defection of the black vote, presented a united front in their campaign for greater black representation in the party's councils. Yet they became resentful of the way in which Baraka, who controlled the machinery of the Black Political Assembly, dominated things, and most of them withdrew. Consequently, the assembly failed to develop into a significant political voice. In fact, the whole movement toward black separatism that the Gary convention seemed to portend waned. And at the second meeting of the Black Political Convention, held in 1974, few elected officials chose to attend. Hatcher, who was present, bitterly called the roll of prominent absent politicians who had decided that black-nationalist leaders like Baraka had few grass-roots votes to deliver at election time and that the brand of separatism represented by the Black Political Convention was not a powerful force.

Separatist and Pan-Africanist sentiment remained a significant element in black thought, but a drift away from nationalist ideology was evident among some of those who had been its warmest advocates. The nationalism of the late 1960's and early 1970's had enjoyed its greatest vogue among young college-educated people; and in fact the black intellectuals who were its spokesmen had, unlike Garvey, proved unable to establish a base among the black masses. Even among college youths, during the years after the peak of nationalist sentiment marked by the Gary convention, the wearing of dashikis, the raising of the clenched fist, and the prevalence of other similar symbolic acts declined. While the interest in black consciousness and black culture retained considerable salience, students turned more toward career concerns. Change also became evident in a very different social stratum—among the Black Muslims. By the time Elijah Muhammad died early in 1975, the organization had been moderating its stance toward whites, who were no longer being denounced as "devils" and "beasts." In fact, Muhammad's son, who succeeded him as head of the sect, announced: "We have caught hell from the white man for four hundred years, but we have grown to where if the white man respects us, we will respect him." And the Nation of Islam dropped its long-standing demand for a separate black state in the United States.

Moreover, some of the most radical nationalists embraced a Marxist position and concluded that justice could only be achieved by united and revolutionary action on the part of lower-income black and white workers. As early as 1968, the Black Panthers had soft-pedaled their nationalist ideology and formed an alliance with Communist and New Left radicals. As we have seen, in Detroit, the League of Revolutionary Black Workers broke apart in the early 1970's, partly because of internal disagreements over whether it should remain a strictly black-nationalist movement or, since capitalism was the enemy, it should ally itself with white revolutionary Marxist groups.

By 1974 there was a serious debate among black-nationalist intellectuals—many of whom were also revolutionary Marxists—over whether race or class was the most important factor in the oppression of blacks. Black revolutionary nationalists had espoused both cultural nationalism and economic revolution, a black socialism that distrusted all whites and envisioned a black nation within America composed of a network of "many Newarks" running their own affairs without the interference of large white corporations. By the end of the year, Baraka had left the nationalist fold. As head of the Congress of African People he had insisted that the primary aim should be to unify the black community through a cultural revolution emphasizing traditional black values and customs and the black American's African heritage. Now, however, he denounced black nationalism as essentially racist and maintained that the black liberation movement was in essence a struggle for socialism. Advocating alliance with poor whites in a common fight against capitalist oppression, he now declared that "nationalism, when it says all nonblacks are our enemies, is sickness or criminality . . . nationalism is reactionary when it becomes simply reverse racism . . . it is a narrow nationalism that says the white man is the enemy." Thus, while black separatism is certainly not passé as an ideology, it is clear that it does not enjoy as much support as it had at the opening of the decade.

6

The number of middle-class blacks has been growing as economic opportunities in business and government open up for those fortunate enough to have obtained an adequate education. On the other hand, nearly one third of black families still have incomes below the official poverty line. There has been in very recent years some token residential dispersal of middle- and upper-class blacks into white neighborhoods and suburbs. Yet demographic studies indicate that residential separation of whites and blacks is still the rule. The largest ghettos exist in the nation's major cities, a rising number of which are becoming predominantly black, and ghettos are also growing in many suburbs. Thus the future of Negroes and of American race relations will revolve around the question of what happens in and to the ghetto. The plantation system has all but disappeared; with the continued mechanization of both tobacco and cotton agriculture, it will vanish completely in the next few years. In cities, both North and South, the political strength of the black ghetto is growing, as is evident in the rising number of Negro officeholders. Will the black protest organizations and the black Democratic politicians be able to harness this political potential and thus help the masses in the ghetto to secure for themselves the power that would compel society to provide them with adequate employment, education, and housing? If this should be achieved will the ghetto, like the plantation, disappear as the focus of Negro life? Or will it remain as a cohesive community, at the core of the nation's largest cities, helping shape the texture and spirit of American life?

Selected Bibliography

THIS BIBLIOGRAPHICAL ESSAY lists significant works, chiefly secondary sources, that are readily available to the general reader and the college student. No attempt is made to include most of the materials on which this book is based.

General Works

The leading and most detailed general historical survey is John Hope Franklin, *From Slavery to Freedom*, 4th ed. (New York, 1974), and it includes excellent and comprehensive bibliographical notes. Benjamin Quarles, *The Negro in the Making of America* (New York, 1964) is an admirable shorter survey. The two major sociological works devoted entirely to the study of black Americans are Gunnar Myrdal, *An American Dilemma*, 2 vols. (New York, 1944), and E. Franklin Frazier, *The Negro in the United States* (New York, 1957). Two important theoretical sociological studies are Hubert M. Blalock, Jr., *Toward a Theory of Minority Group Relations* (New York, 1967) and William J. Wilson, *Power, Racism and Privilege: Race Relations in Theoretical and Socio-Historical Perspectives* (New York, 1973).

There is a growing literature on the history of American racism. Among the more significant works are: William R. Stanton, *The Leopard's Spots: Scientific Attitudes toward Race in America, 1815–59* (Chicago, 1960); Eugene H. Berwanger, *The Frontier against Slavery: Western Anti-Negro Prejudice and the Slavery Extension Controversy* (Urbana, 1967); David Reimers,

White Protestantism and the Negro (New York, 1965); Jacque Voegeli, *Free but Not Equal: The Midwest and the Negro during the Civil War* (Chicago, 1967); Idus A. Newby, *Jim Crow's Defense: Anti-Negro Thought in American Literature, 1900–1930* (Baton Rouge, 1965); Winthrop Jordan, *White over Black: American Attitudes toward the Negro, 1550–1812* (Chapel Hill, 1968); Mary F. Berry, *Black Resistance/White Law* (New York, 1971); and George M. Fredrickson, *The Black Image in the White Mind: The Debate on Afro-American Character and Destiny, 1817–1914* (New York, 1971).

Useful documentaries include Herbert Aptheker, ed., *A Documentary History of the Negro People* (New York, 1951); Leslie H. Fishel, Jr., and Benjamin Quarles, ed., *The Black American: A Documentary History*, 2d ed. (Glenview, Ill., 1970); Gilbert Osofsky, ed., *The Burden of Race: A Documentary History of Negro-White Relations in America* (New York, 1967); John H. Bracey, Jr., August Meier, and Elliott Rudwick, eds., *Black Nationalism in America* (Indianapolis, 1970); Albert B. Blaustein and Robert L. Zangrando, eds., *Civil Rights and the American Negro: A Documentary History* (New York, 1968); and Gerda Lerner, ed., *Black Women in White America* (New York, 1972).

The leading learned journals devoted to black studies are *Journal of Negro History* (Washington, 1916–); *Journal of Negro Education* (Washington, 1932–), whose scope of articles is far broader than its title implies; and *Phylon* (Atlanta, 1940–). In recent years an increasing number of important articles have been appearing in the standard journals of the various disciplines.

Chapter I

There is as yet no satisfactory history of the attitudes of black Americans toward Africa. Suggestive treatments can be found in George Shepperson, "Notes on Negro American Influence on the Emergence of African Nationality," *Journal of African History* 1, no. 2 (1960); John A. Davis, ed., *Africa from* the Point of View of American Negro Scholars (Paris, 1958, a special issue of the magazine Présence Africaine); and Harold R. Isaacs, The New World of Negro Americans (New York, 1963). W. E. B. Du Bois's major work dealing with African history and culture is Black Folk: Then and Now (New York, 1939). Carter G. Woodson's views are found in his African Background Outlined (Washington, 1936). Also pertinent is Louis R. Harlan, "Booker T. Washington and the White Man's Burden," American Historical Review 71 (January 1966).

George Peter Murdock's controversial reconstruction of early West African cultural development is in his Africa: Its Peoples and Their Cultural History (New York, 1959). It should be supplemented with the critical articles "The Spread of Food Production in Sub-Saharan Africa," by J. Desmond Clark and "Comments on the Thesis That There Was a Major Centre of Plant Domestication Near the Headwaters of the River Niger" by H. G. Baker, both in the Journal of African History 3, no. 2 (1962). A general history of West Africa south of the Sahara is J. D. Fage, A History of West Africa (London, 1969). Edward W. Bovill, The Golden Trade of the Moors (London, 1958) is a brilliant history of the western Sudan. An analysis of the characteristics of Sudanese kingship is in Joseph Greenberg, "The Negro Kingdoms of the Sudan," Transactions of the New York Academy of Sciences, 2d ser. 2, no. 4 (1949). Thomas Hodgkin, ed., Nigerian Perspectives: An Historical Anthology (London, 1960) sheds valuable light on the history of an important section of the slaving area.

Useful studies of the people who were the sources of the New World Negro population include three books by Robert S. Rattray, The Ashanti (Oxford, 1923), Religion and Art in Ashanti (Oxford, 1927), and Ashanti Law and Constitution (Oxford, 1929); K. A. Busia, The Position of the Chief in the Modern Political System of Ashanti (London, 1951); Ivor Wilks's exceedingly important multi-disciplinary analysis of the political order among the Ashanti prior to 1900, Asante in the Nineteenth Century: The Structure and Evolution of a Political Order (Cambridge, England, 1975); Melville J. Herskovits,

Dahomey, 2 vols. (New York, 1938); J. A. Akinjogbin, *Dahomey and Its Neighbors, 1708–1818* (Cambridge, England, 1967); Elliott P. Skinner, *The Mossi of the Upper Volta* (Stanford, 1964). C. Daryll Forde and P. M. Kaberry, eds., *West African Kingdoms in the Nineteenth Century* (Oxford, 1967); Jacob Egharevba, *A Short History of Benin*, 3d ed. (Ibadan, 1960); C. Daryll Forde, *The Yoruba-Speaking Peoples of South-Western Nigeria* (London, 1951); Samuel Johnson, *The History of the Yorubas* (Evanston, 1964); and C. Daryll Forde and G. I. Jones, *The Ibo and Ibibio-Speaking Peoples of South-Eastern Nigeria* (London, 1950). A discussion of West African sculpture can be found in William Fagg and Eliot Elisofon, *The Sculpture of Africa* (London, 1958).

The standard reference on African survivals in black-American culture is Melville J. Herskovits, *Myth of the Negro Past* (New York, 1941). Much of the basis for the conclusions reached in that study are in the published accounts of his own field research, but these should be supplemented with James G. Leyburn's extraordinary volume, *The Haitian People* (New Haven, 1941) and Lorenzo D. Turner's pioneering *Africanisms in the Gullah Dialect* (Chicago, 1949). In somewhat popular fashion, Zora Neale Hurston, *Mules and Men* (Philadelphia, 1935) deals with "hoodoo" cults in the United States.

Herskovits's most articulate critic was E. Franklin Frazier, whose views on the subject are summed up in the opening chapter of his *The Negro in the United States* (New York, 1957). For Frazier's influential thesis about black-American family structure see his sociological classic *The Negro Family in the United States* (Chicago, 1939). More recent studies of the influence of matrifocal tendencies on the Afro-American subculture are Lee Rainwater, "Crucible of Identity: The Negro Lower-Class Family," in Talcott Parsons and Kenneth B. Clark, eds., *The Negro American* (New York, 1966), and Elliot Liebow, *Tally's Corner* (Boston, 1967). On the controversy stirred up by Daniel P. Moynihan's famous report on the black family, see Lee Rainwater and William L. Yancey, *The Moynihan Report and the Politics of Controversy* (Cambridge, Mass.,

1967). For a discussion emphasizing family stability and patri-focal patterns, especially among middle- and upper-class Negroes, see Andrew Billingsley, *Black Families in White America* (Englewood Cliffs, 1968).

Chapter II

Though written for a popular audience, Basil Davidson, *Black Mother: The Years of the African Slave Trade* (Boston, 1961) is the best general account available of the slave trade and its influence on African societies. Contrasting views on the extent of slavery among the coastal peoples with whom the Europeans traded can be found in Walter Rodney, "African Slavery and Other Forms of Social Oppression on the Upper Guinea Coast in the Context of the African Slave-Trade," *Journal of African History* 7, no. 3 (1966) and J. D. Fage, "Slavery and the Slave Trade in the Context of West African History," *Ibid.* 10, no. 3 (1969). The role of the Western powers can best be studied in John W. Blake, *European Beginnings in West Africa, 1454–1578* (London, 1937) and in the introductions of the four volumes of Elizabeth Donnan, ed., *Documents Illustrative of the History of the Slave Trade to America* (Washington, 1930–5). A most illuminating and pioneering description of the workings of the slave trade from the African end is the second chapter of K. O. Dike, *Trade and Politics in the Niger Delta, 1830–1885* (London, 1956). Eric Williams, *Capitalism and Slavery* (Chapel Hill, 1944) is a provocative interpretation of the impact of the slave trade on the British imperial economy. The activities of British merchants are described in K. G. Davies, *The Royal African Company* (London, 1957), and Gomer Williams, *History of the Liverpool Privateers and Letters of Marque, with an Account of the Liverpool Slave Trade* (London, 1897). The best eyewitness accounts written by Europeans who participated in the traffic are William Bosman, *A New and Accurate Description of the Coast of Guinea*, trans. from the Dutch (London, 1705); J. Barbot, *A Description of the Coasts of North and South Guinea*, trans. from the French (London, 1746); William Snelgrave, *A New Account of Some*

Parts of Guinea and the Slave-Trade (London, 1754); and Alexander Falconbridge, *Account of the Slave Trade on the Coast of Africa* (London, 1788). For a scholarly analysis of the extent of the slave trade, see Philip Curtin, *The Atlantic Slave Trade: A Census* (Madison, 1969). On Negro participation in the exploration of the New World, see especially Richard R. Wright, "Negro Companions of the Spanish Explorers," *American Anthropologist* 4, no. 2 (1902).

For varying views on the nineteenth-century illicit slave trade, see W. E. B. Du Bois, *Suppression of the African Slave Trade to the United States, 1638–1870* (Cambridge, Mass., 1896); Harvey Wish, "The Revival of the African Slave Trade in the United States, 1856–1860," *Mississippi Valley Historical Review* 27 (April 1941); Warren S. Howard, *American Slavers and the Federal Law, 1837–1862* (Berkeley, 1963); and Ronald T. Takaki, *A Pro-Slavery Crusade: The Agitation to Reopen the African Slave Trade* (New York, 1971).

Most of the older volumes dealing with slavery in the English mainland colonies are hopelessly outdated. The principal exception is Lorenzo J. Greene, *The Negro in Colonial New England* (New York, 1942). The most satisfactory analyses of the evolution of slavery out of indentured servitude are found in Carl N. Degler, "Slavery and the Genesis of American Race Prejudice," *Comparative Studies in History and Society* 2 (October 1959), and Winthrop D. Jordan, *White over Black* (Chapel Hill, 1968). Peter H. Wood, *Black Majority: Negroes in Colonial South Carolina from 1670 through the Stono Rebellion* (New York, 1974) is a path-breaking analysis. Edgar J. McManus, *Black Bondage in the North* (Syracuse, 1973) summarizes scholarly knowledge of the subject. On Pennsylvania, see in addition three important recent articles: Allan Tully, "Patterns of Slaveholding in Colonial Pennsylvania: Chester and Lancaster Counties, 1729–1758," *Journal of Social History* 6 (Spring 1973); Jerome H. Wood, Jr., "The Negro in Early Pennsylvania: The Lancaster Experience, 1730–1790," in Elinor Miller and Eugene D. Genovese, eds., *Plantation, Town, and Country* (Urbana, 1974); and Gary B. Nash, "Slaves and

Slaveowners in Colonial Philadelphia," *William and Mary Quarterly* 30 (April 1973).

The role of blacks in the American Revolution is best described in Benjamin Quarles's scholarly *The Negro in the American Revolution* (Chapel Hill, 1961). The rise of the European and American antislavery movement and the problems it met and overcame in securing the abolition of the slave trade and slavery are analyzed in sophisticated detail in two volumes by David Brion Davis: *The Problem of Slavery in Western Culture* (Ithaca, 1966), and *The Problem of Slavery in the Age of Revolution, 1770–1823* (Ithaca, 1975). On the attitudes of the founding fathers and the early United States antislavery movement, see also Jordan, *White over Black;* Thomas C. Drake, *Quakers and Slavery in America* (New Haven, 1950); Walter H. Mazyck, *George Washington and the Negro* (Washington, 1932); and William W. Freehling, "The Founding Fathers and Slavery," *American Historical Review* 77 (February 1972). Donald G. Matthews, *Slavery and Methodism* (Princeton, 1965), contains a penetrating analysis of how one of the leading antislavery churches came to forsake its original position on the issue. Robert McColley, *Slavery and Jeffersonian Virginia* (Urbana, 1964) argues that plantation slavery remained highly profitable during the late eighteenth century and that there was little sentiment for emancipation among Virginia slaveowners. Arthur Zilversmit, *The First Emancipation* (Chicago, 1967) describes the abolition of slavery in the Northern states during the Revolutionary and post-Revolutionary years.

The best general description of the institution of slavery in nineteenth-century America is Kenneth Stampp, *The Peculiar Institution* (New York, 1956). This should be supplemented by Lewis Gray, *History of Agriculture in the Southern United States to 1860*, 2 vols. (Washington, 1933); the description of the technology of Southern agriculture in Ulrich B. Phillips, *Life and Labor in the Old South* (Boston, 1929); John Hebron Moore, *Agriculture in Ante-Bellum Mississippi* (New York, 1958); Frederic Bancroft, *Slave Trading in the Old South* (Baltimore, 1931); and Carter G. Woodson, *Free Negro Owners of Slaves in the United States in 1830* (Washington, 1925). For a description of Southern slavery in all its variety by a contemporary observer, see Frederick Law Olmsted, *The Cotton Kingdom*, 2 vols. (New York, 1861). Recently the use of slaves in industrial occupations has become a matter of considerable scholarly interest; see especially Robert Starobin, *Industrial Slavery in the Old South* (New York, 1970).

For varied views on the character of American slavery, the nature of slave life and culture, and the question of slave accommodation and resistance, see, in addition to the Stampp and Wood books cited above: Ulrich B. Phillips, *American Negro Slavery* (New York, 1918); Harvey Wish, "American Slave Insurrections before 1861," *Journal of Negro History* 22 (July 1937); Herbert Aptheker, *American Negro Slave Revolts* (New York, 1943); Stanley M. Elkins, *Slavery: A Problem in American Institutional Life* (Chicago, 1959); Eugene D. Genovese, *The Political Economy of Slavery* (New York, 1965), and Genovese, *Roll, Jordan, Roll: The World the Slaves Made* (New York, 1974); Vincent Harding, "Religion and Resistance among Antebellum Negroes, 1800–1860," in August Meier and Elliott Rudwick, eds., *The Making of Black America*, vol. 1 (New York, 1969); Sterling Stuckey, "Through the Prism of Folklore," *Massachusetts Review* 9 (Summer 1968); John W. Blassingame, *The Slave Community* (New York, 1972); Lawrence Levine, "Slave Songs and Slave Consciousness," in Tamara K. Hareven, ed., *Anonymous Americans* (Englewood Cliffs, 1971); Gerald W. Mullin, *Flight and Rebellion: Slave Resistance in Eighteenth Century Virginia* (New York, 1972); George P. Rawick, *The American Slave: A Composite Autobiography* (Westport, Conn., 1972); Charles B. Dew, "Disciplining Slave Ironworkers in the Antebellum South," *American Historical Review*, 79 (April 1974); Robert William Fogel and Stanley L. Engerman, *Time on the Cross*, 2 vols. (Boston, 1974); Hebert G. Gutman, *Slavery and the Numbers Game, A Critique of Time on the Cross* (Urbana, 1975); and Gutman,

Many Children: Afro-Americans and Their Families before and after Emancipation (forthcoming).

The literature relevant to comparative New World slavery and race relations is rapidly growing. Among the significant titles: Frank Tannenbaum, *Slave and Citizen* (New York, 1947); Elkins, *Slavery*; Davis, *The Problem of Slavery in Western Culture*; Sidney Mintz's review of Elkins's *Slavery* in *American Anthropologist* 66 (June 1961); Laura Foner and Eugene D. Genovese, eds., *Slavery in the New World: A Reader in Comparative Slavery* (Englewood Cliffs, 1969); Carl N. Degler, *Neither Black nor White: Slavery and Race Relations in Brazil and the United States* (New York, 1971); Winthrop Jordan, "American Chiaroscuro: The Status and Definition of Mulattoes in the British Colonies," *William and Mary Quarterly* 19 (April 1962); Charles R. Boxer, *The Golden Age of Brazil* (Berkeley, 1962); Stanley J. Stein, *Vassouras* (Cambridge, Mass., 1957); Franklin W. Knight, *Slave Society in Cuba during the Nineteenth Century* (Madison, 1970); Frederick P. Bowser, *The African Slave in Colonial Peru, 1542–1650* (Stanford, 1974); Elsa Goveia, *Slave Society in the British Leeward Islands at the End of the Eighteenth Century* (New Haven, 1965); Richard S. Dunn, *Sugar and Slaves: The Rise of the Planter Class in the British West Indies, 1624–1713* (Chapel Hill, 1972); Jerome S. Handler, *The Unappropriated People: Freedom in the Slave Society of Barbados* (Baltimore, 1974); David W. Cohen and Jack P. Greene, eds., *Neither Slave nor Free: The Freedmen of African Descent in the Slave Societies of the New World* (Baltimore, 1972); Stanley L. Engerman and Eugene D. Genovese, eds., *Race and Slavery in the Western Hemisphere: Quantitative Studies* (Princeton, 1975); and H. Hoetink, *The Two Variants in Caribbean Race Relations* (New York, 1967).

Chapter III

For the antebellum free blacks there is no overall survey, but Leon Litwack, *North of Slavery: The Negro in the Free States, 1790–1860* (Chicago, 1961), Ira Berlin, *Slaves without Masters:*

The Free Negro in the Antebellum South (New York, 1974), and Richard C. Wade, *Slavery in the Cities* (New York, 1964) are pioneering treatments of their respective topics. Among the more specialized studies of value are John Hope Franklin, *The Free Negro in North Carolina, 1790–1860* (Chapel Hill, 1943); Luther P. Jackson, *Free Negro Labor and Property Holding in Virginia, 1830–1860* (New York, 1942) and Jackson, "Religious Development of the Negro in Virginia from 1760–1860," *Journal of Negro History,* 16 (April 1931); William R. Hogan and Elmer A. Davis, *The Barber of Natchez* (Baton Rouge, 1951); E. Horace Fitchett, "The Origin and Growth of the Free Negro Population of Charleston, South Carolina," *Journal of Negro History* 26 (October 1941), and Fitchett, "The Traditions of the Free Negro in Charleston, South Carolina," *Journal of Negro History* 25 (April 1940); Marina Wikramanayake, *A World in Shadow: The Free Black in Antebellum South Carolina* (Columbia, 1973); Donald E. Everett, "Free Persons of Color in Colonial Louisiana," *Louisiana History* 7 (Winter 1966); Loren Schweninger, "John H. Rapier, Sr.: A Slave and Freedman in the Ante-Bellum South," *Civil War History* 20 (March 1974), and Schweninger's illuminating essay on urban slavery, "A Slave Family in the Ante-Bellum South," *Journal of Negro History* 60 (January 1975); Rudolph M. Lapp, "The Negro in Gold Rush California," *Ibid.* 49 (April 1964); Richard C. Wade, "The Negro in Cincinnati, 1800–1830," *Ibid.* 39 (January 1954); Leo H. Hirsch, Jr., "New York and the Negro from 1783–1865," *Ibid.* 16 (October 1931); Emma Lou Thornbrough, *The Negro in Indiana* (Indianapolis, 1957); and two articles by Theodore Hershberg, "Free Blacks in Antebellum Philadelphia: A Study of Ex-Slaves, Freeborn, and Socioeconomic Decline," *Journal of Social History* 5 (Winter 1971–1972), and "The Origins of the Female-Headed Black Family: The Destructive Impact of the Urban Experience," *Journal of Interdisciplinary History* (forthcoming).

An older but stimulating article is Dixon Ryan Fox, "The Negro Vote in Old New York," *Political Science Quarterly* 32 (June 1917). Two surveys by Carter G. Woodson, *The Educa-*

tion of the Negro Prior to 1861 (New York, 1915) and *The History of the Negro Church* (Washington, 1921) contain much useful material, as do the opening chapters of Charles H. Wesley, *Negro Labor in the United States, 1850–1925* (New York, 1927) and Abram L. Harris, *The Negro as Capitalist* (Philadelphia, 1936). Specialized articles of value are Edward N. Palmer, "Negro Secret Societies," *Social Forces* 23 (October 1944) and Dorothy B. Porter, "The Organized Educational Activities of Negro Literary Societies, 1828–1846," *Journal of Negro Education* 5 (October 1936). Descriptions of certain antebellum race riots will be found in Leonard L. Richards, *"Gentlemen of Property and Standing": Anti-Abolition Mobs in Jacksonian America* (New York, 1970).

Carter G. Woodson, ed., *The Mind of the Negro as Reflected in Letters Written during the Crisis, 1800–1860* (Washington, 1926) and the first half of Herbert Aptheker, ed., *A Documentary History of the Negro People in the United States* (New York, 1951) both contain many documents that illustrate the history and thinking of antebellum free Negroes. Useful biographies of black leaders are Carol V. George, *Segregated Sabbaths: Richard Allen and the Rise of the Independent Black Churches* (New York, 1973); Silvio A. Bedini, *The Life of Benjamin Banneker* (New York, 1972); the essays on Samuel Cornish and Henry Highland Garnet in Jane H. and William H. Pease, *Bound with Them in Chains: A Biographical History of the Antislavery Movement* (Westport, Conn., 1972); Arthur Huff Fauset, *Sojourner Truth: God's Faithful Pilgrim* (Chapel Hill, 1938); William F. Cheek, "John Mercer Langston: Black Protest Leader and Abolitionist," *Civil War History* 16 (June 1970); and the books on Frederick Douglass cited below. The antebellum convention movement is treated in Howard H. Bell, *A Survey of the Negro Convention Movement, 1830–1861* (New York, 1969) and in the thoughtful analysis of Frederick Cooper, "Elevating the Race: The Social Thought of Black Leaders, 1827–1850,"*American Quarterly* 24 (December 1972).

In recent years there have appeared the first satisfactory accounts of the role of the black abolitionists in the antislavery movement: Benjamin Quarles, *Black Abolitionists* (New York, 1969), and Jane H. and William H. Pease, *They Who Would Be Free* (New York, 1974). The latter also analyzes other protest and racial-advancement activities during the generation before the Civil War. Two contrasting evaluations of the racial attitudes of the white abolitionists are found in Pease and Pease, "Antislavery Ambivalence: Immediatism, Expediency, Race," *American Quarterly* 17 (Winter 1965) and James M. McPherson, *The Struggle for Equality: Abolitionists and the Negro in the Civil War and Reconstruction* (Princeton, 1964). A discussion of the racial views of the founders of the Republican Party will be found in Eric Foner, *Free Soil, Free Labor, Free Men: The Ideology of the Republican Party before the Civil War* (New York, 1970). Charles H. Wesley has written two helpful articles: "The Negroes of New York in the Emancipation Movement," *Journal of Negro History* 24 (January 1939), and "The Participation of Negroes in Anti-Slavery Political Parties," *Journal of Negro History* 29 (January 1944). Frederick Douglass may be studied through Benjamin Quarles's biography, *Frederick Douglass* (Washington, 1948); Douglass's own recollections, *The Life and Times of Frederick Douglass*, rev. ed. (1893; reprinted several times since); and Philip S. Foner, ed., *The Life and Writings of Frederick Douglass*, 4 vols. (New York, 1950–5). For two perceptive but divergent discussions of John Brown's relationships to blacks, see David Potter, "John Brown and the Paradox of Leadership among American Negroes," in Potter, *The South and the Sectional Conflict* (Baton Rouge, 1968) and Benjamin Quarles, *Allies for Freedom* (New York, 1974).

A brief summary of antebellum colonization thinking is Hollis R. Lynch, "Pan-Negro Nationalism in the New World before 1862," *Boston University Papers on Africa*, vol. 2 (Boston, 1966); the only comprehensive survey of the subject is Floyd John Miller, *The Search for a Black Nationality: Black Colonization and Emigration, 1787–1863* (Urbana, 1975).

On the Underground Railroad, see especially Larry Gara, *The Liberty Line* (Lexington, Ky., 1961). It should be supplemented with Dorothy B. Porter, "David M. Ruggles, An Apostle of Human Rights," *Journal of Negro History* 28 (January 1943); the recollections of William Still, entitled *The Underground Railroad* (Philadelphia, 1879); and the best of the fugitive-slave memoirs: Lunsford Lane, *The Narrative of Lunsford Lane*, 2d ed. (Boston, 1842); Henry Bibb, *The Narrative of the Life and Adventures of Henry Bibb* (New York, 1849); William Wells Brown, *Narrative of William Wells Brown, A Fugitive Slave* (Boston, 1847); Samuel Ringgold Ward, *Autobiography of a Fugitive Slave* (London, 1855); Solomon Northup, *Twelve Years a Slave* (Buffalo, 1853); as well as Douglass's autobiography cited above. These have all been recently reprinted.

Chapter IV

Leading monographs on black participation in the Civil War are Benjamin Quarles, *The Negro in the Civil War* (Boston, 1953) and Dudley T. Cornish, *The Sable Arm: Negro Troops in the Union Army* (New York, 1956). They should be supplemented with Thomas W. Higginson, *Army Life in a Black Regiment* (Boston, 1869; also available in several reprints); James M. McPherson, *The Negro's Civil War* (New York, 1965), and McPherson, *The Struggle for Equality* (Princeton, 1964) and Bell Irwin Wiley, *Southern Negroes, 1861–1865*, rev. ed. (New York, 1953). For the New York City draft riots, see Adrian Cook, *The Armies of the Streets: The New York City Draft Riots of 1863* (Lexington, Ky., 1974).

Two useful general surveys of the Reconstruction period are Kenneth Stampp, *The Era of Reconstruction, 1865–1877* (New York, 1965) and John Hope Franklin, *Reconstruction after the Civil War* (Chicago, 1961). The only general account of the Negro during Reconstruction is W. E. B. Du Bois, *Black Reconstruction in America* (New York, 1935), which gathered together all the data available on the subject and attempted a Marxist analysis of the period. The best monographs on the Negro in individual states are Willie Lee Rose, *Rehearsal for Reconstruction* (Indianapolis, 1964), a superb account of the Sea Island Negroes of South Carolina during the Civil War;

Joel Williamson, *After Slavery: The Negro in South Carolina during Reconstruction, 1861–1877* (Chapel Hill, 1965); A. A. Taylor, *The Negro in the Reconstruction of Virginia* (Washington, 1926); Vernon Lane Wharton, *The Negro in Mississippi, 1865–1890* (Chapel Hill, 1947); and Peter Kolchin, *First Freedom: The Responses of Alabama's Blacks to Emancipation and Reconstruction* (Westport, Conn., 1972). Significant specialized studies on Louisiana are John W. Blassingame, *Black New Orleans, 1860–1880* (Chicago, 1973); Roger A. Fischer, *The Segregation Struggle in Louisiana, 1862–77* (Urbana, 1974); and David Rankin's illuminating investigation, "The Origins of Black Leadership in New Orleans during Reconstruction," *Journal of Southern History* 40 (August 1974).

The work of the Freedmen's Bureau is viewed critically in William S. McFeely, *Yankee Stepfather: General O. O. Howard and the Freedmen* (New Haven, 1968). A related institution is treated in Carl R. Osthaus, *The Freedmen's Savings and Trust Company: The Tragedy of a Black Bank in Reconstruction* (Urbana, 1976). Histories of educational institutions that began during Reconstruction include Rayford W. Logan, *Howard University: The First Hundred Years* (New York, 1969) and Clarence A. Bacote, *The Story of Atlanta University: A Century of Service* (Atlanta, 1969). For a synthesis of materials on blacks and public education during Reconstruction, see William Preston Vaughn, *Schools for All: The Blacks and Public Education in the South 1865–1877* (Lexington, Ky., 1974).

Significant articles include: LaWanda Cox, "The Promise of Land for the Freedmen," *Mississippi Valley Historical Review* 45 (December 1958); Louis R. Harlan, "Segregation in New Orleans Public Schools during Reconstruction," *American Historical Review* 67 (April 1962); Leslie H. Fishel, Jr., "Northern Prejudice and Negro Suffrage, 1865–1870," *Journal of Negro History* 39 (January 1954); James M. McPherson, "Abolitionists and the Civil Rights Act of 1875," *Journal of American History* 52 (December 1965); Bettye C. Thomas, "A Nineteenth Century Black Operated Shipyard, 1866–1884; Reflections upon Its Inception and Ownership," *Journal of Negro History* 59 (January 1974); and C. Vann Woodward, "Seeds of Failure in Radical Race Policy," in Woodward, *American Counterpoint* (Boston, 1971).

Chapter V

General works dealing with the Negro in the period between Reconstruction and the First World War include C. Vann Woodward, *Origins of the New South, 1877–1913* (Baton Rouge, 1951) and Woodward, *The Strange Career of Jim Crow,* 3d ed. (New York, 1966); Rayford W. Logan, *The Negro in American Life and Thought: The Nadir, 1877–1901* (New York, 1954); August Meier, *Negro Thought in America, 1880–1915* (Ann Arbor, 1963); Willard B. Gatewood, *Black Americans and the White Man's Burden, 1898–1903* (Urbana, 1975); and Gilbert T. Stephenson, *Race Distinctions in American Law* (New York, 1910). Otto H. Olsen, ed., *The Thin Disguise: Plessy v. Ferguson, A Documentary Presentation* (New York, 1967) prints the relevant documents concerning the famous *Plessy v. Ferguson* case, with commentary. C. Vann Woodward has reviewed the literature on the controversy surrounding the history of Southern segregation in "The Strange Career of a Historical Controversy," in Woodward, *American Counterpoint.* Research in this topic continues (Boston, 1971); additional light on it is shed by Dale A. Somers's article, cited below, and Howard N. Rabinowitz, "From Exclusion to Segregation: Southern Race Relations, 1865–1890," *Journal of American History* (forthcoming). An important contribution to the history of black farm labor is Pete Daniel, *The Shadow of Slavery: Peonage in the South, 1901–1969* (Urbana, 1972). A recent study of the disfranchisement movement is J. Morgan Kousser, *The Shaping of Southern Politics: Suffrage Restriction and the Establishment of the One-Party South* (New Haven, 1974).

State and local studies of value include Charles E. Wynes, *Race Relations in Virginia, 1870–1902* (Charlottesville, 1961); Clarence A. Bacote, "Negro Proscriptions, Protests, and Proposed Solutions in Georgia, 1880–1908," *Journal of Southern History* 25 (November 1959); Margaret Law Callcott, *The*

Negro in Maryland Politics, 1870–1912 (Baltimore, 1969); George B. Tindall, *South Carolina Negroes, 1877–1900* (Columbia, S.C., 1952); Frenise Logan, *The Negro in North Carolina, 1876–1894* (Chapel Hill, 1964); Henry C. Dethloff and Robert P. Jones, "Race Relations in Louisiana, 1877–1898," *Louisiana History* 9 (Fall 1968); Dale A. Somers, "Black and White in New Orleans: A Study in Urban Race Relations," *Journal of Southern History* 40 (February 1974); Sheldon Hackney, *Populism to Progressivism in Alabama* (Princeton, 1967); John Daniels, *In Freedom's Birthplace* (Boston, 1914), on Boston Negroes; Mary White Ovington, *Half a Man: The Status of the Negro in New York* (New York, 1911); and David Gerber, *Ohio and the Color Line, 1860–1915* (Urbana, 1976).

A model study of a major black enterprise begun in this period is Walter B. Weare, *Black Business in the New South: A Social History of the North Carolina Mutual Life Insurance Company* (Urbana, 1973). The problems of black labor are treated in Sterling D. Spero and Abram L. Harris, *The Black Worker* (New York, 1931); Bernard Mandel, "Samuel Gompers and Negro Workers," *Journal of Negro History* 40 (January 1955); Paul B. Worthman, "Black Workers and Labor Unions in Birmingham, Alabama, 1897–1904," *Labor History* 10 (Summer 1969); Kenneth Porter, "Negro Labor in the Western Cattle Industry, 1866–1900," *Ibid.* 10 (Summer 1969); and Herbert Gutman, "The Negro and the United Mine Workers of America: The Career and Letters of Richard L. Davis and Something of Their Meaning: 1890–1900," in Julius Jacobson, ed., *The Negro and the American Labor Movement* (New York, 1968). Aspects of Negro education in the South are illuminated by Louis R. Harlan, *Separate and Unequal: Public School Campaigns and Racism in the Southern Seaboard States, 1901–1915* (Chapel Hill, 1958); Horace Mann Bond, *Negro Education in Alabama* (Washington, 1939); Kelly Miller, "Education of the Negro," *Report of Commissioner of Education for 1900–1901*, chap. 16 (Washington, 1902); and James M. McPherson, "White Liberals and Black Power in Negro Education, 1865–1915," *American Historical Review* 75 (June 1970). For varying views on the Negro and the agrarian revolt, see the works by Woodward cited above; Jack Abramowitz, "The Negro in the Populist Movement," *Journal of Negro History* 38 (July 1953); Helen G. Edmonds, *The Negro and Fusion Politics in North Carolina, 1894–1901* (Chapel Hill, 1951); V. O. Key, *Southern Politics in State and Nation* (New York, 1949), pp. 530–40; Herbert Shapiro, "The Populists and the Negro: A Reconsideration," Meier and Rudwick, eds., *The Making of Black America*, vol. 2 (New York, 1969), pp. 27–36; William H. Chafe, "The Negro and Populism: A Kansas Case Study," *Journal of Southern History* 34 (August 1968); Lawrence J. Goodwyn, "Populist Dreams and Negro Rights: East Texas as a Case Study," *American Historical Review* 76 (December 1971); and William F. Holmes, "The Demise of the Colored Farmers' Alliance," *Journal of Southern History* 41 (May 1975).

A valuable mine of information on the black community during the late nineteenth and early twentieth centuries is found in W. E. B. Du Bois, ed., *Atlanta University Publications* (1898–1914). An illuminating picture of the Negro in Southern politics is contained in the dissertation by Clarence Bacote, "The Negro in Georgia Politics, 1880–1908" (University of Chicago, 1955). An analysis of the development of the all-black towns is found in Harold M. Rose, "The All-Negro Town: Its Evolution and Function," *The Geographical Review* 4 (July 1965). Late nineteenth- and early-twentieth-century colonization movements are treated in Edwin S. Redkey, *Black Exodus: Black Nationalist and Back-to-Africa Movements, 1890–1910* (New Haven, 1969) and William Bittle and Gilbert Geis, *The Longest Way Home: Chief Alfred Sam's Back to Africa Movement* (Detroit, 1964). A fine urban study is David Katzman, *Before the Ghetto: Black Detroit in the Nineteenth Century* (Urbana, 1973).

Louis R. Harlan, *Booker T. Washington: The Making of a Black Leader, 1856–1901* (New York, 1972), the first volume of a projected two-volume biography, is a major contribution. See also his "The Secret Life of Booker T. Washington," *Journal of Southern History* 37 (August 1971) and "Booker T. Washington in Historical Perspective," *American Historical Review* 75 (October 1970). The interested student should consult Washington's own books: *The Future of the American Negro* (Boston, 1899) and the autobiography, *Up from Slavery* (New York, 1901). For Du Bois, see his volume of essays, *The Souls of Black Folk* (Chicago, 1903), his two autobiographies, *Dusk of Dawn* (New York, 1940) and *Autobiography of W. E. B. Du Bois* (New York, 1968), and two biographies: Francis L. Broderick, *W. E. B. Du Bois: Negro Leader in Time of Crisis* (Stanford, 1959), and Elliott Rudwick, *W. E. B. Du Bois: Propagandist of the Negro Protest*, rev. ed. (New York, 1968 and Philadelphia, 1969). Four biographies of other contemporaries of Washington are Alfreda M. Duster, ed., *Crusade for Justice: The Autobiography of Ida B. Wells* (Chicago, 1970); Eugene Levy, *James Weldon Johnson* (Chicago, 1973); Emma Lou Thornbrough, *T. Thomas Fortune* (Chicago, 1972); and Stephen R. Fox, *The Guardian of Boston: William Monroe Trotter* (New York, 1970). The best representative of the middle-of-the road point of view is Kelly Miller, *Race Adjustment*, 3d ed. (New York, 1910). The transition from a black to an interracial protest and race-advancement movement in the early years of the twentieth century is treated perceptively in Nancy J. Weiss, "From Black Separatism to Interracial Cooperation: The Origins of Efforts for Racial Advancement, 1890–1920," in Barton J. Bernstein and Allen Matusow, eds., *Twentieth Century America* (New York, 1969). The founding and early years of the NAACP are described in Charles Flint Kellogg, *NAACP: A History of the National Association for the Advancement of Colored People, Volume I, 1909–1920* (Baltimore, 1967).

Chapter VI

For a general survey of black migration to the North, see Arna Bontemps and Jack Conroy, *Anyplace but Here* (New York, 1966) and Reynolds Farley, "The Urbanization of Negroes in the United States," *Journal of Social History*, 1 (Spring 1968). For the World War I and postwar migration, the best works are those written by contemporaries: Thomas J. Woofter, *Negro Migration* (New York, 1920); Emmett J. Scott, *Negro Migra-*

tion during the War (New York, 1920); Clyde Vernon Kiser, *Sea Island to City: A Study of St. Helena Islanders in Harlem and Other Urban Centers* (New York, 1932); and Charles S. Johnson, "How Much Is Migration a Flight from Persecution?" *Opportunity* 1 (September 1923). Two of the riots that followed upon the World War I migration are given extended analysis in Elliott Rudwick, *Race Riot at East St. Louis, July 2, 1917* (Carbondale, Ill., 1964) and William M. Tuttle, Jr., *Race Riot: Chicago in the Red Summer of 1919* (New York, 1970).

On the development of the urban ghetto and its subculture, see Robert C. Weaver, *The Negro Ghetto* (New York, 1948); Claude McKay, *Harlem: Negro Metropolis* (New York, 1940); Roi Ottley, *"New World A-Comin'"* (Boston, 1943); Gilbert Osofsky, *Harlem: The Making of a Ghetto* (New York, 1966); Emma Lou Thornbrough, "Segregation in Indiana during the Klan Era of the 1920's," *Mississippi Valley Historical Review* 47 (March 1961); Allan H. Spear, *Black Chicago: The Making of a Negro Ghetto, 1890–1920* (Chicago, 1967); that classic study of the black community in Chicago, St. Clair Drake and Horace Cayton, *Black Metropolis* (New York, 1945); Thomas Philpott, *"The House and the Neighborhood": Housing Reform and Neighborhood Work in Chicago, 1880–1930* (forthcoming); Kenneth Kusmer, *A Ghetto Takes Shape: Black Cleveland, 1870–1930* (Urbana, 1975); Claude Brown, *Manchild in the Promised Land* (New York, 1965); Roger D. Abrahams, *Deep Down in the Jungle: Negro Narrative Folklore from the Streets of Philadelphia* (Hatboro, Pa., 1964); Kenneth Clark, *Dark Ghetto* (New York, 1965); and Elliot Liebow's extraordinary study, *Tally's Corner: A Study of Negro Streetcorner Men* (Boston, 1967).

The extent of residential segregation is analyzed in Karl E. and Alma F. Taeuber, *Negroes in Cities: Residential Segregation and Residential Change* (Chicago, 1965) and in Nathan Kantrowitz, *Ethnic and Racial Segregation in the New York Metropolis* (New York, 1973). On the economic aspects of life in the ghetto, see Abram L. Harris, *The Negro as Capitalist* (Philadelphia, 1936); Sterling D. Spero and Abram L. Harris, *The*

Black Worker (New York, 1931); Horace Cayton and George S. Mitchell, *Black Workers and the New Unions* (Chapel Hill, 1939); F. Ray Marshall, *The Negro and Organized Labor* (New York, 1965); and Brailsford R. Brazeal, *The Brotherhood of Sleeping Car Porters: Its Origin and Development* (New York, 1946). On the impact of urbanization on the black family, see Frazier, *The Negro Family in the United States.* On the political role of Negroes in Northern cities, see Harold F. Gosnell, *Negro Politicians: The Rise of Negro Politics in Chicago* (Chicago, 1935) and James Q. Wilson, *Negro Politics: The Search for Leadership* (Glencoe, Ill., 1960). For a broad analysis of the Negro in politics in the period between the two world wars, both in the North and in the South, see Ralph J. Bunche, "The Political Status of the Negro," 7 vols. (unpublished memorandum for the Carnegie-Myrdal Study, 1940, available on microfilm from the New York Public Library). A revealing biography of a major figure in black politics and journalism is Andrew Buni, *Robert L. Vann of the Pittsburgh Courier* (Pittsburgh, 1974). Aspects of religious life are treated in Arthur Huff Fauset, *Black Gods of the Metropolis: Negro Religious Cults of the Urban North* (Philadelphia, 1944) and Benjamin E. Mays and Joseph W. Nicholson, *The Negro's Church* (New York, 1933).

All these matters are also dealt with most perceptively in Drake and Cayton, *Black Metropolis,* as is the subject of social stratification. For a controversial essay on the Negro class structure, see E. Franklin Frazier, *Black Bourgeoisie* (Glencoe, Ill., 1957). This discussion should be supplemented by two studies of Southern communities: Hortense Powdermaker, *After Freedom* (New York, 1939) and Allison Davis and Burleigh and Mary Gardner, *Deep South* (Chicago, 1941). Also of considerable interest is a more recent study of Negro life in a Piedmont town, Hylan G. Lewis, *Blackways of Kent* (Chapel Hill, 1955).

The best introductions to the Harlem Renaissance are Alain Locke, ed., *The New Negro* (New York, 1925) and Langston Hughes's autobiography, *The Big Sea* (New York, 1940). Incisive analyses of black literature are found in Sterling Brown,

The Negro in American Fiction (Washington, 1937) and Brown, *Negro Poetry and Drama* (Washington, 1937); Benjamin E. Mays, *The Negro's God as Reflected in His Literature* (Boston, 1938); and Robert Bone's controversial *The Negro Novel in America*, rev. ed. (New Haven, 1965). For a critique of the Bone volume, see Darwin T. Turner, "The Negro Novel in America: In Rebuttal," *College Language Association Journal* 10 (December 1966). The best historical survey of the Negro in artistic and theatrical life is to be found in James Weldon Johnson, *Black Manhattan* (New York, 1930). The outstanding biography of Ira Aldridge is Herbert Marshall and Mildred Stock, *Ira Aldridge: The Negro Tragedian* (New York, 1958). The finest anthology of Negro literature is Sterling Brown, Arthur P. Davis, and Ulysses Lee, eds., *The Negro Caravan* (New York, 1941). Also useful are James Weldon Johnson, ed., *Book of American Negro Poetry* (New York, 1922); James Weldon Johnson and J. Rosamond Johnson, eds., *Books of American Negro Spirituals* (New York, 1925, 1926); Arna Bontemps and Langston Hughes, eds., *Poetry of the Negro, 1746–1949* (New York, 1949); Alain Locke, *Negro Art: Past and Present* (Washington, 1936); and James A. Porter, *Modern Negro Art* (New York, 1943). Important articles on two major writers of the last generation are Nathan A. Scott, "The Dark and Haunted Tower of Richard Wright," in Addison Gayle, Jr., ed., *Black Expression: Essays by and about Black Americans in the Creative Arts* (New York, 1969) and Robert Bone, "Ralph Ellison and the Uses of Imagination," *Tri-Quarterly*, no. 6 (Spring 1966).

The Negro and the New Deal is a subject that still remains to be adequately explored by historians. An anthology of available journal literature is Bernard Sternsher, ed., *The Negro in Depression and War: Prelude to Revolution, 1930–1948* (Chicago, 1969). Raymond Wolters, *Negroes and the Great Depression* (Westport, Conn., 1970) examines the policies of certain New Deal agencies. Two valuable recent articles, suggesting important areas for future research, are Christopher G.

Wye, "The New Deal and the Negro Community: Toward a Broader Conceptualization," *Journal of American History* 59 (December 1972) and B. Joyce Ross, "Mary McLeod Bethune and the National Youth Administration: A Case Study of Power Relationships in the Black Cabinet of Franklin D. Roosevelt," *Journal of Negro History* 60 (January 1975). The most substantial literature deals with farm tenancy and sharecropper protests. See especially Charles S. Johnson, Will Alexander, and Edwin R. Embree, *The Collapse of Cotton Tenancy* (Chapel Hill, 1935); Charles S. Johnson, *Shadow of the Plantation* (Chicago, 1935); Arthur F. Raper and Ira DeA. Reid, *Sharecroppers All* (Chapel Hill, 1941); David Eugene Conrad, *The Forgotten Farmers: The Story of Sharecroppers in the New Deal* (Urbana, 1965); Donald H. Grubbs, *Cry from the Cotton: The Southern Tenant Farmers' Union and the New Deal* (Chapel Hill, 1971); and Louis Cantor, *A Prologue to the Protest Movement* (Durham, 1969). Dan T. Carter, *Scottsboro: A Tragedy of the American South* (Baton Rouge, 1969) is a superb account of the Scottsboro case. For a good description of the South during the 1920's and 1930's, with considerable discussion of blacks and race relations, see George B. Tindall, *The Emergence of the New South, 1913–1945* (Baton Rouge, 1967).

On the World War II period, Ulysses Lee, *The Employment of Negro Troops* (Washington, 1966) is an authoritative study of blacks in the army. Richard M. Dalfiume, *Desegregation of the U.S. Armed Forces: Fighting on Two Fronts, 1939–1953* (Columbia, Mo., 1969) traces the history of desegregation in the military services through the Truman era. For varied assessments of the Truman Administration, see Barton J. Bernstein, "The Ambiguous Legacy: The Truman Administration and Civil Rights," in Bernstein, ed., *Politics and Policies of the Truman Administration* (Chicago, 1970); William C. Berman, *The Politics of Civil Rights in the Truman Administration* (Columbus, Ohio, 1970); Harvard Sitkoff, "Harry Truman and the Election of 1948: The Coming of Age of Civil Rights in American Politics," *Journal of Southern History* 37 (November

1971); and Donald R. McCoy and Richard T. Ruetten, *Quest and Response: Minority Rights and the Truman Administration* (Lawrence, Kansas, 1973).

The historical research on twentieth-century Negro protest movements and organizations is still thin, but scholars are working to fill the lacunae. The useful titles are Edmund D. Cronon, *Black Moses: The Story of Marcus Garvey and the Universal Negro Improvement Association* (Madison, 1955), which should be supplemented with the relevant chapters in the books by McKay and Ottley, cited above; B. Joyce Ross, *J. E. Spingarn and the Rise of the N.A.A.C.P.* (New York, 1972); Clement E. Vose, *Caucasians Only: The Supreme Court, the NAACP and the Restrictive Covenant Cases* (Berkeley, 1959); Nancy J. Weiss, *The National Urban League, 1910–1940* (New York, 1974); Arvarh E. Strickland, *History of the Chicago Urban League* (Urbana, 1966); Wilson Record, *The Negro and the Communist Party* (Chapel Hill, 1951); Herbert Garfinkel, *When Negroes March: The March on Washington Movement in the Organizational Politics for FEPC* (Glencoe, Ill., 1959); Richard M. Dalfiume, "The 'Forgotten Years' of the Negro Revolution," *Journal of American History* 55 (June 1968); Harvard Sitkoff, "Racial Militancy and Interracial Violence in the Second World War," *Ibid.* 58 (December 1971). For a Southern interracial protest organization, the Southern Conference for Human Welfare, see Thomas A. Krueger, *And Promises to Keep* (Nashville, 1967). For a critical analysis of the programs of Negro organizations during the 1930's, see Ralph J. Bunche, "The Programs, Ideologies, Tactics and Achievements of Negro Betterment and Interracial Organizations," 4 vols. (unpublished memorandum for the Carnegie-Myrdal Study, 1940, available on microfilm from the New York Public Library). A summary of his conclusions is available in Bunche, "A Critical Analysis of the Tactics and Programs of Minority Groups," *Journal of Negro Education* 4 (July 1935). For illustrative documents, see August Meier, Elliott Rudwick, and Francis L. Broderick, eds., *Black Protest Thought in the Twentieth Century*

(Indianapolis, 1971). A commentary on black participation in radical movements in the twentieth century is found in Harold Cruse, *The Crisis of the Negro Intellectual* (New York, 1967).

Chapter VII

August Meier, Elliott Rudwick, and Francis L. Broderick, eds., *Black Protest Thought in the Twentieth Century* (Indianapolis, 1971), deals with the changes in the character of the civil-rights movement from the turn of the century until the end of the 1960's. Relevant theoretical discussions of the black protest movement in the 1960's are to be found in Joseph S. Himes, "The Functions of Racial Conflict," *Social Forces* 45 (September 1966); Gary T. Marx, ed., *Racial Conflict: Tension and Change in American Society* (Boston, 1971); and in the incisive and provocative Lewis M. Killian and Charles Grigg, *Racial Crisis in America: Leadership in Conflict* (Englewood Cliffs, 1964). Changing attitudes of whites and blacks during the 1950's and 1960's are treated in Leonard Broom and Norval Glenn, *Transformation of the Negro American* (New York, 1965); Thomas F. Pettigrew, *A Profile of the Negro American* (Princeton, 1964), and Pettigrew, *Racially Separate or Together?* (New York, 1971); Ulf Hannerz, *Soulside: Inquiries into Ghetto Culture and Community* (New York, 1967); and Gary T. Marx, *Protest and Prejudice: A Study of Belief in the Black Community*, rev. ed. (New York, 1969).

The best biography of Martin Luther King, Jr., is David Lewis, *King: A Critical Biography* (New York, 1970). King's point of view can be studied in his *Stride toward Freedom* (New York, 1958), *Why We Can't Wait* (New York, 1964), and *Where Do We Go from Here: Chaos or Community?* (New York, 1967). A discussion of the way in which King functioned in the civil-rights movement is August Meier, "On the Role of Martin Luther King," *New Politics*, 4 (Winter 1965). Howard Zinn has sketched the early history of SNCC in *SNCC: The New Abolitionists* (Boston, 1964). The history of CORE can be studied in an account by a long-time member, James Peck, *Freedom Ride* (New York, 1962) and in August Meier and Elliott Rudwick,

CORE: A Study in the Civil Rights Movement, 1942–1968 (New York, 1973). Among the most perceptive analyses of the trends in the civil-rights movement during its direct-action phase are two articles by Bayard Rustin: "The Meaning of Birmingham," *Liberation* 8 (June 1963), and "The Meaning of the March on Washington," *Ibid.* 8 (October 1963). James Farmer, *Freedom-When?* (New York, 1965); Pettigrew, *A Profile of the Negro American*; Inge Powell Bell, *CORE and the Strategy of Nonviolence* (New York, 1968); and Julius Lester, *Look Out Whitey! Black Power's Gon' Get Your Mama!* (New York, 1968), are essential for studying the changes among civil-rights activists during the 1960's. The changing viewpoint of the Urban League is cogently expressed in Whitney M. Young, Jr., *To Be Equal* (New York, 1964) and Young, *Beyond Racism* (New York, 1969). An extremely important article is Gary T. Marx, "Religion: Opiate or Inspiration of Civil Rights Militancy among Negroes?" *American Sociological Review* 32 (February 1967).

Important case studies are Bell, *CORE and the Strategy of Nonviolence*, a careful analysis of developments in a selected group of CORE chapters, 1961–4; Charles V. Hamilton's discussion of the Tuskegee Civic Association, *Minority Politics in Black Belt Alabama* (New Brunswick, 1960); Jack L. Walker, *Sit-Ins in Atlanta: A Study in the Negro Revolt* (New Brunswick, 1964); and William W. Ellis's description of a Chicago group, *White Ethics and Black Power: The Emergence of the West Side Organization* (Chicago, 1969). Pat Watters and Reese Cleghorn, *Climbing Jacob's Ladder: The Arrival of Negroes in Southern Politics* (New York, 1967) describes the Southern voter-registration campaign of 1962–4 and its impact. The changing role of whites is discussed in the books by Bell, Farmer, and Lester, cited above; Charles J. Levy, *Voluntary Servitude: Whites in the Negro Movement* (New York, 1968); Alphonso Pinkney, *The Committed: White Activists in the Civil Rights Movement* (New Haven, 1968); N. J. Demerath, III, Gerald Marwell, and Michael T. Aiken, *Dynamics of Idealism: White Activists in a Black Movement* (San Francisco,

1971); and Gary T. Marx and Michael Useem, "Majority Involvement in Minority Movements: Civil Rights, Abolition, Untouchability," *Journal of Social Issues* 27 (1971).

Changes in the leadership structure of the black community that resulted from the civil-rights revolution are discussed in Lewis M. Killian and Charles U. Smith, "Negro Protest Leaders in a Southern Community," *Social Forces* 38 (March 1960); Jack L. Walker, "The Functions of Disunity: Negro Leadership in a Southern City," *Journal of Negro Education* 32 (Summer 1963); R. H. Hines and James E. Pierce, "Negro Leadership after the Social Crisis: An Analysis of Leadership Changes in Montgomery, Alabama," *Phylon* 26 (Summer 1965); and Gerald McWorter and Robert L. Crain, "Subcommunity Gladiatorial Competition: Civil Rights Leadership as a Competitive Process," *Social Forces* 46 (September 1967).

The economic problems of the black masses and their meaning for the black protest movement are discussed in Arthur Ross and Herbert Hill, eds., *Employment, Race and Poverty* (New York, 1965) and in the books by Whitney Young mentioned above. Among the significant studies dealing with school segregation and desegregation, especially in the North, are United States Commission on Civil Rights, *Racial Isolation in the Public Schools* (Washington, 1967); Raymond W. Mack, ed., *Our Children's Burden: Studies of Desegregation in Nine American Communities* (New York, 1968); and Robert L. Crain, *The Politics of School Desegregation* (Chicago, 1968). Fair-housing law campaigns are described in Lynn W. Eley and Thomas W. Casstevens, eds., *The Politics of Fair-Housing Legislation* (San Francisco, 1968); and Juliet Z. Saltman, *Open Housing as a Social Movement* (Lexington, Mass., 1971). On housing problems of middle-class blacks and their attitudes toward moving to the white suburbs, see L. G. Watts, H. E. Freeman, Helen Hughes, Robert Morris, and Thomas F. Pettigrew, *The Middle-Income Negro Family Faces Urban Renewal* (Boston, 1965).

For varied discussions of Negroes in politics, see John H. Fenton and Kenneth N. Vines, "Negro Registration in Lou-

isiana," *American Political Science Review* 51 (September 1957); M. Elaine Burgess, *Negro Leadership in a Southern City* (Chapel Hill, 1960); Hugh D. Price, *The Negro and Southern Politics: A Chapter of Florida History* (New York, 1957); Harry Holloway, "The Negro and the Vote: The Case of Texas," *Journal of Politics* 23 (August 1961); James Q. Wilson, "Two Negro Politicians: An Interpretation," *Midwest Journal of Politics* 4 (November 1960); Everett C. Ladd, Jr., *Negro Political Leadership in the South* (Ithaca, 1966); Donald R. Matthews and James W. Prothro, *Negroes and the New Southern Politics* (New York, 1966); Samuel D. Cook, "Political Movements and Organization," *Journal of Politics* 26 (February 1964); Bayard Rustin, "From Protest to Politics," *Commentary* 39 (February 1965); and Chandler Davison's study of Houston, *Biracial Politics: Conflict and Coalition in the Metropolitan South* (Baton Rouge, 1972).

The literature on the riots of the 1960's is enormous. The following are among the most significant items: *Report of the National Advisory Committee on Civil Disorders* (Washington, 1968); Robert M. Fogelson and Robert B. Hill, "Who Riots? A Study of Participation in the 1967 Riots," in *Supplemental Studies for the National Advisory Commission on Civil Disorders* (Washington, 1968); Robert M. Fogelson, "From Resentment to Confrontation: The Police, the Negroes, and the Outbreak of the Nineteen-Sixties Riots," *Political Science Quarterly* 83 (June 1968); Robert Blauner, "Internal Colonialism and Ghetto Revolt," *Social Problems* 16 (Spring 1969).

Among the best materials on black nationalism and the varying manifestations of black power and black consciousness are two studies of the Black Muslims: C. Eric Lincoln, *The Black Muslims in America* (Boston, 1961) and E. U. Essien-Udom, *Black Nationalism: The Search for an Identity in America* (Chicago, 1962), and two major books by and about Malcolm X: *The Autobiography of Malcolm X* (New York, 1964) and Peter L. Goldman, *The Death and Life of Malcolm X* (New York, 1973). Other titles include Robert Williams, *Negroes with Guns* (New York, 1962); Stokely Carmichael and

Charles V. Hamilton, *Black Power: The Politics of Liberation in America* (New York, 1967); Charles V. Hamilton, "An Advocate of Black Power Defines It," *The New York Times Magazine* (April 14, 1968); Eldridge Cleaver, *Soul on Ice* (New York, 1968); John O. Killens, "Explanation of the 'Black Psyche,'" *The New York Times Magazine* (June 7, 1964); Joyce Ladner, "What 'Black Power' Means to Negroes in Mississippi," *Trans-Action* 7 (November 1967); Lewis Killian, *The Impossible Revolution?* (New York, 1968); Martin Duberman, "Black Power in America," *Partisan Review* 35 (Winter 1968); and Joel D. Aberbach and Jack L. Walker, "The Meanings of Black Power: A Comparison of White and Black Interpretations of a Political Slogan," *American Political Science Review* 64 (June 1970).

Anthologies illustrative of the literary renaissance of the 1960's are Addison Gayle, ed., *Black Expression* (New York, 1969); LeRoi Jones and Larry Neal, eds., *Black Fire: An Anthology of Afro-American Writing* (New York, 1968); and William Couch, Jr., ed., *New Black Playwrights* (New Orleans, 1968). See also Mercer Cook and Stephen E. Henderson, *The Militant Black Writer* (Madison, 1969).

Chapter VIII

As in the case of the preceding chapter, much of our analysis of recent events is based upon a reading of the black and white press.

The most comprehensive discussion of the relative progress of blacks in American society is Sar A. Levitan, William B. Johnston, and Robert Taggart, *Still a Dream: The Changing Status of Blacks since 1960* (Cambridge, Mass., 1975). Also valuable are reports issued by the United States Civil Rights Commission and an annual publication of the United States Bureau of the Census entitled *The Social and Economic Status of the Black Population in the United States, 1969–* (title varies). Material on Negro business is to be found in the magazine *Black Enterprise* (1970–). For an analysis of the black community today, see also James E. Blackwell, *The Black Community: Diversity and Unity* (New York, 1975).

isiana," *American Political Science Review* 51 (September 1957); M. Elaine Burgess, *Negro Leadership in a Southern City* (Chapel Hill, 1960); Hugh D. Price, *The Negro and Southern Politics: A Chapter of Florida History* (New York, 1957); Harry Holloway, "The Negro and the Vote: The Case of Texas," *Journal of Politics* 23 (August 1961); James Q. Wilson, "Two Negro Politicians: An Interpretation," *Midwest Journal of Politics* 4 (November 1960); Everett C. Ladd, Jr., *Negro Political Leadership in the South* (Ithaca, 1966); Donald R. Matthews and James W. Prothro, *Negroes and the New Southern Politics* (New York, 1966); Samuel D. Cook, "Political Movements and Organization," *Journal of Politics* 26 (February 1964); Bayard Rustin, "From Protest to Politics," *Commentary* 39 (February 1965); and Chandler Davison's study of Houston, *Biracial Politics: Conflict and Coalition in the Metropolitan South* (Baton Rouge, 1972).

The literature on the riots of the 1960's is enormous. The following are among the most significant items: *Report of the National Advisory Committee on Civil Disorders* (Washington, 1968); Robert M. Fogelson and Robert B. Hill, "Who Riots? A Study of Participation in the 1967 Riots," in *Supplemental Studies for the National Advisory Commission on Civil Disorders* (Washington, 1968); Robert M. Fogelson, "From Resentment to Confrontation: The Police, the Negroes, and the Outbreak of the Nineteen-Sixties Riots," *Political Science Quarterly* 83 (June 1968); Robert Blauner, "Internal Colonialism and Ghetto Revolt," *Social Problems* 16 (Spring 1969).

Among the best materials on black nationalism and the varying manifestations of black power and black consciousness are two studies of the Black Muslims: C. Eric Lincoln, *The Black Muslims in America* (Boston, 1961) and E. U. Essien-Udom, *Black Nationalism: The Search for an Identity in America* (Chicago, 1962), and two major books by and about Malcolm X: *The Autobiography of Malcolm X* (New York, 1964) and Peter L. Goldman, *The Death and Life of Malcolm X* (New York, 1973). Other titles include Robert Williams, *Negroes with Guns* (New York, 1962); Stokely Carmichael and

Charles V. Hamilton, *Black Power: The Politics of Liberation in America* (New York, 1967); Charles V. Hamilton, "An Advocate of Black Power Defines It," *The New York Times Magazine* (April 14, 1968); Eldridge Cleaver, *Soul on Ice* (New York, 1968); John O. Killens, "Explanation of the 'Black Psyche,'" *The New York Times Magazine* (June 7, 1964); Joyce Ladner, "What 'Black Power' Means to Negroes in Mississippi," *Trans-Action* 7 (November 1967); Lewis Killian, *The Impossible Revolution?* (New York, 1968); Martin Duberman, "Black Power in America," *Partisan Review* 35 (Winter 1968); and Joel D. Aberbach and Jack L. Walker, "The Meanings of Black Power: A Comparison of White and Black Interpretations of a Political Slogan," *American Political Science Review* 64 (June 1970).

Anthologies illustrative of the literary renaissance of the 1960's are Addison Gayle, ed., *Black Expression* (New York, 1969); LeRoi Jones and Larry Neal, eds., *Black Fire: An Anthology of Afro-American Writing* (New York, 1968); and William Couch, Jr., ed., *New Black Playwrights* (New Orleans, 1968). See also Mercer Cook and Stephen E. Henderson, *The Militant Black Writer* (Madison, 1969).

Chapter VIII

As in the case of the preceding chapter, much of our analysis of recent events is based upon a reading of the black and white press.

The most comprehensive discussion of the relative progress of blacks in American society is Sar A. Levitan, William B. Johnston, and Robert Taggart, *Still a Dream: The Changing Status of Blacks since 1960* (Cambridge, Mass., 1975). Also valuable are reports issued by the United States Civil Rights Commission and an annual publication of the United States Bureau of the Census entitled *The Social and Economic Status of the Black Population in the United States, 1969–* (title varies). Material on Negro business is to be found in the magazine *Black Enterprise* (1970–). For an analysis of the black community today, see also James E. Blackwell, *The Black Community: Diversity and Unity* (New York, 1975).

isiana," *American Political Science Review* 51 (September 1957); M. Elaine Burgess, *Negro Leadership in a Southern City* (Chapel Hill, 1960); Hugh D. Price, *The Negro and Southern Politics: A Chapter of Florida History* (New York, 1957); Harry Holloway, "The Negro and the Vote: The Case of Texas," *Journal of Politics* 23 (August 1961); James Q. Wilson, "Two Negro Politicians: An Interpretation," *Midwest Journal of Politics* 4 (November 1960); Everett C. Ladd, Jr., *Negro Political Leadership in the South* (Ithaca, 1966); Donald R. Matthews and James W. Prothro, *Negroes and the New Southern Politics* (New York, 1966); Samuel D. Cook, "Political Movements and Organization," *Journal of Politics* 26 (February 1964); Bayard Rustin, "From Protest to Politics," *Commentary* 39 (February 1965); and Chandler Davison's study of Houston, *Biracial Politics: Conflict and Coalition in the Metropolitan South* (Baton Rouge, 1972).

The literature on the riots of the 1960's is enormous. The following are among the most significant items: *Report of the National Advisory Committee on Civil Disorders* (Washington, 1968); Robert M. Fogelson and Robert B. Hill, "Who Riots? A Study of Participation in the 1967 Riots," in *Supplemental Studies for the National Advisory Commission on Civil Disorders* (Washington, 1968); Robert M. Fogelson, "From Resentment to Confrontation: The Police, the Negroes, and the Outbreak of the Nineteen-Sixties Riots," *Political Science Quarterly* 83 (June 1968); Robert Blauner, "Internal Colonialism and Ghetto Revolt," *Social Problems* 16 (Spring 1969).

Among the best materials on black nationalism and the varying manifestations of black power and black consciousness are two studies of the Black Muslims: C. Eric Lincoln, *The Black Muslims in America* (Boston, 1961) and E. U. Essien-Udom, *Black Nationalism: The Search for an Identity in America* (Chicago, 1962), and two major books by and about Malcolm X: *The Autobiography of Malcolm X* (New York, 1964) and Peter L. Goldman, *The Death and Life of Malcolm X* (New York, 1973). Other titles include Robert Williams, *Negroes with Guns* (New York, 1962); Stokely Carmichael and

Charles V. Hamilton, *Black Power: The Politics of Liberation in America* (New York, 1967); Charles V. Hamilton, "An Advocate of Black Power Defines It," *The New York Times Magazine* (April 14, 1968); Eldridge Cleaver, *Soul on Ice* (New York, 1968); John O. Killens, "Explanation of the 'Black Psyche,'" *The New York Times Magazine* (June 7, 1964); Joyce Ladner, "What 'Black Power' Means to Negroes in Mississippi," *Trans-Action* 7 (November 1967); Lewis Killian, *The Impossible Revolution?* (New York, 1968); Martin Duberman, "Black Power in America," *Partisan Review* 35 (Winter 1968); and Joel D. Aberbach and Jack L. Walker, "The Meanings of Black Power: A Comparison of White and Black Interpretations of a Political Slogan," *American Political Science Review* 64 (June 1970).

Anthologies illustrative of the literary renaissance of the 1960's are Addison Gayle, ed., *Black Expression* (New York, 1969); LeRoi Jones and Larry Neal, eds., *Black Fire: An Anthology of Afro-American Writing* (New York, 1968); and William Couch, Jr., ed., *New Black Playwrights* (New Orleans, 1968). See also Mercer Cook and Stephen E. Henderson, *The Militant Black Writer* (Madison, 1969).

Chapter VIII

As in the case of the preceding chapter, much of our analysis of recent events is based upon a reading of the black and white press.

The most comprehensive discussion of the relative progress of blacks in American society is Sar A. Levitan, William B. Johnston, and Robert Taggart, *Still a Dream: The Changing Status of Blacks since 1960* (Cambridge, Mass., 1975). Also valuable are reports issued by the United States Civil Rights Commission and an annual publication of the United States Bureau of the Census entitled *The Social and Economic Status of the Black Population in the United States, 1969–* (title varies). Material on Negro business is to be found in the magazine *Black Enterprise* (1970–). For an analysis of the black community today, see also James E. Blackwell, *The Black Community: Diversity and Unity* (New York, 1975).

Index

Index